The Financial Times
Guide to Banking

The Financial Times Guide to Banking

Glen Arnold

Harlow, England • London • New York • Boston • San Francisco • Toronto • Sydney • Auckland • Singapore • Hong Kong
Tokyo • Seoul • Taipei • New Delhi • Cape Town • São Paulo • Mexico City • Madrid • Amsterdam • Munich • Paris • Milan

PEARSON EDUCATION LIMITED

Edinburgh Gate
Harlow CM20 2JE
United Kingdom
Tel: +44 (0)1279 623623
Web: www.pearson.com/uk

First published 2014 (print and electronic)

© Opus Eris Limited 2014 (print and electronic)

Pearson Education is not responsible for the content of third-party internet sites.

ISBN: 978-0-273-79182-9 (print)
          978-0-273-79183-6 (PDF)
          978-0-273-79184-3 (ePub)
          978-1-292-00541-6 (eText)

British Library Cataloguing-in-Publication Data
A catalogue record for the print edition is available from the British Library

Library of Congress Cataloging-in-Publication Data
Arnold, Glen.
 The Financial Times guide to banking / Glen Arnold.
    pages cm
 Includes bibliographical references and index.
 ISBN 978-0-273-79182-9 (pbk.: alk. paper) -- ISBN 978-0-273-79183-6 (PDF) -- ISBN 978-1-292-00541-6 (eText)
 1. Banks and banking. I. Title. II. Title: Guide to banking.
 HG1601.A76 2014
 332.1--dc23
                2013039483

The Financial Times. With a worldwide network of highly respected journalists, *The Financial Times* provides global business news, insightful opinion and expert analysis of business, finance and politics. With over 500 journalists reporting from 50 countries worldwide, our in-depth coverage of international news is objectively reported and analysed from an independent, global perspective. To find out more, visit www.ft.com/pearsonoffer.

13
19

Cover Image: © Peter Lane/Alamy

Print edition typeset in 9/13pt StoneSerITC by 30
Print edition printed and bound in Great Britain by Ashford Colour Press Ltd., Gosport, Hampshire

NOTE THAT ANY PAGE CROSS-REFERENCES REFER TO THE PRINT EDITION

Contents

About the author

Glen Arnold, PhD, has held positions of Professor of Investment and Professor of Corporate Finance, but concluded that academic life was not nearly as much fun as making money in the financial markets. As a wealthy investor in his early 50s Glen now spends most of his time running his own equity portfolio and a small property development company from his office in the heart of rural Leicestershire.

His main research focus explores the question: 'What works in investment?' drawing on the work of the great investors, academic discoveries and corporate strategic analysis. Glen is happy to share his ideas with fellow enthusiasts in the City. He teaches at Schroders Investment Management, and also leads investing seminar days for private investors – see www.glen-arnold-investments.co.uk

Glen is the author of the UK's number one investment book *The Financial Times Guide to Investing* (2nd edn, 2009) as well as the investing classics *The Great Investors* (2010), *The Financial Times Guide to Value Investing* (2nd edn, 2009) and *Get Started in Shares* (2013).

He also wrote the market-leading university textbooks *Corporate Financial Management* (2012), *Modern Financial Markets and Institutions* (2011) and *Essentials of Corporate Financial Management* (2nd edn, 2012). Glen is also author of two definitive books on finance, written for the professional market: *The Financial Times Guide to Financial Markets* (2012) and *The Financial Times Handbook of Corporate Finance* (2nd edn, 2010). All these books are available from Financial Times Publishing.

Preface

Banking is exciting, it is so dynamic and engaged with everyday life. Indeed everyday life as we know it could not exist without modern banks. There are so many areas of interest, from the fun of backing young, entrepreneurial companies with fresh finance to the trading of fancy financial instruments on the ever-moving markets.

This book is designed to provide you with a foundation understanding of the wide variety of activities undertaken by banks. These institutions lie at the heart of any financial system, providing a safe place for people to save and to transfer money to others. They also lend vast amounts of money to people wanting to buy a house or to expand a business. They supply multinational firms with an astonishing array of services, from help with managing foreign exchange to organising a takeover.

Banking activities often take place in the background of our lives and it is only when something goes wrong that we realise just how important these services are to us. Take the financial crisis of 2008 or the euro crisis of 2010–13. All of a sudden some of the functions of banks were turned off and, without government intervention, a calamity worse than the 1930s depression was likely, as banks stopped trusting each other and stopped lending. House buyers and small businesses could no longer borrow, and the fear of economic paralysis spread. The nightly news broadcasts made us acutely aware of the importance of the proper functioning of banks. It became obvious to the politicians, and to all of us, that what banks do for us matters a great deal.

I hope you enjoy learning about what banks do.

Glen Arnold

Author's acknowledgements

I owe a great deal of thanks to Susan Henton, my personal assistant, who has committed much intellectual effort and skill to help write this book.

My editor, Christopher Cudmore, at Financial Times Publishing, not only encouraged me to write this book but took the time to read and improve draft chapters. His suggestions have made for a much better reading experience. Both you, the reader, and I should be grateful to him for the increased clarity he has brought.

The production team at Pearson did a great job of turning a raw manuscript into the book. I would like to thank Lucy Carter, Laura Blake and Angela Hawksbee.

Publisher's acknowledgements

We are grateful to the following for permission to reproduce copyright material:

Figures
Figure 4.1 from www.theukcardsassociation.org.uk, The UK Cards Association; Figure in Article 7.2, Australian banks – high and dry (Lex Column), *FT*, 29/11/2012; Figure in Article 8.1, Bank built on flawed business model, *FT*, 04/04/2013 (Thompson, J. and Jenkins, P.); Figures 9.1 and 9.2 from European Central Bank Financial Stability Review December 2012, http://www.ecb.int/pub/pdf/other/financialstabilityreview201212en.pdf, this information can be obtained free of charge via the ECB website; Figure 15.1 from http://www.bankofengland.co.uk; Figure 23.5 with permission from The WM Company/Reuters; Figure 23.6 © OANDA Corporation. Used with permission. (www.oanda.com); Figure in Article 25.2, Europe's banks turn to capital raising to meet Basel III, *FT*, 13/05/2013 (Jenkins, P. and Schäfer, D.); Figures 25.3 and 25.4 from Bank of England (2013) The Financial Policy Committee's powers to supplement capital requirements: A Draft Policy Statement, www.bankofengland.co.uk/financialstability/Documents/fpc/policystatement130114.pdf under UK Open Government Licence (http://www.nationalarchives.gov.uk/doc/open-government-licence/version/1/open-government-licence.htm).

Tables
Table 8.2 from Standard Chartered; Table 20.1 from UK Debt Management Office website. Contains public sector information licensed under the Open Government Licence v2.0.

Text
Article 1.1 from Damage ripples through Cypriot economy, *FT*, 27/03/2013 (Chaffin, J.); Article 4.1 from Cyprus struggles to cope with lack of coins, *FT*, 20/03/2013 (Hope, K.), Article 4.2 from M-Pesa's cautious start in India, *FT*, 27/12/2012 (Crabtree, J.); Article 4.3 from Banking's handy revolution, *FT*, 27/02/2013 (Davies,

P. J.); Article 4.4 from KFC eyes more orders with 'mobile wallet', *FT*, 03/04/2013 (Dembosky, A.); Article 4.5 from Banking: Finance's fifth column, *FT*, 25/07/2012 (Goff, S. and Palmer, M.); Article 5.1 from Vestas shares jump on refinancing, *FT*, 26/11/2012 (MacCarthy, C.); Article 5.2 from Chinese banks step up lending in the US *FT*, 28/08/2012 (Wong, K.); Article 5.3 from Project finance: Focus turns to overseas opportunities, *FT*, 28/10/2012 (Nakamoto, M; Article 6.1 from Daily fix that spiralled out of control, *FT*, 19/12/2012 (Masters, B. Binham, C. and Scannell, K.); Article 6.2 from FSA says it was slow on Libor, *FT*, 05/03/2013 (Schäfer, D.), Article 6.3 from Australia to use market prices for Libor, *FT*, 27/03/2013 (Hume, N.); Article 7.1 from Liquidity: Banks debate liquidity trade-off, *FT*, 18/03/2013 (Alloway, T.),; Article 7.2 from Australian banks – high and dry, *FT*, 29/11/2012; Article 7.3 from Great and good flex banking muscles, *FT*, 11/03/2013 (Jenkins, P. and Parker, G.); Article 8.1 from Bank built on flawed business model, *FT*, 04/04/2013 (Thompson, J. and Jenkins, P.); Article 8.2 from India's banks face balance sheet decline, *FT*, 31/08/2012 (Crabtree, J.); Article 9.1 from Bank leverage: capital questions, *FT*, 26/04/2013; Article 9.2 from Rift over forcing banks to deal with losses, *FT*, 07/03/2013 (Jones, A; Article 9.3 from Banks glean efficiency tips from industry, *FT*, 27/05/2012 (Schäfer, D.); Article 10.1 from Bankers' pay premium is narrowing, *FT*, 24/03/2013 (Schäfer, D.); Article 10.2 from Barclays recoups £300m in bonuses, *FT*, 27/02/2013 (Schafer, D.); Article 10.3 from Pressure rises for formal bank fees inquiry, *FT*, 26/03/2010 (Burgess, K.); Article 10.4 from Outsized risk and regulation inhibit entrants, *FT*, 24/03/2010 (Jenkins, P.); Article 10.5 from 'Chinese walls' are still porous, study shows, *FT*, 23/03/2011 (McCrum, D; Article 10.6 from Boutiques show their mettle in BAE/EADS, *FT*, 18/09/2012 (Guthrie, J.); Article 11.1 from Goldman faces own goal over link to Man Utd, *FT*, 05/03/2010 (Saigol, L.); Article 11.2 from Banks set aside £700m for swaps scandal, *FT*, 31/01/2013 (Masters, B. and Thompson, J.); Article 12.1 from Co-op £1bn gap puts Lloyds under pressure, *FT*, 26/02/2013 (Thompson, J. and Jenkins, P.); Article 12.2 from Police credit union joins mortgage market *FT*, 09/09/2012 (Allen, K. and Moore, E.); Article 13.1 from Asset-based finance: Follow the money, *FT*, 25/06/2012 (Solman, P.); Article 14.1 from Britain tightens grip on foreign banks, *FT*, 09/12/2012 (Masters, B.); Article 14.2 from Bank watchdog warns on retail branches, *FT*, 03/04/2013 (Masters, B.); Article 15.1 from Banks face threat of portable accounts, *FT*, 15/02/2013 (Parker, G. and Jenkins, P.); Article 15.2 from Capital road eased for new banks, *FT*, 27/02/2013 (Masters, B.); Article 15.3 from Why do people avoid banks?, *FT*, 10/01/2012 (Moore, E.); Article 24.1 from India cuts interest rate to revive growth, *FT*, 19/03/2013 (Kazmin, A.); Article 24.2 from Beijing tightens bank lending reins, *FT*, 18/03/2011 (Anderlini, J.); Article 24.3 from BoE sees inflation staying above target, *FT*, 21/02/2013 (Jones, C.); Article 25.2 from Europe's banks turn to capital raising to meet Basel III, *FT*, 13/05/2013 (Jenkins, P. and Schäfer, D.); Article 25.3 from Barclays bond a key test for cocos market, *FT*, 22/11/2012 (Watkins, M.); Article 25.4

from Fed weighs tighter cap on bank leverage, *FT*, 30/04/2013 (Braithwaite, T. and Nasiripour, S.); Article 26.1 from Santander faces advice probe, *FT*, 13/02/2013 (Powley, T.); Article 26.2 from Twin peaks' regulation to cost £646m, *FT*, 09/04/2013 (Masters, B.); Article 26.3 from Watchdogs keep up pressure on responsibility, *FT*, 26/05/2013 (Masters, B.); Article 26.4 from HSBC to spend $700m vetting clients, *FT*, 11/12/2012 (Jenkins, P. and Braithwaite, T.); Article 26.5 from China pushes lending into the shadows, *FT*, 27/02/2013 (Pilling, D.) © The Financial Times Limited. All Rights Reserved; Example on pp. 85–6 from www.rbcroyalbank.com/commercial/international/im-guarantees.html, RBC Royal Bank.

Different types of banking

1

What is banking?

We were all angry at the behaviour of the bankers in the period leading up to the 2008 crisis. What were their leaders thinking? Didn't they have a brain between them? Millions of people thrown out of work, the misery of a very long recession. And all for what? Because *some* bankers could not see beyond their next bonus round.

Since then there has been much talk (and some action) to modify the rules for bankers, to make the system safer for the rest of us. In this way the users of banks can be reassured and governments are less likely to have to provide the money to rescue those considered too important to fail.

And yet despite the shock and the anger and the all-too apparent dangers that badly run banks can present to our society, very few are calling for the destruction of banks or for them to be removed from the economic scene entirely. Why is that? Why is it that ordinary people can see past the idiocy of a few bank leaders and appreciate the great value they bring to us, each and every day?

The impact of banking on our lives

To gain some perspective on the value of banking I want you to imagine that they do not exist.

Where would we be without being able to pay people?

In this world without banks what are you going to do when you want to make a payment for that sofa you want to buy? How are you going to transfer that £1,000 to your relative travelling in South America? Clearly, someone is going to have to come up with some sort of business model that helps you do these things efficiently. You do not really want to engage in barter for your sofa nor do you want to take along two heavy bags of silver coin. As for sending money abroad the difficulties are legion. Do you give your bags of coin to a stranger to take on an aeroplane who then meets with your relative? Do you post the coin?

Safety of our savings and access to our money

Imagine that you have accumulated a tidy sum in savings and have been keeping it hidden around the house. This money is vital to get you through a rainy day or to have a comfortable retirement. You are worried about leaving it at home. What if there is a fire? What if a burglar comes along? You are also concerned because you can see that every year the price of things in the shops creeps up. You now need twice as many units of currency to buy your weekly groceries as you did ten years ago. If you simply hold onto bags of coin then inflation might crumble their value. It would be good to receive some interest that at least compensated for inflation.

You could invest in land, as many of your friends have done. You could invest in a business, but these are not growing very well because they do not have access to reasonably priced loans (banks do not exist) and other financial services. And anyway you need the safety of access to your money at short notice – land may take months to sell and you may never find a buyer for a stake in a business.

Want a loan on reasonable terms?

Before banks were invented lending did take place between individuals and between organisations and individuals. Loans can be arranged in a world without banks, but there will be far fewer of them, because of the difficulties of borrower and potential lender finding each other. Where do you go to find someone able and willing to lend? Also, lenders are going to be very nervous. How can they be sure that they will be repaid? This fear might lead to a demand for a high level of **collateral** (backup of some asset they could take and sell if the agreement is reneged on) and for high interest rates. How can an ordinary person assess the viability of a business plan and the likelihood of cash flows being sufficient to repay the loan plus interest? Do you need to hire expensive lawyers to draw up the loan agreement? And what if the borrower requires such a large loan that it can only be provided if a dozen lenders band together? The complications go on and on. The amount available for entrepreneurs, for homebuyers and for students is very small and very expensive.

Helping companies with financial market transactions

Imagine that your business has an order for 2,000 garments from a company overseas. The company is not willing to simply send money for payment before you have delivered the goods to it. The owners seem nice people, but you know that it would not be good business practice to simply send the goods without far more reassurance that you will be paid. You need an organisation that you trust which not only vouches for the import company, but guarantees that you will be paid.

You allow the customer to pay in its own currency three months after delivery, standard practice if you want to compete. But this leads to a risk. What if the value of the importer's currency goes down between the time of despatch and you getting paid? You will end up with less money than you first thought. You might end up making a large loss on the deal. Perhaps you could do with an organisation that will agree at the time of despatch to exchange the expected currency from your overseas company to your currency at a point in the future (three months later?) at an exchange rate agreed at the outset.

There are many other areas where a business needs help, e.g. in organising a merger with another company or raising new money by selling shares. Who understands the financial markets and the rules and regulations sufficiently to help you?

Article 1.1 highlights the trauma caused by an absence of banking in Cyprus in 2013.

Article 1.1

Damage ripples through Cypriot economy

By Joshua Chaffin in Nicosia

On Monday, EU officials pronounced Cyprus saved after the country agreed terms with international lenders on a €10bn bailout. Laiki, the country's second-largest bank, as a condition of the bailout, is now in liquidation.

The most immediate problem confronting businesses was a scarcity of cash. As of Tuesday, banks had been closed for 11 days and were not expected to reopen until Thursday.

"The problem is that the market is operating on a cash basis – everybody wants cash – but how can you create cash without banks?" said Iacovos Iacovou, chairman of Iacovou Brothers Group, the construction company that built the international airport.

Mr Iacovou said he was seeing a shortage of building materials because suppliers were demanding cash. "If the banks do not open in two days, we will have a problem," he said.

One Cypriot businessman said the situation was so severe because every company he dealt with had accounts at either Laiki or Bank of Cyprus or both. The former is being split up and wound down, with accounts over €100,000 frozen. The latter is being restructured.

As a result, uncertainty has spread to every corner of the commercial world.

"It's a nightmare," the businessman said. "If companies lose their existing overdraft facilities the logistics will be very difficult."

Mr Papadopoulos [the owner of Politis, a newspaper] was devising a plan to make partial payment to his 50 employees on Friday after many of Politis' advertisers failed to settle bills with their agencies, and kiosks stopped reimbursing the paper's distributor.

"It's just total paralysis of the system," he said. "If this goes on for another month, there will be nothing left."

FT Source: Chaffin, J. (2013) 'Damage ripples through Cypriot economy', *Financial Times*, 26 March.

Thousands of years of banking

Clearly, there are real difficulties in going about everyday life in the absence of banks. In this section we look at a series of problems people faced and how they overcame them by inventing new types of institutional arrangements or new instruments. This historical journey will give us some insight into the key issues in banking and help your understanding of the reasoning behind the way things are in modern banking.

Money to tide you over

We start with the problem of short-term cash flow shortages.

You are a farmer in Mesopotamia, 4,400 years ago. You need to buy seed, expecting a harvest in six months. You also need to feed and clothe your family between now and harvest. Worse than that, the government insist on taxes now. You need to find someone who will lend money (silver or goods) on the promise that you will repay after harvest. Thus, some people became lenders. Some of the earliest known writing of any form is on fired clay tablets for the purpose of recording loan deals. The interest charged seems to be fixed regardless of the length of time to harvest. Here is one of those agreements, from the mid-twenty-fourth century BC[1]

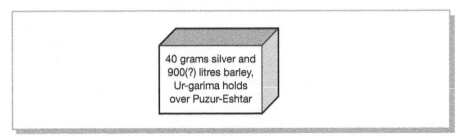

40 grams silver and 900(?) litres barley, Ur-garima holds over Puzur-Eshtar

Ur-garima might well have been an institution rather than an individual lender. Other borrowers were long-distance traders who needed capital for their businesses. Property such as homes were often pledged as collateral. Note that the financiers at the centre of these businesses were not like modern banks; in particular they did not take in deposits. They were closer to modern door-step lenders, probably using their own savings to generate the loans, employing a few 'heavies' just in case of non-payment. The more respectable were linked to the temples and charged more modest interest rates.

A couple of millennia later and over the other side of the Himalayas, on the Chinese part of the Silk Road, another arrangement for short-term loans was developed, that of the pawn shop. Just like the high street pawn shops of today, portable security items (e.g. clothing, pearls, mirrors) were held at the shop until repayment of capital and interest was made. Two thousand year old paper contracts still exist which instead of being signed, show imprints of finger joints below the names to indicate acceptance of the terms. Interest extracted by these professional lenders could be 13% per month or more. This was so lucrative that there is a record of a princess supplementing her income by opening pawnshops. To get lower rates as a borrower you could persuade someone to act as a guarantor for your loan, so that if you failed to pay, the pawnbroker could collect from, say, your rich uncle.

New types of money

At that time bolts of silk (40 feet by 8 feet long) were used as one of the **mediums of exchange**, a type of currency, alongside bronze coin and silver. Bronze coin was a pain to carry around because it was so heavy relative to silk; the unit was one string, which is one thousand coins, weighing four kilos. Gold coin predominated in international trade because traders could take payment in one country and then spend it a thousand miles away.

Now here is a problem: you are the king in a southern regional kingdom of China in the tenth century. You are used to issuing bronze coins as the main currency, but the copper mines are located in war-torn and chaotic Northern China and the copper stopped flowing south to the royal mint. What do you do? You have plenty of iron, so you start minting iron coins, which become currency alongside the bronze ones. However, this solution brings its own problems. If you thought hauling around a string of bronze coins was burdensome then try iron for size: each coin was worth about one-tenth that of a bronze one. For merchants travelling to do deals in different parts of the country this was too much. Housewives had to bring a kilo and a half of iron coin to market to buy a kilo of salt.

Solution: the authorities set up depositories where merchants could deposit coin. They received in return a piece of paper promising that a sum of money could be taken away from any one of the depositories in the provincial capitals. Thus 'flying cash' was created. Paper substituted for hard currency. Tea merchants wanting to send money back to their home town were delighted that they could do so with **paper money**, which had a fixed value in bronze coin.

Merchants are always looking for a new way of generating a return. They figured that, given the amount of coin they had in their vaults, they could issue paper money themselves to buy things for their businesses. These would be exchangeable into coin when the holder wanted. However, there are rogues in every business and it wasn't long before conmen persuaded others to take paper payment without having sufficient back-up of real bronze or iron.

The market needed to be regulated. In the eleventh century the government stepped in to say that only 16 merchant houses deemed to have sufficient financial resources could issue paper money. They also insisted on standardised colour, size and format of the paper. These then circulated around the economy, exchanging hands several times much like our paper money today.

The sceptical Europeans and too much money

While the Chinese were getting increasingly comfortable with paper money, over in Europe the idea behind the use of a thing as money was that it had to have value as a commodity in its own right. Gold and silver currencies had worth based on their intrinsic value as commodities, not just because the monarch said that they were money. Paper money is called **fiat money**; it is money simply because it is declared by a government to be legal tender. It is money without intrinsic value other than the potential for others to trust it and accept it as money.

In China a problem arose because the government did not impose limits on the amount of paper money created. Also, some of the merchant houses, accepting clients' money as deposits giving them paper money in return, got greedy. They used the deposited cash to buy assets with high returns such as property, and speculated on luxury commodities. They reduced the stock of coins in the vault to such an extent that they did not have enough liquidity to redeem the notes they had issued. **Liquidity** means the extent to which an asset can be sold quickly for cash, at low transaction cost without moving the price against you. In trying to sell land in a hurry the merchant houses found the prices falling and, of course, high transaction costs.

Coin itself is the most liquid – but the merchant houses did not have enough of it to pay depositors. If depositors get a whiff of a rumour that their financial institution may have difficulty delivering on its promise of returning their hard currency when they demand it, they rush to be first in the queue to withdraw, while the organisation still has some cash left. The queues around Northern Rock branches in 2008 were not a new phenomenon – **bank runs** have been with us a long time.

On top of the liquidity problem, there were counterfeit notes in circulation. Clearly the Chinese authorities needed to get a grip. A state-run currency bureau was established and given the exclusive right to print paper money. Counterfeiting was reduced by removing the currency from circulation after two years.

The Chinese also improved matters in other ways. Whereas the old paper could have an odd denomination, say 32 or 13 strings of coin, the new notes were denominated as 1 and 10. To give you some idea of the size and importance of this new money in people's lives consider the total number of strings that just the first print run of official notes (in 1024) represented: 1,880,000 were needed to oil the wheels of commerce. By 1264 there were over 270 million in circulation in a country with roughly the same population as the UK today. By the 1290s the Chinese State had declared that the paper was no longer convertible to metal coins, it was the monetary standard on its own – a pure fiat currency. Silver continued to be used unofficially as currency but, scholars think that paper use predominated.

Treasury bills

The Chinese had another problem: they needed to station one million soldiers on their northern borders to fend off invaders. Merchants had to be encouraged to supply the men with goods. Instead of paying with coin the authorities insisted on paying them with a 'promissory note'; that is a piece of paper that declares that the State will pay them a certain amount a few days later. Surprisingly perhaps, or as a indicator of the sophistication and trustworthiness of the State, the merchants were happier to receive the promissory notes than to have to lug all the coin down the mountain trails. Thus was born the idea of **Treasury bills** – a promise on a piece of paper that the Treasury of the nation will pay the holder in a few days. When they returned to the capital the merchants could exchange the bills for bronze coin.

It was only natural that the merchants would start to sell the right to receive a quantity of coin to other merchants rather than going and collecting it themselves. Thus a **secondary market** was created in which Treasury bills changed hands before the redemption date at a price less than their nominal value. (The **primary market** is when the original deal is done with the finance raiser – the State in this case – and the lender.) Today the Treasury bill markets are enormous and a key aspect of modern banking.

Inflation

There is a problem with the State printing money – political leaders sometimes find it difficult to control themselves. It does not take much of a crisis for them to think that the way to pay for state spending when tax receipts are too low is to turn on the printing presses. If the volume of new currency is not matched by increased output of goods and services then the value of the currency depreciates relative to real goods and services and we have the phenomenon of inflation. The Chinese did it in the twelfth century, Germany in the 1930s and Zimbabwe in the twenty-first century. Later we discuss the role of central banks in the control of money supply and inflation; these organisations are generally able to take decisions independently of politicians.

Tallies and stocks

Have you ever wondered where the word 'tally', meaning a record of how much you owe, comes from? Well, **tally** sticks were thought by the medieval English to be a much more reliable way for a lender and a borrower to keep tabs on the deal than the clay tablets used by the Mesopotamians.[2] They are sticks of wood, often 5–8 inches long, but could be up to 8 feet long. If the stick had a 'V' cut into it this indicated a pound owed, grooves indicated shillings and notches pence. The borrower's name and a brief note about the deal was written on the side of the stick and it was then split vertically, so that each party could take away a record of cuts and grooves representing money owed. The debtor retained the 'foil' and the lender held the 'stock'. (The term stock is still used for modern financial instruments to mean an obligation.) In the old days, to hold 'stock' in the Bank of England literally meant keeping sticks of wood there, and dividends could be collected by presenting your half of the stick to the bank every few months.

If a government ran short of money they could resort to issuing tallies to creditors, e.g. suppliers to the Royal Household. This right to receive a payout from the State a few days in the future is the English version of Treasury bills. These could then be sold in a secondary market – sticks were bought and sold for six centuries, until the nineteenth century.

Long-term borrowing

European governments often needed to borrow large sums of money and wanted to do so for many years. Venice solved this problem by forcing its wealthy citizens to buy its bonds in 1171 to construct a fleet to fight Byzantium; brutal but effective. The buyers received paper in return, which stated an interest of 5% per year payable in two halves, every six months. The principal sum was to be paid back when it was to be paid back – in other words, probably never (**irredeemable bonds** or **perpetuities** we call them today). Even without a solid promise of redemption this right to receive interest regularly had value to people other than those who had been forced into buying the bonds, so they could be sold in the secondary market to other investors. Specialists acted as **brokers**, charging around 0.5%, to transfer ownership – modern day investment banks do much the same, but a bit cheaper. This is the start of the **government bond markets** which today are vital for economic progress. Just ask the modern day Greeks, Irish and Spaniards how vital it is to raise money here, and to keep the trust of your lenders.

A few hundred years later, in the 1530s, the Italian city states decided to switch to voluntary purchasing of bonds. They were snapped up; they offered high interest which was not taxed. They appealed particularly to retired folk who wanted a regular annual income until they died. These became known as **annuities**.

A king loses his head, a kingdom gains banks

Imagine you are a wealthy Londoner in the seventeenth century. You have a problem: much of your wealth is in metal coins and you need somewhere safe to keep these. You have heard of a group of merchants known as goldsmiths who have long experience, strong vaults, high reputation and the latest technology to keep valuables safe. They've been dealing in gold for decades. You could strike up a deal with them whereby they looked after your gold and silver for a small fee.

The goldsmith gives you a written receipt. This piece of paper states the value of the coins deposited. If you wanted to buy something in a shop you could take your piece of paper to your goldsmith to receive coins to spend. But what happened next led to the development of goldsmiths as banks. The shop keeper, as likely as not, would deposit your coins with a goldsmith for safekeeping, receiving a receipt in return. It did not take long for shopkeepers to realise that a receipt from a reputable goldsmith was worth taking from a customer rather than insisting on the usual merry-go-round of collecting coin and depositing it again. The shopkeeper could simply accept the receipt and collect the coins at a later date (or get them transferred to their account at the goldsmiths). The paper receipts increasingly became accepted as a form of money.

These private depositories of coin got a real boost when the rival depository, the Royal Mint, on Tower Hill, was raided by Charles I at the start of the English civil war. He decided to 'borrow' the huge sum of £200,000. He later repaid, but the damage was done: trust was gone. The goldsmiths not only had higher reputations, but paid interest.

Fractional-reserve banking

Goldsmiths noticed that most of the deposited coins were never taken out. On a typical day, or even a typical month, only a very small proportion of depositors turned up to demand their coins. So, reasoned the bankers, if for every £100 deposited only around £20 would need to be kept in the vault to satisfy those who turned up at the bank, why not lend out the other £80 and gain some interest? Hence only a fraction of the money deposited is held in reserve: this is **fractional-reserve banking**.

Money creation

Now we can move to another stage; we can actually create money. The borrowers of the money from goldsmiths were usually content to take a piece of paper – call it a **bank note** – instead of taking coins out of the bank. They could then use that as currency to buy things. The goldsmiths could just create these pieces of paper off their own bat. Thus, a goldsmith bank might have a total of, say, £1,000 deposited, but hand out £500 of the coin as loans and issue another £5,000 or £6,000 of new paper money to borrowers.

You can see the obvious danger here: depositors might all come at the same time to demand their money; they want £1,000 back when there is only £500 in the vault. Illiquidity! But, what are the chances of a high proportion of depositors wanting cash back at the same time? Miniscule, thought the bankers, and so they carried on lending beyond their **deposit base** – and this is what bankers do today. They create money out of thin air (just so long as there is a deposit base on which to build) – see Figure 1.1. Initially there is only £100, but after seven actions there is £100 + £80 + £64 + £51.20 = £295.20 in the economy (we look at money creation further in Chapter 24).

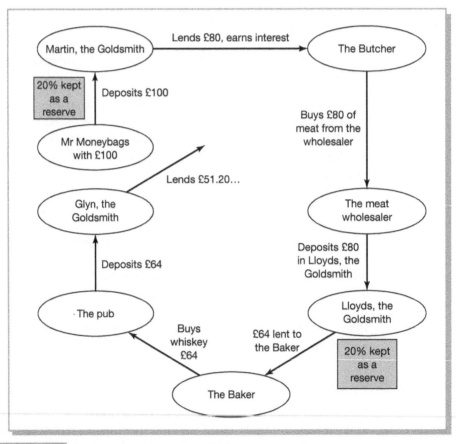

Figure 1.1   Money creation by bankers

This new money is actually debt. And it only works if people are willing to accept **bankers' promissory notes**. They do this because they are perceived as being 'payable on demand'. If you turn up at a bank you would be able to swap your notes for coins. Today UK notes still state 'I promise to pay the bearer on demand the sum of twenty pounds'. However, unlike in the seventeenth century, if you went to collect from the Bank of England today you would only get another note in exchange – we have moved right over to pure fiat money. To be useful the notes issued then and now have to carry a legally enforceable unconditional right to payment. Also, they should be **negotiable** – that is, transferable – between people.

Of course there is another danger: if you are working off a deposit base of £1,000 and you lend £4,000, and then 30% of your borrowers are unable to pay, you are bankrupt. This thought should limit the amount you lend given your deposit base (a **capital reserve** is kept), but bankers occasionally misjudge this.

Many of the goldsmith bankers developed into today's famous banking firms, such as Coutts & Company.

The cheque is invented

If a depositor wanted to make a payment he could write a letter to his goldsmith bank asking that the person named in the letter be allowed to receive in cash the sum stated in the letter. Alternatively, the letter could authorise the transfer from one deposit account at the goldsmith's to another. The earliest handwritten **cheques** appeared after the English civil war. The early 1700s saw the first fully-printed cheques, and the first personalised printed cheques were produced in 1810.

A clearing house

But what if the payee banks with another goldsmith bank? Then there had to be a way of communicating between the two. At first this process would have been laborious, as clerks from each bank would visit all the other banks to exchange cheques and then settle between them, but in 1770 the London bankers got together in one place (a tavern) to handle the cheques from many banks. This eventually became the **Bankers' Clearing House** in the early nineteenth century. When the railways linked up the rest of the country in the 1840s the cheque system really took off, linking up over 150 banks.

Over in America

The first modern fiat paper money issued by *a government* was by Massachusetts in 1690. To pay off soldiers who had contributed to the latest round of plundering expeditions in Quebec £7,000 was printed. The pieces of paper handed out were to be redeemed in gold or silver out of tax receipts in a 'few years' (in fact, they had to wait 40 years). Massachusetts' politicians loved this way of paying for things and so kept issuing paper – by 1748 there was £2.5m in circulation. By the late 1750s all the other colonies had followed suit. It was only natural that the Continental Congress chose the tool of fiat paper money to finance the Revolutionary War (1775).

Paper money in the UK

Britain was somewhat slower in gaining government control over the issue of paper money. In 1694 the **Bank of England** was founded but at this stage its job was to act as the government's banker (managing its account) and to raise money for it. It immediately raised £1.2m for the government by getting people to subscribe to a share issue to set up the new bank (the government needed to pay for a war with France). The subscribers became the Governor and the Company of the Bank of England (BoE). While other banks were restricted in size by being limited to six partners (if they were to issue currency), the BoE, being a joint-stock company with shareholder limited liability, could issue shares to investors around the country to raise capital. Also, being so big and strong it attracted plenty of deposits. Its strength meant that by the 1780s it was acting as banker to other banks.

During the Napoleonic wars the government was borrowing so much paper money from the BoE that it ran out of gold to back the notes. The government thus declared that the notes need no longer be convertible to gold. The result of all this spending and the creation of so much fiat money was high inflation. The lesson was learned again: you need to limit the quantity of paper money.

To develop a more sustainable group of banks the Country Bankers Act 1826 was passed. This permitted companies to have more than six members if they operated more than 65 miles from London. Thus we have the development of major banking organisations across the country. The creation of many banks with extensive branch networks brought the added benefit of geographical convenience, that is, a customer could deposit and borrow from a range of locations. Also, previously the deposits of people in one county would tend to be borrowed in the same county. Now deposits in Liverpool could be used for investment in Manchester.

There continued to be many small banks issuing bank notes. Many were unsound, irresponsibly creating notes. In 1844 the BoE was emphasised as the main issuer of notes. From then on, there were to be no new issuers of notes and those whose issues lapsed, or who were taken over, forfeited their right to issue. Other issuers gradually died out. The notes issued by the BoE were mostly backed by its holdings of gold or silver bullion, but another £14m was permitted (equal to the BoE capital raised from shareholders). The backing of gold (the **gold standard**) created a long period of price stability.

In addition to the issue of notes and being banker to the government, the BoE took on roles such as being **lender of last resort** to the banking system and was called on to stabilise the banking system in crises, which happened fairly often.

Banks help with the flow of money

We round off the chapter by describing the way in which modern banking and other financial services help us all today. We start by considering what happens to people's savings. Households generally place the largest proportion with financial institutions. These organisations then put that money to work. Some of it is lent back to members of the household sector in the form of a mortgage to purchase a house, or as a personal loan – see Figure 1.2. Some of the money is used to buy securities (e.g. bonds, shares) issued by the business sector. The institutions will expect a return on these loans and shares, which flows back in the form of interest and dividends. However, they are often prepared for businesses to retain profit within the firm for further investment in the hope of greater returns in the future.

The government sector enters into the financial system in a number of ways. For example, taxes are taken from individuals and businesses and, secondly, governments usually fail to match their revenues with their expenditure and therefore borrow significant sums from the financial institutions, with a need to return that money with interest. Figure 1.2 remains a gross simplification; e.g. it has not allowed for overseas financial transactions but it does demonstrate a crucial role for financial institutions in an advanced market economy.

Primary investors

Typically the household sector is in financial surplus. This sector contains the savers of society. It is these individuals who become the main providers of funds used for investment in the business sector. **Primary investors** tend to prefer to exchange their cash for financial assets which:

▣ allow them to get their money back quickly should they need to with low transaction costs,

▣ have a high degree of certainty over the amount they will receive back.

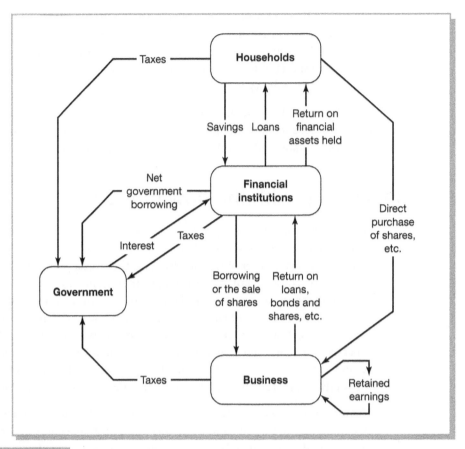

Figure 1.2   The flow of funds and financial intermediation

In other words, primary investors like high liquidity and low risk. Lending directly to a firm with a project proposal to build a North Sea oil platform which will be in production for five years is not a high-liquidity and low-risk investment. However, putting money into a sock under the bed is (if we exclude the possibility of the risk of theft).

Ultimate borrowers

In our simplified model the **ultimate borrowers** are in the business sector. These firms are trying to maximise the wealth generated by their activities. To do this, companies need to invest in capital equipment, in real plant and other assets, often for long periods of time. The firms, in order to serve their social function, need to attract funds for use over many years. Also these funds will be at risk, sometimes very high risk. (Here we are using the term 'borrower' broadly to include all forms of finance, even 'borrowing' by selling shares.)

Conflict of preferences

We have a **conflict of preference** between the primary investors wanting low-cost liquidity and certainty, and the ultimate borrowers wanting long-term risk-bearing capital. A further complicating factor is that savers usually save on a small scale, £100 here or €200 there, whereas businesses are likely to need large sums of money. Imagine some of the problems that would occur in a society which did not have any financial intermediaries. Here lending and share buying will occur only as a result of direct contact and negotiation between two parties. If there was no organised market where financial securities could be sold on to other investors then the fund provider, once committed, would be trapped in an illiquid investment. Also the costs that the two parties might incur in searching to find each other in the first place might be considerable. Following contact a thorough agreement would need to be drawn up to safeguard the investor, and additional expense would be incurred obtaining information to monitor the firm and its progress. In sum, the obstacles to putting saved funds to productive use would lead many to give up and to retain their cash. Those that do persevere will demand exceptionally high rates of return from the borrowers to compensate them for poor liquidity, risk, **search costs, agreement costs** and **monitoring costs**. This will mean that few firms will be able to justify investments because they cannot obtain those high levels of return when the funds are invested in real assets. As a result few investments take place and the wealth of society fails to grow. Figure 1.3 shows (by the arrow on the right) little money flowing from savings into investment.

The introduction of financial intermediaries

The problem of under-investment can be alleviated greatly by the introduction of financial institutions (e.g. banks) and financial markets (e.g. a stock exchange). Their role is to facilitate the flow of funds from primary investors to ultimate borrowers at a low cost. They do this by solving the conflict of preferences.

There are two types of financial intermediation: the first is an **agency** or **brokerage type operation** which brings together lenders and firms; the second is an **asset-transforming type of intermediation,** in which the conflict is resolved by the creation of **intermediate securities** which have the risk, liquidity and volume characteristics which investors prefer. The financial institution raises money by offering these securities for sale, and then uses the acquired funds to purchase primary securities issued by firms.

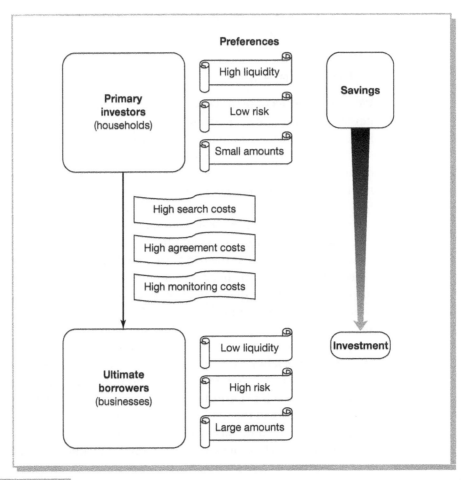

Figure 1.3   **Savings into investment in an economy without financial intermediaries**

Brokers

At its simplest an intermediary is a 'go-between', someone who matches up a provider of finance with a user of funds. This type of intermediary is particularly useful for reducing the search costs for both parties. Stockbrokers, for example, make it easy for investors wanting to buy shares in a newly floated company. Investment banks act as brokers in the bond market. Brokers may also have some skill at collecting information on a firm and monitoring its activities, saving the investor time. They also act as middlemen when an investor wishes to sell to another, thus enhancing the liquidity of the fund providers.

Asset transformers

Asset transformation is the creation of an intermediate security with character-istics appealing to the primary investor to attract funds, which are then made available to the ultimate borrower in a form appropriate to them. Intermediaries, by creating a completely new security – the intermediate security – increase the opportunities available to savers, encouraging them to invest and thus reducing the cost of finance for the productive sector. The transformation function can act in a number of different ways.

▧ **Risk transformation.** Instead of an individual lending directly to a business with a great idea, such as manufacturing a new silicon chip, a bank creates a deposit or current account with relatively low risk for the investor's savings. Lending directly to the firm, the saver would demand compensation for the probability of default on the loan and therefore the business would have to pay a very high rate of interest which would inhibit investment. The bank acting as an intermediary creates a special kind of intermediate security called a bank account agreement. The bank intermediary then uses the funds attracted by the new financial asset to buy a security issued (e.g. a bank loan deal) by the chip producer (the **primary security**), allowing the manufacturer to obtain long-term debt capital. Because of the extra security that a lender has by holding a bank account as a financial asset rather than by making a loan direct to a firm, the lender is prepared to accept a lower rate of interest and the ultimate borrower obtains funds at a relatively low cost. The bank reduces its risk exposure to any one project by diversifying its loan portfolio among a number of firms. It can also reduce risk by building up expertise in assessing and monitoring firms and their associated risk.

▧ **Maturity (liquidity) transformation.** The fact that a bank lends long term for a risky venture does not mean that the primary lender is subjected to illiquidity. Liquidity is not a problem because banks maintain sufficient liquid funds to meet their liabilities when they arise. You can walk into a bank and take the money from your account at short notice because the bank, given its size, exploits economies of scale and anticipates that only a small fraction of its customers will withdraw their money on any one day. Banks play an important role in borrowing 'short' and lending 'long'. The ability to maintain only small cash amounts is assisted by (a) a large number of depositors providing a steady inflow and outflow to their accounts each day, and (b) the portfolio of loans can be arranged to mature in a reasonably steady fashion so that a small proportion is always close to being repaid, thus assuring a steady flow of cash.

▧ **Volume transformation.** Banks gather small amounts of money from numerous savers and re-package these sums into larger bundles for investment in the business sector.

Bank economies of scale

A bank is able to accept lending to companies at a relatively low rate of return because of the economies of scale enjoyed compared with the primary investor. These economies of scale include:

- **Efficiencies in gathering information on the riskiness of lending to a particular firm and subsequent monitoring.** Individuals do not have access to the same data sources or expert analysis.

- **Risk spreading.** Intermediaries are able to spread funds across a large number of borrowers and thereby reduce overall risk. Individual investors may be unable to do this.

- **Transaction costs.** Intermediaries are able to reduce the search, agreement and monitoring costs that would be incurred by savers and borrowers in a direct transaction. Banks, for example, are convenient, safe locations with standardised types of securities. Savers do not have to spend time examining the contract they are entering upon when, say, they open a bank account. How many of us read the small print when we opened a bank account? Borrowers have the convenience of numerous bank branches to approach and the procedure for obtaining a loan is fairly standardised within the different categories of loans (mortgage, personal loan, business overdraft, etc.) and so the legal and other transaction costs are kept low.

- **A regular flow of liquidity.** Banks are able to lend long, partly because they can anticipate the regular receipt of deposits, or borrow to make up shortfalls.

The reduced information costs, convenience and passed-on benefits from the economies of operating on a large scale mean that primary investors are motivated to place their savings with intermediaries.

The effects of the financial intermediaries and markets are shown in Figure 1.4 where the flow of funds from savings to investment is increased.

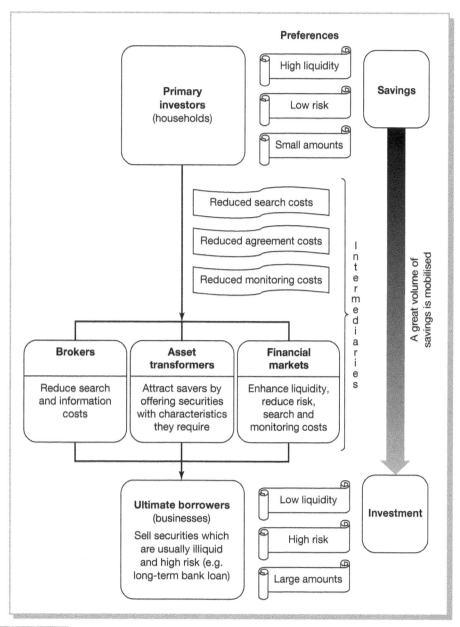

Figure 1.4 Savings into investment in an economy with financial intermediaries and financial markets

2

An overview of different aspects of banking

Banks started out as fairly straightforward businesses, taking in deposits, making loans and providing a payment mechanism. But they grew. They now conduct a much wider range of activities, and it can be difficult to define banking activity in the modern world. Figure 2.1 provides some clarity by grouping the activities into four different types of banking. Some organisations concentrate on providing services in just one, or perhaps two, of the segments, others are **universal banks** offering a full range of banking. This classification is not perfect – there are many banks that do not neatly fit into these groups, and there are other 'banking' activities not listed here – but it does allow us some understanding of what it is that banks do.

Put at its simplest, the **retail banks** take (small) deposits from the public which are re-packaged and lent to small businesses and households. This is generally high-volume and low-value business which contrasts with **wholesale banking** which is low volume but each transaction is for a high value. For example, wholesale banks obtain a great deal of the money they use from the sale of financial instruments in the markets, in values of tens or hundreds of millions of pounds, dollars, euros, etc.

The retail banks operate branch networks and a subset of banks provide a cheque and electronic clearance system – transferring money from one account to another. These are the clearing banks. For example, in the UK the clearing banks are Bank of Scotland (part of Lloyds), Barclays, Clydesdale (part of National Australia), Co-operative, HSBC, Lloyds, National Westminster (part of RBS), Nationwide,[1] Royal Bank of Scotland and Santander. Until 2008 retail banks tended to reduce their reliance on retail deposits year by year, raising more whole-sale funds from the financial markets. Northern Rock is an example of a bank that became over-reliant on wholesale funding. When those short-term loans became due for payment in 2008 it found that it could not obtain replacement funding. This caused its collapse.

Until recently the trend was toward the creation of increasing numbers of universal banks through the merger of banks. This was boosted by the panicky

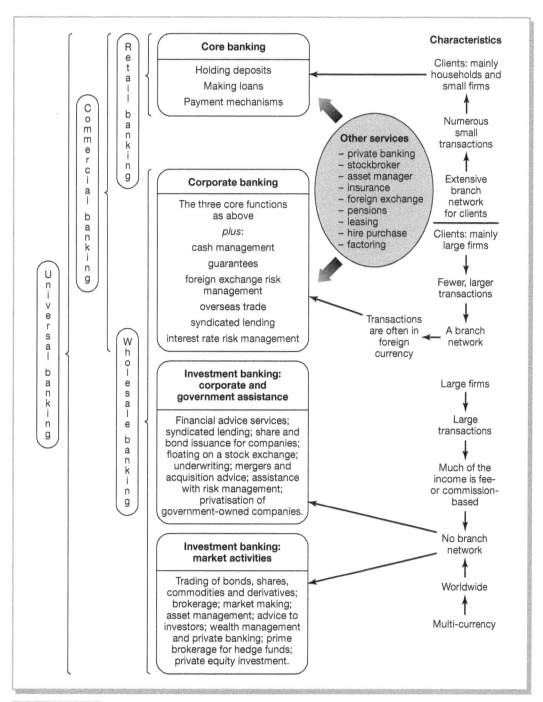

Figure 2.1   An overview of the different types of banking

authorities, who, in the midst of the financial crisis, encouraged mergers, and also by ambitious bankers thinking they could build overwhelmingly big empires to dominate banking segments and have diverse sources of income and thus greater stability. For example, we now have JPMorgan (investment bank) joined with Chase, Washington Mutual and Bear Stearns; Merrill Lynch (investment bank) joining Bank of America so that it could be the client's 'everyday banker as well as your big deal banker'; Lloyds absorbing Bank of Scotland and Halifax (mostly commercial banking).

Doubts about universal banking

However, a number of factors have made some banks think hard about whether being a universal bank is a good idea. UBS, the Swiss giant, has already decided to give up most of its bond trading and many other investment bank businesses to concentrate on retail and wealth management (looking after rich people's money – see Chapter 4) which is seen as more stable and profitable. The few investment banking operations remaining support its wealth management and commercial banking operations. The UK government has told RBS to move away from universal banking and become a more UK-focused commercial bank.

Factors weighing on the universal model are:

- **Capital reserves.** To embark on riskier investment banking activities, such as trading bonds, banks are now required to have more shareholders' money held in reserve to operate with a greater degree of safety, without needing bailouts. The raised amount of money kept in the businesses makes it more difficult to obtain a high enough return on shareholders' equity capital employed.

- **Scandal.** There have been a series of scandals due to rogue investment bankers losing vast amounts of money. The fines for manipulating LIBOR interest rates (see Chapter 6) are high enough, but the amount lost by, say, JPMorgan in a supposedly safe part of its operations, or UBS's investment bankers' loss on stock market bets run into billions. Bank directors are earnestly questioning whether the profits reported by their investment bank divisions are real, rather than just picking up nickels in front of steam-rollers. One day the risk will be manifest, resulting in one event wiping out years of supposed profits.

- **Splitting.** UK and European authorities are debating whether to insist that universal banks separate ('**ring-fence**') the retail/commercial banking operations from the investment bank/trading operations. These ring-fenced businesses will have separate boards of directors and separate pots of safety capital in case something goes wrong (but only one holding company). The idea is that these pots of capital will be called on first in the event of a future crisis. As a back-up the regulators/government will come to the rescue of the commercial banking arms, but will leave the investment banking part to sink or swim. The danger remains that the investment bank part will bring down a substantial part of the financial system, as Lehman Brothers did in 2008. There are other safeguards put in place to counter this (see Chapters 25 and 26) but these impose even more cost on banks operating in many areas seen as higher risk.

◼ **Banned.** Even without ring-fencing the regulators are toughening up and banning many activities. In the USA banks are working under the 'Volcker Rule' which imposes a ban on **proprietary trading** (buying and selling using the bank's money to try to make a profit from risk taking – see Chapter 10). The more limited definition of 'trading' permitted is that which is necessary to match buyers with sellers, rather than taking on the risk of one side of a trade. US investment banks are also banned from investing in hedge funds and private equity by more than 3% of the total assets of the fund or 3% of the bank's capital.

◼ **Poor economic conditions.** Many areas of banking have become unprofitable and so banks are withdrawing from product and geographical areas. In many cases they are focusing on their home markets and nearby countries, and no longer have serious global ambitions. Citigroup is one of the exceptions here. It gets the majority of its business from emerging markets, serving emerging-market multinational companies as well as a large cohort of developed market multinationals.

◼ **Running out of capital.** The dwindling of profitable activities on top of the massive write-offs of loans to clients has weakened many banks so that they simply cannot do as much as they want to.

◼ **Local capital required.** Many banks are withdrawing from operating in a number of countries because the regulators are insisting on a high level of capital and plenty of liquid assets being held in their areas. Dedicating capital and liquidity to multiple local subsidiaries is much more costly than drawing off a central pool of money and moving it around the world at will. (The regulators were stunned in 2008 when, allegedly, Lehman Brothers, transferred $8bn of cash from Europe to the firm's New York headquarters days before the bankruptcy. Also, the government of Iceland agreed to reimburse local customers while leaving British and Dutch depositors trying to recoup more than $5bn following the collapse of its banks.)

Some strategic moves

As a result of all this pressure, soul-searching and costs, many banks are going through a transition phase. Some have decided to withdraw from most areas of investment banking. Others are scrutinising each area of the business for profitability, e.g. Credit Suisse has decided to focus on serving businesses and its private bank clients, rather than proprietary trading.

Some are making noises suggesting that they truly believe in the cost efficiencies, cross-selling of services and other customer benefits, as well as the increased stability of diversified sources of income, and so are determined to stick with the universal model, e.g. Deutsche Bank still wants to be a **'full-service investment bank'**; Société Générale and BNP Paribas continue to be universal banks, and Barclays, while reviewing its various investment banking operations and closing down the unprofitable and those with high reputational risk (e.g. its tax management division, accused of helping the wealthy avoid taxes through complicated legal structures), is likely to continue to emphasise its strengths in bond markets. Bank of America, Citigroup, JPMorgan Chase remain strong universal banks too.

Others were always more cautious about too much emphasis on the investment banking side and so did not allow these aspects to grow big relative to the rest of the bank, e.g. HSBC, Standard Chartered, Santander and BBVA. Of course, where they have the critical mass and high reputation, leading to high profits in particular areas of investment banking (e.g. HSBC in bond trading and cross-border trade) they intend to carry on. But they are not determined to be top of the league tables in all aspects of investment banking, unlike some more macho counterparts.

Others are just trying to stay alive and are looking critically at any area of the bank that uses large amounts of capital showing a poor risk-return ratio, e.g. RBS and Lloyds, which are selling off or closing down bits of their businesses, while keeping high market shares in commercial banking – Lloyds has over one-quarter, and RBS (including NatWest) almost one-fifth, of UK current accounts. Nomura is also retreating after an expedition to buy the investment banking operations of Lehman Brothers in Europe failed to produce the goods. It is scaling back unprofitable overseas businesses and reallocating resources to Japan and Asia.

This is very much a situation of flux and by the time this book is published banks will have made major strategic moves – so you need to keep watching. What we can say is that the glory days of ever-expanding investment banks, and those 'masters of the universe', is, at least for the foreseeable future, in abeyance. The pendulum has swung back towards an emphasis on traditional, humdrum commercial banking rather than what politicians refer to as the 'casino' activities of the investment bank side.

The American banking industry is somewhat different to the structure in much of Europe and Asia where a very small group of large banks dominate the retail and wholesale side. The Americans have thousands of small commercial banks often restricted to operating only in particular States, and a handful of universal banks – although currently the breadth of their activities is being curtailed by angry politicians and regulators in the wake of the financial crisis (see Chapter 19 of *The Financial Times Guide to Financial Markets* (2012) by Glen Arnold for an explanation of the causes and consequences of the crisis).

We also find organisations concentrating almost exclusively on investment banking, e.g. Goldman Sachs and Morgan Stanley. These two became, technically, **'bank holding companies'** rather than **broker-dealer investment banks** in 2008 to save themselves in the meltdown. This way they gained access to emergency lending facilities from the Federal Reserve Bank (the US central bank – see Chapter 25) in a crisis. Despite rapidly expanding commercial bank divisions, lending to wealthy clients and taking their deposits and managing their money, they remain focused on the activities listed in the third and fourth boxes of Figure 2.1. They are a long way from retail banking. On the other hand, there are still some large US banks that prefer to concentrate on old-fashioned servicing of ordinary people's financial needs without a significant investment banking presence, such as Wells Fargo.

All in all, the banking sector consists of a mixed bunch, there is no typical bank or typical national structure of banking. Some are purely home-country bankers with little or no investment banking activities, others are or aspire to be, giants on the world stage with the power to move vast amounts of money around the globe, to intimidate governments and the power to greatly damage economies if they mess things up. What is clear is that we are entering a period of unprecedented change. Ordinary people, while recognising the benefits of good banking practice, are fed up with the disasters they are asked to pay for. They want reform, they want more humility and greater safety, they want concentration on socially useful activities. It will be an interesting period to live through.

Retail banking

At the heart of banking is the acceptance of deposits, the making of loans and enabling customers to make payments. This chapter describes the deposit-taking function of banks and introduces lending methods and structures for individuals and small and medium-size businesses. The next chapter looks at payment systems and the wide variety of other activities performed by retail banks.

Assets and liabilities

The main source of funds for banks is deposits, as shown in Table 3.1; this provides a very crude breakdown of the sources of funds available to banks. The proportions vary from bank to bank depending on whether the bank is purely retail banking focused or has moved into corporate or investment banking (indeed many investment banks would have no deposits at all). Also some banks deliberately choose to obtain most of their money from deposits whereas others obtain a high proportion from issuing securities on the financial markets.

Table 3.1   **Typical liabilities of banks – a rough breakdown**

	Proportion of assets (%)
Current accounts, also called sight deposits	10–40
Time deposits, also called savings accounts	10–50
Money market borrowing[1] (repos, interbank, certificates of deposit)	10–40
Bank capital	5–15

Banks recognise that any money deposited (or lent to them via the purchase of a financial market security) will have to be repaid one day; thus deposits and other borrowings by the bank are classified as liabilities. If you deposit money in a bank it is an asset for you and part of your wealth because you can withdraw it, but it is an obligation for the bank. (When the bank says that you are in credit, it means that you are a creditor – it owes you the money.) We will discuss money market borrowing and bank capital later in the book. For now we will concentrate on deposits.

Deposits

Current account (cheque (check) account, demand deposits or sight account)

An individual can walk into a bank branch and withdraw the money held in their **current account** at very short notice. Alternatively, they can transfer the money to someone else's account, either using a paper-based method or electronically. These accounts usually pay very low (or no) rates of interest and so are a low-cost source of funds for the bank from that point of view, but the bank will need to spend a considerable amount in processing transfers, monthly statements, providing conveniently located branches, etc. In some countries a fee for each cheque may be charged above a threshold number each month. Banks often run current accounts at a loss in order to build up a relationship with a customer so that other services can be sold.

Current accounts are the lifeblood of high street banking. In the UK, for example, 98% of households have at least one current account. Paying bills was traditionally done by writing out cheques and visiting a bank branch. Times have changed. According to TheCityUK, a body promoting UK financial services, 44 million British are registered for online banking and 38 million for telephone banking, thereby removing the need to visit a branch except on rare occasions. Cheque issuance in 1990 was 11 million daily and in 2011 it was 2.7 million; by 2018 this is predicted to be less than 1.6 million per day. In 2000 one in 12 payments was made by cheque; by 2018 this is expected to be less than one in 110.

Time or savings deposit accounts

Depositors agree to place money with a bank on the understanding that a set period of notice is required to withdraw cash ranging from a few days to several months. Alternatively, the customer may place the money in the account for a fixed period. There are usually substantial penalties for early withdrawal and the accounts rarely provide a cheque facility. In return for losing the flexibility to withdraw cash at short notice these accounts offer higher interest rates than current accounts. Minimum amounts may have to be maintained.

Lending

Some bank lending is short term, such as an overdraft, but most of it is long-term lending – certainly longer than the notice periods on most deposit accounts. Loans to individuals and to corporations typically account for 50–70% of a commercial bank's assets. Another 10–35% might be lent out to other banks and institutions in the financial markets on a short-term basis, i.e. money market instruments, or loans such as interbank lending or repos (see Chapters 6 and 20). Some is likely to be invested in long-term governments bonds, shares or other long-term investments, but this is usually below 20%. Somewhere between 1% and 10% of the bank's assets may be in the form of buildings, equipment, software or other assets such as gold.

It is possible for banks to lend out most of the money deposited despite a high proportion of deposits being repayable on demand because depositors usually do not all ask for their money back at the same time. However, just in case they need to meet unexpected large outflows, banks hold a fraction of their capital in the form of liquid reserves. This is cash (the same as in your wallet or purse) in the vault, at the tills and in automated teller machines (ATMs) as well as cash deposited at the central bank (banks need bank accounts too) such as the Bank of England, the Federal Reserve in the USA or the Bundesbank in Germany, or very liquid assets. The cash holdings usually account for a very small percentage of a bank's assets.[2] Funds kept in a highly liquid form (but not cash) may also include assets that can quickly be turned into cash such as lending to another bank for 24 hours or seven days (interbank lending) or government Treasury bills (lending to a government for, say, 3 or 6 months) that can be sold to other investors within minutes in a very active secondary market if money is needed.

Household lending

Consumer loans

Consumer loans (personal loans) are often **unsecured**, meaning that nothing is being used as specifically assigned collateral to be seized by the bank should the borrower fail to pay. In the UK these loans can be up to £25,000 if not secured by collateral and are usually repayable within five years. The interest rate is usually fixed at a constant percentage of the outstanding amount throughout the period.

Mortgages

Loans secured on property, such as a **house mortgage**, are typically repaid month by month over 20–25 years and carry a lower rate of interest than a consumer loan because of the lower risk for the bank. Annual mortgage lending by banks is very big business – over £140bn in the UK, where there are 11.3 million mortgages, with loans worth over £1,200bn[3] (£20,000 per person). Home mortgages outstanding in the USA are over $13,000bn ($42,000 per person).[4] About one-half of US households hold a mortgage on their main residence, compared with roughly one-fifth in the euro area. It is thought that Americans are more likely to view mortgages as a way of obtaining cash from their property through re-mortgaging than Europeans.

Mortgages can be arranged where the interest rate is at a **fixed rate** for its entire life (popular in the USA), or, more commonly in the UK, fixed for a period of say two or five years; for the remaining 20 years or so the rate of interest will vary when the mortgage lender changes, say, its **standard variable rate (SVR)**. The SVR is strongly influenced by, but not entirely determined by, the base rate interest rates targeted by the Bank of England. (The Bank of England is willing to lend to other banks. The interest rate it is willing to charge influences the individual bank's base rate, which is the benchmark interest rate. Bank loans of various types are set as so-many percentage points above the base rate.)

An alternative is a **tracker mortgage**. This is a type of variable interest rate mortgage, but during the tracking period (first few years) the interest rate tracks the Bank of England base rate at a set margin (e.g. 2%) above or below it. After that the rate is the SVR.

And, of course, there is the **variable rate mortgage ('adjustable-rate' or 'floating rate')** where the interest rate varies from the start of the mortgage depending on the lender's SVR. To try and entice borrowers banks often offer **discounted variable rate mortgages** where the interest rate is set at a certain 'discount' below the lender's SVR for a set period of time. For example, if a lender has an SVR of 4% and the discount is 1%, the rate you'll pay will be 3%. Discount mortgage deals typically last between two and five years, following which the lender will transfer the borrower onto its SVR. While UK base rates remain at 0.5%, SVR-based mortgages are typically 2.5–5.5%, i.e. 2–5% above the base rate. There is a danger here. When base rates rise to more normal levels, say 4% or 5%, borrowers may find themselves paying over twice as much each month.

Prior to the 2008 crisis lenders were keen to lend over 90% of the market value of the property – a 10% or less down payment. In some case they would lend 100% or even, unbelievably now, 110%. They were also not too fastidious about ensuring applicants really did have the income required to afford the repayments (a typical benchmark is a loan three times the annual income of the applicant). They have now gone the other way, charging very high interest rates if the borrower wants a **loan-to-value ratio** greater than 90%, if they are willing to lend at all. The UK government has devised schemes to encourage banks to lend at higher loan-to-value ratios, e.g. the 'Help to Buy' scheme allows 5% deposits from home buyers, with the government guaranteeing the next 15% of the loan.

Buy-to-let mortgages is a very important sub-category in the UK. The borrower uses a property as collateral which will be rented out to tenants. The lender may examine the borrower's income other than rent to judge the safety of the loan; however, many lenders will only focus on the extent to which the monthly rent is greater than the mortgage payments (usually 1.3 times) and the loan-to-value ratio (usually 75%).

As well as loan-to-value ratios, the lender may measure creditworthiness by considering the affordability of the monthly payments expressed relative to the borrower's income. Also, **debt to income ratio** might be considered (all debt payments, including mortgage payments, as a percentage of income) and various net-worth measures. In many countries, credit scores may be used as well.

Credit scoring

Credit scoring is estimating the creditworthiness (likelihood of repaying debt) of a person using numerical data. Credit scores, often compiled by specialist firms (**credit bureaus**) such as Experian and Equifax, are often used to determine who qualifies for a loan, credit card, store cards, car lease, etc. It may also determine the interest rate and the **credit limit** (maximum extent of borrowing). A statistical analysis is conducted making use of a wide variety of information, including:

- Paid past bills and debts on time?
- Large amount of debt outstanding from various sources?
- A long or short history of borrowing and then repaying?
- Many applications for credit?
- Experience at managing a mix of credit from various sources?

Other household lending

Banks also lend via credit cards – discussed later in the next chapter. (For leasing and other asset-based finance – see Chapter 13.)

Lending to businesses

For most companies banks remain the main source of **externally** (i.e. not retained earnings) **raised finance**. Banks make it attractive for companies to borrow from them compared with other forms of borrowing:

- ▓ **Administrative and legal costs are low.** Because the loan arises from direct negotiation between borrower and lender the marketing, arrangement and regulatory expenses involved in, say, a bond issue are avoided.

- ▓ **Quick.** The key provisions of a bank loan can be worked out speedily and the funding facility can be in place within a matter of hours.

- ▓ **Flexibility.** If the economic circumstances facing the firm should change during the life of the loan banks are generally better equipped – and are more willing – to alter the terms of the lending agreement than bondholders. Negotiating with a single lender in a crisis has distinct advantages. Bank loans are also more flexible in the sense that if the firm does better than originally expected a bank loan can often be repaid early without penalty. Contrast this with many bonds with fixed redemption dates, or hire purchase/leasing arrangements with fixed terms.

- ▓ **Available to small firms.** Bank loans are available to firms of almost any size whereas the bond market is for the big players only.

An **arrangement fee** may be payable by the borrower to the bank at the time of the initial lending, say 1% of the loan, but this is subject to negotiation and may be bargained down. The interest rate can be either fixed (same for the whole borrowing period) or floating (variable). If it is floating then the rate will generally be a certain percentage above the bank's **base rate** or **LIBOR**. LIBOR is the London Inter-Bank Offered Rate, that is, the rate of interest charged when a bank lends to a highly reputable and safe bank in London (see Chapter 6). Because the typical borrowing corporation is not as safe as a high-quality bank it will pay say 1% (also referred to as 100 **basis points, bps**) more than LIBOR if it is in a good bargaining position.

In the case of **base-rate-related lending** the interest payable changes immediately the bank announces a change in its base rate. This moves irregularly in response to financial market conditions, which are heavily influenced by the central bank in its attempt to control the economy (see Chapter 24). For customers in a poorer bargaining position offering a higher-risk proposal the rate could be 5% or more over the base rate or LIBOR. The interest rate will be determined not only by the risk of the undertaking and the bargaining strength of the customer but also by the degree of security for the loan and the size of loan – economies of scale in lending mean that large borrowers pay a lower interest rate.

A generation ago it would have been more normal to negotiate fixed-rate loans but most loans today are variable rate. If a fixed rate of interest is charged this is generally at a higher rate of interest than the floating rate at the time of arrangement because of the additional risk to the lender of being unable to modify rates as an uncertain future unfolds.

Overdraft

Usually the amount that a depositor can withdraw from a bank account is limited to the amount put in. However, business and other financial activity often require some flexibility in this principle, and it is often useful to gain permission to take more money out of a bank account than it contains up to a certain limit – this is an **overdraft**.

Overdraft facilities are usually arranged (authorised) for a period of a few months or a year and interest is charged on the excess drawings. They are popular in Germany and the UK and are frequently used by people and businesses whether by prior arrangement or accidentally. If the borrower goes **overdrawn without authorisation** (an **unauthorised overdraft**) then additional fees/penalties are charged. In other countries (e.g. France) banks take a very tough line if you try to remove more than what you have deposited in an account, unless you have prior authorisation.

Overdrafts have the two following advantages:

1 **Flexibility.** The borrowing firm (individual) is not asked to forecast the precise amount and duration of its borrowing at the outset but has the flexibility to borrow up to a stated limit. Also the borrower is assured that the moment the funds are no longer required they can be quickly and easily repaid without suffering a penalty.

2 **Cheapness for businesses.** Banks usually charge 2–5 percentage points over base rate (or LIBOR) depending on the creditworthiness, security offered and bargaining position of the borrower. There may also be an arrangement fee of, say, 1% of the facility, but many banks have dropped arrangement fees to attract borrowers. These charges may seem high but it must be borne in mind that overdrafts are often loans to smaller and riskier firms which would otherwise have to pay much more for their funds. Large and well-established borrowers with low **financial gearing** (low borrowing relative to the amount put in by the business owners – also called **leverage**) and plenty of collateral can borrow on overdraft at much more advantageous rates. A major saving comes from the fact that the banks charge interest only on the daily outstanding balance. So, if a firm has a large cash inflow one week it can use this to reduce its overdraft, temporarily lowering the interest payable, while retaining the ability to borrow more another week.

A major drawback to an overdraft for the borrower is that the bank retains the right to withdraw the facility at short notice. Thus a heavily indebted firm may receive a letter from the bank insisting that its account be brought to balance within a matter of days. This right lowers the risk to the lender because it can quickly get its money out of a troubled company, allowing it to lower the cost of borrowing. However, it can be devastating for the borrower and so firms are well advised to think through the use to which finance provided by way of an overdraft is put. It is not usually wise to use the money for an asset which cannot be easily liquidated; e.g., it could be problematic if an overdraft is used for a bridge-building project which will take three years to come to fruition.

Term loans

A **term loan** is a business loan with an original maturity of more than one year and a specified schedule of principal and interest payments. These loans are normally for a period of between three and seven years, but the period can range from 1–20 years. It may or may not be secured with collateral and has the advantage over the overdraft of not being repayable at the demand of the bank at short notice (if the borrower sticks to the agreement). The specified terms will include provisions regarding the repayment schedule.

Alternative repayment arrangements

In setting up a term loan the bank can be very flexible with regard to the conditions it sets for the borrower. For example, a proportion of the interest and the principal can be repaid monthly, or annually, and can be varied to correspond with the borrower's cash flows. It is rare for there to be no repayment of the principal during the life of the loan but it is possible to request that the bulk of the principal is paid in the later years. It could be disastrous, for instance, for a firm engaging in a project which involved large outlays for the next five years followed by cash inflows thereafter to have a bank loan which required significant interest and principal payments in the near term. If the borrower is to apply the funds to a project which will not generate income for perhaps the first three years it may be possible to arrange a **grace period** or **repayment holiday** during which only the interest is paid, with the capital being paid off once the project has a sufficiently positive cash flow.

Other arrangements can be made to reflect the pattern of cash flow of the firm or project: e.g. a **'balloon' payment structure** is one where only a small part of the capital is repaid during the main part of the loan period, with the majority repayable as the maturity date approaches. A **'bullet'** repayment arrangement takes this one stage further and provides for all the capital to be repaid at the end of the loan term. Banks generally prefer **self-amortising term loans** with a high proportion of the principal paid off each year. This has the advantage of reducing risk by imposing a programme of debt reduction on the borrowing firm.

Instalments and drawdowns

Not all term loans are drawn down in a single lump sum at the time of the agreement. In the case of a construction project which needs to keep adding to its borrowing to pay for the different stages of development, an **instalment arrangement** might be required with, say, 25% of the money being made available immediately, 25% at foundation stage and so on. This has the added attraction to the lender of not committing large sums secured against an asset not yet created. From the borrower's point of view a **drawdown arrangement** has an advantage over an overdraft in that the lender is committed to providing the finance if the borrower meets prearranged conditions, whereas with an overdraft the lender can withdraw the arrangement at short notice.

Reducing risk for the bank

Information flows

When banks are considering the provision of debt finance for a firm they will be concerned about the borrower's competence and honesty. They need to evaluate the proposed project and assess the degree of managerial commitment to its success. The firm will have to explain why the funds are needed and provide detailed cash forecasts covering the period of the loan. Between the bank and the firm stands the classic gulf called **asymmetric information** in which one party in the negotiation is ignorant of, or cannot observe, some of the information which is essential to the contracting and decision-making process. The bank is unable to assess accurately the ability and determination of the managerial team and will not have a complete understanding of the market environment in which the team proposes to operate. Companies may overcome bank uncertainty to some degree by providing as much information as possible at the outset and keeping the bank informed of the firm's position as the project progresses.

Bankers encourage the finance director and chief executive to consider carefully both the quantity and quality of information flows to the bank. An improved flow of information can lead to a better and more supportive relationship. Firms with significant bank financing requirements to fund growth will be well advised to cultivate and strengthen understanding and rapport with their bank(s). The time to lay the foundations for subsequent borrowing is when the business does not need the money, so that when loans are required there is a reasonable chance of being able to borrow the amount needed on acceptable terms.

Relationship banking and transactional banking

There are two types of interaction a company might have with a bank. The first is **relationship banking** in which there is an understanding on both sides that there will be a long-term relationship in which the company provides information regularly to the bank and the bank can reduce its screening and monitoring costs compared with new customers. Over time, the bank develops special knowledge of the firm and its needs and as a result can be more supportive when the need for borrowing or forbearance in hard times is needed. The other type is **transactional banking** in which the company shops around for services looking for the lowest cost for individual tasks. This has the advantage of obtaining cheaper individual services, but the absence of a long-term relationship can make the firm vulnerable in tough times.

Collateral

Another way for a bank to reduce its risk is for the firm to offer sufficient **collateral** for the loan. Collateral provides a means of recovering all or the majority of the bank's investment should the firm fail to repay as promised. If the firm is unable to meet its loan obligations then holders of **fixed charge** collateral can seize the specific asset used to back the loan. With a **floating charge** the legal right to seize assets 'floats' over the general assets of the firm so they can be bought and sold or rented without specific permission from the lender. The charge only **crystallises** at the point of default on the loan – the assets are frozen within the firm and made available to repay lenders. On liquidation, the proceeds of selling assets will go first to the secured loanholders, including floating-charge bank lenders.

Bankers may look at a firm on two levels. First, they might consider a **liquidation analysis** in which they think about their position in a scenario of business failure. Secondly, they will look at a firm on the assumption that it is a **going concern**, where cash flows rather than assets become more important.

Collateral can include stocks (inventories) of unsold goods, debtors and equipment as well as land, buildings and marketable investments such as shares in other companies. In theory, banks often have this strong right to seize assets or begin proceedings to liquidate. In practice, they are reluctant to use these powers because such draconian action can bring adverse publicity.

Banks are careful to create a margin for error in the assignment of sufficient collateral to cover the loan because, in the event of default, assigned assets usually command a much lower price than their value to the company as a going concern. A quick sale at auction produces bargains for the buyers of liquidated assets and usually little for the creditors. Instead of rushing to force a firm to liquidate, banks will often try to **reschedule** or **restructure** the finance of the business (e.g. grant a longer period to pay).

Loan covenants

Another safety feature applied by banks is the requirement that the borrowing firm abides by a number of **loan covenants** which place restrictions on managerial action until the debt has been repaid in full. Some examples are:

- **Limits on further debt issuance.** If lenders provide finance to a firm they do so on certain assumptions concerning the riskiness of the capital structure. They will want to ensure that the loan does not become more risky due to the firm taking on a much greater debt burden relative to its equity base, so they limit the amount and type of further debt issues – particularly debt which is higher (**senior debt**) ranked for interest payments and for a liquidation payment. **Subordinated debt** – with a low ranking on liquidation – is more likely to be acceptable.

- **Dividend level.** Lenders are opposed to money being brought into the firm by borrowing at one end, while being taken away by shareholders at the other. An excessive withdrawal of shareholder funds may unbalance the financial structure and weaken future cash flows.

- **Limits on the disposal of assets.** The retention of certain assets, e.g. property and land, may be essential to reduce the lenders' risk.

- **Financial ratios.** A typical covenant here concerns the **interest cover**, e.g.: 'The annual pre-interest pre-tax profit will remain four times as great as the overall annual interest charge.' Other restrictions might be placed on working capital ratio levels,[5] and the debt to net assets ratio. If these financial ratio limits are breached or interest and capital is not paid on the due date the bank has a right of termination, in which case it could decide not to make any more funds available or, in extreme cases, insist on the repayment of funds already lent.

While covenants cannot provide completely risk-free lending they can influence the behaviour of the management team so as to reduce the risk of default.

Guarantees

Lenders' risk can be further reduced by obtaining guarantees from third parties that the loan will be repaid. The guarantor is typically the parent company of the borrower. Finally, lenders can turn to the directors of the firm to provide additional security. They might be asked to sign **personal guarantees** that the firm will not default. Personal assets (such as homes) may be used as collateral. This erodes the principle of limited liability status and is likely to inhibit risk-taking productive activity. However for many smaller firms it may be the only way of securing a loan and at least it demonstrates the commitment of the director to the success of the enterprise.[6]

The five C's for qualitative assessment of risk

Bankers often use a checklist of factors when considering a business loan or, indeed, a personal loan – see Table 3.2.

Table 3.2	The five C's for credit analysis
CHARACTER	An assessment of creditworthiness considers important factors such as character and talents of the individuals leading the organisation. Traits such as trustworthiness and honour are relevant alongside a consideration of business experience, education and history of loan repayments and ability to stick to a task even in troubled times.
CAPACITY	Will the business (individual) be able to pay back? When and how? Cash flow forecast and profit projections are evaluated for realism as well as alternative ways of repayment if the business plan does not work out. Do the forecasts make sense in light of any past cash flows?
COLLATERAL	As well as seizable physical assets, personal assets need to be evaluated if they are the source of security for a personal guarantee. Banks will not lend pound for pound against assets held, giving a margin for error and allowing for discounted sales values in a liquidation, e.g. they might lend up to 80% of accounts receivable, 50% against inventory, 80% against equipment and 75% against property.
CONDITIONS	A review of the business environment facing the firm: e.g. degree of competition, prospects for the economy, potential for new entrants to this industry, risks due to being heavily dependent on one customer or source of supply.
CAPITAL	Is the business owner making a serious commitment of his or her own capital (equity) to the business; enough 'skin in the game'? If he or she is able to do so, but chooses not to, then why should the bank have high faith in the prospects for the venture? Equity is needed to withstand adverse conditions, to absorb losses before the debt portion of the capital is impaired.

Transferring money and other retail bank services

By way of introduction and to demonstrate the importance of the services discussed in the first part of this chapter I ask you to consider the devastation wrought by a virtual closing down of the payments system in Cyprus in 2013 – see Article 4.1. Clearly, we are very dependent on the efficient and continuous running of the mechanisms behind the transfer of money.

After describing payments systems the chapter moves on to the amazing range of other services banks now offer to retail (and big business) customers. They have the high street presence, the technological infrastructure, expertise and (notwithstanding the troubles in investment banking) the trust of customers to offer much more than deposit, loan and payment services. The banks enjoy the additional income these extra activities bring.

Payment mechanisms

Banks facilitate payments between people and organisations using either paper or electronic means.

Cheques

While still a popular means of settling indebtedness the cheque is increasingly giving way to direct debits, credit and debit cards. A **bank draft** is somewhat different to a standard cheque because it is drawn on a bank (it is paying) and so there is a very high likelihood that the payment will be made. The bank customer wanting to buy something (e.g. car) will prearrange the creation of the draft and will be charged a fee.

Giro

Even before the electronic age people without cheque books could still transfer money to others by using a giro slip which instructs their bank to pay, say, the

Cyprus struggles to cope with lack of coins

By Kerin Hope in Nicosia

Popi, the owner of a kiosk selling newspapers and cigarettes in a central Nicosia square, was turning customers away on Wednesday because she had run out of change.

"If you've got a €5 note to spend, that's fine," she said. "Otherwise, I'm keeping tabs for a few regulars, but I'm losing a lot of business."

Banks across the island were closed on Wednesday for a second day as the government struggled to find ways of raising its €5.8bn share of an international bailout.

Online banking shut down last Friday. "It is frightening how Cyprus turned into a cash economy in just a few days," said Anthimos Evgenides, an economics student trying to change a €100 banknote at a pharmacy.

"I am sitting with my team working on different scenarios while we wait for the government to come up with some decisions," said the chief executive of a corporate communications company with franchises in the Balkans and Gulf states. "We had some of our people abroad go and open new bank accounts in their capitals today, so we can avoid routing transfers through Cyprus... There's going to be a huge back-up of electronic transactions when the banks reopen."

Hotels, restaurants and some supermarkets have stopped accepting credit cards for transactions as suppliers in turn demand cash from clients.

"Some wholesalers have just suspended the 45-day payment schedule and want cash upfront," said Olga, a Ukrainian immigrant managing a mini-market in Nicosia's old town.

Andreas Papaellinas, a leading importer, warned that the island's supply chain could seize up by the weekend.

"Since Friday we have seen retailing down, wholesalers suffering and imports starting to pile up at the ports. We cannot operate our business for more than a day or two without a functioning banking system."

electricity company. Bank giro credits (credit transfers) remain a popular means of payment to this day in Germany, The Netherlands, Austria and Japan. Giro banks were set up in many European countries using their post offices to allow those without a bank account, let alone a cheque book, to make payments. The bill could be paid at the post office counter and the money transferred to the payee. Post offices can be surprisingly big players in the financial system. Indeed, the largest deposit-taking institution in the world is not a bank but the Japanese post office. It holds around £2,000bn in savings accounts (one-quarter of all Japanese household assets) and has bought one-fifth of all the Japanese government bonds in issue. That is a lot of bonds given that the Japanese government has outstanding borrowings of over 200% of annual gross domestic product (GDP).

Standing orders and direct debits

These are used for recurring payments. With **standing orders** the account holder instructs his or her bank to pay a fixed regular amount to a beneficiary's account. It is only the account holder who can change the order instructions. **Direct debits** are similar to standing orders except that the supplier of a good or service which is due to be paid (e.g. gas or water company) gets the customer to sign the direct debit which allows the supplier to vary the amount and the time of payment.

Plastic cards

We have got so used to transferring money using plastic that it no longer seems remarkable. A bank card allows us to use ubiquitous ATMs (automated teller machines), providing a quick way of obtaining cash, checking balances or other services. The **debit card** (usually the same card as the ATM-enabled card) allows us to make payments by providing the information the retailer needs to set up what is in effect an electronic cheque to credit the retailer's account while debiting our account. They use an **EFTPOS (electronic funds transfer at point of sale)** terminal to initiate the debiting of our accounts. EFTPOS are even more numerous than ATMs.

Credit cards allow users to pay for goods, wait for a statement of indebtedness to the credit card company, and then decide whether to pay off the whole amount outstanding that month or pay only, say, 5% of the debt owed and borrow the rest until the user is in a better position to pay back. Users are allowed a fixed maximum borrowing. The credit card company gains income from charging the retailers (usually 1–3% of the transaction value) as well as charging the user interest if he or she fails to pay off the full amount outstanding each month. The rates on money borrowed this way can be very high. For example, while secured mortgages can be obtained for around 3–6% per year, credit cards typically charge over 18%. Much of this extra interest is to cover bad debts and fraud. Visa and Mastercard process transactions for the retailer and card issuer. Just how much we use these two types of cards can be seen in Figure 4.1, which shows the monthly amount the British spend.

Thousands of commercial organisations, such as high-street retailers, issue their own versions of credit cards, known as **store cards**. The retailer usually lacks the infrastructure to process the store card transactions and so works with a bank or a specialist organisation. American Express and Diners Club cards are different – they are **charge cards**. Here, the user is expected to pay off the balance every month.

Smart cards (electronic purses, chip cards) store information on a microchip. This might be an amount of cash (**e-money**) loaded onto it using an ATM, personal computer or telephone/tablet download. The retailer is able to take money

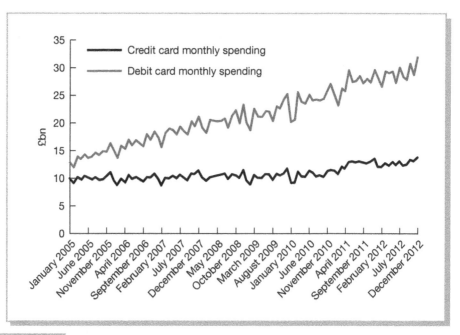

Figure 4.1   **Monthly expenditure on debit and credit cards in UK**

Source: www.theukcardsassociation.org.uk

from the customer's card and load it onto its own, ready for paying into its bank account. To purchase goods on the internet **e-cash** is often used, which is created by setting up an account with a bank which then transfers credits to the user's internet-enabled device. When the user wants to buy something cash is taken electronically from the user's device and transferred to the merchant's computer.

Landlines and mobile phones

Telephone banking has been with us a long time now. Some banks are principally telephone (with internet) based, e.g. First Direct in the UK, but mostly telephone banking is an extra service available for standard branch-based accounts. Not only is telephone banking available 24 hours a day but transactions such as bill paying can be conducted quickly and loans can be arranged.

Banks encourage customers to use telephone banking because the cost of undertaking a transaction can be one-quarter to one-half that of using the branch. In many parts of Africa people, many of whom do not have bank accounts, are transferring money to each other using mobile phones.[1] In Kenya over 70% of adults use the system, with 25% of the economic output flowing through it. It is convenient and safer than carrying cash on public transport. It allows people to save small amounts without a bank account and money transfers are more traceable than cash (useful where there are corrupt government officials). India has great potential for mobile banking – see Article 4.2.

M-Pesa's cautious start in India

By James Crabtree

Rajasthan seems an improbable setting for a technology revolution. Yet for the past year the historic northern state has provided the testing ground for an idea that some believe could help bring basic financial services to hundreds of millions of Indians for the first time – in the form of mobile money.

In November 2011 just outside Jaipur, a city better known for its hill-top forts and charming pink buildings, Vodafone, the UK-based mobile phone company, announced plans to pilot M-Pesa. This service, pioneered in Africa, lets users store cash on their phones and use it either to shop, pay bills or send money to others.

Since then Vodafone, which is India's second-largest mobile operator, has been busily signing up agents in nearby villages, who are often simply small shop owners in dusty roadside shacks, who then sell the product to locals. The trial went well, and last month the company announced plans to roll it out nationwide.

Mobile money's admirers talk up its many benefits, which include the possibility of ending financial exclusion across the developing world. These champions point especially to successes in Kenya, where M-Pesa has become a virtual currency, used by more than seven in 10 adults.

In India the opportunity is clear enough. More than half the country's 1.2bn population have no bank account, but it is the world's second- largest mobile phone market, with more than 900m subscribers. If only a fraction of these customers sign on, India could easily become the world's mobile money leader.

Mobile money's ponderous start in India means it is much further advanced in neighbouring countries such as Bangladesh and Pakistan. Poorer users might start off by simply transferring money to friends or relatives, but they can move up to more complex savings and investment products.

As well as being convenient for customers, mobile money can have wider economic benefits:

- Increased remittance (from overseas relatives) flows, lower transaction costs for small businesses and a move towards the formal banking sector are all positively associated with growth.

- In Kenya, M-Pesa's success has helped spawn a small start-up scene, known as 'silicon savannah'.

- It can cut graft. In Afghanistan mobile money is used to pay policemen, removing corrupt intermediaries, while other countries use it to send state welfare payments. As India completes its Aadhaar project, an ambitious government programme to provide every citizen with a unique biometric identification number, these uses have potential.

Internet, smartphones and tablets

Millions of people now use internet-based accounts as an extra facility attached to their usual account. Transaction costs for banks can be a tenth of those for branch-based activity, so expect to see banks promoting greater use of the internet. Smartphones allow customers to engage in bank transactions online almost anywhere and at almost any time – as a result the number of interactions with a bank, such as checking balances or transferring money, each month have risen significantly. Internet, smartphone and tablet banking is even more important in rapidly growing Asian countries – see Article 4.3.

Article 4.3

Banking's handy revolution

By Paul J Davies in Hong Kong

The battle to win bank customers across Asia is not taking place on its high streets or even through its televisions and computer monitors – increasingly it is taking place in the palms of people's hands.

As the region's economies grow, become more urban and more middle-class, many industries are skipping stages of technological development that took years – even decades – to pass through in the west. Some banks have woken up to the fact that their industry is not just skipping a bit of history but that the people who should be their customers are coming to financial services from an entirely different starting point.

China alone already accounts for 40 per cent of mobile banking users worldwide. Aside from the brute numbers, Asia's youthful demographics and rapid adoption of smartphones and other mobile technologies influence the character of the markets. "Asia is leading the way in mobile banking because consumer behaviour is leading the banks, but also because there is much more upside to making an investment [in consumer

technology] where you have growth markets and lower branch numbers," says Kenny Lam, a partner at McKinsey, the consultancy.

For the wider market the key for banks, as in so many other sectors, is being able to collect and use data – on what consumers earn, what they owe, where and on what they spend their money. "Where there is a real arms race is on the customer analytics front, to deliver a service that is bespoke," he says. "The predictive capabilities of Amazon around recommendations for books or music are the example to follow."

Across the region, the use of mobile and internet for banking overtook branch and telephone use for the first time last year.

The bank is fighting to keep its place "in the value chain", an executive explained – battling to prevent the loss of consumer data and to maintain low but steady revenues from ordinary transactions that might otherwise be claimed by non-bank competitors such as Alibaba, the internet group that is also offering loans to small businesses.

➡

Article 4.3   Continued

Smartphones connect with new customers

In Asia, mobile banking is potentially the touch paper for people to begin using financial services, both more regularly and for the first time. Some simple numbers illustrate this.

Across Asia, 55% of adults have a bank account, according to the World Bank. In China, the number is slightly higher with almost 64% of people having one, while in Vietnam and Indonesia the figure is about 20%.

In the USA, that number is almost 90% – and in the UK it is nearing 100%.

But China has almost 1 billion mobile phone users, up to a third of which have smartphones, according to various industry estimates. In the USA, the total number of mobile phones of all kinds is 320 million, according to the CTIA, a US trade body.

According to Juniper Research, east Asia boasts 240 million mobile banking users versus the USA's 54 million, and it reckons that the region will make up almost half the projected 1 billion users it forecasts for 2017.

 Source: Davies, P. J. (2013) 'Banking's handy revolution', *Financial Times*, 27 February.

Smartphones are increasingly being used as mobile wallets, with apps allowing people to pay for items – see Article 4.4. The mobile operators and retailers may step on the toes of banks here. Banks value the close relationship they have with customers when handling their payments and want to charge retailers for electronic payments. The retailers and phone operators would like to reduce the cut going to banks and to have full access to details about consumers' shopping habits through monitoring their payments; thus they are setting up alternative systems.

Article 4.4

KFC eyes more orders with 'mobile wallet'

By April Dembosky in San Francisco

Kentucky Fried Chicken has become the latest company to allow customers to use a "mobile wallet" to order and pay for food before they arrive at an outlet.

The company has joined McDonald's, Starbucks and other quick service restaurants trying to attract new customers and boost sales through smartphone apps and mobile payment systems.

Forest Research estimates that mobile payments are expected to reach $90bn by 2017.

"When you have a very comfortable ordering environment, like a smartphone, you just order more," said Jeremie Leroyer, chief executive of Airtag, which built the app for KFC.

He said mobile ordering for fast food restaurants would count for about 5 per cent of transactions

Continued

in the next year, but expected that to "grow drastically" in the next two to three years.

KFC implemented its technology in 10 locations in the UK on Wednesday, with the goal to extend it across the country, then to the US and the rest of the world.

The move comes as companies from Google to start-ups race to build the default technology, in what analysts now refer to as the "digital wallet wars".

PayPal, the payment arm of e-commerce company eBay, is developing apps that allow people to order and pay in sit-down restaurants without having to wait for the server to bring the bill. It is also running a test with Jamba

Juice that allows people to order and pay for smoothies from their mobile phones, then pick them up in the store, bypassing the line and cash register.

Last year Starbucks began replacing the payment systems in its 7,000 US locations with mobile payments technology built by Square, a San Francisco start-up.

Carrefour, the second-largest retailer in the world by sales after Walmart, has deployed a version of the technology in its grocery stores in France. It allows people to order and pay for all their groceries from their mobile phone or a computer, then pick them up in the store, where everything is bagged and waiting for them at a set time.

Source: Dembosky, A. (2013) 'KFC eyes more orders with "mobile wallet"', *Financial Times*, 3 April.

Clearing systems

After a cheque (or electronic payment) has been written and handed over to the payee there needs to be a system for transferring the money from one bank account to another. This is **clearing**. Banks within countries came together long ago to work out a way of ensuring accurate and timely settlement of payments. Usually central banks led the process. Those banks linked into the system are referred to as **clearing banks**. These are usually only the large banks with extensive retail banking operations. Smaller banks may make a deal with one of the clearing banks for it to handle its cheque (electronic) clearance.

If a cheque or debit card draws money from one account for it to be credited to another person's account at the same bank then the bank will deal with clearing itself. If, however, money needs to be transferred to an account at another bank the cheque will be put through the central clearing system. This is mostly electronic because the cheque has computer-readable information such as the branch sort code, account number and cheque number displayed – the amount of money is the missing element that needs to be input. Of course, direct debits, standing orders and other regular payments are already inputted into computer systems to permit electronic clearance.

Clearing in the UK

In the UK all clearing is overseen by the **UK Payments Council** which acts as controller of various payment services: **BACS Ltd.** (originally the **Bankers' Automated Clearing Services**) clears electronic payment for direct debits and credits, standing orders, salaries, etc.; the **Cheque and Credit Clearing Company (C&CCC)** manages the cheque clearing system. The time taken to clear a cheque, three working days at best, is a constant cause for complaint, given that funds transferred over the internet or telephone can be virtually instantaneous. The reason for the time taken is that cheques must be returned physically to the paying bank, whose responsibility it is to detect discrepancies or fraud. Some banks speed up the process but it is still a far from rapid one – see Figure 4.2.

CHAPS (Clearing House Automated Payment System) allows money to be electronically transferred the same day (this costs a minimum of £25–£30 but is frequently worth it for large or urgent payments). It is a **real-time gross settlement (RTGS)** system meaning that payments are settled individually and continuously throughout the day within two hours, rather than waiting until the end of the day (thus avoiding the risk associated with a bank going bust half way through the day and not completing the deal). The average payment under CHAPS is about £2m compared with a few hundred under BACS and C&CCC.

Europe and US clearing

The **TARGET2 (Trans-European Automated Real-time Gross-settlement Express Transfer)** system is the most important large-value euro system for cross-border transfers within the EU.

A large group of banks own an international electronic payments system called **SWIFT (Society for Worldwide Interbank Financial Telecommunication)**, a messaging service that sends payment orders between banks and 10,000 other financial institutions and corporations which then settle payments between themselves. In the USA high-value payments go through a different electronic system called **CHIPS (clearing house interbank payments)** and **Fedwire**; there are a number of systems for small payments clearing.

Banks invest billions to ensure good payment systems. Even then the computers sometimes go wrong and everyone realises just how dependent we have become on efficient bank plumbing, and how much we take it for granted. Customers were irate at the failure of RBS to make payments on time in 2012; wages and supplier bills were left unpaid – see Article 4.5.

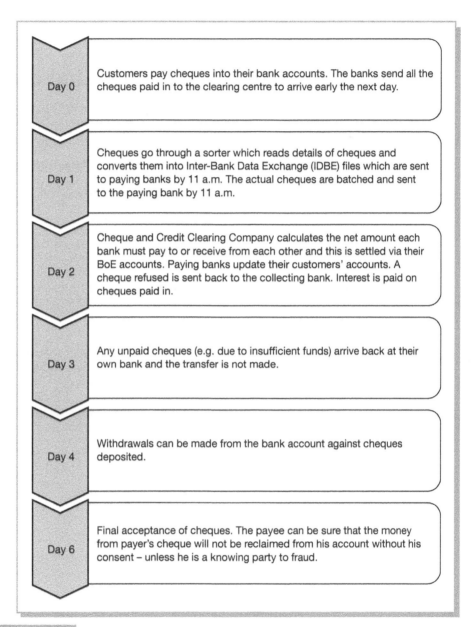

Day 0 Customers pay cheques into their bank accounts. The banks send all the cheques paid in to the clearing centre to arrive early the next day.

Day 1 Cheques go through a sorter which reads details of cheques and converts them into Inter-Bank Data Exchange (IDBE) files which are sent to paying banks by 11 a.m. The actual cheques are batched and sent to the paying bank by 11 a.m.

Day 2 Cheque and Credit Clearing Company calculates the net amount each bank must pay to or receive from each other and this is settled via their BoE accounts. Paying banks update their customers' accounts. A cheque refused is sent back to the collecting bank. Interest is paid on cheques paid in.

Day 3 Any unpaid cheques (e.g. due to insufficient funds) arrive back at their own bank and the transfer is not made.

Day 4 Withdrawals can be made from the bank account against cheques deposited.

Day 6 Final acceptance of cheques. The payee can be sure that the money from payer's cheque will not be reclaimed from his account without his consent – unless he is a knowing party to fraud.

Figure 4.2   **The cheque clearing process**
Source: Cheque and Credit Clearing Company

Article 4.5

RBS systems failure: Machines that can become banks' enemies within

By Sharlene Goff and Maija Palmer

Last month's computer problems at Royal Bank of Scotland plunged the company into a Kafkaesque tangle of unmanageable bureaucracy.

RBS said the initial problem was rectified within a couple of days but it lost track of which payments had been processed and had to draft in a team to check manually. With a backlog of about 20m transactions building up every day, it was drowning. At one point the bank had 100m unprocessed payments.

These difficulties had started with a fairly minor change. On Sunday June 17 the bank launched a routine upgrade of the "batch processing" software that allows it to process the millions of ordinary payments and cash withdrawals that customers make every day. The following night when its system started working through that day's transactions it became clear something was wrong. The process was slow, eating through too much memory. So 24 hours later, RBS attempted to unwind the upgrade – and the technology collapsed.

IT specialists who know RBS's systems well believe the glitch was probably the result of a simple human error – the wrong button being pressed at the wrong time. They have questioned whether RBS had the appropriate disciplines in place to ensure actions were properly supervised and approved by senior IT staff.

Such severe outages are rare at banks, although a number have suffered less extreme IT failures, largely as a result of bedding down acquisitions. Santander encountered problems when it integrated Abbey, the UK building society, for example. Bank of Scotland customers also suffered disruption when they joined the Lloyds TSB platform last year.

Other retail banking services

Although some banks are state-owned, as in China, or are owned by their customers, e.g. co-operative banks, the majority are run as commercial operations with the profit motive driving them forward. They are keen on finding new sources of revenue and over the past 30 years or so have done remarkably well in using the competitive advantages they possess, such as knowledge of long-standing customers, trust and presence on the high street, to sell an ever widening range of products and services to individuals and businesses. Customers often find when walking into a branch that the original activities of the bank (e.g. paying in money) are demoted to a corner while staff are encouraged to sell other services to customers. A phrase has been coined to describe the shift to a wide-ranging operation: **financial supermarkets.**

Stockbroking

In many countries, e.g. the UK, most buying and selling of shares and bonds by retail (individuals) investors takes place using independent stockbrokers as agents, rather than the banks. Having said this, the banks have established an impressive stockbroking business since they were permitted to enter the industry following the Big Bang of financial reforms in 1986. In other countries, e.g. many continental European countries, such as Germany and Switzerland, banks have long dominated the buying and selling of financial securities on behalf of investors. (See *The Financial Times Guide to Investing* by Glen Arnold, Chapter 4, for more on stockbrokers.)

Asset management

Banks often establish their own range of mutual funds, unit trusts or investment trusts to offer to investors, allowing investors to place their money in a wide range of shares or other securities in a portfolio under professional management (see *The Financial Times Guide to Financial Markets* by Glen Arnold, Chapter 7, for more on collective investments). The fees on these funds are usually over 1.5% per year and they can generate a lot of money for the bank. Alternatively banks may act as agents for outside fund management groups receiving a commission for sales made. In Spain the banks sell *Super Fondos*, in France they provide *SICAVs,* and most of these mutual funds can now be marketed across European borders.

Custody and safety deposits

Share and bond owners often do not want to receive and look after certificates of ownership. The banks provide a service of safekeeping and ensure interest or dividends are claimed. They will also notify the owner of annual general meetings of companies, rights issues and other events. The bank is paid a fee for acting as **custodian.** As well as the local retail custodianship there is also the big league of **global custodians** (mostly owned by banks) who safeguard the investments of enormous investment funds run by institutional investors – the amounts are measured in billions. In addition to dealing with the technicalities of transfer of ownership of shares and other securities, in a number of countries they collect income, reclaim tax and assist with other aspects of fund administration. They provide a very necessary protection for investors against illegal or fraudulent activities of the fund manager, who could be tempted into dishonest behaviour simply by the enormous sums involved. The idea is to keep the assets at arm's length from the individuals running the funds.

Banks may also provide safety deposit boxes for people to keep items such as jewellery in a vault. To open a box two keys are required, the customer's and the one kept at the bank.

Insurance and pensions

Most banks in continental Europe also own insurance operations or have a close relationship with an insurance company. The French have coined the term **bancassurance** for the selling of insurance and banking services alongside each other; the Germans have the term **Allfinanz**. Banks often know their customers well and can tailor insurance offerings to their needs. For example, if a couple with children take out a mortgage with a bank it is an easy sell to point out the need for life insurance to pay off the mortgage should one of the parents die, and for buildings and contents insurance. Banks are also increasingly selling pension savings schemes to their customers. (Chapters 7 and 8 of *The Financial Times Guide to Financial Markets* by Glen Arnold has more on insurance and pensions.)

Foreign exchange

There is a thriving business in exchanging currency for people going on holiday or for business transactions. Small and large corporations trading overseas need to deal with foreign exchange and risks associated with their movements. Banks assist here (see Chapter 23). **Traveller's cheques** are also available. These are pre-printed cheques of a fixed amount in various denominations issued by a bank. They are signed by the customer when first bought and then signed again when used for payment abroad. If lost or stolen the bank may reimburse.

Wealth management and private banking

Wealth management and **private banking** (terms that are used interchangeably)[2] are undertaken by a number of banks. This involves services and advice to improve the management of the financial affairs of high-net-worth individuals, including their investments, current and deposit accounts (possibly in numerous currencies and jurisdictions), obtaining of loans and tax issues. They may also offer advice on topics as wide-ranging as buying a jet to selecting private schools.

The definition of a high-net-worth individual varies, but usually means the person has over $1m in net wealth besides the main home. Annual fees may be charged (around 1% of assets managed) or/and each transaction is charged. There are some old and venerable names in this business such as C. Hoare and Co. and Pictet & Cie, but most of the high street banks also have private banking arms for their wealthier customers. The Swiss banks, with their tradition of confidentiality, integrity and long experience of good service, are particularly strong in this market segment.

5

Corporate banking: lending

Corporate banking builds on the foundation of retail banking because larger non-financial corporations also need the services provided by retail banks such as overdrafts, term loans and payment systems. However, larger and more complex companies seek more from their banks including loans for multi-million pound overseas projects or the ability to access funds from dozens of banks simultaneously. This chapter outlines various forms of borrowing that corporates obtain from their banks. The next chapter examines other aspects of commercial banking, ranging from operations in the interbank market (including the now infamous LIBOR) to help with overseas trading and managing day-to-day cash inflows/outflows.

Line of credit

An **uncommitted line of credit (credit line)** allows a company (or individual) to borrow up to a maximum sum for a given period (a month, months or years), repay and borrow again as needed within that time period. The bank is **uncommitted** because it merely has to make its best efforts to make the sum available and it has discretion to remove the facility at short notice. The interest rate is often set as a number of basis points over the interbank lending rate (see Chapter 6). A line of credit is very useful for short-term working capital or seasonal borrowing needs because interest is charged only on the outstanding balance at any one time and there is usually no penalty for paying off the balance early. It can be secured against collateral or unsecured.

If the line of credit description sounds very familiar, then you are right, it is similar to overdrafts (discussed in Chapter 3). But there is a subtle difference. Whereas the overdraft allows the borrower to have a negative balance on a current account, the line of credit is set up as a separate account. Then borrowed funds can be drawn on from the line of credit by transfer to the normal business account by phoning the bank, online or by visiting a branch. It may also be possible to obtain a credit card that draws from the line of credit.

Revolving credit facility

A **revolving credit facility (RCF)** is a term used for financial products very similar to a line of credit, except they are usually on a much larger scale.[1] The lender(s) enters into an obligation to provide funds upon request by the borrower, provided any agreed conditions and covenants in the loan agreement have been and are being met (a **committed** form of lending). They generally permit larger credit limits than overdrafts, and have the advantage over hire purchase and leasing (see Chapter 13) of not requiring the borrower to make a number of fixed payments to the bank. RCFs are usually for between one and five years.

Businesses often use RCFs alongside term loans to provide a borrowing facility for the less predictable week-by-week borrowing requirements or for cyclical cash flow challenges, such as VAT bills or seasonal work. Often, the borrowing can be available in a variety of currencies.

The bank is committing some of its assets to providing the facility to the corporation (legally enforceable) whether or not, in the end, the borrowing is actually needed. This uses up some of the bank's loan capacity and therefore it demands fees. **Front end** or **facility fees** are for setting it up and **commitment fees** on the undrawn amount are for providing the option to the borrower while the commitment remains in place. Of course, the borrower will also be charged interest on the amounts drawn under the facility, usually a number of basis points over an interbank rate (see Chapter 6).

A **bilateral facility** is a deal with a single lender, used for small credit limits. With a **syndicated facility**, two or more lenders each lend a proportion of the money. They are often used for larger deals where a single lender may not be willing and/or able to lend the whole amount. Bilaterals have less documentation and lower fees.

The insider's view   A syndicated facility

Simon Melliss, Chief Financial Officer of Hammerson, the property company, put together a large revolving credit facility:

'Hammerson plc announces the successful syndication and signing of a £505m five-year revolving credit facility. The facility carries a margin of 150 basis points over LIBOR. It will be used for general corporate purposes. The facility was increased from £400m to £505m following an over-subscription. BNP Paribas acted as co-ordinator for the facility, alongside 11 other prominent financial institutions:

▶

	Sterling (£)
BNP Paribas	50,000,000
Barclays Bank PLC	50,000,000
Bank of America Merrill Lynch	50,000,000
The Bank of Tokyo-Mitsubishi UFJ, Ltd.	50,000,000
HSBC Bank plc	50,000,000
JPMorgan	50,000,000
The Royal Bank of Scotland plc	50,000,000
Santander UK plc	50,000,000
Crédit Agricole Corporate and Investment Bank	35,000,000
Deutsche Bank AG, London Branch	35,000,000
Société Générale	35,000,000

'This new facility will replace existing undrawn facilities of £670m due to expire 2011–2013. Hammerson's third existing revolving credit facility of £340m will be maintained to maturity. Following this, the total medium-term committed financing available to Hammerson is approximately £2.7bn.

'I am delighted with the excellent response we have received from our bankers for this facility, which provides flexibility going forward.'

Source: www.hammerson.com

Whether collateral is required usually depends on the borrower's creditworthiness. Borrowers are keen to minimise the interference with day-to-day business that might arise with fixed security charges on specific assets and from lender's attempts to monitor the borrower's activities, e.g. through covenants, but may be forced to concede these points. Vestas had lowered bargaining power when negotiating for a new credit facility – see Article 5.1.

Article 5.1

Vestas shares jump on refinancing

By Clare MacCarthy

Shares in Vestas, the wind turbine maker, jumped sharply after it secured fresh funding to avert an impending credit squeeze.

The Danish company has lurched from crisis to crisis in recent years and earlier this month announced a further round of job cuts.

Monday's deal involves the replacement of a €1.3bn syndicated credit facility with a new one worth €900m in total. The nine Nordic and international banks that were its existing lenders all participated in the new syndicate.

The company said €250m of these loans will be repaid by January 2015 while there is an option to extend a revolving €650m credit facility for another two years beyond that date.

Vestas also secured a €200m loan from the European Investment Bank and another of €55m with the Nordic Investment Bank.

One analyst in Copenhagen said that the fact that the new facility was smaller meant Vestas was "paying the price" for deferring a covenant test earlier this year.

Vestas has suffered frequent setbacks in the highly unpredictable market for wind turbine manufacturing, but its problems were exacerbated after 2008 when it started an expansion drive just as the global economy began to falter.

This wiped some 90 per cent off its share value over the past three years and forced it to reduce its workforce to 16,000 employees – about the same level as in 2008.

 Source: MacCarthy, C. (2012) 'Vestas shares jump on refinancing', *Financial Times*, 26 November.

Even US-based lending is frequently related to interest rates set in London – see the following case study.

Case study   A syndicated facility

Cypress Semiconductor Corp. today [27 June 2012] announced that it has entered into a five-year senior secured revolving credit facility with a group of lenders led by Morgan Stanley Senior Funding, Inc. as administrative agent and collateral agent. The facility enables the company to borrow up to $430m on a revolving basis. The credit facility bears interest at LIBOR plus 2.25% on the drawn amount. There is a commitment fee payable of 0.375% per annum on any undrawn amounts.

Source: http://investors.cypress.com

Syndicated lending

Syndicated lending is not just for revolving credit facilities. It is also used for large long-term loans (usually 5–10 years) where a single bank may not be able or willing to lend the whole amount. To do so would be to expose the bank to an unacceptable risk of failure on the part of one of its borrowers. Bankers like to spread their lending to gain the risk-reducing benefits of diversification. Thus they participate in a number of syndicated loans in which a few banks each contribute a portion of the overall loan. For example, with a large multi-national company loan of £500m, a single bank may provide £70m, with perhaps 30 other banks contributing the remainder.

The bank originating the loan will usually manage the syndicate and is called the **lead manager** (there might be one or more lead banks or **arranging banks**). This bank (or these banks) may invite a handful of other banks to **co-manage** the loan; these then persuade other banks to supply much of the funding. That is, they help the process of forming the **syndicate group** of banks in the general syndication. The managing bank also usually **underwrites** much of the loan while inviting other banks to underwrite the rest – that is, guaranteeing to provide the funds if other banks do not step forward.[2] The lead managers(s) and co-managers generally lend 50–70% of the loan themselves.

As well as the lenders gaining diversification benefits through participating in numerous syndicates they might benefit from the collective expertise and information within the group. Also, because the borrower fears reputational damage and therefore restricted future access to the financial markets if it defaults there is less risk for the lenders than for private loan arrangements.

The City of London is the world centre for syndicated lending, even when the arrangements are made elsewhere. This is so that the participants can make use of the well-developed Euromarket (international currencies rather than euros) funding facilities there, with deep markets in a range of currencies (see Chapter 14). The loans are generally based on a floating benchmark interest rate, usually LIBOR. Interest payable is adjusted each 'rollover day', usually every three or six months depending on LIBOR for that period, e.g. a borrower may agree to pay 120 basis points over LIBOR – a **'spread'** (**risk premium**) over LIBOR. If two years after the loan is taken LIBOR is 2.5% for a three-month period then the borrower will be charged 3.7% for that three months (this is expressed as an annual rate – the borrower pays one-quarter of this for three months).

Syndicated loans are available at short notice (within one week),[3] can be provided discreetly (helpful if the money is to finance a merger bid, for example) and are usually cheaper to arrange than a bond issue. While they can be a cheap form of borrowing for large well-established firms there will be various fees to pay, from management and commitment fees to underwriting fees for guaranteeing the availability of the funds and the agent's fee (usually a flat amount, say £100,000 per year of the loan). The **management fee** is paid on signing as a flat percentage of the loan (e.g. 1%). This will be shared among the managing banks. The **participation fee** is a flat percentage of each bank's amount lent. **Commitment fees** are generally flat percentages (e.g. 0.5%) of the *undrawn* portion of the loan. The **agent bank** (usually one of the banks with sizeable loan commitment) collects the loan money to transfer it to the borrower, and collects interest and other payments from the borrower to transfer them to the syndicate banks. It performs various other administrative tasks such as periodically fixing the LIBOR rate and observing compliance with loan conditions including collateral valuation. In the event of default the agent liaises with the participant banks and helps create conditions for a '**workout**' to be accomplished, i.e. a negotiated agreement between borrowers and lenders to put a delinquent borrower back on track, which may involve rescheduling payments, some element of debt forgiveness or additional collateral.

There is a secondary market in syndicated loans: a lending bank may later sell its portion of a syndicated loan to another financial institution, thus creating some liquidity for the bank. This benefit helps to lower the interest rates they can offer to borrowers.

The lead manager may offer one of three types of syndication – see Table 5.1.

Table 5.1	Types of syndication mandate
Fully committed (underwritten) syndication	Even if the lead bank fails to attract other banks to participate in the syndication it will provide the full amount of the loan.
Partially committed syndication	The lead bank only guarantees to lend a part of the loan. The rest will depend on the reaction of other banks to the proposal.
Best-efforts syndication	The borrower may not obtain the desired loans if there is insufficient participation from other banks despite the good faith efforts of the lead bank to generate interest.

Borrowers can usually draw down portions of the overall loan according to a draw-down schedule. Grace periods of several years are often granted in which no principal is repayable. The syndicated market is usually only available for loans of more than £50m. For around one-third of syndicated loans the credit rating agencies (e.g. Moody's – see Chapter 20) are paid to rate the likelihood of default. The volume of new international syndicated loans now runs into hundreds of billions of pounds per year – see Article 5.2 for some examples.

Project finance

A typical project finance deal is created by a corporation (or number of corporations) providing some equity capital for a separate legal entity (a **special purpose vehicle (SPV)**) to be formed to build and operate a project, e.g. an oil pipeline. The **project finance borrowings** are then provided as bank loans or through bond

Article 5.2

Chinese banks step up lending in the US

By Kandy Wong

China's top banks are stepping up their lending activities in the US as large US companies diversify their funding sources and seek to penetrate more deeply into the world's second-largest economy.

Chinese banks' share of US syndicated lending has risen to 6.1 per cent of the total market so far in 2012, up from 5.1 per cent last year, according to data from Dealogic. So far this year, the total value of syndicated loans from Chinese banks into the US has reached $51bn.

Liao Qiang, Chinese banking analyst at Standard & Poor's, said: "Many global banks have been deleveraging as a result of the 2008 global financial crisis and the debt crisis in Europe. Their retreat in lending markets provides opportunities for Chinese banks to deepen relationships with the multinational companies and steadily increase their international presence."

The increased syndicated lending by Chinese banks comes as their balance sheets compare favourably with US counterparts.

Among the latest deals, Bank of China is involved in a $1.4bn syndicated loan to Zimmer, the medical device company, and Bank of East Asia is part of a $575m loan syndication to Constellation Brands, the wine and beer group. Industrial and Commercial Bank of China took part in an $11.8bn syndicated loan for Walmart, the US retailer.

Bi Mingqiang, general manager of ICBC's New York branch, said the bank was seeking long-term lending relationships with US companies which had a presence in China and elsewhere.

issues direct to the separate entity. The significant feature is that the loan returns are tied to the cash flows and fortunes of a particular project rather than being secured against the parent firm's assets. For most ordinary loans the bank looks at the credit standing of the borrower when deciding terms and conditions. For project finance, while the parent company's (or companies') credit standing is a factor, the main focus is on the financial prospects of the project itself. Many of the small companies which develop oil fields and pipelines, for example, would not be able to participate in this industry on the strength of their existing cash flow and balance sheet, but are able to obtain project finance secured on the oil or fees they would later generate in a SPV. To make use of project finance the project needs to be easily identifiable and separable from the rest of the company's activities so that its cash flows and assets can offer lenders some separate security. Project finance has been used across the globe to finance power plants, roads, ports, sewage facilities, telecommunications networks and much more.[4] It is a form of finance that has grown rapidly over the past 25 years; globally, about $300–400bn is lent annually in this form.

There is a spectrum of risk sharing in project finance deals. At one extreme there are projects where the parent firm (or firms) accepts the responsibility of guaranteeing that the lenders will be paid in the event of the project producing insufficient cash flows. This is referred to as **recourse finance** because the lenders are able to seek the 'help' of the parent. At the other extreme, the lenders accept an agreement whereby, if the project is a failure, they will lose money and have no right of recourse to the parent company; if the project's cash flows are insufficient the lenders only have a claim on the assets of the project itself rather than on the sponsors or developers. Between these two extremes there might be deals whereby the borrower takes the risk until the completion of the construction phase (e.g. provides a completion guarantee) and the lender takes on the risk once the project is in the operational phase. Alternatively, the commercial firm may take some risks such as the risk of cost overruns and the lender takes others such as the risk of a government expropriating the project's assets.

The sums and size of projects are usually large and involve a high degree of complexity and this means high transaction and legal costs. Because of the additional risk to the lenders the interest rates charged tend to be higher than for conventional loans. Whereas a well-known highly creditworthy firm might pay 80 basis points over LIBOR for a 'normal' parent company loan, the project company might have to pay 200 bps (2%) above LIBOR.

The salient points of project finance are:

- ▦ **Combining skills and spreading the risk.** It often makes sense to tap into the varied skills and risk appetites of a number of sponsor companies for high-capital cost projects with long development phases.

- ▦ **Transfer of risk.** By making the project a stand-alone investment with its own financing, the parent can gain if it is successful and is somewhat insulated if it is a failure, in that other assets and cash flows may be protected from the effects of project losses. This may lead to a greater willingness to engage in more risky activities, which may benefit both the firm and society. Of course, this benefit is of limited value if there are strong rights of recourse.

- ▦ **Off-balance-sheet financing.** The finance is raised on the project's assets and cash flows and therefore is not recorded as debt in the parent company's balance sheet. This sort of off-balance-sheet financing is seen as a useful 'wheeze' or ploy by some managers, e.g. borrowing limits can be bypassed. However, experienced lenders and shareholders are not so easily fooled by accounting tricks.

- **Political risk.** If the project is in a country prone to political instability, with an anti-transnational business attitude and acts of appropriation, a more cautious way of proceeding may be to set up an arm's-length (separate company) relationship with some risk being borne by the banking community, particularly banks in the host country.

- **Simplified banking relationship.** In cases where there are a number of parent companies, it can be easier to arrange finance for a separate project entity than to have to deal with each of the parent companies separately. Also, some of the parents may not be creditworthy enough to take on more debt, whereas the robust contractual framework of the SPV (e.g. regular income from road tolls) can support borrowings.

- **Managerial incentives.** Managers of projects may be given an equity stake in the project if it is set up as a separate enterprise. This can lead to high rewards for exceptional performance.

From the bankers' viewpoint project finance does away with their maxim of 'obtain two sources of repayment', because the assets held by the SPV usually have little alternative use and therefore have a low second-hand value (and recourse to the security of the parent's assets is usually limited). Thus, bankers need to focus on cash flow expectations and, once the project is underway, to be willing to work with managers to solve problems as they arise. **Step-in** procedures may also be agreed, whereby the lenders take control of a project from management if it is running into trouble.

Project finance requires a complex web of contracts to reduce risk for the parents and for the borrowers. Customers for the output (gas pipeline, railway or use of hospital) are usually tied in to a long-term purchasing contract, and key raw material inputs may be subject to long-term supply contracts – see Figure 5.1. Due to the complexity of organising the risks and rewards to various parties and the taxation, foreign exchange, legal and regulatory issues, the financial design might be assigned to a financial adviser, who is neither one of the sponsors nor a lending bank, but an investment banker.

Japanese banks currently dominate the project finance market as western banks retreat after the financial crisis while they rebuild capital – see Article 5.3.

Note issuance facility

Note issuance facilities (NIFs) – variously known as **revolving underwriting facilities (RUFs), note purchase facilities** and **Euronote facilities** – were developed as services to large corporations wanting to borrow by selling commercial

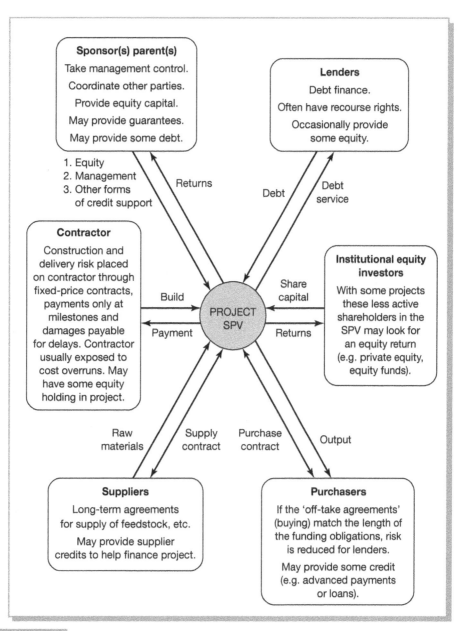

Figure 5.1   An example of project structure

paper (CP) or medium-term notes (MTNs) into the financial markets. The paper and notes are merely legal documents stating that the borrower agrees to pay sum(s) of money in the future, say three months from now. Thus a company could

Article 5.3

Project finance: Focus turns to overseas opportunities

By Michiyo Nakamoto

When the Saudi Arabian government decided to privatise Medina Airport, it awarded the contract to build a passenger terminal and operate the airport for 25 years to a consortium led by TAV Airports, the Turkish group.

No Japanese companies were involved in the first ever airport privatisation in Saudi Arabia, but Sumitomo Mitsui Banking Corporation won the contest to become sole financial adviser on the deal.

The Medina agreement is one of countless project finance deals in overseas markets that Japanese banks are seeking and winning.

"We believe there is huge potential in this market," says Yasuhiro Oka, head of the planning and co-ordination team in Mizuho's global structured finance division.

Although Japanese banks have been participating in project finance deals for decades, their focus on the business in overseas markets has grown, as lending at home has stagnated.

SMBC, for example, has expanded its team from fewer than 40 people in 1997 to more than 360 globally today.

Japan's proximity to the rest of Asia is an advantage.

"The centre of gravity of this business has moved from the west to Asia, and Japanese banks are the centre of the business," says Rajeev Kannan, general manager of SMBC's project and export finance department. Project finance deals were down in all regions in the first nine months of this year. Nevertheless, Asia, including Japan, maintained the lead in total proceeds, at $55.2bn in that period, compared with $26.2bn in the Americas and $50.7bn for Europe, the Middle East and Africa.

Japanese banks are particularly well suited to project financing, says Makoto Kobayashi, global head of structured finance at BTMU. "Project finance depends on stable cash flow over a long period and we prefer deals that provide stable revenues, rather than short-term gains," which have been the focus of western investment banks.

What is more, project financing deals lead to other banking businesses, such as deposit accounts and cash settlement services. "We provide interest rate hedging, cash management, transaction banking and other services. So if I put all these together in a basket, the overall return of this business is quite good," says Mr Kannan.

Mizuho has been investing at an early stage in large projects to ensure it is better placed to participate in the financing. For example, it has invested equity in Ascendas, a Singaporean company, developing an industrial park and multipurpose site in Chennai, India.

"It will probably take 10 years for the Chennai project to generate returns," says Ko Isaki, manager of the strategic projects department. "But we are getting involved at an early stage because, by the time the project gets to the financing stage, there is huge competition and the returns become quite competitive," he says.

sell for £1.95m commercial paper that gave the investor the right to receive £2m in six months. The investor gains £50,000 over six months. No explicit interest is paid other than an effective interest from the difference between the buying price and the sum received when it comes to the end of its life, its maturity date.

Medium-term notes (MTNs) are financial instruments issued by borrowing companies to investors in the financial markets. By issuing a note a company promises to pay the holders a certain sum on the maturity date, and in many cases a coupon interest in the meantime. These instruments are typically unsecured and may carry floating or fixed interest rates. MTNs have been sold with a maturity of as little as nine months and as great as 30 years, so the term is a little deceiving. They can be denominated in the domestic currency of the borrower (MTN) or in a foreign currency (**Euro MTN**).[5] MTNs normally pay an interest rate above LIBOR, usually varying between 0.2% and 3% over LIBOR.

The largest corporations often expect to be selling a series of different CP or MTN issues over the next 5–7 years. Instead of handling each individual issue themselves as the need arises they make a deal with an **arranging bank(s)** at the outset, who will, over the, say, five years, regularly approach a panel of other banks to ask them to purchase the debt as it becomes needed. The loan obligation can be in a currency that suits the borrower at the time. The borrower can also select the length of life of the paper (say, 14 days or 105 days) and whether it pays fixed or floating interest rates.

If there is a time when it is difficult to sell the paper to the banks then the borrower can turn to those banks that have signed up to be underwriters of the facility to buy the issue or, depending on the deal, borrow from the bank or banks in the syndicate. Underwriters take a fee for these guarantees. Most of the time they do not have to do anything, but occasionally, often when the market is troubled, they have to step in.

Some people draw a distinction between an NIF and an RUF: with an RUF the underwriting banks agree to provide loans should one of the CP/MTN issue fail, but under an NIF they could either lend or purchase the outstanding CP or notes. However, these definitions do not seem to be rigidly applied.

By allowing borrowers the choice at each point of borrowing, of either drawing a loan from the bank(s) at an agreed spread over LIBOR or selling CP/ MTN through banks, the borrower gets the best of both worlds; a bank loan (committed bank facility) fallback or access to the financial markets in corporate debt instruments. The choice depends on interest rates at the time. One-off fees are payable for the arrangement and annual fees for the bank's participation (actual lending) and commitment (standing ready to lend).

Opus plc agrees a £300m NIF with a bank for six years. This lead bank asks other banks to join the syndicate. Opus obtains a credit rating (see Chapter 20) for commercial paper that it might issue. Opus can repay funds drawn down under the NIF at will, without penalty. Opus decides it would like to borrow £150m starting in eight days for a six-month period. It tells the lead bank that it would like either to take a six-month loan at the rate stated in the NIF loan agreement, which is LIBOR + 95 bps or to issue CP to a predetermined syndicate of banks and dealers at the rate currently being offered by that dealer group. Currently, a six-month LIBOR is 1.4%, thus the loan will cost 2.35% (annual rate) for six months. The lead bank comes back with the CP interest rate of 2.56%, so Opus decides to exercise its right under the NIF to borrow the £150m from the banks. For the remaining five and a half years Opus will have the right to repay and then take out fresh loans or issue fresh CPs as the need arises.

Really well-known creditworthy issuers can opt to avoid the cost of maintaining the backstop option of access to loans (arrangement and participation fees) and simply rely on their ability to periodically attract lenders in the CP market under the NIF framework, but they still pay for 'swinglines' and 'back-up'. That is, to obtain a credit rating CP issuers must have unused credit lines from banks to provide liquidity in the event of an interruption to the CP market preventing roll over (the issue of new CPs as old ones mature). Swinglines are bank commitments to provide same-day credit facilities to cover a few days of the CP maturities. Back-up lines, sometimes uncommitted, are available for the longer maturities. There are a variety of liquidity back-ups that can be acceptable for this purpose, including cash and securities, but most CP issuers rely on credit lines from banks.

Ranking (seniority) of debt

When lending, bankers need to be aware that if a corporate borrower gets into trouble and cannot repay all its debts, then there is a hierarchy or pecking order for who gets paid back first should the company be forced to liquidate (sell-off) its assets. This is bargained for at the time of the loan, thus those high up the ranking, with **seniority**, accept lower interest rates because they have less risk of loss of some or all of the principal borrowed because a **junior debt** is only paid off if the senior debtholders have been satisfied – see Table 5.2.

Table 5.2	Debt ranking
Senior	Top precedence.
	Senior notes or senior loans.
	Often secured by specific collateral (fixed charge) – i.e. the senior debtholders have 'first lien'. But unsecured senior debt also exists.
	Senior debtholders are likely to insist on an intercreditor agreement before allowing a borrower to obtain a junior loan to make sure they remain top of the pecking order. Each class of lender agrees to specific procedures and order of precedence in the event of a bankruptcy or liquidation. The terminology in some intercreditor agreements is confusing because the subordinated secured debt may rank higher than the senior unsecured debt. Also, you may see 'senior subordinated' debt lower ranked than subordinated secured. It all depends on the contractual terms, and the propensity for lawyers to confuse!
Subordinated	A junior form of debt.
	Specific assets may be pledged as collateral. But may be unsecured.
	Within this category there will be a pecking order of different types of subordinated debt.
Share capital	Equity or preference shares.

Banker's acceptances

Banks also lend by signing a document stating that the bank will pay a sum of money at a date some time in the future, say in 90 days. This is a **banker's acceptance**, also known as an **acceptance credit**, which because it is a document stating the signatory will pay at a future date is called a **time draft**.

Say, for example, that an importer has agreed to buy goods from an exporter with an agreement to pay in three months. Instead of sending the bill to the importer, the exporter is instructed to send the document, which states that the signatory will pay a sum of money at a set date in the future, to the importer's bank. This is 'accepted' by the importer's bank, by signing it, rather than by a customer. Simultaneously the importer makes a commitment to pay the accepting bank the relevant sum at the maturity date of the bill.

The exporter does not have to wait three months to receive cash despite the importer's bank not paying out for 90 days. This is because it is possible to sell this right to investors in the **discount market** long before the three months are up. This bank commitment to pay the holder of the acceptance credit allows it to be sold with more credibility in the money markets to, say, another bank (a discounter) by the exporter after receiving it from an importing company's bank. It is sold at a **discount** price to the face value; that is less than the amount stated to be paid in the future. So, say, the acceptance states that €1m will be paid to the holder on 1 August. It could be sold to an investor (perhaps another bank) in the discount market for €980,000 on 15 June. The importer is obliged to reimburse the bank €1m (and pay fees) on 1 August; on that date the purchaser of the acceptance credit collects €1m from the bank that signed the acceptance, making a €20,000 return over six weeks.

Not all banker's acceptances relate to overseas trade. Many are simply a way of raising money for a firm. The company in need of finance may simply ask its bank to create a banker's acceptance and hand it over. Then the company can sell it in the discount market at a time when it needs to raise some cash. They are very useful for companies expanding into new markets where their names are not known, and therefore their creditworthiness is also unknown. They can take advantage of the superior creditworthiness of the bank issuing the acceptance, which guarantees that payment will be made.

There are three costs involved:

1 The bank charges **acceptance commission** for adding its name to the acceptance.

2 The difference between the face value of the acceptance and the discount price, which is the effective interest rate.

3 Dealers take a small cut as they connect firms that want to sell with companies that wish to invest in banker's acceptances.

These costs are relatively low compared with overdraft costs. However this facility is only available in hundreds of thousands of pounds, euros, etc. and then only to the most creditworthy of companies. Figure 5.2 summarises the acceptance credit sequence for an export deal.

Example   **The use of a banker's acceptance**

A Dutch company buys €3.5m of goods from a firm in Japan and draws up a document promising to pay for the goods in 60 days' time. The Dutch company asks its bank to accept the document. Once the bank has stamped 'accepted' on the document, it becomes a negotiable (sellable) instrument. The exporter receives the banker's acceptance. After 15 days, the Japanese company decides it needs some extra short-term finance and sells the acceptance at a discount of 0.60%, receiving €3,479,000. The exporter has been paid by banker's acceptance immediately the goods are dispatched. It can also shield itself from the risk of exchange rates shifting over the next 60 days by discounting the acceptance immediately, receiving euros, and then converting these to yen. And, of course, the exporter is not exposed to the credit risk of the importer because it has the guarantee from the importer's bank.

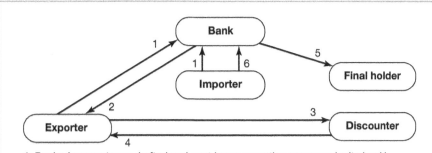

1 Banker's acceptance drafted and sent by an exporting company (or its bank) demanding payment for goods sent to an importer's bank. Importer makes arrangements with its bank to help it. Acceptance commission paid to the bank by importer.
2 The bank accepts the promise to pay a sum at a stated future date.
3 The banker's acceptance is sold at a discount.
4 The discounter pays cash for the banker's acceptance.
5 The bank pays the final holder of the banker's acceptance the due sum.
6 The importer pays to the bank the banker's acceptance due sum.

Figure 5.2 Banker's acceptance sequence – for an export deal

Corporate banking: key activities

Banks borrow and lend a great deal of money to each other, every working day. When lending to the most creditworthy banks they charge very low interest rates compared with those charged to corporate customers. These interbank lending rates form fundamental benchmarks for a great deal of other borrowing. For example, corporations are charged interest rates that are a number of basis points (one-hundredth of a per cent) above the rates the safest banks are charged for borrowing. These benchmark rates are determined in the interbank market, the dominant one being in London, with its London Interbank Offered Rate (LIBOR). This market is crucial for loans all over the world, so we need to get to grips with LIBOR – and better than the regulators did in the noughties!

This chapter also introduces a range of other commercial banking activities, from foreign exchange management to cash management. Most are discussed in more detail later in the book, but we take a particular look at overseas trade assistance here.

The interbank market

Originally, the **interbank market** was defined as the market where banks lend to each other, in both the domestic and international markets. This is a rather old-fashioned definition. Increasingly, as well as banks being depositors this group includes other financial institutions, such as money market funds (see Chapter 20) and non-financial corporates. The interbank markets exist so that a bank or other large institution which has no immediate demand for its surplus cash can place the money in the interbank market and earn interest on it. In the opposite scenario, if a bank needs to supply a loan to a customer but does not have the necessary deposit to hand, it can usually borrow on the interbank market.

There is no secondary trading in the interbank market; the loans are **non-negotiable** – thus a lender for three months cannot sell the right to receive interest and capital from the borrower (a bank) to another organisation. The lender has to wait until the end of the agreed loan period to recover money. If a bank needs its funds, it simply ceases to deposit money with other banks. The loans in this market are not secured with collateral. However, the rate of interest is relatively low because borrowers are respectable and safe banks. Banks with lower respectability and safety will have to pay more than the benchmark rates set by the safest institutions.

Interest rates

In the financial pages of serious newspapers you will find a bewildering variety of interest rates quoted from all over the world. The following is an explanation of some of the terms in common use.

LIBOR

LIBOR or **Libor**, the **London Interbank Offered Rate**, is the most commonly used benchmark rate, in particular the three-month LIBOR rate, which is the interest rate for one bank lending to another (very safe) bank for a fixed three-month period. Obviously any actual lending deals are private arrangements between the two banks concerned, but we can get a feel for the rates thought to be charged by surveying the leading banks involved in these markets. This is done every trading day, between 11 a.m. and 11.10 a.m.

Until 2013 the official LIBOR rates were calculated by Thomson Reuters for the **British Banking Association (BBA)** by asking a panel of 23 UK and international banks at what rates they could borrow money unsecured loans of various maturities. The size of the panel for a particular currency varied from seven (e.g. New Zealand dollar) to 18 (e.g. US dollar). For Sterling it was (and is) 16. Contributor banks were (and currently still are) asked to base their LIBOR submissions on the following question: 'At what rate could you borrow funds, were you to do so by asking for and then accepting interbank offers in a reasonable market size just prior to 11 a.m.?' The rates from the submitting banks were ranked in order from the highest to the lowest and the average of only the middle two quartiles is taken, i.e. with 16 submitting, the top four and bottom four quoted each day were removed and then the middle eight rates were averaged to calculate LIBOR. The LIBOR figures appeared on a million computer screens around the world at mid-day.

For over two decades the BBA produced LIBOR interest rates for borrowing in ten currencies with a range of 15 maturities from overnight (borrowing for 24 hours) to 12 months quoted for each currency, producing 150 rates each business day. The rates were (are) expressed as an annual rate even though the loans may only be for a few days or weeks, e.g. if an overnight sterling rate from a contributor bank is given as 2.00000%, this does not indicate that a contributing bank would expect to pay 2% interest on the value of an overnight loan. Instead, it means that it would expect to pay 2% divided by 365.

In 2013 it was decided that there was not enough data to keep calculating 150 benchmarks – for some, such as nine-month sterling, a big bank may only do 50 borrowing deals per year, but, nevertheless, had to submit a new estimate every day – and so the less frequently used currencies/maturities have now been dropped. The data shown in Table 6.1 are for those currencies and maturities that are currently available.

Table 6.1   **LIBOR Rates for 26 February 2013**

Euro Libor	%	Japanese Yen Libor	%
Overnight	0.01714	Spot/next	0.09214
1week	0.02757	1week	0.10143
1month	0.05571	1month	0.12571
2months	0.09429	2months	0.14143
3months	0.13071	3months	0.16143
6months	0.24000	6months	0.26429
12months	0.45286	12months	0.45786

US Dollar Libor	%	Swiss Franc Libor[1]	%
Overnight	0.15650	Spot/next	−0.0010
1week	0.17320	1week	−0.0010
1month	0.20370	1month	−0.0010
2months	0.24300	2months	0.00700
3months	0.28660	3months	0.02200
6months	0.45690	6months	0.09440
12months	0.75250	12months	0.27440

UK Pound Libor	
	%
Overnight	0.48125
1 week	0.48500
1 month	0.49250
2 months	0.50000
3 months	0.50813
6 months	0.62188
12 months	0.94375

Source: www.bbalibor.com

Because the LIBOR rate is calculated in different currencies, its influence is spread worldwide. In all, LIBOR is used to price around £200tn financial products; for comparison, the output of all UK citizens in one year (GDP) is around £1,400bn. Remarkably, about 90% of US commercial and mortgage loans are thought to be linked to the LIBOR rates, usually 2–3% over LIBOR.

Scandal

The fact that LIBOR was not necessarily based on actual transactions because there were simply not enough lending transactions in each of the currencies/maturities every day meant that a bank was asked to 'estimate' or to 'predict accurately' the correct rate for currencies or maturities based on its knowledge of its credit and liquidity risk profile. This inability to base many LIBORs on recorded loans gave all the leeway needed for unscrupulous bankers to manipulate the reported rate to further their own ends. This led to the now infamous LIBOR scandal and fines amounting to billions imposed on the banks.

There were two main elements to the manipulative behaviour. First, the value of billions of pounds/dollars worth of derivatives is determined by the level of LIBOR. If derivative traders could persuade those in their bank (and in some of the other banks) who had responsibility to submit daily LIBOR rates to change the submission slightly, they could make a fortune on the movements in derivatives. From 2005 on (and perhaps earlier) rate-submitters were regularly cajoled, bribed and leant-on to do the derivative guys a favour – and senior bankers encouraged this. It was an international game with many interlocking personal relationships in the very small world of rate submitters and derivative traders located in the major financial centres. More than 20 banks were involved in the network of deceit. [2]

Second, following the financial crisis of 2007–08 banks did not want to appear weak. A clear sign of weakness, higher risk, is to admit that you have to borrow from other banks at high interest rates. Thus, the rate submitters were lent-on to 'lowball' their submissions to make them appear healthier than they really were. Admittedly, there was so little confidence in banks generally at this time that actual tangible inter-bank lending became very thin, if not completely shut down, and so submitters had to fall back on their judgement of what they might have to pay to borrow *were you to do so*. They were caught out by email records showing that far from merely using good judgement about what rate the bank might have to pay they were deliberately underestimating borrowing rates to fool outsiders – they falsified.

The insider's view

In the tight-knit world of interest rate derivatives and LIBOR submissions, the bankers know each other by first name, regularly phoning, texting, messaging and emailing. They were ridiculed in the Press as crass, money-obsessed, shallow people. Their confidence and bonuses knew no bounds at a time when millions suffered in a recession created by greedy bankers, an image that was not helped by the email correspondence made public, for example:

- 'Dude, I owe you big time! Come over one day after work and I'm opening a bottle of Bollinger.'
- 'When I write a book about this business your name will be written in golden letters.'
- 'If you keep the 6s [the six-month Yen LIBOR rate] unchanged today … I need you to keep it as low as possible … if you do that … I'll pay you … I'm a man of my word.'
- 'It's just amazing how LIBOR-fixing can make you that much money or lose it if opposite. It's a cartel now in London.'

And from the submitters:

- 'Always happy to help.'
- 'Done … for you big boy.'
- 'You know, scratch my back yeah an all.'

The response from bank leadership is interesting. Here is a quote from the Economist:[3]

'Risibly, Bob Diamond, [Barclays] chief executive, who resigned on July 3rd as a result of the scandal, retorted in a memo to staff that "on the majority of days, no requests were made at all" to manipulate the rate. This was rather like an adulterer saying that he was faithful on most days.'

The authorities are on the warpath – see Article 6.1.

Article 6.1

Daily fix that spiralled out of control

By Brooke Masters, Caroline Binham and Kara Scannell

UBS traders and managers on three continents used phone calls, electronic chat rooms and emails to manipulate benchmark interest rates in five currencies on an almost daily basis, according to documents filed by US, UK and Swiss authorities.

The web of activity spanned the globe, taking in traders in Japan and the US, brokers in London and elsewhere and rate submitters based in London and Switzerland.

About 40 UBS employees, traders at five other banks and 11 employees at six interdealer brokers were directly involved or aware of efforts to manipulate interbank lending rates in various currencies.

US authorities have charged two former UBS traders, Tom Hayes and Roger Darin, with criminal conspiracy, and Mr Hayes also faces a criminal price-fixing charge in connection with allegations he "colluded" with another bank to manipulate the yen Libor rate.

The charging and settlement documents include excerpts from myriad emails and chat room messages focused on the daily fixing process for Libor,

and Euribor and Tibor, similar rates set in Brussels and Tokyo.

All of the benchmarks rely on averaging daily estimates from panels of banks, so they can in theory be moved if one or more banks deliberately aim high or low.

That was not a problem in Libor's infancy in the mid-1980s when it was used primarily to price corporate and other lending. But the interbank lending rates became a crucial benchmark for derivatives in the late 1990s, transforming the importance of the daily fixings. A swing of only a few basis points changed from being a rounding error on a loan rate to making the difference between a bonanza trading day and devastating losses.

UBS traders, according to the Swiss regulator Finma, could triple or even sextuple their annual salaries with bonuses for good results.

The FSA documented more than 2,000 requests to move rates. The internal contacts were so pervasive that one submitter responded to a January 2007 rate request with "standing order, sir", the FSA said.

UBS traders also reached out directly to their counterparts

at other banks and they sometimes worked in concert.

But the vast majority of external requests, particularly for yen Libor, went through the interdealer brokers. The FSA said four UBS traders based in Tokyo used 11 employees at six brokerages as conduits, asking them to pass on requests for specific rates to traders and more broadly influence the market.

Although brokers do not participate in the rate setting process directly, they were frequently contacted for market information by submitters at some panel banks. So UBS traders also asked the brokers to report false bids and offers – known as "spoofs" – and asked them to manipulate the rates shown on their trading screens to skew market perceptions, according to the FSA.

The brokers were repaid for their assistance in two ways: "wash trades" – transactions that have no purpose other than to generate fees – with the helpful party. [Secondly,] corrupt payments of £15,000 per quarter to brokers to reward them for their assistance.

The new regime

In 2013 the BBA was stripped of its 'sponsor' role and a new administrator created. This benchmark administrator is overseen by the Financial Conduct Authority (FCA), the financial regulator (formerly the Financial Services Authority) – see Figure 6.1.

Despite the new system placing more emphasis on actual market transactions there are voices saying this is not going far enough, that no quotes should be based on banks estimating the rate at which they think they could borrow, but that all submissions should be on actual deals. Other prominent people such as regulators ponder whether it is best to move toward two systems running in parallel: (1) the estimated LIBOR, as in Figure 6.1, allowing financial deals based on LIBOR to continue as well as allowing a wider range of LIBOR maturities/currencies, even those with fewer transactions, and (2) a purely transaction-evidenced LIBOR.

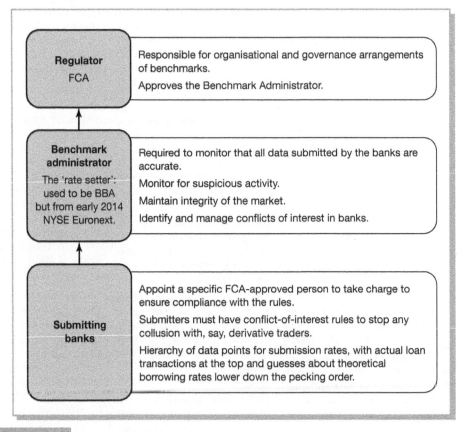

Figure 6.1   The new LIBOR structure

The regulators have learned a lot from the LIBOR scandal – see Article 6.2.

FSA says it was slow on Libor scandal

By Daniel Schäfer

The City's regulator has admitted it was slow off the mark when the first indications emerged six years ago that banks were submitting artificially low Libor rates.

Officials at the Financial Services Authority received dozens of clues over possible lowballing of the benchmark interest rate in 2007 and 2008 but they were "too narrowly focused" on the financial crisis, an internal review by the FSA has found.

After combing through 97,000 emails and other documents spanning a more than two-year period until May 2009, the internal audit found 26 direct references to lowballing and a further 48 that could have been interpreted as such references.

It included a market update by the Bank of England saying that banks were "making a mockery of the fixings" and another one saying Libor submissions had been "a finger in the air exercise for some months".

The review had been commissioned by Lord Turner, FSA chairman, after the Commons Treasury committee criticised the regulator for failing to react to warning signs in the years before it opened its formal investigation in early 2010.

Lord Turner said the FSA had been focused on the direct fallout of the financial crisis while also not being formally responsible for the Libor submissions, which in the past has been an unregulated process.

"As a result, the FSA did not respond rapidly to clues that lowballing might be occurring," he said.

But the review did not find evidence that the authority had received any clues indicating that traders were manipulating Libor for profit. Lord Turner said this showed that more intense supervision might not be the most appropriate way to uncover such wrongdoing.

"Better whistleblowing procedures, greater accountability of top management, and more intense requirements for self-reporting of suspicious activity may turn out to be more effective tools."

Now that LIBOR is no longer calculated for the Australian dollar (or NZ or Canadian dollars, or Danish and Swedish krona) the Australians have decided to obtain interbank rates from market transactions – see Article 6.3.

Article 6.3

Australia to use market prices for Libor

By Neil Hume in Sydney

Australia will use prices displayed electronically by brokers and trading venues to set the price of the country's benchmark interbank borrowing rate.

The Australian Financial Markets Association, which represents 130 Australian and international banks, brokers and fund managers, announced on Wednesday it would "bypass the panel requirement by adopting a process to extract these rates directly from trading venues – brokers and electronic markets. This proposal has the support of market participants".

The BBSW is the Australian equivalent of the scandal-plagued Libor and is used to set interest payments on floating rate securities, derivatives and Australian dollar-denominated loans.

The decision to take rates directly from the market, rather than from submissions, comes after two more banks – Citigroup and HSBC – said they would no longer contribute to the BBSW panel. JPMorgan and UBS withdrew earlier this year.

Banks are quitting rate-setting panels around the world because of tougher scrutiny and a rise in compliance costs brought about by the Libor scandal.

Australia's BBSW rate differs from Libor in that panellists are asked for the actual rates they observe in the market rather than an indicative quote.

 Source: Hume, N. (2013) 'Australia to use market prices for Libor', *Financial Times*, 27 March.

EURIBOR and some other BORs

A benchmark similar to LIBOR in common use is **EURIBOR (Euro InterBank Offered Rate)** which is the rate at which euro interbank term deposits are offered by one prime bank to another prime bank within the eurozone (not London) for periods of one week to one year. It does not cover overnight lending – see EONIA below for that. EURIBOR is calculated as a weighted average of unsecured lending transactions undertaken within the euro area by 37 eurozone banks daily at 11 a.m. The highest and lowest 15% of all the quotes collected are eliminated and the remaining rates averaged. It is calculated by Euribor-EBF.

There is also a **US dollar Euribor (USD InterBank Offered Rate)**, also organised by the Euribor-EBF, which is the rate at which USD interbank term deposits are being offered by one panel bank to another panel bank for a range of maturities from overnight rates up to 12 months.

Many other countries have market setting rates for lending between domestic banks. **TIBOR (Tokyo InterBank Offered Rate)** is the rate at which Japanese banks lend to each other in Japan. In Singapore we have **SIBOR** and in Hong Kong we have **HIBOR**.

Federal Funds Rate and Prime Rate

In the USA, the equivalent to very short-term LIBOR, is the **Federal Funds Rate (fed funds)** and is the average rate at which domestic financial institutions lend to each other for a period of one day (overnight). This is strongly influenced by intervention by the US central bank, the Federal Reserve. Banks often need to borrow from other banks to maintain a minimum level of cash reserves at the Federal Reserve (see Chapter 7). The lending banks are happy to lend because they receive a rate of interest and the money is released the next day (usually). This borrowing is unsecured and so is only available to the most creditworthy. The Federal Reserve can influence the fed funds rate by increasing or lowering the level of cash or near cash reserves the banks have to hold and other methods. (There is more on the role of the Federal Reserve and the fed funds rate in Chapters 24 and 25.)

The fed fund interest rate (borrowing in the US) and the overnight US dollar LIBOR rate (borrowing in the UK) are usually very close to each other because they are near-perfect substitutes. If they were not close then a bank could make a nice profit borrowing in one overnight market and depositing the money in another. If the US dollar LIBOR rate is higher, banks needing to borrow will tend to do so in the fed funds market; the increased demand will push up interest rates here, while the absence of demand will encourage lower rates in the US dollar LIBOR market.

The US **prime rate** is the interest rate US banks charge the best corporate customers. It is also used as a benchmark for other loans, e.g. consumer credit loan interest rates are often set as so-many basis points above the prime rate. The prime rate, in approximate terms, is around 3% more than the fed funds rate.

EONIA

EONIA (Euro OverNight Index Average) is the effective overnight rate for the euro, computed as a weighted average of all overnight unsecured lending transactions in the interbank market, initiated within the euro area by the contributing 37 panel banks. It is calculated with the help of the **European Central Bank (ECB)**.

EURONIA

EURONIA (Euro OverNight Index Average) is the UK equivalent of EONIA, a weighted average of euro interest rates on unsecured overnight euro deposits arranged by money brokers in London.

SONIA

SONIA (Sterling OverNight Interbank Average) tracks the actual sterling overnight rates experienced by money brokers in London.

Overseas trade

Banks provide various services to assist companies when buying and selling across borders.

Documentary letters of credit

A **letter of credit** (also called an L/C or **documentary credit** or **import letter** of **credit**)is a promise from a bank that an exporter will be paid after shipping goods to an importer. This reassures the exporter and allows an importer to buy without up-front payment even though it might not be well-known to the exporter. While an L/C is similar to a bank guarantee, it differs in that the bank pays out if the transaction proceeds as planned, while a bank guarantee is to make payment if the transaction does not go as planned. With a guarantee the issuing bank waits for the buyer to default before paying out. With an L/C the obligation to pay is transferred to the bank, which it will do at the contracted time; even if the importer's finances are perfectly healthy and it could pay from its own resources the bank will make the payment. Thus the exporter has much greater reassurance of getting paid because a safe bank has taken on the obligation to pay rather than an unknown importer in a distant land. Naturally, the bank will expect its client (the importer) to pay it the amount concerned plus some fees and interest to cover the provision of this service.

Thus, in return for reassurance (evidence) that all the documents needed for the goods to be exported and received abroad, documents showing actual shipment of the goods and official licences, etc., are present and correct, the exporter receives full payment from the importer's bank. A key requirement is a **bill of lading**, which is a document issued by a carrier (e.g. airline, shipping firm) to an exporter or its bank confirming that the goods have been received by the carrier, that the carrier accepts responsibility to deliver the goods to the importer, evidence of ownership of the goods, insurance certificates and commercial invoices.

The importer's bank normally arranges for a bank in the exporter's home country to transfer the money to the exporter, so once shipment has occurred exporters are able to receive payment for their goods in their own country. In some cases cash may not be received. Instead a promise to pay at a fixed future date is received from the bank (a **time** or **date L/C**). With a **sight L/C** payment is made immediately to the exporter upon presentation of the correct documents.

The importer has reassurance that payment will not be made unless the exporter has complied with the terms of the contract to the satisfaction of its bank, and so can expect to receive the goods when they are required. Thus, for a fee(s) and interest banks have made arrangements so that neither the importer nor the exporter need accept high risk with regard to payment. However, the risk to the importer of receiving goods from the exporter of lower quality than those stated in the documents remains. A further safeguard: once an L/C (and the documents) is in place the exporter may have the option of asking its own bank to add its reassurance of payment, so even if the importer's bank does not pay the exporter's will.

Bills of exchange/banker's acceptances

Bills of exchange and banker's acceptances oil the wheels of international commerce. They enable corporations to obtain credit from suppliers or raise money, and, due to the assistance of banks, to trade with foreign corporations at low risk of financial inconvenience or loss. Banker's acceptances were dealt with in the last chapter, so we'll concentrate on bills of exchange here.

On sending goods abroad an exporter draws up a bill of exchange (called a **trade bill**). This is a legal document showing the indebtedness of the buyer. The exporter also obtains a bill of lading from the carrier to show that the goods have been appropriately despatched. At this point the bill of exchange may be forwarded directly to, and **accepted** by the customer, which means that the customer signs a promise to pay the stated amount and currency on the due date (a **time draft**). The due date is usually 90 days later, but 30-, 60- and 180-days bills are not uncommon. However, note that some bills of exchange are **sight drafts (documents against payment drafts)**, payable on demand immediately.

More usual is for the bill first to be sent to the exporter's bank, which, in turn, sends the draft and the documents to a bank in the importer's country with which the exporter's bank has an ongoing relationship. This 'correspondent bank' will be instructed to get the draft signed, that is, accepted, by the importer, or to receive payment in the case of a sight draft. Then the correspondent bank will hand over the bill of lading documents permitting the importer to claim the goods. With payment on a sight draft the correspondent bank will transfer the funds received from the importer to the exporter's bank, which will credit the exporter's account. Fees will be charged for facilitating these transactions. With time bills the exporter will receive a promise to pay in, say, 90 days.

The banks have reduced the risk for the exporter by ensuring that the goods are not released to the importer until money or a promise is in place. Also, for the time draft, there is a legal acknowledgement that a debt exists facilitating easier access to the legal systems in the event of non-payment.

As well as the benefit of a potential credit period before paying on a time draft, the risk for the importer is reduced because payment will only be made if the goods are present and correct with all the documentation.

Trading time drafts

With a time draft the bill is returned to the exporter who can either hold it until maturity, or sell it at a discount. Many bills of exchange are traded in an active secondary market. The purchaser (discounter) in this market pays a lower amount than the sum to be received at maturity from the customer. The difference represents the discounter's interest payment. For example, the customer might have signed the bill promising to pay £300,000 in 90 days. The bill is sold immediately by the exporter to a discount house or bank for £297,000. After 90 days the discounter will realise a profit of £3,000 on a £297,000 asset. Through this arrangement the customer has the goods on 90 days credit terms, the supplier has made a

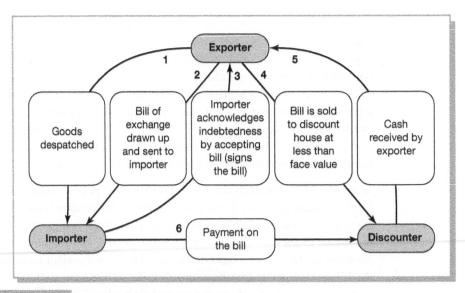

Figure 6.2   The bill of exchange sequence

sale and immediately receives cash from the discount house amounting to 99% of the total due. The discounter, if it can borrow at less than 1% over 90 days, turns a healthy profit. The sequence of events is shown in Figure 6.2.

Despite the simplification of Figure 6.2, many bills of exchange do not remain in the hands of the discounter until maturity but are traded a number of times before maturity. Also, despite the figure showing direct communication between importer and exporter, usually banks on both sides facilitate these actions. An alternative scenario is where the importer's bank 'accepts' the bill (promises to pay). It can then be sold at a discount in the local banker's acceptance market. The full proceeds from this are sent to the exporter.

Bills of exchange are normally only used for large transactions (more than £100,000). The effective interest rate charged by the discounter is usually a competitive 150 to 400 basis points over interbank lending rates (e.g. LIBOR). The holder of the bill usually has recourse to both of the commercial companies: if the customer does not pay then the seller will be called upon to make good the debt. This overhanging credit risk for the exporter can sometimes be transferred (to, say, a bank) by buying credit insurance. If the bill is guaranteed by another bank or the importer has a very high credit standing it may not carry recourse rights for the holder to force the exporter to pay.

Another service: some banks will purchase bills from their customers, e.g. the bank advances 75% of the face value of the bill. When the importer pays, say after 60 days, this will be used to repay the advance together with any accrued interest on the advance.

Forfaiting

Forfaiting is designed to provide immediate finance to exporters using the security of an obligation or a series of obligations owed to it by one or more importers to be paid in the future. Under forfaiting the importer will not be paying for at least six months, but more typically will pay over a period of time up to ten years, but the exporter can have cash now in exchange for assigning the rights to receive the importer's money over to the forfaiter.

So, if an exporter holds a series of bills of exchange (or letters of credit or promissory notes), indicating legally enforceable acceptance by an importer of an obligation to pay in the future, at say six-monthly intervals over the next four years, then this series of rights can be sold to a forfaiting company, usually a bank, at a discount. For additional safety the payment obligations are usually guaranteed by the importer's bank – such a reassurance lowers the charge imposed on the exporter by the forfaiter for providing funds in advance.

The forfaiter then assumes responsibility for collecting the debts from the importer as they fall due. Because the forfaiter pays for the bills, L/C or notes straightaway the exporter now has finance for production. Financing can be arranged in any of the major currencies, usually at a fixed interest rate, but a floating rate option is also available.

The exporter receives guaranteed payment for the goods less the forfaiter's charges and its discount from the face value of the debt, thus passing-on risk such as political interference and commercial trouble and protecting against exchange rate fluctuations. This system also helps sellers to do business in countries where the risk of non-payment would otherwise be a matter of too much concern. The importer obtains extended credit – which enhances the exporter's sales promotion.

Forfaiting deals are large transactions of a value in excess of $100,000 and frequently tens of millions and are non-recourse, i.e. the exporter will not be called on by the forfaiter to make up the difference should an importer or its bank fail to pay. Thus, the exporter has no further interest in the transaction. It is the forfaiter who collects the future payments due from the importer and it is the forfaiter who runs all the risks of non-payment.

The forfaiter may keep the bills or notes until payment is due, or may sell them on in the financial markets. Unlike factors (see below), forfaiters typically work with exporters who need to offer extended credit periods from 180 days to seven years or more.

Factoring

In return for a fee, **factors** (often a bank) agree to collect short-term (less than 180 days) importer's credit payments (invoices, 'current accounts receivables') that are due to an exporter, and the exporter receives from the factor immediately, say, 80% of the outstanding trade debtor balance owed by importers. The remainder is handed over when the factor receives full payment of the debt from the importer. However, this is reduced from the full importer's debt because factors charge fees and interest on the amount advanced to the exporter.

Companies are able to take advantage of the advanced receipt of cash, and the risk of non-payment is negated because the factor usually takes on the risk of failure of the importer to pay. Factoring is suited for a continuous stream of short-term export sales of consumer goods on **open account** terms (i.e. simply shipping the goods/services with an invoice asking for delayed payment). Note that it does not revolve around letters of credit, bills of exchange or promissory notes, with their extra risk-reducing properties.

A disadvantage for the exporter of the factor taking on debt collection may be that the factor could adopt aggressive tactics to get paid by the importer, which may damage relationships with a customer. Factors work with other factors in relevant countries who help with assessing the importer's creditworthiness and the handling of the collection of payments. (There is more on factoring in Chapter 13.)

Foreign exchange risk management

Companies usually learn through bitter experience that shifts in exchange rates can lower profits significantly, sometimes to the point of endangering the firm. There are various risk management tools that a bank can offer a client to mitigate these problems. These usually involve the use of derivatives such as forwards and options. Banks can assist companies in using these prudently to reduce risk. (These are considered in Chapter 23.)

More corporate banking services

Guarantees

Banks are sometimes prepared, for a fee, to guarantee that a transaction by a third party will take place or that compensation will be paid if the transaction does not take place. For example, a bank may grant a guarantee to an exporter that an importer will pay for goods supplied. To give you some idea of the range of guarantees offered by banks the following Example is the list shown on the Royal Bank of Canada's website.

Example   **Some bank guarantees available to corporates**

RBC Offers a Variety of Guarantee Solutions:
Guarantees for Common Business Transactions

- ▪ **Borrowing Money** – When negotiating a loan or mortgage, an RBC Global Services' guarantee will assure the lender of repayment.
- ▪ **Purchase or Lease Agreements** – When you are purchasing goods or acquiring or leasing a property, an RBC guarantee assures the seller or lessor of your ability to honour the terms of the agreement.
- ▪ **Utility Service Contracts** – Guarantees can facilitate contracts with public utilities, gas companies, etc. that may need assurance of your ability to pay for their services.
- ▪ **Financial Clout for Commercial Paper** – If you wish to issue commercial paper to raise funds (and if you qualify for credit) an RBC guarantee will help you borrow at better rates.

▶

Bid, Performance and Advance Payment Guarantees

- **Bid Bonds or Tender Guarantees** – To ensure that suppliers submit serious offers, tenders often call for up-front cash deposits or irrevocable guarantees. With our bid guarantee, you can establish your credibility without tying up your cash.
- **Performance Bonds or Guarantees** – Successful bidders often require a performance guarantee for a percentage of the contract amount. RBC enables you to meet your contract requirements and assures your client of your ability to perform.
- **Advance Payment Guarantees** – If you require an advance payment from your client, an RBC guarantee assures the client that their advance will be repaid by RBC if you fail to meet your contractual obligations.
- **Advance Payment of Holdback Under Contract** – Payment retentions or holdbacks can extend years after the completion of a project. If you require cash before the end of the holdback period, you can arrange to have your client pay the holdback in advance, in exchange for RBC issuing a guarantee to the client.

Source: www.rbcroyalbank.com

Cash management

Corporations with large day-to-day cash flows soon realise that they need to employ efficient systems to ensure that the potential to earn interest on the cash is not lost while also keeping back enough cash in an easily accessible form to support the business. Banks can help with this. They provide daily information on the firm's cheques/electronic transfers that have been paid and account balances so that money can be moved out of a no-interest account if the balance starts to build up. They can be given the task of automatically redirecting money held in a number of accounts at different banks and branches to a few centralised accounts at one branch. They can also provide software to assist firms in handling money in a variety of currencies and investing it short term.

Asset-based lending

Banks also provide finance for companies (or individuals) to obtain the use of, say, a car, by leasing it or buying it on hire purchase. (Asset-based lending is discussed in Chapter 13 under finance house activities.)

Interest rate risk management

If a corporate (or individual) takes out a medium- or long-term loan with interest rates that move up and down with a benchmark, e.g. LIBOR, then there is a risk of severe profit impact if rates unexpectedly shoot up. Many businesses have been killed as a result. Banks have devised all sorts of means of assisting a firm to eliminate or mitigate this form of risk. (We look at some of them in Chapters 21 and 22.)

7

How a bank operates

The aim of this chapter and the next is to show how core banking works. There are a few basic things bankers have to get right. First, they must avoid lending out via long-term loans a very high proportion of the money they attract without regard for the potential for depositors and other creditors to suddenly demand their money back instantly. That is, banks must retain reserves of cash (and other liquid assets) to satisfy creditors as the need arises. On the other hand, holding too much cash leads to the loss of opportunities to lend that money (acquire assets) to earn interest. This **liquidity management** involves a delicate balance.

Second, banks must protect themselves against the possibility of their assets falling below liabilities (what the bank owes depositors and other creditors of the bank). Such an eventuality would make a bank insolvent and unable to carry on. This might happen, for instance if say 10% of the loans it has made to businesses go sour and are never repaid (as happened with HBOS following the financial crisis). If a bank was to play it ultra-safe it would always hold assets worth at least 20% more than its liabilities. This level of safety is being called for by some experts in the wake of the 2008 financial crisis, but very few banks come anywhere near that level; more typical levels are 3–4%. This **capital management** issue is a much debated topic.

The third issue is the quality of the lending decisions banks make – **asset management**. Obviously, banks want high interest rates from borrowing customers, but this has to be weighed against competitive pressure on lending rates, greater risk (chance of default) and illiquidity of these bank assets. Sensible diversification comes in here too.

The fourth issue is selecting different forms of money to raise – **liability management**. What is the best mix, e.g. to raise more from depositors or from the financial markets? Low cost must be weighed against a host of other considerations.

Finally, we have banking income from trading financial instruments, fees for services and other activities that do not appear on balance sheets. These **off-balance sheet activities** need careful handling, as became evident when dozens of banks found their shareholder value wiped out by instruments/deals kept off the balance sheet, such as derivatives of bonds based on sub-prime mortgages.

We deal with the first two issues, liquidity and capital management, in this chapter.

Capital

The fundamentals are that a bank starts out with some money put in by its owners to pay for buildings, equipment, etc. Shareholders' funds, obtained by the selling of shares in the firm, have the advantage that the shareholders do not have the right to withdraw their money from the company – it is **permanent capital** – although they might sell their shares to other investors. As well as paying for the initial set-up, shareholders' capital also provides a buffer of capital acting as a safety margin against the event of a significant number of the loans granted to borrowers going wrong. The buffer is referred to as **capital** and loans made are **assets** of the bank. Deposits (and other loans to the bank) are **liabilities**.

Total assets = Total liabilities + Capital

In addition to capital being raised at the foundation of the business it can be augmented over the years through the bank making profits and deciding to keep it within the business rather than distributing it as dividends to shareholders – **retained earnings**. It can also be increased by selling more shares. Capital is also called **net worth** or **equity capital**.

Another worry – liquidity risk

A bank is also likely to be concerned about the possibility of a high proportion of the depositors/other lenders withdrawing their money on a single day and not being able to replace those funds with fresh funding. To reduce the chance of **liquidity risk** – running out of liquid assets – it thus keeps a proportion of the money it raises in the form of cash (and near-cash) rather than lending it all.

Let us assume for now that a bank, BarcSan, is required by the central bank (its regulator) to hold 8% of the value of its customer deposits in reserves. These are the regulatory **required reserves**. However, the bank may judge that 8% is not enough and decide to add another 4% of the value of its customer deposits as **excess reserves**. Reserves consist of both the cash that the bank is required to hold in its account with the central bank plus cash that it has on its own premises, referred to as **vault cash**. Note that we are referring here to cash reserves and not the capital reserves (the difference between assets and liabilities). Cash reserves are there to avoid running out of cash, a short-term phenomenon, whereas capital reserves are there to avoid running out of net assets (assets minus liabilities).

Cash reserves of 12% of customer deposits is fairly typical. In rough terms cash held is generally 6–9% of overall liabilities (not just customer deposits), and another 10% or so might be held in assets that can quickly be converted to cash, such as very short-term loans to other banks (the interbank market is discussed in Chapter 6), certificates of deposit for money placed with other banks in tradable form (see the box below) and government Treasury bills (lending to the government for a few days, say 30 or 91 days); these are termed near-cash. The term for reserves that includes near-cash is **liquid reserves**.

Certificates of deposit (CDs)

Certificates of deposit are issued by banks when funds are deposited with them by other banks, corporations, individuals or investment companies. The certificates state that a deposit has been made (a **time deposit**) and that at the maturity date the bank will pay a sum higher than that originally deposited. The maturities can be any length of time between a week and a year (typically one to four months)[1] and can be negotiable, that is, they can be sold on to other investors,[2] or non-negotiable. There is a penalty for savers withdrawing the money before the maturity date (they are **term securities**). CDs are normally issued in lots ranging from £50,000 to £500,000 in the UK, or $100,000 to $1m in the USA, with similar-sized lots in the eurozone and Japan.

Non-negotiable CDs must be held by the depositor until the CD reaches maturity. The advantage of negotiable CDs is that although they cannot be redeemed at the issuing bank without a penalty, they can be traded in a secondary market, so the original depositor can achieve liquidity but the bank issuing the certificate has a deposit held with it until the maturity date. The rate of interest paid on negotiable CDs is lower than a fixed deposit because of the attraction of liquidity.

A company or a bank with surplus cash can put it into a CD knowing that if its situation changes and it needs extra cash, it can sell the CD (if negotiable) for cash. At the centre of the secondary market are a network of brokers and dealers in CDs, striking deals over the telephone.

To understand the working of a bank we will start with a very simple example of a change in the cash held by a bank. Imagine that Mrs Rich deposits £1,000 of cash into her current account at the BarcSan Bank. This has affected the bank's balance sheet. It has an increase of cash, and therefore reserves, of £1,000. This is an asset of the bank. At the same time it has increased its liabilities because the bank owes

Mrs Rich £1,000, which she can withdraw any time. We can illustrate the changes by looking at that part of the balance sheet which deals with this transaction. In the T-account below, the asset (cash) is shown on the left and the increased liability is shown on the right.

BarcSan partial balance sheet

ASSETS		LIABILITIES	
Vault cash (part of reserves)	£1,000	Current account	£1,000

This increase in reserves could also have come about through Mrs Rich paying in a £1,000 cheque drawn on an account at, say, HSBC. When BarcSan receives the cheque it deposits it at the central bank which then collects £1,000 from HSBC's account with the central bank and transfers it to BarcSan's account at the central bank, increasing its reserves. Remember: cash reserves include both those held at the central bank and in the bank vault, tills, ATMs, etc.

Given that BarcSan has required reserves of 8% of current account deposits, following the receipt of £1,000 it has increased assets of £80 in required reserves and £920 in excess reserves.

BarcSan partial balance sheet

ASSETS		LIABILITIES	
Required reserves	£80	Current account	£1,000
Excess reserves	£920		

These reserves are not paying interest to BarcSan.[3] What is even more troubling is that the bank is providing an expensive service to Mrs Rich with bank branch convenience, cheque books, statements, etc. This money has to be put to use – at least as much of it as is prudent. One way of making a profit is to lend most of the money. It does this by lending to a business for five years. Thus the bank borrows on a short-term basis (instant access for Mrs Rich) and lends long (five-year term loan). The bank decides to lend £880 because this would allow it to maintain its required reserve ratio of 8% and its target excess reserve of 4%.

BarcSan partial balance sheet

ASSETS		LIABILITIES	
Required reserves	£80	Current account	£1,000
Excess reserves	£40		
Loan	£880		

Liquidity management and reserves

A bank has to keep enough cash on hand to satisfy current account holders and other customers withdrawing money from their accounts. There may be times when a large volume of cash is withdrawn and the bank has to be ready for that – this is what we refer to as **liquidity management**. Let us look at the (simplified) balance sheet for BarcSan as a whole, all its asset and all its liabilities. We will assume that all deposits are current account deposits and so it keeps 8% of those as required reserves and *aims* to have a further 4% as excess reserves (either at the central bank or as vault cash). As well as £10bn in deposits the bank has £900m in capital accumulated mostly through retaining past profits. It has lent £5.7bn and bought £3.1bn of marketable securities such as government bonds and bills (actually another form of lending).

BarcSan's balance sheet

ASSETS		LIABILITIES	
Required reserves	£800m	Deposits	£10,000m
Excess reserves	£1,300m	Bank capital	£900m
Loans	£5,700m		
Securities	£3,100m		

To satisfy its own rule of 12% of customer deposits held as reserves it needs only £1.2bn but it currently has £2.1bn (£800m + £1,300m). It has a 'spare' £900m. If there is a sudden rise in withdrawals from bank accounts as people worry about the bank system collapsing and a bank not being able to repay its deposit liabilities (as with Northern Rock in 2007 or Cypriot banks in 2013) this will have an impact on BarcSan. If £900m of cash is withdrawn from BarcSan its balance changes to:

BarcSan's balance sheet after a sudden withdrawal of £900m

ASSETS		LIABILITIES	
Required reserves	£728m	Deposits	£9,100m
Excess reserves	£472m	Bank capital	£900m
Loans	£5,700m		
Securities	£3,100m		

The bank still has cash reserves above its target because 12% of £9,100m is £1,092m,[4] whereas the bank has £1,200m (required reserves of £728m plus excess reserves of £472m). Because it started with plentiful reserves the public panic to withdraw funds has not affected the other elements in BarcSan's balance sheet.

Now take a different case, where BarcSan has already lent out any reserves above its prudential level of 12% of deposits.

BarcSan's balance sheet if actual reserves equal target reserves

ASSETS		LIABILITIES	
Required reserves	£800m	Deposits	£10,000m
Excess reserves	£400m	Bank capital	£900m
Loans	£6,600m		
Securities	£3,100m		

Now imagine a financial panic: many depositors rush to the bank's branches to take out their money. In one day £900m is withdrawn. At the end of the day the balance sheet is looking far from healthy.

BarcSan's balance sheet after £900m is withdrawn (after the bank just met its reserve target)

ASSETS		LIABILITIES	
Required reserves	£300m	Deposits	£9,100m
Excess reserves	£0m	Bank capital	£900m
Loans	£6,600m		
Securities	£3,100m		

Another day like that and it might be wiped out. It is required to hold 8% of £9,100m as reserves, £728m, but now has only £300m. Where is it going to get the shortfall from? There are four possibilities.

1. Borrow from other banks and other organisations

There is an active market in interbank loans as well as banks borrowing by selling commercial paper or certificates of deposit to corporations and other institutions. Perhaps BarcSan could borrow the £428m it needs here.

BarcSan's balance sheet if it borrows £428m from the markets

ASSETS		LIABILITIES	
Required reserves	£728m	Deposits	£9,100m
Excess reserves	£0m	Borrowed from banks and corporations	£428m
Loans	£6,600m	Bank capital	£900m
Securities	£3,100m		

However, given the cause of the crisis was a system-wide loss of confidence BarcSan may have difficulty raising money in these markets at this time. This was a problem that beset many banks around the world in 2008, and then many eurozone banks in Greece, Cyprus, Portugal and Spain in 2011–13. They had grown used to quickly obtaining cash to cover shortfalls from other banks. But in the calamitous loss of confidence following the sub-prime debacle and the eurozone crisis banks simply stopped lending – those that were caught with insufficient reserves failed or were bailed out by governments.

2. Securities could be sold

Of the securities bought by a bank most are traded in very active markets where it is possible to sell a large quantity without moving the price. Let us assume that the bank sells £428m of government Treasury bills and bonds to move its reserves back to 8% of deposits.

BarcSan's balance sheet if it sells £428m of securities

ASSETS		LIABILITIES	
Required reserves	£728m	Deposits	£9,100m
Excess reserves	£0m	Bank capital	£900m
Loans	£6,600m		
Securities	£2,672m		

The short-term securities issued by respectable (safe) governments held by banks are classified as **secondary reserves** because they tend to be very easy to sell quickly, at low transaction cost and without moving the market price, even if sold in fairly high volume. Other securities held by the bank will have higher transaction costs of sale and are less easy to sell and so are not classed as secondary reserves.

3. Borrowing from the central bank

One of the major duties of a central bank is to act as **lender of last resort**. It stands ready to lend to banks that lack cash reserves (there is more on this in Chapters 24 and 25). However, it will do this at a high price only (high interest rate) to deter banks from calling on it in trivial circumstances. If BarcSan borrows the £428m shortfall from the central bank to take it back to the regulator's minimum of 8% its balance sheet now looks like this:

BarcSan's balance sheet if it borrows £428m from the central bank

ASSETS		LIABILITIES	
Required reserves	£728m	Deposits	£9,100m
Excess reserves	£0m	Borrowings from central bank	£428m
Loans	£6,600m	Bank capital	£900m
Securities	£3,100m		

4. Reducing lending

Banks receive principal repayments on loans every day as the period of various loan agreements come to an end, or as portions of loans are repaid during the term of the loan. To raise some money the bank could simply refuse any more loans for a period. I was on the sharp end of this in February 2007 when trying to complete a business property deal. Suddenly Halifax Bank of Scotland refused to lend on what was a pretty safe deal for the bank. I was nonplussed. What were they playing at? Didn't they know they would lose my company as a customer? Of course, with hindsight we all know that this was the start of the crisis when HBOS was desperately short of cash (it only avoided complete annihilation by allowing itself to be bought by Lloyds). Another possibility is to sell-off some of its loan book to another bank – but the purchasers are unlikely to pay full value, especially in uncertain times. An even more drastic solution is to insist that borrowers repay their loans immediately. This is possible with some types of loans such as overdrafts but it results in much resentment and damage to long-term relationships. If BarcSan raised £428m in one of these ways its balance sheet would look like this:

BarcSan balance sheet after reducing loans by £428m

ASSETS		LIABILITIES	
Required reserves	£728m	Deposits	£9,100m
Excess reserves	£0m	Bank capital	£900m
Loans	£6,172m		
Securities	£3,100m		

Of course, there are a few more moves that need to be made if the bank wants to reach its target of 12% reserves, rather than simply get to 8%, but after such a crisis in the financial markets this may take a few years to achieve.

A difficult balance

A bank has a trade off to manage. If it ties up a very high proportion of its money in reserves it loses the opportunity to lend that money to gain a return, but the managers can feel very safe, as they are unlikely to run out of cash. Yet if it goes for maximum interest by lending the vast majority of the money deposited, it could face illiquidity. Thus it has to have enough reserves to avoid one or more of the following costly ways of quickly raising money: (a) borrowing from other banks; (b) selling securities; (c) borrowing from the central bank; or (d) reducing its loans. Excess reserves provide insurance against incurring liquidity problems due to deposit outflows, but like all insurance it comes at a high price.

Some rules for liquidity management

Many banks adopt these rules to reduce liquidity risk:

1 **Illiquid assets should be funded with customer deposits.** The alternative funding of borrowing in the wholesale financial markets (interbank, commercial paper, etc.) is more risky because the lenders here may switch off the funding tap very quickly at any hint of trouble, whereas deposits are more stable, less likely to be withdrawn in times of financial stress.

2 **After customer deposits are exhausted as a funding source, use mostly long-term not short-term wholesale funding sources.** This reduces the risk of failing to roll over funding as it matures.

3 **Never rely extensively on wholesale funding.** Do not expand the asset base such that wholesale funding comes to dominate. One way of checking on this is to have a moderate ratio of loans to deposits, say 100%, implying that wholesale funding is not financing a high proportion of illiquid loans. A **loan-to-deposit** ratio below 70% is regarded as excessively liquid, producing lower returns for shareholders.

4 **Maintain a good stock of almost instantly liquid assets.** Requires a greater emphasis on owning shorter-dated government bills rather than, say, bonds issued by corporate, local authorities or financial institutions, or even CDs.

5 **Diversify sources of liquid funding** (e.g. selling financial instruments to a variety of different types of organisation, from central banks to other banks) and **have a contingency plan** to switch to alternatives as the need arises.

International standards

Over the next few years the bank supervisors in most countries are likely to impose the new international minimum standards they agreed under the leadership of the **Basel Committee on Banking Supervision** in 2013. This focuses on the **liquidity coverage ratio (LCR)**, which is the quantity of cash and high-quality liquid assets relative to its commitments to repay funding (after allowing for some inflows) over the next 30 days in a stress situation, e.g. a panic by depositors.

A big debate took place in 2012 over what assets should count as liquid, with many saying that stockmarket-listed shares were not sufficiently reliable as a source of liquidity. There was even more fuss over the decision to include bonds whose interest and capital repayments depended on mortgage holders continuing to pay their mortgages ('mortgage-backed bonds' – see Chapter 11). In the end the LCR target was more permissive than many thought it would be – see Figure 7.1 and Article 7.1.

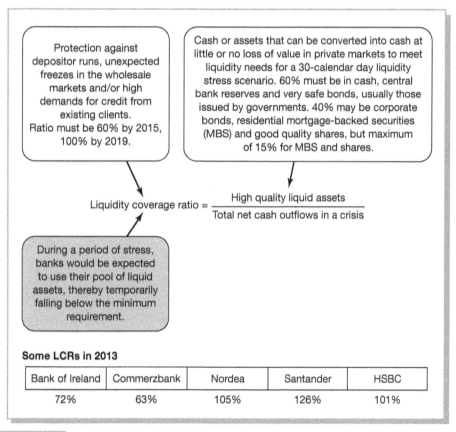

Some LCRs in 2013

Bank of Ireland	Commerzbank	Nordea	Santander	HSBC
72%	63%	105%	126%	101%

Figure 7.1   Liquidity coverage ratio – Basel Committee rules

Article 7.1

Liquidity: Banks debate liquidity trade-off

By Tracy Alloway

When Basel banking supervisors unveiled loosened liquidity requirements in January, one could practically hear the cheers emanating from financial centres around the world. Not only did the regulators widen the types of assets that could be included in banks' so-called liquidity buffers, they also extended the deadline for compliance.

The watered-down liquidity requirements meant that US banks' collective liquidity coverage ratio shot up from 81% to 94%. That is just 6 percentage points shy of the 100% they will ultimately need to achieve.

Under the proposed rules, banks have to hold a buffer of high-quality and liquid assets to cover their estimate of the amount of funding they might lose over a 30-day period.

It is a key plank in regulators' attempts to prevent the kind of market turmoil witnessed during the depths of the financial crisis.

While holding large war chests of ostensibly liquid assets makes sense from a financing perspective, there is an economic trade-off. Liquid assets tend to be less profitable for banks. ... restricting financial institutions' ability to lend.

Regulators say they had this trade-off in mind when they opted to soften their original LCR proposals.

Banks will now be able to include a host of assets, from residential mortgage-backed securities (RMBS) to different types of corporate bonds, when building their buffers.

"Since we attach great importance to try to make sure that banks can indeed finance a recovery, it does not make sense to impose a requirement that might damage the recovery," says Mervyn King, Bank of England governor.

Risk experts say whether banks opt to go over and above the LCR rules will depend

on a multitude of factors, including their perceived risk profile, jurisdiction and type of business. Banks that are aiming to attract retail depositors, for instance, may find that holding a big buffer of liquidity could be a selling point to customers.

Basel has yet to set out the penalties for not complying with the liquidity rules, for instance. "My guess would be that if the consequences are quite severe then the banks will have a bigger buffer," says Joo-Yung Lee, at Fitch Ratings. "If the consequences are light they may move towards the minimum."

Few wish to be on the low end of the LCR once markets go awry. That might mean many banks end up clamouring for more liquid assets just when markets are beginning to turn.

"You really don't want to have a number 100 when the stuff is hitting the fan," says one risk manager at a top European bank, "So maybe you want to get to 120 before this happens."

Capital adequacy management

How much capital should the bank hold? In deciding this managers need to trade off the risk of bank failure by not being able to satisfy its creditors (depositors, wholesale market lenders, etc.) against the attraction of increasing the return to the bank's owners by having as little capital as possible relative to the asset base. The fear here is of **insolvency** – an inability to repay obligations over the longer course of events – rather than illiquidity, which is insufficient liquid assets to repay obligations falling due if there is a sudden outflow of cash (e.g. large depositor withdrawals on a particular day, borrowers defaulting, unexpectedly drawing down on lines of credit, or large payments under derivative deals).

To understand the difficulty with this trade-off we can compare BarcSan's situation with a less well-capitalised bank, Mercurial.

BarcSan's opening balance sheet

ASSETS		LIABILITIES	
Required reserves	£800m	Deposits	£10,000m
Excess reserves	£1,300m	Bank capital	£900m
Loans	£5,700m		
Securities	£3,100m		

BarcSan's capital to assets ratio is £900m/£10,900 = 8.3%. Mercurial has exactly the same assets as BarcSan, but it has only £400m in capital. It has raised an extra £500m from deposits. It has a ratio of capital to assets of 3.7% (£400m/£10,900m).

Mercurial's opening balance sheet

ASSETS		LIABILITIES	
Required reserves	£800m	Deposits	£10,500m
Excess reserves	£1,300m	Bank capital	£400m
Loans	£5,700m		
Securities	£3,100m		

Now consider what happens if we assume a situation similar to that in southern Europe in 2013. Both banks invested £500m in bonds issued by Cypriot financial institutions. These now become worthless as the borrowers stop paying.[5] BarcSan can withstand the loss in assets because it maintained a conservative stance on its capital ratio.

BarcSan's balance sheet after £500m losses on Cypriot bonds

ASSETS		LIABILITIES	
Required reserves	£800m	Deposits	£10,000m
Excess reserves	£1,300m	Bank capital	£400m
Loans	£5,700m		
Securities	£2,600m		

Its **capital-to-assets ratio** has fallen to a less conservative 3.8% (£400m/£10,400), but this is a level that still affords some sense of safety for its providers of funds. (Some writers refer to the capital-to-assets ratio as the **leverage ratio**, others take its inverse as the leverage ratio.)

Mercurial is insolvent. Its assets of £10,400 are less than the amount owed to depositors.

Mercurial's balance sheet after £500m losses on Cypriot bonds

ASSETS		LIABILITIES	
Required reserves	£800m	Deposits	£10,500m
Excess reserves	£1,300m	Bank capital	–£100m
Loan	£5,700m		
Securities	£2,600m		

A course of action is to write to depositors to tell them that it cannot repay the full amount that was deposited with the bank. They might panic, and rush to the branch to obtain what they are owed in full. More likely is that the regulator steps in to close or rescue the bank. Occasionally the central bank organises a rescue by a group of other banks – they, too, have an interest in maintaining confidence in the banking system. In 2009 Royal Bank of Scotland and Lloyds Banking Group, following the sudden destruction of balance sheet reserves when the value of their loans and many securities turned out to be much less than what was shown on the balance sheet, were rescued by the UK government which injected money into them by buying billions of new shares. This was enough new capital to save them from destruction but the banks are still clawing their way back to health by holding onto any profits they make to rebuild capital reserves.

Why might banks sail close to the wind in aiming at a very low capital to assets ratio?

The motivation to lower the capital to assets ratio is to boost the returns to shareholders. To illustrate: imagine both BarcSan and Mercurial make profits after deduction of tax of £150m per year and we can ignore extraordinary losses such as the sub-prime fiasco. A key measure of profitability is **return on assets (ROA)**.

$$ROA = \frac{\text{Net profit after tax}}{\text{Total assets}}$$

Given that both firms (in normal conditions) have the same profits and the same assets we have a ROA of £150m/£10,900m = 1.376%.[6] This is a useful measure of bank efficiency in terms of how much profit is generated per pound of assets.

However, what shareholders are really interested in is the return for each pound that *they* place in the business. Assuming that the capital figures in the balance sheet are all provided by ordinary shareholders then the **return on equity (ROE)** is:

$$ROE = \frac{\text{Net profit after tax}}{\text{Equity capital}}$$

For BarcSan:

$$ROE = \frac{£150m}{£900m} = 16.7\%$$

For Mercurial:

$$ROE = \frac{£150m}{£400m} = 37.5\%$$

Mercurial appears to be super-profitable, simply because it obtained such a small proportion of its funds from shareholders. Many conservatively-run banks were quizzed by their shareholders in the mid-2000s on why their returns to equity were low compared with other banks, and 'couldn't they just push up returns with a little less caution on the capital ratio?' Many were tempted to follow the crowd in the good times only to suffer very badly when bank capital levels were exposed as far too daring. You can understand the temptation, and that is why regulation is needed to insist on minimum levels of capital – this is discussed in Chapter 25. Article 7.2 shows ROEs are much reduced.

Australian banks – high and dry

Lofty returns on equity but low on excitement

Yeah, yeah. Bank targets 15 per cent return on equity. We've heard that one before. What looked like a disappointing return in the boom years has in the past five become a reminder of how far banks in the US and Europe have sunk. But, for Gail Kelly of Westpac who repeated the target on Thursday, it looks all too possible, as it does for Australia's other big banks.

Aussie banks, along with their Canadian peers, are held up as examples of what regulators think others should look like. And their ROEs are something rivals can only dream of: since 2008, Australia's big four – Commonwealth Bank, Westpac, ANZ and NAB – have averaged 14 per cent ROE, from 17 per cent in the boom.

Top US and western European names, meanwhile, are producing about 6 per cent these days, against an average 16 per cent before. Only China's banks, at 20 per cent now and 18 before, look better.

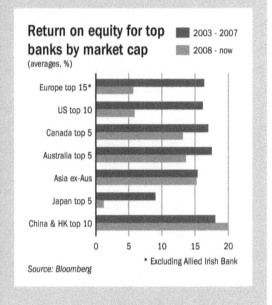

Return on equity for top banks by market cap
(averages, %)

■ 2003 - 2007
■ 2008 - now

Source: Bloomberg

* Excluding Allied Irish Bank

The equity multiplier

There is a mathematical relationship between the return on assets, ROA, and return on equity, ROE. This is determined by the equity multiplier (gearing multiplier) which is the amount of assets per pound of equity:

$$\text{Equity multiplier} = \frac{\text{assets}}{\text{equity capital}}$$

For BarcSan:

$$\text{Equity multiplier} = \frac{£10{,}900m}{£900m} = 12.11$$

For Mercurial:

$$\text{Equity multiplier} = \frac{£10,900m}{£400m} = 27.25$$

Return on equity = Return on assets × Equity multiplier
BarcSan: 16.7% = 1.376% × 12.11
Mercurial: 37.5% = 1.376% × 27.25

The Archbishop of Canterbury (formerly a finance man) and other knowledgeable people think that the government has proposed a leverage ratio (inverse of equity multiplier) requirement that provides insufficient capital relative to assets – see Article 7.3.

Article 7.3

Great and good flex banking muscles

By Patrick Jenkins and George Parker

The Parliamentary Commission on Banking Standards has flexed its muscles more forcefully than George Osborne ever expected.

When the chancellor gave the commission power to scrutinise his banking reform bill, he did not foresee a rebellion by his fellow Conservative MPs, a former chancellor and even the archbishop of Canterbury.

In a report on Monday, the commission, chaired by Conservative MP Andrew Tyrie, objects to the proposed law's requirement that a bank's equity capital must exceed 3 per cent of its assets.

The commission, which includes Lord Lawson, former chancellor, and Justin Welby, archbishop of Canterbury, said it is "wholly unconvinced" that a 3 per cent leverage ratio is sufficient.

A leverage ratio is seen as a powerful backstop to more manipulable capital ratios, which depend on banks applying often controversial "risk-weights" to different categories of loans [see Chapter 25]. That risk judgment, the focus of concern among regulators in the UK and internationally, is stripped out by leverage ratios.

The original Vickers review recommended a leverage ratio of at least 4 per cent.

Two of Britain's banks, HSBC and Barclays, last week published their Basel III leverage ratios for the first time, although they will not be enforceable until 2018. Although HSBC exceeded 4 per cent, Barclays' was only 2.8 per cent.

What to do if your bank holds too much or too little capital

The objective is to select an amount of capital sufficient to maintain the bank as a going concern taking into account both expected losses and a reasonable margin of safety for unexpected losses (often informed/imposed by regulators). Exceeding this results in excess capital and lowered ROEs.

There are three ways for bank directors to reduce the amount of capital relative to assets:

1 Pay out a high dividend(s) to shareholders to reduce their equity in the business.

2 Buy back some of the bank's shares.

3 Increase assets by ramping up lending, financed by borrowing more, e.g. issue CDs, long-term bonds, commercial paper or attract more deposits.

There are four ways to increase the amount of capital relative to assets:

1 Reduce dividends to increase retained earnings (many UK, European and US banks have done this over the past five years).

2 Sell new shares in the bank (again, a popular move recently).

3 Reduce assets by lowering borrowing, selling off existing loans to other financial institutions, and selling securities. Many politicians, regulators and economists are frustrated that so many banks opted for this solution post-2008 (rather than solution 4), resulting in a slowing economy as consumers found it hard to obtain mortgages and small businesses were refused loans.

4 Reduce costs to increase retained profits. Policymakers and the press have been screaming at the bankers to reduce pay, bonuses and other costs. Apparently, this is very difficult to do, according to the bankers. The pace may be glacial, but it now seems to be happening.

Which is riskier?

Take a look at the balance sheet summaries for Company A and Company B in Figure 7.2. Which company do you think is taking the most risk?

Clearly, A is safer from a liquidity point of view. Its liabilities mature later and it has a greater proportion of liquid assets. Thus it could better withstand a sudden outflow of cash if there is a crisis in the funding markets. However, it is vulnerable

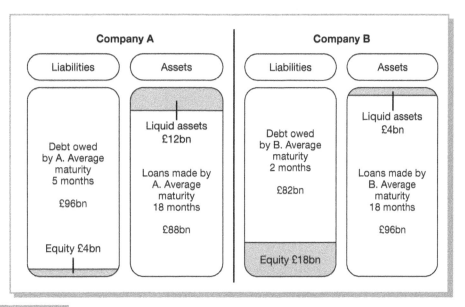

Figure 7.2 Trade off: Capital strengths or liquidity strength

in a different way: with only £4bn of equity capital, if only a small fraction of its borrowers failed to pay it would find itself insolvent. Furthermore, while it was on the road to insolvency, and rumours started to circulate, the suppliers of funds to A might take fright and back away from supplying fresh funds as old debts mature, thus precipitating a liquidity crisis.

B, on the other hand, may find itself with the markets doubting its ability to meet its debts as they fall due: a liquidity issue. These doubts may manifest themselves in a market reluctance to refinance maturing liabilities. This may force B to sell off a significant proportion of its assets at knock-down prices to survive a liquidity crisis. If, as a result, a large amount of asset value has to be written off the balance sheet then the crisis may morph into a capital crisis as the equity buffer diminishes.

There is no right answer as to which is the safer company. Both are vulnerable in different ways. It depends whether the future will bring a liquidity crisis or a capital loss crisis. Without reliable crystal balls we need to protect against both dangers.

Asset and liability management

We have already examined lending and other asset management from the perspective of individual deals. Now we turn to bankers considering the overall approach to managing the bank's assets.

Likewise, when it comes to selecting the appropriate mixture of funding types we need to take an overview of the bank's approach, rather than the details of individual transactions.

The final topic dealt with in this chapter is off-balance activities, ranging from derivative position risks to bank guarantees which create problems for the bank if contingent events occur, such as a customer failing to pay a supplier.

Asset management

In managing a bank's assets the senior team must balance out the three factors shown in Figure 8.1 to try and maximise shareholder returns in the long run. The highest returns usually come from tying up bank money in long-term loans and securities where it is difficult and/or costly to release the money quickly. Also, higher returns are usually associated with higher risk-taking by the bank. However, within those generalisations it makes sense for bank loan officers to search for potential borrowers who are least likely to default and most likely to accept a high interest charge.

The skill in asset management comes from assessing who is a good credit risk and who is not. Banks generally like to take a very low risk approach and anticipate that only around 0.6–1% of their loans will go bad. However, they occasionally engage in riskier prospects. When they do, they charge a higher interest rate to compensate for the expectation that a higher proportion of these loans will default.

Credit risk is the risk that a customer will default, but it also covers the possibility that the credit quality of the obligor will deteriorate, short of actual default. Thus,

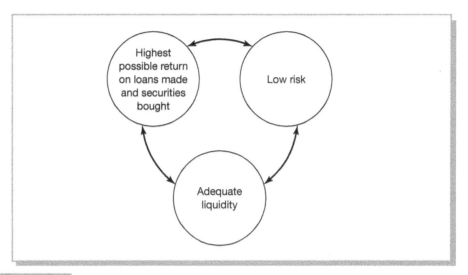

Figure 8.1   The three objectives to be traded off in asset management

the mere probability of a borrower eventually defaulting under a syndicated loan, for instance, may rise due to trouble facing the obligor's business. This may be reflected in a downgrading of the company's credit rating, either calculated by the bank internally or by a credit rating agency (see Chapter 20).

Loan policy and credit culture

A bank's formal **loan policy** must be reinforced by a supportive **credit culture.** This concerns behavioural/set of beliefs factors that run throughout the bank. The policy might state a high-quality, low-risk, low default-type lending. The training, messages and rewards employees receive should reinforce that culture. Alternatively, the bank may specialise in lending for projects at the forefront of technology where more risk is accepted together with higher interest rates and fee income. If so, understanding the dynamics of clients and their market environment, as well as a greater risk-taking attitude, may be a cultural necessity to win business.

Senior managers need to state explicitly the bank's approach to risk, define the limits of exposure to trading instruments and type of borrower, and set clear lines of responsibility and accountability. Steadfastness in sticking to the policy through the ups and downs of an economic cycle will bring greater expertise and clarity to decision-making. Many banks lowered their lending criteria in the mid-2000s on both sides of the Atlantic, particularly for mortgages where loans greater than the value of the property were offered to people on low and unstable incomes; then, in the subsequent recession they became reluctant to lend unless a very large deposit was provided. Article 8.1 describes the failed banking policy and culture of HBOS – it raises a few other issues, which we address later in the chapter.

Bank built on flawed business model

By Jennifer Thompson and Patrick Jenkins

Looking to the past to learn lessons for the present can be a dismal, if ultimately constructive, exercise. But if unpicking the litany of failures that led to the ruin of HBOS at the height of the financial crisis is to serve any purpose, it must highlight the dangers of ill-judged lending, poor risk control and slack regulatory scrutiny.

That is the conclusion of the Parliamentary Commission on Banking Standards in its damning report on the bank.

"This is a case study of how not to run a bank and how not to regulate one," said Andrew Tyrie, chairman of the commission. [The] lessons are clear.

The first could be summed up as the importance of culture and strategy in preventing reckless lending policies and weak risk management.

Lending across all the bank's divisions had shot up in the years between its creation in 2001 from Bank of Scotland's merger with Halifax and the start of the financial crisis in 2008. But ultimately, this "strategy for aggressive, asset-led growth ... sowed the seeds of [HBOS's] destruction", the commission said.

"This culture was brash, underpinned by a belief that the growing market share was due to a special set of skills which HBOS possessed and which its competitors lacked."

The results were particularly bad in the bank's corporate lending division, which had loans of £123bn at the end of 2008, up from about £55bn in 2001.

The commission estimates that impairments on loans originating from this division, whose expansion focused on lending to riskier sectors such as property and construction, were at least £25bn between 2008 and 2011. "The picture that emerges is of a corporate bank that found it hard to say 'no'," the commission said.

Nor was the corporate division an isolated case. HBOS's activities in Australia and Ireland were cited as particularly painful examples of how skewed risk judgment had cost it dear as the bank embarked on a "wildly ambitious growth strategy".

In those two markets alone it incurred impairments of £14.5bn in the period from 2008 to 2011.

The commission presents a compelling case that HBOS's whole business model was flawed from the start. The merger that created the bank in 2001 brought together two banks that already had an unusually high reliance on wholesale market funding – essentially bond issuance – rather than more conservative deposit finance. But the mismatch was exacerbated by the strategy embarked upon by the then chief executive Sir James Crosby and chairman Lord Stevenson to grow lending aggressively.

HBOS's loan-to-deposit ratio of 143 per cent in 2001 had jumped to 198 per cent by the end of 2008, sending its wholesale funding needs rocketing from £61bn to £213bn. The report highlights an internal report to the board that characterised this funding position as "untenable", "unsustainable" and described HBOS as "structurally illiquid".

Article 8.1   Continued

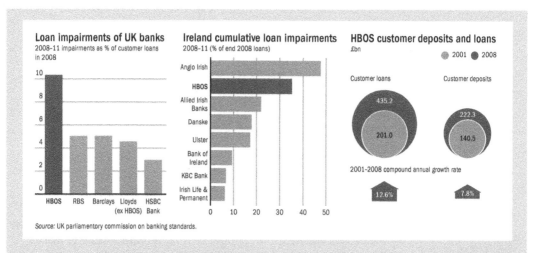

Loan impairments of UK banks
2008–11 impairments as % of customer loans in 2008

Ireland cumulative loan impairments
2008–11 (% of end 2008 loans)

HBOS customer deposits and loans
£bn

Source: UK parliamentory commission on banking standards.

The commission castigat[es] the bank's "flawed strategy, inappropriate culture and inadequate controls", which it blamed on the bank's two successive chief executives, and "particularly the chairman".

In addition to HBOS's excessive vulnerability to wholesale funding – more than half of which was very short-term in nature, in contrast to the long-term lending commitments on its balance sheet – the report says the most fundamental problem was the poor quality of loans.

It described the risk function as a cardinal area of weakness in the bank. "This is a story of a retail and commercial bank, rather than an investment bank, brought down by ill-judged lending, poor risk control and inadequate liquidity," said Lord Turnbull, a Commission committee member and leader of its panel on HBOS. "Its strategy was flawed from the start."

 Source: Thompson, J. and Jenkins, P. (2013) 'Bank built on flawed business model', *Financial Times*, 5 April.

Existing client lending

A policy of lending to existing clients has many advantages. Information such as the way in which the customer has run his or her current account, or behaved when granted a loan in the past can give vital clues on credit risk, as can knowledge of a person's character. Reputation is also likely to be of great importance to borrowers, who will be less likely to blot their copybook by applying for a loan for a low-risk venture and then switching to a high-risk business if they are looking for long-term future relations with the bank. It is fair to say that this kind of constraint is usually more significant in controlling adverse behaviour than all the legal covenants set out in the loan agreement. HBOS's aggressive loan growth led its loan book to be disproportionately weighted to new customers.

Credit rationing

Credit rationing is declining to lend even if the borrower is willing to pay the stated interest.

There are two forms:

1   No loan at all to that particular borrower. Some proposals are just too risky for the bank, even with very high interest rates. Indeed, raised interest rates for a high-risk venture can actually make the problem worse as the borrower struggles to pay the extra outflow. In 2001–08 HBOS stretched its criteria to allow lending to marginal cases.

2   A loan is made, but it is less than the borrower requested. This may be because the bank estimates that borrowers may expose themselves too much by over-borrowing, e.g. limits on credit card borrowing. Another example is the maximum mortgage available to a household. Alternatively, the borrower may not have sufficient collateral. Or it might be that the bank wishes to place a limit on its exposure to any one customer, industry or country.

Diversification

Banks should construct a portfolio of loan assets and financial security assets to diversify credit risk. No one loan or category of loans (e.g. property-related or retail-related) or securities should dominate the portfolio. The benefit of diversification is very much influenced by the degree to which defaults on a number of loans and securities are likely to happen at the same time, i.e. are they highly **correlated**? Obviously, the less correlated (lower **co-variability** or **covariance**) the better.

To avoid over-exposure to a single sector banks often set **concentration limits**, restricting the proportion of the bank's assets in an area of activity, with upper limits for countries or sectors. Diversification for its own sake is not recommended because the bank may stray into areas beyond its circle of competence. It should, however, be able to develop thorough knowledge and competitive advantage in a sufficient number of banking areas to produce good results even when some sectors are suffering from shocks.

Foreign exchange risk

Many banks choose to lend in currencies other than their home currency to take advantage of better interest rates. However, they need to be aware of the possibility that a loan denominated in an overseas currency will not retain its value in the home currency if the foreign currency depreciates; then it will buy fewer home currency units at loan maturity. Thus, a bank faces foreign currency risk on the assets side.

Likewise, if it obtains funding in a foreign currency repayments will rise if the foreign currency appreciates. Banks carefully estimate their net asset/liability positions in various currencies and for various maturities to ensure that the risk is limited – risk amelioration may be assisted with derivatives (see Chapters 21, 22 and 23).

Non-performing loans

Non-performing loans (NPLs) are those where the debtor is failing to make contractual payments, usually interest and/or principal. The non-payment period before a debt is declared an NPL depends on local regulations. In many countries banks will usually wait 90 days after a payment is due before declaring it non-performing, and to do so they might require other reasons to doubt that payments will be made in full. By failing to make a scheduled payment of interest or principal such loans are in **debt service default**. A **technical default** is when loan covenants are violated but payments are made, e.g. failure to supply obligatory information, or the profits-to-interest ratio falls below the level stated in a covenant. If, after being declared non-performing, the debtor starts making payments again it becomes a **re-performing loan**, even if the debtor has not caught up on all the missed payments.

A **bad debt** is when a portion (or all) of a loan will ultimately be uncollectable. Perhaps the borrower's assets have already been liquidated and there is plainly not enough left to pay all creditors in full. Even before a loan is declared bad the bank will normally set aside money to cover the potential loss. These are **loan loss provisions**, also called **impairment allowances/charges,** which lower profit and balance sheet assets to reflect the loss in value. Note that the bankers have not identified a specific loss, merely that from experience they judge that a certain proportion in that class will default, and so an amount of money is earmarked as a buffer in the balance sheet so that the bank can withstand the losses when they occur. This reduces profits now even though the losses may not yet have occurred to protect against having to take a large loss to profits as they occur in an uneven way in the future. Barclays' impairment allowances are shown in Table 8.1.

Table 8.1   Barclays allowance for impairment by asset class, 2012

	£m
Home loans	855
Credit cards, unsecured and other retail lending	3,780
Corporate loans	5,041

Source: Barclays Annual Report 2012

While many loans are not serviced exactly as agreed, the bank may recover much of the debt either through agreeing a rescheduling of payments (**restructuring**) or from **recovery** of value after default, e.g. selling off collateral following liquidation or home repossession. The percentage of the default loan recovered is the **recovery rate**.

Estimating individual loan and portfolio default and recovery rates is very difficult, especially at times of market downturns and recessions. In normal times the bank may have the starting point of historical data of default and recovery rates gathered over, say, five years and then make tweaks using experienced judgement to suit the current circumstances. But a major shift in the economic outlook (e.g. economic growth, interest and exchange rates, level of home repossessions and corporate failures) leads to so much uncertainty that the models used are of limited validity. Default rates and recovery rates differ from one recession to the next, depending on depth and length of the slowdown, response of the authorities on such issues as company/household bailouts, emergency tax breaks, lowered interest rates, altered bankruptcy procedures, etc.

The Indian government is concerned that its banks have poor lending practices leading to high levels of non-performing loans – see Article 8.2.

Article 8.2

India's banks face balance sheet decline

By James Crabtree in Mumbai

The term "lazy banking" has dogged Indian financial services for the past decade since a senior regulator used it to describe an industry dominated by lumbering, risk-averse, state-backed institutions.

Yet many of these same banks have begun lending much more energetically, heightening concerns among regulators and analysts about weak risk management and declining asset quality.

Analysts have been worried about a sharp increase in gross non-performing assets, which rose from 2 per cent a year ago to 3.4 per cent at the end of the last quarter. Debt restructuring between lenders and borrowers is on the rise, too – zooming up threefold in the past year to Rs680bn ($12bn) – raising analysts' suspicions that banks are using these agreements to fudge the true level of their bad debts.

Both trends are partly cyclical, as corporate credit quality drops in the face of slowing growth, high interest rates and rising input costs. However, there is also evidence of a structural change, with sharp increases in the concentration of bank exposure to the debts of a group of large corporates.

India's banks have enjoyed an annual compound growth rate of about 20 per cent over the past five years, but this has increasingly been driven by a fivefold debt increase at just 10 large conglomerates.

India's state-backed banks, which account for about three-quarters of lending, have borne the brunt of this balance sheet deterioration with all four of the largest groups reporting weaker asset quality.

"The next phase of this credit cycle will see large corporates come under greater pressure,

Continued

with restructuring set to rise further," says Anish Tawakley, a banking analyst at Barclays in Mumbai, "and, here, many of the private banks are just as exposed."

Such trends have regulators worried. In a stinging speech this month, KC Chakrabarty, of the Reserve Bank of India, attacked public sector banks in particular for weak risk management and inappropriate use of restructuring agreements.

If current trends continue, India's government will soon need to inject fresh capital into its public lenders, while private banks will have to seek new funding from wary markets.

Capital tied up in restructured loans, meanwhile, will not be available to lend elsewhere, hobbling an economy that badly needs funds to restart investment and increase infrastructure spending.

"The banks need to call a spade a spade when there is a problem," says Rana Kapoor, chief executive of Yes Bank, a fast-growing private outfit launched eight years ago.

Purchasing securities

With the money allocated to investing in securities managers are seeking high returns, but also need to consider the market risk as well as the credit risk they are taking. **Market risk (price risk)** is the effect of market prices or rates on shareholder value. If short-term (e.g. commercial paper) or long-term (e.g. bonds) assets are to be held to maturity and then redeemed by the borrower the market risk is minimal as the bank is unlikely to need to sell in the market. Short-term trading, on the other hand, to make a gain on differences in prices over a period of days or weeks of bonds, commodities, currencies, derivatives, shares, etc., can contribute to profits, but there is often a high risk of a price decline.

Despite many bankers thinking they have a trading edge, misjudgements of markets are commonplace; economic and other events unpredictable. Rival bank traders might merely be playing a zero-sum game against each other, so if one is gaining another is losing an equal amount. Also, there is the threat of a rogue trader making large bets seeking prestige, praise and high bonuses if the bets go right, but potentially jeopardising the bank.

Assets and liabilities may have to be **'marked to market'** for the purposes of annual (or quarterly) accounts. That is, instead of the asset (or liability) being recorded at its original cost it is changed as time goes on depending on market prices. Thus the balance sheet figures can be pushed up or down even before the position is closed. This will affect profits reported too. Banks exposed to high market price risk are required by supervisors to hold more capital.

Liability management

Liability management is focused on judgements made about the composition of the liability book as well as the adjusting of interest rates offered to lenders to the bank to obtain the target mix of borrowing. Banks are generally advised to be diversified in terms of where money is obtained. Many banks (e.g. Northern Rock, HBOS) found in 2008 that they had become over-reliant on obtaining funding from the wholesale markets (e.g. selling bonds, commercial paper or borrowing from other banks) and not enough of their money came from ordinary depositors with current or time deposits.

A balance needs to be struck. Retail depositors tend to be more reliable in leaving their money with a bank, whereas lenders in the wholesale markets move money from place to place quickly if there is any sign of trouble or low rates of return are offered. On the other hand, wholesale money can allow a bank to grow its balance sheet rapidly, whereas it takes time to attract deposits – all those advertisements, high street branches, teaser interest rates, etc.

Going back 50 years, liability management was a much simpler operation because banks tended to focus on core banking, which meant that liabilities were over-whelmingly deposits. Now banks borrow billions from each other and other financial institutions in various ways, from the interbank market to CDs and bonds. The sophisticated wholesale markets for purchasing instruments allow banks to raise finance easily so they can set fast asset-growth targets.

Interest rate risk

A high proportion of loans today are made at floating rates of interest, going up or down periodically with a benchmark, e.g. base rate or LIBOR. To understand the risk associated with this we need to return to BarcSan (first introduced in Chapter 7). The balance sheet below has been broken down in a different way, to show the proportions of assets and liabilities subject to floating rates or with a fixed interest rate for the whole life of the loan/security.

There is a mismatch in interest rate sensitivity: whereas £5.5bn of liabilities fluctuate with general interest rates, only £2.5bn of assets do. Now imagine that interest rates rise by 4 percentage points. The change in income from assets is an extra £2.5bn × 0.04 = £100m per year. However, this is much less than the additional interest paid out on the liabilities: £5.5bn × 0.04 = £220m. For a bank that made profits of £150m this loss of £120m can be quite a burden.

You might be thinking that this works in favour of BarcSan if interest rates fall by 4%, and you would be right, the bank would gain a net £120m. Perhaps BarcSan

BarcSan's assets and liabilities, split by type of interest

ASSETS	*LIABILITIES*
Interest rate sensitive assets	**Interest rate sensitive liabilities**
Including short-term loans and overdrafts and some long-term loans and mortgages linked to base rate/ LIBOR. Also financial market securities with variable rates: £2.5bn	Variable rate borrowings in the financial securities market (e.g. interbank) and variable rate deposit accounts: £5.5bn
Fixed rate assets	**Fixed rate liabilities**
Including some long-term loans, securities and reserves: £8.4bn	Many deposit accounts and securities markets' instruments and equity capital: £5.4bn

will take a win-some-lose-some attitude and accept the fluctuation, but wild swings in profits are usually not acceptable to shareholders and so attention is paid to avoiding a large difference in amounts of rate sensitive assets and liabilities.

Gap analysis

Banks often refer to **basic gap analysis**, which is a summary of the two calculations we have done: the quantity of rate sensitive liabilities is deducted from the quantity of rate sensitive assets. Thus, £2.5bn – £5.5bn = –£3bn. This can be multiplied by the change in interest to obtain the effect on bank profits. If rate sensitive assets exceed rate sensitive liabilities the bank is vulnerable to a fall in general market interest rates. When rate sensitive liabilities exceed rate sensitive assets, however, the vulnerability is to a rise in interest rates.

Maturity gap (maturity bucket) analysis takes things a little further by splitting the fixed versus floating assets and liabilities into different maturity buckets. Thus, it could be that for assets and liabilities maturing between overnight to one week the gap is £2bn with assets less than liabilities, but between one and two years assets outweigh liabilities by £2bn, and so on. See Figure 8.2 for an example focused on the rate sensitive assets and liabilities. Clearly, this bank is not following a **'matched book'** approach, where assets and liabilities in their time profiles (and floating/fixed rates) are matched, but following the typical pattern of mostly borrowing short term and lending long. Typically, longer-term interest rates are higher than in the short term – there is an upwardly sloping **yield curve** – thus it make sense for the bank to benefit from these higher rates of lending. By knowing the current position management can plan future asset growth in various maturity buckets along with funding needs. Also consideration can be given to risks arising from movements in the yield curve, e.g. short-term rates rise but long-term rates do not.

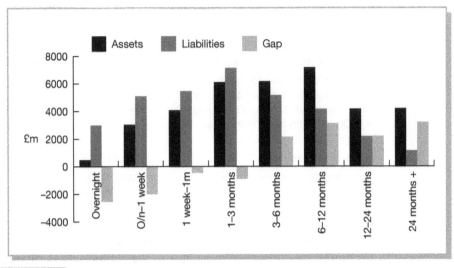

Figure 8.2   Interest rate gap by maturity bucket for interest sensitive assets and liabilities

Refinancing risk

One of the main functions of a bank is maturity transformation (see Chapter 1): banks generally borrow, e.g. via current accounts, on a short-term basis and tie the money up in loans granted to clients for many years. Thus the principal on a five-year loan to a borrowing business may not be repaid until the loan period is up. Yet short-term funding sources, such as deposits, interbank borrowing and certificates of deposit will have to be rolled over every few days or weeks to maintain the money in the bank. **Refinancing risk** is the risk that the cost of these rolled-over funds will rise above the return being earned on the asset (say a five-year fixed-rate loan). The inability to refinance short-term debt led to the failure of many financial institutions in the crash.

Simulation approach

In the **simulation approach** the impact on bank cash flows is examined in the context of a number of alternative possible future paths of interest rates and non-interest income/expense. Various scenarios are considered, the most significant being the '**stress test**'. Here plausible, but fairly extreme, events are assumed. Then the impacts on the bank's cash flows, capital and liquidity reserves are calculated. For example, a stress test might assume that bond prices fall by 10% at the same time as house prices, decline by 20% at the same time as the short-term markets in money (interbank, etc.) freeze so banks cannot roll over debt as it becomes due.

How much would the bank lose in a stress scenario and can it survive? Regulators around the world have examined their banks regularly under stress assumptions after the appalling failures in 2008–10. As a result many have been required to beef up their capital and liquidity buffers.

Asset and Liability Committee (ALCO)

The ALCO co-ordinates the decisions on sources of funding and acquisition of assets across the bank simultaneously, taking an overarching view of the bank's risk. It helps to set policy and guidelines. This function becomes particularly important and difficult when a universal bank has dozens of overseas branches and hundreds of lending/market operations each running risks which need to be aggregated at the bank centre. Interest rate, foreign exchange and liquidity risk management are transferred to the centre, but credit and individual market risk are usually left to the business unit, where the managers can be held to account for those decisions. Those risks transferred to the ALCO, such as interest rate gap risk, will often be hedged using derivative deals, e.g. interest rate futures (discussed in Chapter 21).

Risk-adjusted return on capital (RAROC)

A useful performance ratio for judging different parts of the bank is RAROC, basically a measure of profit divided by capital allocated to that area:

$$RAROC = \frac{\text{Revenue} - \text{expenses} - \text{expected loss on loans} + \text{return on capital set aside}}{\text{Economic capital tied up in that activity}}$$

Imagine that the bank has a division with £100m of loans. To finance the loans it will use £100m of deposited money. It also has to set aside economic capital of 8% of assets for this activity; this is an equity cushion to cover *unexpected* losses. Note that the cost of *expected* losses is allowed for in the calculation. The £8m (£100m × 0.08) of capital will be used to buy very safe government bonds yielding a return of 2%. These will be kept separate to act as a safety buffer. Thus we have our first number going into the calculation: The 'return on capital set aside' is £8m × 0.02 = £0.16m.

Assume the loan granted will generate interest of 6% or £6m. This provides the 'revenue' number.

'Expenses' have two parts: (a) the interest paid out to depositors, say this is 3% or £3m; and (b) general administration, overhead costs, etc., say £1.2m.

'Expected loss on loans' is the mean or average loss anticipated – estimated from past experience of defaults in this type of lending. Say this is 1% of the amount lent, or £1m.

We now have all the data needed to calculate RAROC for this segment of the bank:

$$RAROC = \frac{£6m - £4.2m - £1m + £0.16m}{£8m} = 12\%$$

Where, you might be asking, does the risk element come in? It is in two places:

1   It is in the economic capital number. Economic capital is the cushion needed to protect against large (unexpected) losses for risk-taking in this type of business. If the activity is more risky the economic capital set aside to cover unexpected losses will rise from 8% or £8m in this case to say 10% or £10m. If the activity is lower risk the capital allocated might be only £6m or 6% of assets. The economic capital buffer allocated depends on the level of market risk, credit risk and **operational risk** (risk of loss from failed internal processes, people, systems and external events, such as human error, fraud, technology failure, etc.).

2   Also the numerator 'return' includes an adjustment for 'risk costs', that is the expected loss, in our example £1m.

Bankers and academics can get carried away with mathematical apparent sophistication here, with complex measures of volatilities, correlations and goodness knows what. However, at the base of it all is a series of judgements (guesses), drawing on historical experience, about the level of expected and unexpected losses hitting the bank.

RAROC can be estimated for each activity, portfolio of loans, portfolio of securities, division and product centre. Capital is not directly allocated, but is imputed. For example, a portfolio of small-company loans generally requires (by the regulators) a larger amount of capital per £ lent than say a portfolio of high grade mortgages (see Chapter 25).

The RAROC is compared with a hurdle rate. For the bank as a whole this might be the bank's 'cost of equity' which is the return required by shareholders to induce them to hold the bank's shares, based on their opportunity cost, i.e. return available elsewhere for the same level of risk.[1] Typically this is 8% to 12% in 2013. If the bank is generating, say, 15% on equity capital then it is creating shareholder value overall.

Off-balance-sheet management

There are many modern bank activities that do not get fully reflected in balance sheets.

Income from fees

As discussed in earlier chapters there is a panoply of fee-earning commercial banking activities, from foreign trade assistance to commitment fees for lines of credit facilitation to custody fees to wealth management charges. Furthermore, as we will see (in Chapters 10 and 11), investment bankers rely on fee income from merger advice, bond issue arrangement, new share flotations, to name but a few activities.

Some of these expose the bank to considerable risk, e.g. guarantees (underwriting) of commercial paper/bond/share purchases in the event of poor take-up from other institutions. The guarantees do not appear on the balance sheet because they are merely **contingent commitments** dependent on an event occurring. But there is still the risk of the client defaulting or a simultaneous call from an overwhelming number of borrowers insisting on access to arranged credit facilities at a time of low bank liquidity or deterioration in the borrower's credit risk position. When the **contingent event** occurs the asset or liability will be written in the balance sheet and the profit numbers affected are reported. Table 8.2 shows the off-balance items for Standard Chartered.

Table 8.2 Contingent liabilities and commitments for Standard Chartered Bank 2012

	31 Dec 2012 $million	31 Dec 2011 $million
Contingent liabilities		
Guarantees and irrevocable letters of credit	34,281	27,022
Other contingent liabilities	10,168	15,858
	44,449	42,880
Commitments		
Documentary credits and short-term trade-related transactions	7,752	8,612
Forward asset purchases and forward deposits placed	711	733
Undrawn formal standby facilities, credit lines and other commitments to lend:		
One year and over	39,309	28,507
Less than one year	17,388	24,193
Unconditionally cancellable	110,138	88,652
	175,298	150,697

Source: Standard Chartered Annual Report 2012

*Includes amounts relating to the Group's share of its joint ventures

Income from selling loans

Many banks have become adept at originating loans but then shortly afterwards selling the right to receive interest and principal to another financial institution. These are often bundled up with other loans, e.g. the right to receive payments on 1,000 mortgages from householders for the next 20 years could be sold in the active mortgage-backed securities (MBS) market. The bank can make a profit by selling the 1,000 mortgages for more than was originally loaned. In other words, mortgagees are charged a higher interest rate than the MBS' holders receive. Thus the asset of 1,000 loans is removed from the balance sheet and cash is put there instead, at least temporarily until an alternative use is found, such as originating another 1,000 mortgages. (There is more on this repackaging of debt (securitisation) in Chapter 11.)

Trading financial instruments

Banks trade in a wide range of financial instruments on behalf of clients as agents, as market makers allowing buyers and sellers to trade and as proprietary traders trying to make profits from taking positions buying and selling on their own account in the markets (see Chapter 11). Also greater volatility in financial markets has led bankers to attempt to manage interest rate risk, foreign exchange movement risk and other risks through the use of futures, options, swaps and other derivative products. The availability of these liquid markets has also led to a greater propensity to speculate, to out-guess the markets. The huge bets made expose banks to enormous risks from time to time. There have been some spectacular failures as a result: (Barings Bank in 1995, Lehmans in 2008) and large losses e.g. UBS in 2011.

Value at risk used to estimate the overall risk of on- and off-balance-sheet exposures

Because banks hold a very wide range of assets from corporate loans to complicated derivatives, and they bear a number of obligations, senior managers can lose track as to the extent to which the firm as a whole is exposed to risk. One division might be building up large holdings of bonds while another is selling options and swaps, and yet another is packaging up mortgage bonds and selling MBS. Perhaps what one division is doing will offset the risk that another is taking on. On the other hand, it might be that risk is merely compounded by the combination of positions. Each day the mix of assets and liabilities changes and therefore the risk exposure changes.

Back in the 1990s some bankers[2] thought it would be a good idea to produce a single number that encapsulated the overall risk profile of the bank each evening. The senior managers could look at that and be reassured that they were not taking excessive risk. If the number started to look dangerously high then they could instruct a reweighting of assets and obligations until a safety margin was restored. The measure that they came up with is called **value at risk**, or **VaR**, which asks: 'If tomorrow is a bad day (e.g. different asset classes, such as shares and bonds, fall in market price significantly) what is the minimum that the bank will lose?' VaR is an estimate of the loss on a portfolio over a period of time (usually 24 hours is chosen) that will be *exceeded*[3] with a given frequency, e.g. a frequency of one day out of 100, or five days out of 100.

Another way of looking at the frequency element is called the **confidence level**. Thus with a 99% confidence level set the VaR might turn out to be $100m. Therefore for 'one-day VaR' there is a 1% chance that the portfolio could lose more than $100m in 24 hours. A 95% confidence level means that there is a 95% chance that the loss will be less than the derived figure of say $16m for a day, and a 5% chance that it will be greater than $16m.

Calculating VaR

So, how does a bank calculate VaR estimates? It needs some numbers and some assumptions. One assumption often made is that returns on a security (share, derivative, bond, etc.) follow a particular distribution. The usual assumption is the **normal distribution** where there is a large clustering of probabilities of returns around the average expected return and then very small probabilities of the extremes ('thin tails'). This is rather like the distribution in the heights of 14 year olds: most are clustered around 5' to 5'6", with decreasing numbers of children at 4'9", 4'8", 4'7" and very few in the 'tail region' of 4' on the downside; and decreasing numbers at 5'7", 5'8" and 5'9" with very few in the tail region of greater than 6'1". And the pattern of decrease is symmetrical around the mean observation, say 5'3".

For banks the distribution of possible outturns is symmetrical about the mean too – there is the same chance of being, say, £3m above the average expected return as of being £3m below it. See Figure 8.3 for a normal distribution of probabilities, a bell-shaped symmetrical curve. The usual source of data, whether combined with a normal distribution assumption or not, is a long time series of an historical data set of daily return data for the securities. Then the mathematicians assume that this represents the future distribution of returns. Another important source of information is the calculation of the extent to which asset returns move together – e.g. do corporate bond prices move in step with prices for MBS? Then it is assumed that these correlations remain true for future estimations.

Figure 8.3 shows a possible output from using VaR. On the right-hand side the return numbers increase but the probability of earning those high returns decrease significantly the further we move away from the average expected return (as would the probability of finding a 6'3" 14 year old). The probabilities for returns below average are symmetrical with those above average in this case where we assume 'normality'. (If we have used real past return data the distribution may not be quite normal and the maths for calculating the confidence level becomes more complicated, but it can still be handled. A skewed distribution just creates more fun for the mathematicians.) You can read off the 99% chance of not losing more than the amount marked by the dashed line. If the dashed line is at –$200m then one day out of 100 we would lose more than –$200m, in theory.

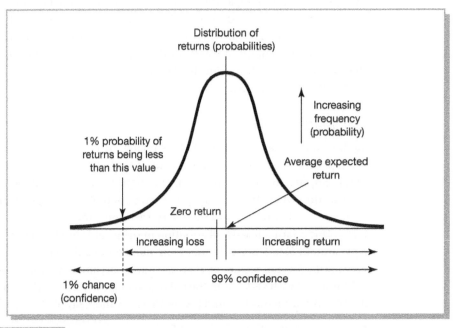

Figure 8.3   A VaR analysis assuming a normal distribution of the probabilities of return on an asset or collection of assets

Is past data enough?

A key assumption is that the past data has a very close bearing on the future prob-abilities. Even using the normality method you need past data to estimate the size of the various probabilities. So, you might gather data from the previous three years. If unusual/infrequent events are not present in that data set you might be missing some extreme positive or negative possibilities. This event might have a massive impact on risk, but might be missed if the data set is limited to a period of stability. Indeed it might be missed even if the data set is extensive if the event is very rare. An influential writer on derivatives and market players, Nicolas Taleb[4] was warning us long before the crisis that the mathematicians were not allowing for the possibility of extreme events (dubbed **black swans**) – that the tails of the distribution are in fact much bigger, 'fatter', than generally supposed, because extreme things hit us more often then we anticipate. There are 'high-impact rare events', often caused by human reactions to apparently insignificant triggers; reactions such as exuberance, fear and panic. Asset returns and liabilities which appeared to be uncorrelated suddenly all move together to a much greater extent than short-memory players in financial markets expect. There are risks out there that we did not know existed, until it is too late. The more experienced old-hands know that unexpected and unimaginable events shape the markets, leaving them with question marks concerning the extent to which they can trust historical data to be the only guide.

Led astray

VaR led many senior bankers into a false sense of security prior to the crisis. They were thus emboldened to double and triple their bets on securities such as mortgage-backed bonds and the related derivatives because they appeared to produce high profits without raising VaR much. Many regulators insisted on the disclosure of VaR. Indeed, under the supervisory capital rules for banks VaR could be used as an argument for lowering capital requirements. Banks jumped at the chance of lowering capital buffers so as to increase return on equity (see Chapter 7) – they leveraged themselves up. They particularly liked to stock up on 'high-quality' mortgage-based derivatives because the model told them that they had trivial VaR and so they were required to hold only trivial capital reserves. Yes, the regulators have much to answer for, too. They placed far too much faith in these mathematical models. They even allowed banks to do their own calculations of risk exposure, and more or less accepted these for setting capital limits.

The crisis

Although we may have moved on from the global financial crisis which began in 2007 and the economic climate is very different, it is still an important event in any discussion on banking and finance. Prior to the summer of 2007 banks tended to use historical evidence going back between one and five years to estimate VaR. By then a large part of their exposure was to the mortgage market. In the mid-2000s this had been as placid as the sea was when the Titanic was crossing the Atlantic – no trouble encountered for day after day. It would seem that VaR gave little indication of real likely losses. For example, in the autumn of 2007 Bear Stearns reported an average VaR of $30m[5] which is tiny for a bank with so many assets. It could withstand days and days of such losses and barely notice. So according to VaR it was hardly at risk at all. And yet within weeks it was bust, losing $8bn of value. As the complete failure of the bank approached, the VaR number did rise slightly to $60m because it started to incorporate data for the most recent days when securities became more volatile as the market mayhem started – but it still had lots of older placid data pushing the number down.

It turned out that 'highly unlikely events' such as a correlated fall in house prices all over the USA, and the fall in market prices of derivatives and bonds, can all happen at the same time. The average person on the street could have told them that, but these mathematicians and financial economists could not see past their complex algebra. The guys over at Merrill Lynch were perplexed: 'In the past these AAA CDO securities [mortgage based derivatives – see Chapter 11] had never experienced a significant loss in value.'[6] But how long was that 'past' – if they could find a decade of data they would have been lucky, because these instruments were so young.

As the crisis got under way most of the large banks experienced losses that should only happen once in 1,000 years (according to their models) day after day. In their language these were six-sigma (standard deviation) events, which were virtually impossible from their faithful-to-the-algebra perspective. Indeed, in August 2007 the market experienced several 25-sigma events – these should happen only once every 14 billion years. How confusing for them – the model let them down when it really mattered. Triana[7] likens VaR to buying a car with an air bag which protects you 99% of the time, that is when conditions are moderate, but if you have a serious crash it fails.

Bear Stearns understood the problems with VaR. Take this statement from their filing with the Securities and Exchange Commission on February 29 2008:

> VaR has inherent limitations, including reliance on historical
> data, which may not accurately predict future market risk, and
> the quantitative risk information generated is limited by the
> parameters established in creating the models. There can be no
> assurance that actual losses occurring on any one day arising
> from changes in market conditions will not exceed the VaR
> amounts shown below or that such losses will not occur more
> than once in 20 trading days. VaR is not likely to accurately
> predict exposures in markets that exhibit sudden fundamental
> changes or shifts in market conditions or established trading

relationships. Many of the Company's hedging strategies are structured around likely established trading relationships and, consequently, those hedges may not be effective and VaR models may not accurately predict actual results. Furthermore, VaR calculated for a one-day horizon does not fully capture the market risk of positions that cannot be liquidated in a one-day period.[8]

Despite this list of doubts they had used it because everyone else did (and the regulators allowed them to get away with it).

Once faith in VaR had evaporated those lending to banks became afraid that the risk metrics they publicly announced under-reported their real exposure. They took the action that you or I would take when told that borrowers might default on what they owe: stop lending any more money and try to call in old loans. The problem is the entire banking system was a complex web of loans to each other and once confidence had gone the whole system collapsed. Notice the key words here are not quantifiable – 'afraid', 'confidence' – these fuzzy things are just as important to understand about banking as the maths, if not more so.

There is more on the causes of the financial crisis in *The Financial Times Guide to Financial Markets* by Glen Arnold (Pearson: 2012).

Bank financial statements

Banks need to measure how well they perform in trying to obtain a good return for shareholders. They do this through the income (profit) statement for a period. They also need to examine the total asset and liability position at a point in time, as well as the mixture of those assets and liabilities. These are summarised in the balance sheet. This chapter describes the main components of bank's income statements and balance sheets. It looks at the results of two banks, Lloyds and Barclays, and uses the published numbers to explain some key metrics used by the banks themselves to judge performance and stability.

Also, an important form of both borrowing and lending is through the very active sale and repurchase agreement, 'repo', market. This allows a bank to fund shortages of money over a matter of a few days or weeks by borrowing in the repo market. Alternatively a bank can earn interest on otherwise idle money when it has a temporary surplus of cash by lending via the repo market. Repurchase agreements thus feature prominently in most banks' balance sheets and so this market needs to be explained here.

Balance sheet

A balance sheet states the bank's assets, liabilities and capital on a certain day. In other words, it lays out what the company is owed and what it owes. This leads to the **net worth** on that day – if the assets and liabilities could be converted to cash at their stated values. These values assume that the bank is a **going concern**, i.e. it will continue in existence for the foreseeable future, usually defined as 12 months. The significance of this is that the assets are valued in their normal use and not at a value they might fetch when sold off in a liquidation sale at knockdown prices. Balance sheets are now often called **a statement of financial position** following the adoption of international financial reporting standards by the large companies.

Barclays has many things in common with Lloyds Banking Group (Lloyds, Bank of Scotland, Halifax), including an extensive high street presence in retail and corporate banking, but there is one major difference: Barclays has built up a substantial investment banking business. The differences are reflected in their respective balance sheets (see Tables 9.1 and 9.2) because Barclays shows that a much smaller proportion of its assets are loans to customers, 28% versus 56%, and a much lower proportion of its funding is from customer deposits, 26% versus 46%.

Table 9.1 Lloyds Bank balance sheet, 31 December 2012 (items as a percentage of the total)

ASSETS		LIABILITIES	
Cash and balances at central banks	9%	Deposits from banks	4%
Trading and other financial assets	17%	Customer deposits	46%
		Trading and other financial liabilities	4%
Derivative financial instruments	6%	Derivative financial instruments	5%
		Debt securities in issue	13%
Loans to banks	3%	Liabilities arising from insurance contracts	15%
Loans to customers	56%		
Debt securities	<1%	Other liabilities	8%
Available-for-sale financial assets	3%		
Property and other assets	5%	Equity (capital)	5%
Total £924.5bn	100%		100%

Source: Lloyds Bank Annual Report and Accounts 2012

Table 9.2 Barclays Bank balance sheet, 31 December 2012 (items as a percentage of the total)

ASSETS		LIABILITIES	
Cash and balances at central banks	6%	Deposits from banks	5%
Trading and other financial assets	13%	Customer accounts/deposits	26%
		Repurchase agreements and other similar secured borrowing	15%
		Trading and other financial liabilities	8%
Derivative financial instruments	31%	Derivative financial instruments	31%
Loans & advances to banks	3%	Debt securities in issue	8%
Loans & advances to customers	28%	Other liabilities	3%
Available-for-sale financial assets	5%		
Reverse repurchase agreements & other similar secured lending	12%		
Property and other assets	2%	Equity (capital)	4%
Total £1,490.3bn	100%		100%

Source: Barclays Bank Annual Report and Accounts 2012

Note the much higher derivative activity at Barclays. Almost one-third of its balance sheet is devoted to derivative assets and liabilities, compared with a mere 6% for Lloyds. Whereas Barclays uses derivatives to make profits by trading in and out of positions – proprietary trading – as well as assisting clients, Lloyds is more focused on customer needs and lowering risk rather than searching for high profits. The company states:[1]

> The Group holds derivatives as part of the following strategies:
>
> - customer driven, where derivatives are held as part of the provision of risk management products to Group customers;
> - to manage and hedge the Group's interest rate and foreign exchange risk arising from normal banking business; and
> - derivatives held in policyholder [insurance] funds as permitted by the investment strategies of those funds.

Barclays uses the money market much more than Lloyds, in particular for repurchase agreements (see below) and other similar secured borrowing. Clearly the balance sheet of a commercial bank differs from that of a universal bank; and is dramatically different to that of a pure investment bank.

Lloyds has a large insurance (with pension services) division (e.g. Scottish Widows and Clerical Medical) and therefore 15% of its balance sheet is devoted to insurance and related savings-type products.

Liquidity and capital reserves

Only small proportions of the assets of both banks are kept as cash (9% and 6%). But Lloyds has other liquid assets to reduce liquidity risk: 'The total liquid asset portfolio of £205 billion represents approximately four times our wholesale funding with a maturity of less than one year at the end of 2012, providing a substantial buffer in the event of market dislocation.'[2]

The capital/total assets ratio or leverage ratio, 4% for Barclays and 5% for Lloyds, gives some indication of the size of the safety buffer these banks hold against say a large loss on loans, securities held or other trouble. It would take a fall of only 4% or 5% in the value of assets to wipe out the bank – at least it is better than for Deutsche Bank in early 2013 which only needed a 2.7% fall to be insolvent.

This simple measure is considered too crude by many bankers because you could have two banks with the same ratio but one holds nothing but high-risk assets and the other nothing but low-risk assets. Thus bankers and regulators allow for greater risk by insisting on higher capital reserves (this risk-adjustment is discussed in Chapter 25). Article 9.1 shows that there is a lively debate as to the minimum leverage ratio for banks. (For the Article: 'Basel III' is the international organisation linking bank regulators, 'core tier one capital' can be regarded as equity capital for now.) This is not an easy problem to solve!

Article 9.1

Bank leverage: capital questions

Calls for more capital ignore drawback of radically higher leverage ratios

This could get expensive. A US bill unveiled this week would require banks with more than $500bn in assets to hold equity equivalent to 15 per cent of that. That is a big jump from the current 5.6 per cent average. Meanwhile, UK lawmakers say that the Basel III leverage ratio (equity as a proportion of total assets) of 3 per cent is too low. And a recent book from academics Anat Admati and Martin Hellwig says that leverage ratios should rise to 20–30 per cent.

The banks say they have enough capital, and they might be right. In the UK, the sector has written off £210bn since the start of the crisis. The five big banks now have £250bn of core tier one capital, more than enough to cover a repeat. Add that to the higher cost of equity – which could be passed to customers via higher charges – and there are reasons to leave equity alone.

Nonsense, argue the banks' detractors. They say that in no other industry would a funding mix of 3 per cent equity and 97 per cent debt be considered prudent, and that the mix benefits shareholders at the expense of society, which ends up guaranteeing much of the debt. Too much debt increases funding costs as the possibility of bankruptcy looms. More equity in the mix would therefore reduce the cost of that equity.

What is absent from the debate is discussion of how banks would get the extra equity. Getting to a 7 per cent leverage ratio in the UK (as suggested by a 2011 Bank of England paper) would require an extra £168bn, or 15 years' worth of retained earnings at last year's rate. Getting to the 30 per cent that Messrs Admati and Hellwig demand would require £1.6tn, close to the value of the FTSE 100. According to Standard & Poor's, implementation of this week's US bill would require $1.4tn.

This is the real drawback of radically higher leverage ratios. They might make the sector a little safer but in the process would require equity investors substantially to increase their exposure to banks, at the expense of investment elsewhere. That is not good for the investors, or for the economy as a whole.

 Source: Lex Column (2013) 'Calls for more capital ignore drawback of radically higher leverage ratios', *Financial Times*, 26 April. © The Financial Times 2013. All rights reserved.

Repurchase agreements (repos)

A **repo** is a way of borrowing for a few days using a **sale and repurchase agreement** in which securities such as government bonds are sold for cash at an agreed price with a promise to buy back the securities at a specified (higher) price at a future date. The interest on the agreement is the difference between the initial sale price and the agreed buy-back, and because the agreements are usually collateralised by government-backed securities such as Treasury bills, the interest rate is low. While collateral back-up for the lender is usually provided by the borrower handing over (selling) very safe government issued securities, other very safe securities might be used. If the borrower defaults on its obligations to buy back on maturity the lender can hold on to or sell the securities.

Repos (RPs) are used regularly by banks and other financial institutions to borrow money from each other. Companies do use the repo markets, but much less frequently than the banks. This market is also manipulated by central banks to manage their monetary policy (see Chapter 24). The best way to understand the repo market is through an example.

Example   **Repurchase agreement**

Barclays has the need to borrow £6m for 14 days. It agrees to sell a portfolio of its financial assets, in this case government bonds, to a lender for £6m. An agreement is drawn up (a repo) by which Barclays agrees to repurchase the portfolio 14 days later for £6,001,219.73. The extra amount of £1,219.73 represents the interest on £6m over 14 days at an annual rate of 0.53%. The calculation is:

$$\text{Interest} = \text{Selling Price} \times \text{Interest Rate} \times \frac{\text{Days to Maturity}}{\text{Days in Year}}$$

$$\text{Interest} = 6{,}000{,}000 \times \frac{0.53}{100} \times \frac{14}{365} = £1{,}219.73$$

The term for repos is usually between one and 14 days, but can be up to a year and occasionally there is no end date, this is called an **open repo**.

Reverse repo

A **reverse repo (RRP)** is the lender's side of the transaction, an agreement in which securities are *purchased* with a promise to *sell them back* at an agreed price at a future date. Banks/traders may do this to gain interest. Alternatively, it could be to cover another market transaction. For example, a bank may need to obtain some Treasury bills (T-bills) or bonds temporarily because it has shorted them – sold them before buying – and needs to find a supply to meet its obligations, and so it places a reverse repo order to get an inflow of the securities now. In a transaction, the terms repo and reverse repo are used according to which party initiated the transaction, i.e. if a seller initiates the transaction, it is a repo; if the transaction is initiated by a buyer, it is a reverse repo.

Repos are very useful for banks and other financial institutions that hold large quantities of money-market securities such as T-bills. They can gain access to liquidity through a repo for a few days while maintaining a high level of inventory in short-term securities.

Table 9.3 shows the repo rates recorded by the Bank of England for borrowing in pounds.

Table 9.3	Repo rates in March 2013				
	18 March	19 March	20 March	21 March	22 March
Annualised percentages					
Overnight	0.465	0.465	0.465	0.465	0.455
1 week	0.455	0.465	0.465	0.46	0.465
2 week	0.455	0.455	0.465	0.45	0.465
1 month	0.455	0.455	0.465	0.46	0.465
3 month	0.455	0.455	0.455	0.455	0.455
6 month	0.425	0.425	0.435	0.43	0.445
1 year	0.395	0.38	0.405	0.395	0.415

Source: www.bankofengland.co.uk

Haircuts

Although the securities bought and sold are considered safe collateral for the lender of the cash, there is always the danger that the price of the bills, etc. might fluctuate during the period of the agreement to the detriment of the buyer; the value of the collateral might decrease. Therefore it is common practice to impose a **haircut** on the collateral, where the seller receives the amount of cash secured on the collateral less a margin (the haircut). So, if we take the repurchase agreement example above, even if the securities handed over are valued at £6m the borrower may receive £5.9m, allowing the lender an extra degree of safety should the value of the securities decrease and the borrower fails to buy them back at the agreed price.

Income statements

An **income statement** (or **profit and loss account**) shows the revenue and expenses of a particular period, leading to the calculation of **net income** or **net profit**.

There are two sources of income and three types of operating expense.

Income can be:

1 **Interest income.** This can be interest on loans granted, securities purchased (e.g. a government bond paying interest) or other interest.

2 **Non-interest income.** Banks charge for various services ranging from current account charges to fees on underwriting securities, insurance and asset management commission. They may also generate **income from trading** in the markets.

Operating expenses can be:

1 **Interest expense.** Banks pay interest on many deposit accounts and when they borrow in the markets from other banks, corporations or the central bank.

2 **Non-interest expense.** Expenses associated with fee and commission generation, buildings, computer systems, salaries, etc.

3 **Provisions for loan losses (impairment loses).** Banks are required to estimate the likely losses they will make when a proportion of loans default and write this off as an expense even though borrowers have not yet actually defaulted (see Chapter 8). And, of course, actual loan losses incurred need to be included.

A bank may choose to separate out particularly large non-banking income sources, e.g. insurance.

Income statement examples

Now let us examine the income statements of Lloyds and Barclays – see Table 9.4.

| Table 9.4 | Extracts from Lloyds Bank Group and Barclays income statements for the year to 31 December 2012 |

	Lloyds (£ million)	Barclays (£ million)
Interest and similar income	23,535	19,199
Interest and similar expense	(14,460)	(7,560)
Net interest income	9,075	11,639
Fee and commission income	4,731	10,216
Fee and commission expense	(1,438)	(1,634)
Net fee and commission income	3,293	8,582
Net trading income	13,554	3,025
Investment income	–	817
Insurance premium income	8,284	896
Other operating income	4,700	332
Total income	38,906	25,291
Insurance claims	(18,396)	(600)
Total income net of insurance claims	20,510	24,691
Regulatory provisions	(4,175)	
Expenses	(11,756)	(20,989)
Trading surplus	4,579	
Impairment losses on loans and receivables	(5,149)	(3,596)
Profits from associate companies etc.	–	140
(Loss) profit before tax	(570)	246
Taxation	(773)	(482)
Loss for the year	(1,343)	(236)

Sources: Lloyds Banking Group Annual Report and Accounts 2012; Barclays Bank Annual Report and Accounts 2012.

Note that non-interest income is split into a number of parts: (a) fee and commission income, (b) net trading income, i.e. after taking away the costs of generating that income, and (c) various other types – in the case of Barclays this is separated into 'investment income', 'insurance premium income' and 'other'. For those smarting from high unauthorised overdraft fees you might like to know that of the £4,731m charged by Lloyds in fee and commission around one-fifth was current account fees, and one-fifth was credit and debit card fees. (Barclays do not break down its fee income to the same degree in the **Notes to the Accounts.**)

Regulatory provisions was extraordinarily high in 2012 because Lloyds wrote off the expenses associated with the payment protection insurance scandal of £3,575m.

People were mis-sold insurance policies to cover payments on borrowing should they become redundant, fall ill, etc. These deals were often of no value to the customer.

Credit impairment rates (writing down loan values) differ between different types of assets. For example, Lloyds had an impairment charge for personal retail banking of 0.36% of advances made in 2012, whereas for business loans it was 1.85%. Barclaycard had a loan loss rate of 2.82% compared with 0.21% for Barclays UK retail and business banking. Bank managers have quite a lot of flexibility in the choice of impairment rates, but the accounting regulators are toughening the rules – see Article 9.2.

Article 9.2

Rift over forcing banks to deal with losses

By Adam Jones

International accounting standard-setters have unveiled a fresh plan to force banks to set aside money earlier against lending losses, but their revisions failed to bridge a damaging transatlantic rift in this key area of financial regulation.

The International Accounting Standards Board also admitted that it was unlikely that its proposed new rules would be in force before 2016, allowing banks yet more breathing space to repair their balance sheets.

The London-based IASB sets the IFRS accounting rules followed by listed companies in the European Union, Canada, Australia, Brazil, Russia and other countries.

Its current mechanism for totting up losses on bad loans has been criticised for allowing banks to ignore the consequences of reckless lending for years and then get swamped by a sudden wave of losses.

At the behest of governments around the world, the IASB had been working with the organisation that sets US accounting norms – the Financial Accounting Standards Board – on a global reform of these "impairment" rules.

However, the two standard-setters are now pursuing different approaches, with the FASB preferring to recognise more losses up front than the IASB, which argues that such a regime could discourage lending [because it reduces the capital base].

The model announced by the IASB on Thursday further solidified this dispute. It would involve IFRS banks setting aside a certain amount of money on all loans to reflect the likelihood of them going sour over a 12-month period.

More losses would be taken if credit quality "significantly" deteriorated. The IASB said this would trigger losses markedly earlier than the current "incurred loss" model that came in for vilification during the financial crisis.

Under the incurred loss model, banks tend to delay the pain of impairment losses until a borrower has come close to default, the IASB said.

The standard-setter said its latest "expected loss" model was simpler than its previous thinking and more in tune with the way banks managed their loan portfolios.

Tony Clifford, an Ernst & Young specialist on accounting for loans and other financial instruments, said the proposed change would probably lead to bigger credit loss provisions at many financial institutions.

"However, the increase in provision will vary by entity, and entities with shorter term and higher quality financial assets are less likely to be affected," he added.

Some important bank metrics

Net interest margin

A vital measure of bank performance is the difference between interest earned and interest paid as a percentage of assets. This is the net **interest margin (NIM)**:

$$\text{NIM} = \frac{\text{Interest income} - \text{Interest expense}}{\text{Assets}}$$

A typical NIM is between 1% and 4%. So if a bank is paying 3.5% on average on its deposit accounts and other borrowings, but charges the average borrower 6% it has a net interest margin of 2.5%.

Banks and the financial press also report the **Net interest income (NII)** which is simply the top half of the NIM ratio, interest income minus interest expense. Of course this is a measure in absolute amounts of pounds, euros, etc., rather than a percentage. An example of interest income and expense: Lloyds paid an average interest rate of 1.96% on deposit accounts and charged an average of 3.91% on loans and advances to customers in 2012. Figure 9.1 shows the net interest margins made by eurozone banks as a percentage of total assets. In the post-eurozone crisis years the margins were slightly over 1%.

Cost-income ratio

Another frequently quoted measure is the **cost-income ratio (C/I)**, which measures the bank's efficiency in holding down its costs relative to income: the lower it is, the more profitable.

$$\frac{\text{Cost}}{\text{Income}} = \frac{\text{Non-interest expenses}}{\text{Net interest income} + \text{Net non interest income}}$$

'Cost' covers administrative and fixed costs, such as wages and property expenses, but not bad debts. Net (after expenses) non-interest income includes net trading revenues, net fee income from services such as funds management, net insurance revenues and net income from financial instruments.

Look for a rise in the ratio over time because this might indicate potential problems: costs are rising at a higher rate than income, which could mean that the managers are letting costs run away as they chase more business. To give some

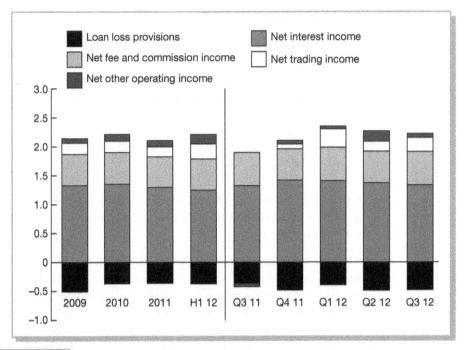

Figure 9.1   **Breakdown of operating income for euro area large and complex banking groups, 2009–third quarter (Q3) 2012; percentage of total assets**

Source: European Central Bank Financial Stability Review December 2012
www.ecb.europa.eu/pub/html/index.en.html

perspective, some 2012 UK bank cost-to-income ratios and net interest margins are shown in Table 9.5:

Table 9.5   **Cost-income ratios and NIMs for some UK banks**

	Barclays	RBS	Lloyds	HSBC	Standard Chartered
Cost/Income	80.3%	64.0%	54.3%	57.5%	52.3%
NIM (basis points)	189	192	193	237	230

Source: UK Banks' Performance Benchmarking Report: Half year results 2012 kpmg.co.uk/banking

Given all the fuss in the press about banker's pay and bonuses, you may find it surprising that the investment banking division of Barclays has a C/I ratio lower than the bank as a whole, at 64%. At the time of writing the cost-income ratio numbers are unusually high – see Article 9.3.

Banks glean efficiency tips from industry

By Daniel Schäfer

When the financial crisis plunged investment banks globally into big losses that threatened the existence of some, they set out to drastically reduce their often overblown cost structures.

But several years and tens of thousands of staff cuts later, the sector is back to square one.

Investment banks' average cost-income ratio – a key measure of efficiency – has ballooned to 80 per cent last year from 60 per cent in 2007, according to data by Morgan Stanley and Oliver Wyman.

It comes after tighter regulatory capital requirements, lower leverage and falling revenues have eaten into returns while costs for back-office functions such as risk management and information technology have been stubbornly on the rise.

Fixed salaries have also increased by 37 per cent over four years, according to a survey by the Association for Financial Markets in Europe, a lobby organisation.

UK bank Barclays last year embarked on a cost-cutting drive, combining payment systems, human resources and other functions across its wealth management, investment bank and corporate and retail arms as part of a programme to slash £2bn in costs by next year.

In the past few years, banks have already merged previously scattered IT operations and other back-office functions such as human resources.

But despite that, back-office costs have increased since 2007, as regulatory and market requirements have driven up costs for risk management and information technology.

"IT costs have increased by 30 per cent for tier one banks and by 45 per cent for tier two banks over the past three years, largely driven by regulation," the Boston Consulting Group wrote in a recent study.

Tom Gosling, partner at PwC in London, says: "There's a view that high levels of profitability pre-crisis led to lack of focus on costs, which is now proving tough to shift."

One big factor is pay, but the issues are not necessarily the same as the public debate might suggest. "All the political focus is on bonuses, but further reductions in bonus pools won't really shift the dial on returns. Banks now need to focus on more fundamental cost issues," says Mr Gosling.

Analysts estimate that Goldman Sachs is around a fifth more efficient than rivals in its back office thanks to higher productivity (and despite high salaries), while JPMorgan has cut pay levels by outsourcing such functions to places like Mumbai.

Mr Gosling said European investment banks would need to follow suit. "Return on equity needs to double in many banks to get back above cost of capital. This means productivity needs to double or pay needs to halve. Neither is realistic so in reality it will need to be a mixture of the two."

Loan to deposit ratio

The **loan to deposit ratio** is the amount of loans lent out divided by the amount of funds attracted to bank accounts. These deposits are 'stickier' than funds obtained from the wholesale markets, e.g. from other banks. Lloyds has been trying to get its loan to deposit ratio down; it has succeeded in reducing it from 154 in 2010 to 121 in 2012. The management are conscious of the dangers:[3]

> The Group has completed the transformation of its funding profile, with customer deposit growth and non-core reduction [getting rid of businesses it no longer wants] driving a reduction in our wholesale funding requirement to £170billion, a 32% reduction in the year. At the same time the maturity profile of our wholesale funding further improved with only 30% of total wholesale funding now having a maturity of less than one year.

Barclays seems content with its loan to deposit ratio of 102% when discussing the aggregate of Retail and Business Banking, Corporate Banking and Wealth and Investment Management (i.e. outside of Investment Banking).

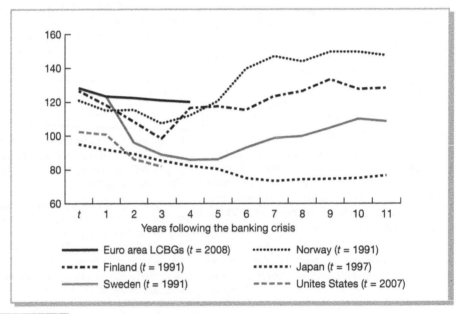

Figure 9.2   Evolution of banks' loan to deposit ratio following various banking crises, percentages; loans to customers (other than banks) divided by customer deposits (LCBGs are large and complex banking groups)

Source: European Central Bank Financial Stability Review December 2012
www.ecb.europa.eu/pub/html/index.en.html

Note that eurozone banks were particular dependent on financial market funding in 2008 to finance their loans; loans were over 125% of their deposits. Even by the beginning of 2013 the figure was 120% indicating a difficulty in switching to greater deposit-based funding – see Figure 9.2.

10

Investment banking: services to companies and governments

Most of us do not encounter investment banks in our daily lives. Despite them operating in the background, working with companies, governments, financial institutions and wealthy individuals, they are highly influential. The extent of their importance was harshly brought home with the financial crisis of 2008. Even those of us that work in the field of finance had hardly heard of US sub-prime mortgages or the repackaging of these mortgages into bonds issued by investment bankers, let alone the repackaging of the repackaged bonds. And yet all this financial engineering led to a calamity with enormous implications for us all.

The greedy re-engineering of financial claims is to look on the dark side of the role of investment banks; their bread and butter jobs are far more down to earth and far more useful. For example, corporate executives go to investment bankers when contemplating a once-in-a-career corporate move, such as buying another company. They lack the knowledge and skills to cope with the regulations, the raising of finance or the tactics to be employed, so they turn to the specialists at the bank who regularly undertake these tasks for client companies. Another area where executives need specialist help is in raising money by selling bonds or shares. The sums raised can be in the tens or hundreds of millions, and all the details have to be right if investors are to be enticed and the regulators to be satisfied. Investment bankers also assist companies in managing their risks. For example they may advise a mining company on the use of derivatives to reduce the risk of commodity prices moving adversely, or interest rates, or currency rates. Then there are their roles in assisting the workings of the financial markets, acting as brokers, market makers and as fund managers. The list of people they help is long, despite most of us being unaware of their activities.

What do investment bankers do to earn so much money?

Investment banks are complex organisations selling a wide range of services as well as trading securities for their own profit. Not all of them are active in the full range discussed in this chapter and the next; many are content to specialise in certain services or trading areas. It is also important to note that of the services they offer companies and governments many are regarded as loss-leaders (e.g. reports on valuations of company shares, or even lending by the bank to companies) so that they can engage with potential clients over a long period of time, gain their trust and then offer highly lucrative services when the company makes a major move, such as the takeover of another firm. Thus for investment banks to maximise profits they need to be very good at co-ordinating their various activities so that they can sell a number of different services to a client company or government.

Talent

It is people that form relationships rather than organisations, so investment banks have to employ talented employees who can form strong bonds with clients. Such talent is expensive, especially once they have some leverage with their employers because the client executives trust them as individuals, rather than the bank, to help them with, say, a **rights issue**[1] – there is always the possibility of an investment banker taking his or her client contact list to another employer. This partly explains the high bonus culture at investment banks. And then, on the trading side, the talented individuals who make good bets on the movements of securities, commodities, exchange rates, etc. can also command high bonuses.

Investment banks typically put aside around 35–60% of income for employee compensation (salary + bonuses, etc.). Just to give you some idea, the ratio of compensation and benefits to net revenues was 37.9% ($12.9bn paid to employees) for Goldman Sachs in 2012. The average for each Goldman Sachs employee in 2012 was $399,506, at Morgan Stanley it was $273,777. This includes all employees, from secretaries to IT staff – the true bankers will be on a lot more.

Oh! The shame of it: investment banking pay is now only five times greater than the average, what a come down – see Article 10.1.

New rules imposed in the major economies limit the amount of remuneration that can be taken as cash to less than 20% if the bonus is over £500,000 or 30% if under £500,000, with the rest deferred for a lengthy time, and much of it in

Article 10.1

Bankers' pay premium is narrowing

By Daniel Schäfer

Investment bankers still get paid much more than other professionals, including doctors and engineers, but for the first time in a generation, the gap is narrowing.

In what remuneration experts say marks only the beginning of potentially the largest adjustment in decades, average pay per head in a sample of nine European and US investment banks has fallen from 9.5 times the private sector average in 2006 to 5.8 times last year, according to research compiled by PwC.

The study shows that the pay premium that was built up amid the deregulation wave since the 1980s and the debt-fuelled bonanza in the past decade is waning six years after the financial crisis.

"Bank pay has fallen further and faster than many people think, and 2012 has seen a material reallocation of returns from employees to shareholders," said Tom Gosling, a partner at PwC.

Last year, European banks in particular have cut pay, despite strongly rising profits, in a stark sign of how the changes go beyond cyclical adjustments.

"There is somewhat less pressure at US banks. They still pay more overall and they pay a much higher cash bonus," said Stéphane Rambosson, a partner at Veni Partners.

The FT research compares a sample of nine investment banks with global companies in the FTSE 100 index, which given that two-thirds of these companies' revenues are derived from outside the UK is seen as a valid gauge.

The finding that investment bankers continue to earn £212,000 on average – more than a decade ago – may add fuel to the heated European debate about the sector's pay levels.

shares of the bank. This is an attempt to align the interests of the bankers with the long-term interests of their shareholders and wider society. It was felt that they had been focusing on short-term gains and taking high risks so that they could get a large bonus – if it all went wrong then the government would bail them out, they reasoned. And anyway, after a year of two of high bonuses they already had the house in Mayfair and a bulging Swiss bank account. Under the new system the fancy house may have to wait until it is proven that their deals have not left a time-bomb in the bank. The new (UK) rules are as follows:

Bonuses under £500,000

- 30% immediate cash, maximum
- 30% immediate shares (which the employee cannot sell for 6 months)
- 20% deferred cash (held by the employer for 3 years)
- 20% deferred shares (held by the employer for 3 years and then by the employee for 6 months).

Bonuses over £500,000

- 20% immediate cash, maximum
- 20% immediate shares (which the employee cannot sell for 6 months)
- 30% deferred cash (held by the employer for 5 years)
- 30% deferred shares (held by the employer for 5 years and then by the employee for 6 months).

Clawing bonuses back

- If it transpires that any employee took reckless risks or behaved illegally, then the deferred bonus can be cut or cancelled.

Source: British Bankers Association, www.bba.org.uk

Barclays has already clawed back some bonuses after staff were accused of behaving against customers' and shareholders' interests – see Article 10.2.

Article 10.2

Barclays recoups £300m in bonuses

By Daniel Schäfer

Barclays has recouped about £300m in promised bonuses from its bankers in the biggest ever effort by a global bank to strip staff of previous years' awards.

The move by the UK lender underlines how banks are enforcing clawback provisions on a much broader scale than in the past as they seek to show regulators and investors they are taking tough action to deal with past failures.

The move comes after Barclays was rocked by a series of scandals that included manipulation of Libor and mis-selling of various financial products.

The bank has reduced last year's group-wide bonus pool by 14 per cent to £1.85bn as its new management seeks to restore Barclays' image and redistribute some of the spoils from employees to shareholders.

Article 10.2   **Continued**

Antony Jenkins, who replaced Bob Diamond as chief executive amid the Libor scandal, has promised to turn Barclays into a bank that is "doing well financially and behaving well".

About half of the clawbacks will be enforced in relation with the manipulation of the Libor benchmark interest rate, which prompted the bank to pay a £290m fine to regulators in the UK and US last summer.

The other half will be clawed back because of the bank's involvement in the mis-selling of payment protection insurance and other misconduct.

Barclays had more than £2.9bn in outstanding deferred bonus payments at the end of last year, giving Mr Jenkins leeway to claw back a sizeable amount without risking a series of staff defections.

Banks globally from HSBC and Royal Bank of Scotland in the UK to JPMorgan in the US have started to claw back bonuses from a limited number of staff in recent years after rules to hold employees financially accountable for illicit or loss-making behaviour came into force in 2009.

Source: Schäfer, D. (2013) 'Barclays recoups £300m in bonuses', *Financial Times*, 27 February.

The EU proposed going further in 2014 by limiting bonuses to no more than the amount of the employee's salary. (This one-to-one ratio can be doubled with the approval of a supermajority (75% in UK) of shareholders.)

Small number of high-reputation banks

However, then there is the question of why investment banks generate such high pre-wage profits to be able to pay bonuses in the first place.[2] One place to look would be the small number of players in the field with high reputations for handling complex financing and deals – corporate executives are often willing to pay a great deal for what they perceive as the 'best'. On the investing side, when contemplating whether to invest some money, institutions often look for a big-name investment bank's stamp of approval of a firm issuing new securities (e.g. shares) or committing to a merger deal. The big names will refuse to handle an issue of shares or bonds for a company if there is a real risk of the issue upsetting investors by subsequently underperforming.

The industry looks very much like an oligopoly for many areas of activity – for some services there might be only three banks in the world able to offer them. Lord Myners, who has decades of experience in the City before becoming a government minister, is certainly suspicious – see Article 10.3.

Article 10.3

Pressure rises for formal bank fees inquiry

By Kate Burgess

Political pressure for a formal inquiry into investment banking fees mounted as Lord Myners, City minister, said there was clear evidence of restricted competition in the market.

"Certain aspects of investment banking in equity underwriting exhibit features of a semi-oligopolistic market."

His comments come less than a week after the Office of Fair Trading revealed it was looking at the fees charged by investment banks to decide whether to launch a formal probe.

He criticised institutional investors for complaining about the rising fees but doing "little or nothing about it themselves – they have, for the most part, acquiesced".

He told the FT: "Here is a real opportunity for investment managers to show they are acting on behalf of their clients and launch an inquiry."

Lord Myners spoke out following shareholder complaints to ministers asking for government reviews. The Association of British Insurers [called for] pressure on companies to clamp down on fees paid to banks.

The "enormous" fees paid to investment banks for advising companies on deals might be skewing the outcome of takeovers, the ABI letter warned, and acted as a "deadweight cost" on shareholders that could swallow part of savings derived from mergers and acquisitions.

Lord Myners said it was clear investment banks had profited from raising margins on trading and intermediating between companies and investors in capital markets.

He noted that while banks were charging higher fees for assuring companies that a share issue went well, they have reduced their own risks by advising companies to issue shares at a discount and warming up investors to the issue in advance.

Lindsay Tomlinson, chairman of the National Association of Pension Funds, said: "Shareholders are extremely vexed about fees charged by banks for equity issues and mergers and acquisitions, but whether they would set up their own probe is another matter."

Source: Burgess, K. (2010) 'Pressure rises for formal bank fees inquiry', *Financial Times*, 26 March.

Article 10.4 discusses the difficulties of introducing more competition into investment banking. Any new entrant challenging the current leaders would need large amounts of capital to be able to do the deals that clients expect. They would also need to attract the best employees, those capable of inspiring confidence and of maintaining a long-term relationship of trust with corporate executives, offering exceptional expertise. They would need to offer the broad range of services that multinational corporate clients now expect. These barriers to entry are considered so strong that they rarely allow a newcomer to seriously attack the market shares of the leaders.

Article 10.4

Outsized risk and regulation inhibit entrants

By Patrick Jenkins

In all the furore over bankers' bonuses and bulging bank profits in recent months, one big question seems to have been forgotten: why is it that banks make so much money in the first place? Is there a cartel in investment banking, as the UK's Office of Fair Trading last week implied?

The titans of Wall Street and the City of London have long seemed unassailable. The need for vast amounts of capital, a strong enough brand to attract staff and a compelling enough suite of products and services to draw customers has proved too big an obstacle for all but a tiny clutch of challengers. If Barclays Capital and Deutsche Bank have been winners, their number is dwarfed by the losers. The still-trying category stretches from France (Crédit Agricole, Natixis) to Japan (Nomura, Mizuho).

"The barriers to entry have always been pretty high," says Rob Shafir, who heads Credit Suisse in the Americas. "It takes years to build the technology, the human capital, and make the client investment."

There is certainly space for more players, bankers admit. "In the old days, before the financial crisis, there were 14 or 15 firms," says Colm Kelleher, co-head of Morgan Stanley's investment banking operations. "Now, there are seven or eight. So, perversely you've ended up with less competition."

The investment banking chief of one European bank agrees. "Our industry is too consolidated, it is frightening," he confesses, before adding: "[Profit] margins in this business are fantastic."

It is one of the unintended consequences of the post-crisis world that as regulators seek to make the financial sector safer, they are also insulating it from fresh competition.

"We'd love to have smarter competitors," says one Wall Street boss. "But every time they ratchet up the regulations, it gets tougher."

"The structural barriers are certainly higher than they were," says David Weaver, president of Jefferies International. "But it's not only regulatory capital that has got more demanding. If you're a lender, in these markets, you have to step up and provide capital on your balance sheet."

Even HSBC, which boasts one of the most powerful brands internationally, threw in the towel in 2006. Executives say it was impossible to compete with rivals that had a greater appetite for risk, particularly when it came to backing transactions with balance-sheet lending, or to break down their historic relationships with clients.

The big hope for those banks outside the bulge bracket is to find profitable niches. HSBC, for example, has retrenched to focus on servicing its core corporate clients, with a bent towards emerging markets.

"If you want to be everywhere in Europe, Asia, the US, it's true that the barriers are very high," agrees Sergio Ermotti, head of investment banking at Italy's UniCredit. "But our focus is on Europe and there we have big opportunities."

At the centre of an information web

Another place to look for an explanation for the exceptional profits/pay is the extent of the variety of tasks undertaken by the banks – perhaps they gain some special advantage in doing so many different things for other traders, for investors or for companies. So, while helping a company issue bonds they might also act as a market maker in the bond market and provide research to clients. They might also be dealing in that company's shares and acting as a broker for its derivatives trades, while selling its commercial paper, managing its foreign exchange deals and buying commodities for it. They might also be running large investment funds for pension funds and other investors. Like spiders at the centres of information webs they can detect movements long before others and are in a position to benefit themselves from that superior knowledge. How much of this 'special knowledge' tips over into conflict of interest territory (or even insider dealing) is difficult for us to know – but some people suspect that quite a lot of it does, see Article 10.5.

Article 10.5

'Chinese walls' are still porous, study shows

By Dan McCrum

Equity analysts at large banks benefit from inside information provided to the institutions' corporate lending desks, according to a study.

The analysis throws fresh light on the weakness of so-called Chinese walls, internal processes and procedures designed to stop price-sensitive client information passing between different parts of conglomerate banks.

Based on an examination of bank loans and analysts' earnings per share estimates between 1994 and 2007, the study found forecast accuracy improved significantly if a loan deal was signed by a bank's commercial lending arm. Assistant Professor Martin, a co-author: "The lead arranger of a loan is in regular contact with the borrower; they have more inside information."

The report sampled 382 syndicated loan deals in which the lead arranger also had an affiliated research division and had not lent money to the target company in the preceding three years. The study captures 16 banks that both lend and publish stock research.

The authors compared 4,500 earnings estimates published by analysts at the lending banks in the three years before and after a loan deal, against 19,400 estimates published by the same analysts for non-borrowing companies, as well as a control group of independent analyst estimates.

High pay is one thing; but these people often work ridiculously long hours from 7 a.m. to very late. Work–life balance just does not come into it. As for job security, consider the following insider's view.

As a UBS banker arriving for work on Tuesday 30th October 2012 I was shocked to find that my entry card no longer worked. Blocked from my office, along with a few hundred others, I was asked to go to a room on the fourth floor, where I was told we had been put on leave while the bank figured out its redundancy plans. It seems that UBS chose a particularly brutal way to make redundancies, I'm told it's usually a bit more civilised. I guess they were worried that if they gave us a notice period we might then physically trash the place or trash the bank by completing financial deals that would lose them money. I've heard of others finding out they have been sacked by reading about it in the *FT* on the morning tube journey. 'Couldn't they at least have texted them?' said a fellow City worker when hearing of our layoffs. That's life in some investment banks I guess. What do I do now?

Source: Based on Pickford, J. (2012) 'Tradition of a swift and brutal end', *Financial Times*, 2 November. © The Financial Times 2012. All rights reserved.

Balance sheet structures

The balance sheet of an investment bank is somewhat different to that of a commercial bank. Investment banks do not (generally) hold retail deposits – unless they are part of a universal bank, of course. Their liabilities come in the form of promises to pay on securities such as bonds or short-term wholesale money market instruments. Also they would use money placed in the company by shareholders (or by partners in a partnership – some investment banks are still partnerships rather than companies). Most of the money lent to investment banks is for repayment at a fixed date in the future and so they are less vulnerable to the risk of unforeseen withdrawals than retail banks. However, their reliance on wholesale market funding makes them vulnerable to a loss of confidence in the money and bond markets leading to a lenders' strike – the bank may have to pay off old loans as per the original agreement but not be able to replace the money by borrowing again. This happened throughout the western world in 2008–09, and again in Southern Europe in 2012–13.

Global investment banks and boutiques

'**Bulge bracket**' investment banks are those that are regarded as the leaders. They are dominant in key activities such as assisting corporations with bond and equity issuance, underwriting and mergers and acquisitions, particularly for larger companies. Goldman Sachs and Morgan Stanley are examples of bulge bracket firms. **Global banks** are those active in a number of countries. **Full-service** investment banks offer a large range of services including merger advice, trading, underwriting, loans and investment products.

The US investment banks became very large in the USA between the 1930s and 1990s because after the Great Depression US banks could either become commercial banks or investment banks, they could not do both. Investment banks were not allowed to take deposits, but they were allowed to assist with the issuance of securities, underwriting, securities dealing and other market-related activities. Commercial banks could take deposits and lend but were restricted in their business activities, in particular they were not to engage in underwriting and trading of securities.[3] Thus, as corporations grew and realised they needed investment banking-type services they went to the few Wall Street investment banks that dominated the scene. In addition, the USA is an economy that is very much oriented to financial markets when it comes to raising finance – much more so than Europe where bank loans and equity investments by banks into companies are much more normal. Thus, the USA developed enormous bond markets (corporate, local authority, government) and enormous equity markets; and at the heart of these markets grew a handful of investment banks.

As countries around the world reduced the restrictions inhibiting cross-border banking in the 1980s and 1990s the US investment banks became dominant in many other countries too. They bought up many of the local operators and integrated them into a global business, leading to more economies of scale and even greater dominance. Having said that, the Americans do not have it all their own way – there are some other large investment banks around, e.g. Barclays of the UK, Credit Suisse of Switzerland, Deutsche Bank of Germany and Daiwa Securities of Japan.

The **Glass–Steagall Act 1933**, named after the Congressmen who steered it into US law, separating commercial banks from investment banks, was repealed in 1999, but following the 2008 crisis new rules were judged necessary because the commercial banking arms which provide vital services to society were dragged down to near-bankruptcy due to the 'casino-type' activities of the investment banking wing of the universal banks. The US **Dodd–Frank Act** in 2010 contained prohibitions and restrictions on the ability of banks to engage in proprietary trading for speculative investments (the so-called 'Volcker Rule'). There are some loopholes though: exemptions include trading in certain government debt; underwriting and market making related activities; risk-mitigating hedging activity; and trading on behalf of customers. In practice it is sometimes very difficult to say when a transaction tips from being classified as relating to market-making (a regular investment bank activity – see the next chapter) or 'risk-mitigating' to being proprietary trading. At the time of writing US banks are busy finding ways of evading the restrictions or ignoring them. Expect disputes with the regulators. The Act also restricts bank involvement with hedge funds and private equity. Banks cannot invest more than 3% of their capital in such enterprises – this is just in case bankers thought they might carry on as normal, but with the proprietary trading diverted through these type of structures that they control. The regulators have been slow to implement these new 'rules' and we are still not sure where we stand.

Notably, the new US rules do not insist on splitting universal banks into commercial and investment banking entities, nor on a ring-fenced structure such as the Europeans and UK regulators are heading towards, in which one organisation controls two separate banks. The **Liikanen Report** of 2012 for the EU recommends mandatory separation of proprietary trading and other high-risk trading under a ring-fence structure. The trading division will have to hold its own capital, meaning that it stands or falls by its own activities and cannot, in theory at least, destroy the vital commercial banking operations.

The UK **Independent Banking Commission**, chaired by Sir John Vickers, recommended in 2011 that the retail banking activities be ring-fenced to protect them from the riskier activities of the investment banking arms. Ring-fenced banks would also be prohibited from carrying out a range of investment and wholesale banking activities, including the sale of complex derivatives, and should have independent boards with a separate chairman and independent directors. They should also have higher capital requirements. At the time of writing a **Banking Reform Bill** is working its way through Parliament, supposedly based on Vickers'.

Boutiques

There are two main types of investment bank. Firstly, there are the huge, global banks that perform the wide variety of functions described in this chapter and the next. Secondly, there are much smaller outfits that specialise in particular areas. Thus you might have a **'boutique' investment bank** that simply advises companies on financing issues and mergers, but does not raise finance for the firm, or underwrite, or engage in securities trading. Lazard and Evercore are two of the more established names, who, while not exactly boutique, do have fewer potential conflicts of interest as they concentrate on advice and do not undertake second-ary-market trading or many other aspects of the securities business conducted by the global investment banks – see Article 10.6.

Article 10.6

Boutiques show their mettle in BAE/EADS

By Jonathan Guthrie

Independent M&A advisers are playing an intriguingly prominent role in merger discussions between EADS and BAE Systems. The continental aerospace group has retained two of this fast-growing breed in hopes they will help it pull off the tricky €38bn transaction. Perella Weinberg and rival Evercore dug in long ago as advisers to the owner of Airbus, with BNP Paribas and Lazard France featuring as later additions.

Gleacher Shacklock, meanwhile, figures as an independent counsellor to BAE alongside a couple of bulge bracket groups. Corporate finance watchers credit the firm's Tim Shacklock with early involvement in the proposal, even if he has to share the credit with Simon Robey of Morgan Stanley and Karen Cook of Goldman Sachs.

According to their fans, independents provide a good sounding board for chief executives seeking feedback on a merger or takeover plan. At its best, the service is reputedly personal,

conflicts of interest are few and its small scale reduces scope for leaks. The latter claim seems a bit unfair on corporate financiers at big investment banks, thus smeared as gossips. However, nervous chief executives sometimes agree with the truism that the more people you let into a secret, the less secret it becomes.

Less controversially, knowledgeable bankers with the right contacts will always win mandates. An independent house is a good place to do it from if working for a big bank palls.

Dietrich Becker of Perella Weinberg is a longstanding adviser to EADS chief executive Tom Enders, having acted for the German side in the original combination as a Morgan Stanley executive. Bernard Taylor of Evercore, an ex-Flemings man, has a similar record with the French contingent. And Mr Shacklock, formerly of Kleinworts, has advised BAE for upwards of 20 years. Useful CVs to have, given the fat fees payable for a successful deal in an otherwise depressed market.

Corporate and government assistance

Advice on financing and raising finance

A corporation reaching the point when it needs to raise capital from outside the firm (i.e. not rely on retained profits) faces a confusing array of alternative types of finance and ways of raising that finance, from a syndicate bank loan to a bond to selling new shares. Investment banks can advise on the advantages and disadvantages of each and suggest paths to take.

Furthermore the bank often has the knowledge, contacts and reputation to be able to bring a company needing finance to potential investors. They can help price a new issue of bonds or shares, having awareness of market conditions. They can assist in selling those securities, often roping in a number of other financial institutions to have a greater impact in attracting investors. They know the legal and regulatory hurdles that have to be stepped over or manoeuvred around. They will also **underwrite** new security issues – guaranteeing to buy any not purchased by other investors. Just to confuse everybody the Americans commonly refer to the entire process of organising an equity or bond issue on behalf of a firm as 'underwriting' even though true underwriting (the guarantee of a sale) is only a part of it. To confuse even more: the US (and some other countries') investment bankers describe the process of 'underwriting' shares or bonds as meaning that the investment bank purchases the entire issue at an agreed price and then resells the issue in the market. In the UK and elsewhere the bank does not usually buy and then sell, but merely insures that the issue will be sold.

Investment banks help with **initial public offerings, IPOs (new issues)**, when a company issues shares on the stock market for the first time. The investment bank will co-ordinate the whole process, advise on price and try to find buyers for the shares. When underwriting it usually gets other institutions to take most of the underwriting risk for a fee. Total underwriting fees are typically 6–7% in the USA and 3–4% in Europe.

Investment banks also assist with **seasoned equity offerings (SEOs)** – the issue of new shares for a company already listed or publicly traded on the exchange, also called **follow-on offerings**. This may be through a rights issue. Again, the investment bank(s) will charge fees for many services, including advice, finding buyers and underwriting.

Companies often need to raise short- and medium-term finance through the issue of financial instruments such as commercial paper and medium-term notes: investment banks stand ready to help them – for a fee, of course. There are also many other types of finance investment banks advise on and assist companies with, including project finance and **sale and leaseback** (in which the firm sells an asset, say a building, and then rents it back so it can continue to use it).

The origin of many investment (merchant) banks was as providers of services to assist overseas trade in the eighteenth and nineteenth centuries. Importers and exporters have always been nervous about trading with each other; goods are sent to a foreign country with a different legal system and payment is made months later. This exposes the exporter to all kinds of risk, from the importer simply not paying to the risk of running out of money before being paid and the risk of currencies moving adversely. One way of reducing risk is for the exporter to get the importer to sign a document guaranteeing that in, say, 90 days it will pay say $1m to the holder of the document. In most cases the exporter does not even have to wait 90 days; it can sell the right to receive $1m in a discount market (run by investment banks) and then the purchaser of the bill can collect the $1m – this is the **bill of exchange market**. The risk for the importer and for the potential purchaser in the discount market can be lessened if the guarantor for the payment is a respected bank; thus a bank '**accepts**' the bill (for a fee) from the importer (bank acceptances are discussed in Chapter 5).

A number of banks were given boosts hundreds of years ago when governments in Europe were keen to borrow money outside their home territory – they organised the borrowing. Still today, there are dozens of governments faced with poorly developed domestic capital markets who need to raise funds by selling bonds on the international markets, and they often turn to investment banks to assist – thus they issue **emerging market bonds**.

Mergers, acquisitions, corporate restructuring

Investment banks often have departments ready to advise companies contemplating a merger or acquisition (M&A). This sort of help can be very lucrative for the bank – it would seem that for once-in-a-blue-moon corporate actions like this directors do not look too carefully at the amount they have to pay for what is supposedly the best advice available. Indeed, the M&A departments of the banks attract some very able people, but the fees do seem on the high side for handholding and guidance. But then, they offer, besides expertise on say takeover regulation and tactics, a recognised 'name' respected by investors should the acquiring company need to raise additional finance through a bond issue or a rights issue. The fees for a bundle of services like this can run into tens of millions. For pure advice (without fund raising) the fees for smaller company deals are around 3–4% of the total sale value; for larger deals (billions) they are generally in the range of 0.125–0.5%. When you consider that Goldman Sachs and Morgan Stanley each assist over $400bn of M&A each year even 0.125% fees amount to a large income for advice. And they make a lot more on top by raising finance for the deal-makers. Players in this market who are usually near the top of the rankings are shown in Table 10.1. In some cases fees are only payable by the bidder if the bid is successful or by the target if there is a successful defence.

Table 10.1   Fees paid to the top 10 investment banks in 2012 for assistance with
M&A, equity raising, bond issuance and loan organisation

		Percentage of fees collected by product			
	($m)	M&A	Equity	Bonds	Loans
JPMorgan	5,505.42	23	18	34	25
Bank of America Merrill Lynch	4,695.86	19	19	34	28
Goldman Sachs	4,171.14	41	21	27	11
Morgan Stanley	3,738.53	32	24	32	11
Citi	3,622.18	19	19	40	22
Credit Suisse	3,476.67	32	17	30	20
Deutsche Bank	3,342.76	22	20	38	20
Barclays	3,256.05	27	15	36	22
UBS	2,193.81	28	26	34	13
Wells Fargo	1,997.40	10	14	40	36
Total for all banks	77,650.76	33	17	28	22

Source: www.ft.com

Corporate restructuring comes in many forms, from selling off a subsidiary (a
divestiture) to assisting a company that has borrowed too much, found itself in
difficulties and needs to 'restructure its debt'. This kind of **balance sheet restructuring** usually means lenders accepting a reduction in their claim on the firm (e.g.
a £100m loan is reduced to £70m, or the interest in arrears is written off), an extension of the time period to pay, the acceptance of shares in the company in return
for writing off debt (**debt for equity swap**) or the replacement of one bunch of
debt agreements with others more suited to the company's reduced circumstances.

Investment banks can assist with valuation and procedural matters for bolt-on
acquisitions – e.g. the purchase of a subsidiary from another firm. They might also
help with organising an alliance or joint venture of firms or represent the interests
of one of the firms in an alliance or joint venture.

Sometimes the chief executive of a corporation announces that they are undertaking a **strategic review** of the company. This is usually code for 'at the right price
we might be in favour of someone buying the company, in the meantime we will
try to improve matters'. The review is often assisted/conducted by an investment
bank that is likely to receive telephone calls from prospective buyers. Of course,
the bankers will have to work out the value of the firm as a revitalised creature and
its value to other companies, and will have to polish up their negotiating skills. A
confidential memorandum presenting detailed financial information is likely to

be prepared for prospective buyers and the bankers may screen enquiries to narrow them down to serious potential future owners only.

Relationship managers

The corporate finance bankers within investment banks are generally sophisticated, suave communicators, who nurture long-term relationships with key executives in the large corporations. These '**relationship managers'** tend to spend their time visiting chief executives and chief financial officers of companies, either those that already work with the investment bank or prospective clients. They are not trying to push one particular product onto clients, but give advice on the most suitable from across the bank's full range for the client at that stage of its development – offering the right solution at the right time.

The very best relationship managers (often part of the **corporate broker** function in the UK) put the needs of the client first at all times. Over a period of years they develop a good understanding of the client's business strategy and financing needs. They are then in a position to draw on the various product specialists within the bank to put together a suitable package of services. They are focused on a very distant horizon, often providing financing advice without a fee for many years in the hope that when the time is right for the corporation to launch an IPO, a SEO or a merger bid it will pay large fees to the bankers it has trusted for so many years.

This is crude stereotyping, but the traders within the banks tend to have different personalities and culture, and there can be a degree of suspicion and mutual misunderstanding between them and the corporate bankers. Traders are focused on making money over short time periods. Corporate bankers sometimes characterise the traders as pushy and uncouth. On the other hand, the traders shake their heads at the corporate bankers' lack of impatience in making money.

Risk management

The treasury departments of large companies have to deal with significant amounts of temporary cash and try to earn a return on this cash for short periods. They also need to manage various risk exposures of the firm, e.g. the problems that can be caused by shifts in interest rates, commodity prices or foreign exchange rates. Investment banks are able to assist with the investment of temporary cash surpluses and discuss with corporate treasurers the outlook for risk exposures and advise them on how to mitigate the risk – this often involves derivatives.

Lending

With a syndicated loan the investment bank may do more than simply advise and arrange the deal; it might participate as a lender. Investment banks may make other loans available to firms. The fact that most investment banks are part of universal banks is used as a competitive weapon – they can use the big bank's enormous balance sheet to offer low-cost loans to help win investment banking business.

Privatisation

The Thatcher government in the 1980s hit upon the idea of selling off state-owned assets such as Rolls-Royce, British Airways and British Gas. Investment banks assisted in this process, advising and organising the selling-offs, and thus built up a specialised knowledge of **privatisation** which they were then able to take to other countries as the idea caught on around the globe. Banks have also helped set up **public–private partnerships (PPPs)** in which governments persuade private firms to build and operate, say, a school or a prison in return for an income flow in subsequent years. Investment banks are looking forward to helping in the sale of the banks that were rescued by governments around the world and taken into public control; thus investment banks benefit from the aftermath of a crisis they helped create.

Investment banking within investment banking

Here is a point of confusion: in order to distinguish the central activities of financial advice, raising funds for companies/governments, underwriting issues of shares/ bonds, risk management transactions and mergers/acquisitions/corporate restructuring these are sometimes collectively referred to as 'investment banking' within investment banks – they are also titled corporate finance. But (as you can see in Chapter 11) there are many activities within investment banks other than 'investment banking'. I suppose, at least it separates some of the core elements focused on helping companies (and governments) from the rest. And don't ask what 'merchant banking' is: this depends on who you are speaking to – it's too confusing to even attempt a differentiation.

11

Investment banking: market trading activities

Alongside great skill in assisting companies with primary market issuance of bonds and shares, investment banks have developed experience and superior capability in secondary market dealing for equities, bonds, derivatives, commodities, currencies, etc. They perform one, two or all three of the following roles in market trading:

- **Broker.** Act on behalf of clients to try and secure the best buy or sell deal in the market place.

- **Market maker.** Quote two prices for a security, the price at which they are willing to buy and a (slightly higher) price at which they are willing to sell the same security. They 'make a market' in an instrument and expect to make numerous purchases and sells during a day, taking an income from the gap between the two prices.

- **Proprietary trading.** The bank takes positions in securities in order to try and make a profit for itself rather than for its customers from subsequent favourable movements of prices.

Brokers

As **brokers** investment banks earn commissions on completing purchases and sales of a wide range of securities. As brokers they do not own the securities but merely act as middlemen helping buyers and sellers to match up and do a deal. They mainly serve wholesale institutional (e.g. pension funds) and corporate clients rather than individuals, although they may own retail brokerage organisations that serve private investors.

An investment bank may also have a **corporate broker** arm, which acts on behalf of companies, e.g. providing advice on market conditions, representing the company to the market to generate interest, advising on the rules and regulations applying to stockmarket-quoted companies. They can also gauge likely demand should a company be interested in selling bonds or shares to investors. And then, during the process of a new issue they can gauge a suitable price and organise underwriting. They work with the company to maintain a liquid and properly informed market in a client company's shares and bonds. They often stand ready to buy and sell the company's securities when market makers and others are refusing to deal. Companies are charged periodic fees by the corporate broker for regular services but he or she keeps this to a minimum. The idea is to build up a long-term relationship so that the bank might earn a substantial amount should the client need advice and services during a major move such as a rights issue. The corporate broker can also be a bridge linking the client executives to other product providers within the bank.

Market making

Market makers, also known as **dealers**, fulfil a crucial role in the markets: in those securities in which market makers agree to make a market there will always be someone available who will quote a price at which they will buy or sell – as a purchaser or seller you may not like the price but at least someone is making a trade possible. To take share trading as an example, imagine if you wanted to invest in a small company's shares and there were no market makers, then you might hesitate because the shares would fail to have the important quality of liquidity. Investors in companies lacking an active secondary market will demand higher rates of return (lower share prices) to compensate for the inability to quickly find a counterparty willing to trade.

We refer to a trading system with market makers at the centre as '**a quote-driven system**' because client investing firms can obtain firm **bid** and **offer (ask)** prices on a security and the dealers stand ready to trade. A bid price is one that the market maker will buy at (what the client firm could get from selling). An ask or offer price is what the market maker is willing to sell at (what the client firm would have to pay should it want to trade). Naturally because the market maker is trying to make a profit, the bid price is always lower than the offer price. If the gap gets too wide then clients will be lured away by better prices being offered by competing market makers in that security. The difference between the prices is known as the **trader's spread** or **bid-offer spread**. Many of these prices are displayed on electronic systems so that clients can see them displayed on their computer screens throughout the day. Other security bid-offer prices are only given to you (or your broker) if you telephone the market maker and ask for a quote.

Market makers take a considerable risk: they have to hold inventories of shares and other securities to supply those who want to buy. Tying up a lot of money in inventories of shares, bonds, etc. can be very expensive, and there is always the possibility of downward movement in price while they hold millions of pounds or euros in inventory. The degree of risk varies from one security to another and this helps explain the differences in the size of the bid-offer spread. For some securities it is significantly less than 1% of the value, in others it can be 20% or more.

The other major factor influencing the spread is the volume of trade that takes place relative to the amount that has to be held in inventory – high volume gives access to a liquid market for the market maker. Thus Marks & Spencer has millions of shares traded every day and so the market maker is not likely to have M&S shares on its hands for long, because they are going out of the door as fast as they are coming in – spreads here can be around a tenth of 1%. Shares of a small engineering company on the other hand might trade in lots of only a few hundred at two- or three-day intervals. Thus the market maker has money tied up for days before selling and is fearful of a price fall between trading days.

We can see how the quote-driven system works through Figure 11.1. This could apply to markets in a wide variety of securities and instruments, from bonds to commodities, but we will assume that it is company shares. The demand curve shows that as the price declines the amount demanded to buy from the market maker rises. The supply curve shows rising volume offered by investors with higher prices. The **clearing price** is 199p: this is where the demand from clients wanting to buy and the supply of the securities from those wanting to sell is evenly matched. Naturally, the market makers in this security will be taking a spread around this clearing price so the true price to the buying client might be 199.5p, whereas the price that a seller to the market makers can obtain is only 198.5p.

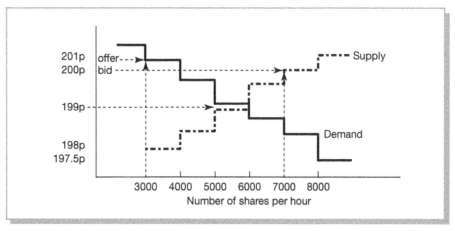

Figure 11.1   Supply and demand in a quote-driven market

If one of the market makers is currently quoting prices of 200p–201p (offering to buy at 200p and sell at 201p) then he will experience a flood of orders from sellers because investors are willing to sell 7,000 shares per hour if offered 200p. On the other hand demand at 201p is a mere 3,000 shares. The market maker will thus end up buying a net 4,000 shares per hour if he takes all the trade. In fact it is even worse than this for our market maker because the potential buyers can pick up their shares for only 199.5p from other market makers and so he ends up buying 7,000 per hour and not selling any.

Even if our market maker is exceptionally optimistic about the market equilibrium price rising significantly above 201p in the next few hours he is not doing himself any favours by quoting such high prices because he could buy a large number of the shares he wants at a price a lot less than this. Thus there is a strong incentive for our market maker to move his prices down toward the intersection of the supply and demand curves.

Now consider a market maker who quotes 198p–197.5p. She will experience a flood of buy orders from clients given the prices offered by other market makers in this competitive market. Under the rules governing market makers she is obliged to deal at the prices quoted up to a maximum number of shares (decided by the exchange that controls this particular market). Perhaps this obligation to sell 8,000 shares per hour to clients when she is attracting few (no) clients to sell to her may lead to problems in satisfying demand. She will thus be tempted (unless she has a lot of shares to shift) to move her bid and offer prices to around the market equilibrium.

A market maker that tries to maintain an unusually large bid-offer spread will fail when there are many market makers for a security. For example, consider the five market makers offering the following prices:

Market maker	Bid price	Offer price
1	198.5p	199.5p
2	197.3p	199.5p
3	197.0p	200.0p
4	198.5p	199.7p
5	198.3p	202.0p

Any potential seller (or broker for the seller) would look at the various market makers' prices and conclude that they would like to trade with either market maker 1 or 4 at 198.5p. Any buyer of shares would want to trade with 1 or 2. Market maker 4 may be temporarily under-stocked with these shares and is content to see inventory build up – he is not going to get many to buy from him at 199.7p when buyers can get away with paying only 199.5p. On the other hand market maker 2 will see more sales than purchases – perhaps she has excessive inventory and wishes to allow an outflow for a while.

Of course, for most companies the intersection of the supply and demand 'curves' moves over time. Perhaps the company announces that it has won a large export order at 2 p.m. Immediately the investors see this news on their computer screens and the demand curve shifts upwards while the supply curve shifts downwards. Market makers also read the news and anticipate the shifts and quickly move their price quotes to where they think they can trade with a reasonable balance between bid deals and offer deals, aiming for a large number of each making a profit on the spread.

Proprietary trading

Proprietary trading ('**prop trading**') uses the bank's capital in order to try to make capital gains called **trading income** which consists of both **realised gains** where the trade is completed (there has been both a buy and sell) and **unrealised gains** – say a buy has taken place and there is a **paper gain** but it has not yet been turned into cash by selling, thus all the accountant has to go on is the **marking to market** of the value at the current price. Proprietary trading grew in volume significantly in the 20 years to 2010, but now governments and regulators around the world are clamping down on what can be risky, highly-geared (lots of borrowing or using derivatives) bets; there is a fear that if a number of large bets go wrong in one bank it can lead to a domino-like collapse of other banks as one after the other reneges on its obligations, i.e. **systemic risk**.

You may think there might be some conflict of interest between advising a firm on its finances or acting as a broker to a pension fund, thus gaining advanced and special knowledge of client actions on the one hand, and trying to make profits by trading the same or similar securities on their own account on the other. You may think that, but I could not possibly comment. The banks themselves protest that they have strong and high 'Chinese walls' that separate the individuals who act as advisers or brokers (and others) from the proprietary traders within the banks – see Article 11.1 for some people's views on conflicts of interest.

Fixed income, currencies and commodities (FICC) trading

The **FICC** operations of an investment bank concentrate on sales and trading (e.g. market making) of debt securities and their derivatives, currencies and commodities on behalf of client firms, rather than on their own account. They may also encompass assisting with risk-management strategies often involving complex

Article 11.1

Goldman faces own goal over link to Man Utd

By Lina Saigol

Sir Alex Ferguson, Manchester United's manager, is not slow to react when a player incurs his wrath. It seems that the club's owners take the same approach with investment banks.

The Glazer family are considering severing ties with Goldman Sachs after Jim O'Neill, the bank's chief economist, was revealed as a member of a consortium looking to buy the football club.

Goldman insists that Mr O'Neill is working in a personal capacity, but his role brings back uncomfortable memories of a clash United had with JPMorgan four years ago when Malcolm Glazer first bid for the club.

At the time, JPMorgan Cazenove was acting as United's stockbroker while its parent company, JPMorgan, had been arranging £265m of debt for Mr Glazer's bid.

The dual role infuriated Sir Roy Gardner, then chairman of United, who claimed it represented a clear conflict of interest and was hostile in nature.

The row also had wider repercussions. Two months later, Centrica dropped JPMorgan Cazenove as its joint broker. Sir Roy happened to be chief executive of the UK energy supplier at the time.

In the same year, Roger Carr, who was chairman of Centrica, had his own clash with Goldman Sachs.

Mr Carr was also chairman of Mitchells & Butlers when Goldman made an indicative £4.6bn debt-and-equity offer for the pub group, on behalf of a consortium in which it was one of the largest participants.

Mr Carr described the offer as "hostile and inappropriate", the bank withdrew from the consortium, and the bid evaporated.

Mr Carr's anger struck a chord with Goldman – the bank acted as corporate broker to both Centrica and Cadbury, where Mr Carr was also a board member.

Goldman's private equity fund had also been involved in unsolicited approaches to ITV and BAA. Those episodes prompted Hank Paulson, Goldman's then chairman and chief executive, to warn its bankers not to use its principal investment funds in hostile situations.

The potential for conflicts of interest for banks has intensified in recent years in tandem with the rapid development of new financial products.

Full-service banks incorporating private equity funds, advisers, traders and asset managers under one roof are likely to run more risks than single-discipline boutiques.

Banks have so-called "Chinese walls", which are supposed to limit the flow of information between different businesses, such as proprietary trading and investment banking.

In reality, these walls are only as sound as the integrity of the banks that erect them.

financial instruments and market analysis. Members of these teams might also assist other teams with bond and other security origination and syndication, underwriting, pricing and placement of new issues. The big players in the this market are Goldman Sachs, Bank of America, JPMorgan, Deutsche Bank, Citigroup and Barclays.

The fixed-income section of a bank specialises in deals in interest-rate securities. This includes:

▦ **High-grade,** low-risk (**investment-grade**) corporate bonds: **domestic bonds** (under the laws and regulations of the country where they are issued where the issuer is a local firm); **foreign bonds** (the issuer comes from abroad but the bond is under the jurisdiction of the country of issue) **Eurobonds,** where the bond is issued outside the jurisdiction of the country in whose currency it is denominated; and convertible bonds, where the bond may be converted into another security, usually shares. (Bonds are discussed in Chapter 20.)

▦ **Sovereign bonds** – issued by governments.

▦ Credit derivatives such as credit default swaps (see Chapter 22) which allow investors to buy a kind of insurance against the possibility of a bond failing to pay the agreed interest and/or principal amounts.

▦ High-yield securities such as high-yield bonds. These have low credit ratings (below BBB–) and so offer high interest rates (see Chapter 20).

▦ Bank loans – yes, there is a secondary market in bank loans.

▦ Bonds issued by local authorities/municipalities.

▦ Emerging market debt – bonds, etc. issued by governments or corporations in developing markets (some might be economically developed but under-developed with regard to financial markets).

▦ Distressed debt – borrowers are not meeting their obligations under a debt agreement.

▦ Mortgage-backed securities and other asset-backed securities – see securitisation later in the chapter.

▦ Interest-rate derivatives such as interest rate futures (see Chapter 21).

▦ Money market instruments, such as Treasury bills, commercial paper and repurchase agreements.

There are other divisions dealing and advising in currencies and currency derivatives (see Chapter 23). There is usually yet another division that specialises in commodities and commodity derivatives, such as energy, metal and agricultural product trading.

In all these FICC areas the bank often acts as a market maker in these products, creator of many of them, as an adviser and broker for clients and as a proprietary trader. How they manage the conflicts of interest inherent in this I cannot tell you – but I can tell you that there are scandals from time to time.

Equities

The equities section of an investment bank helps clients with their investing and trading strategies in shares and equity-linked investments. The more exotic instruments they deal in include:

- **Futures in shares** and **futures in market indices** (e.g. the FTSE 100 index), giving the right to buy (or sell) a number of shares or an entire index of shares at a fixed date in the future at a price agreed upon now.

- **Equity options,** giving the right but not the obligation to buy or sell shares at a pre-agreed price sometime in the future (see Chapter 22).

- **Warrants,** giving the holder the right to subscribe for a specified number of shares at a fixed price during or at the end of a specified time period. If a company has shares currently trading at £3 it might choose to sell warrants, each of which grants the holder the right to buy a share in the company at, say, £4 over the next five years. If by the fifth year the share price has risen to £6 the warrant holders could exercise their rights and then sell the shares immediately, gaining £2 per share, which is likely to be a considerable return on the original warrant price of a few pence. Warrants are frequently attached to bonds, and make the bond more attractive because the investor benefits from a relatively safe (but low) income on the bond if the firm performs in a mediocre fashion, but if the firm does very well and the share price rises significantly the investor will participate in some of the extra returns through the 'sweetener' or 'equity kicker' provided by the warrant. There is no requirement for investors to hold warrants until exercised or they expire. There is an active secondary market on the London Stock Exchange.

- **Preference shares** which usually offer their owners a fixed rate of dividend each year. However, if the firm has insufficient profits the amount paid may be reduced, sometimes to zero. Thus, there is no guarantee that an annual income will be received, unlike with debt capital. The dividend on preference shares is paid before anything is paid out to ordinary shareholders – indeed, after the preference dividend obligation has been met there may be nothing left for ordinary shareholders. Preference shares are attractive to some investors because they offer a regular income at a higher rate of return than that available on fixed-interest securities, e.g. bonds. However this higher return also comes with higher risk, as the preference dividend ranks after bond interest, and upon liquidation preference holders are further back in the queue as recipients of the proceeds of asset sell-offs. The holders are not usually able to benefit from any extraordinarily good performance of the firm – any profits above expectations go to the ordinary shareholders. Also preference shares usually carry no voting rights, except if the dividend is in arrears or in the case of liquidation.

Again the bank will often act as market maker in these products, creator of many of them, as a broker for clients and as a proprietary trader.[1]

Derivatives

Investment banks not only act as market makers or brokers in the derivative markets but also create new derivatives (**originating**) and market them to clients. Much of the commodity market trading by investment banks is via derivatives such as futures, whereby the buyer enters into a contract to buy or to sell the underlying commodity at a fixed priced at a point in the future, say three months hence (see Chapter 21). They may assist firms trying to hedge in these markets, e.g. an airline trying to fix the future price of its aviation fuel, or they may conduct proprietary trades to make a profit for the bank. Of course, investment banks will also assist with non-derivative commodity trading by helping a client buy for immediate use some quantity of a commodity – '**spot trading**'.

It has been known for investment bankers to get too enamoured of the fancy derivative strategies they devised for companies and governments. They can be very complex and it can be almost impossible for the client to understand the full implications of the risks they are exposed to. Whether the lack of understanding is to be blamed on the clients or on the lack of effort on the part of the bankers to explain themselves is a moot point – see Article 11.2 (Chapter 22 explains swaps).

Asset management

Many investment banks have fund management arms that manage assets on behalf of pension funds, charities or companies. They try to generate high returns relative to risk by selecting investments for the funds. The investments selected vary widely from shares and bonds to property and hedge funds. They also manage the savings of private individuals through the unit trusts, open-ended investment companies (OEICs), mutual funds and investment trusts[2] that they set up and market. As managers they will receive a fee and, possibly, a bonus for exceptional performance.

Banks set aside £700m for swaps scandal

By Brooke Masters and Jennifer Thompson

Barclays, HSBC, Royal Bank of Scotland and Lloyds have set aside about £700m for compensation for mis-selling complex derivative products to small businesses.

The Financial Services Authority ordered the four banks to review all their sales of interest rate hedging products, including swaps and more complicated products, to small businesses that it concluded were "unlikely to understand the risks associated with those products".

They had already agreed to compensate mis-selling victims after an earlier probe found "serious failings" in the way customers were sold products meant to protect them from swings in loan-repayment costs. The latest FSA study will determine how many cases the banks will have to look at.

Interest rate derivatives are supposed to protect businesses against rising interest rates. But in a pilot study of 173 interest rate products, the FSA found that nine out of 10 products sold to small and medium-sized businesses by the four

banks failed to meet regulatory requirements and that a "significant" portion of customers should receive compensation.

The FSA said banks had sold about 40,000 derivatives to "non-sophisticated" customers since 2001.

The Federation of Small Businesses said the banks need to take "swift and decisive action" to compensate businesses caught up in the scandal.

The contracts were designed to protect companies from interest rate rises by fixing rates on their loans. However, when the base interest rate dropped to historic lows, some businesses were hit with fees and others complained they faced huge penalties for cancelling the hedges or refinancing their loans to take advantage of lower rates.

Some SMEs also said they were told that buying the swaps was a condition of taking out a loan, while others complained of high-pressure sales tactics and large fees to exit the swaps.

Investment advice

Many investment banks have teams of investment analysts examining accounts and other data relating to companies, so that they can make recommendations on whether their shares, bonds or other securities are good value for potential investors. Alongside the analysts there might be **private-client representatives** talking to individual investors and an **institutional sales force** assisting professionally-managed funds, e.g. pension funds, to find good investments and manage risk. As well as analysing companies they will provide analysis of industries, markets, macroeconomics and currencies worldwide.

Unfortunately, such research may be tainted because analysts within an investment bank are sometimes in contact with the section of the bank that advises the same companies on financing strategy. The corporate finance section may be keen on encouraging the analysts to provide positive research about an issuer of shares or bonds (or a company that they are advising in a merger deal) – if they succumb to this pressure their independence is compromised.

A further pressure comes from the fact that company managers do not like to read that their shares are regarded by an investment bank analyst as being over-valued. They may retaliate by refusing to speak to analysts from that bank, and this can mean that in-depth reports on that company cannot be compiled. Thus we have another incentive for analysts to accentuate the positive and downplay the negative in their reports. In the USA, where this problem seems to be most acute, it can be that there are nine positive reports on companies for every negative one. Despite the availability of many unbiased bankers' analyses the trend is increasingly for the investing institutions (the **'buy-side'**) to employ their own analysts rather than rely on the **'sell-side analysts'** who might be assisting the sale of securities.

Wealth management and private banking

Wealth management and **private banking** involve services and advice to improve the management of the financial affairs of high-net-worth individuals, including their investments, current deposit accounts (possibly in numerous currencies and jurisdictions), obtaining of loans and tax issues – see Chapter 4.

Prime brokerage for hedge funds

Some investment banks have **prime brokerage** arms that provide services for hedge funds such as acting as a broker buying and selling blocks of shares, derivatives, etc. for the fund (**trade execution**); clearing and settlement of trades; risk management; back-office accounting services; cash management: and custodial services. The main sources of income for the bank from prime brokerage usually come in the form of interest charged for lending to the hedge fund, fees for arranging debt supplied by others and income from stock (share) lending to enable the hedge fund to **sell securities short** (i.e. sell without first buying – the buying comes later, hopefully at a lower price than they were sold for).

Another role for prime brokers is in helping their hedge fund clients find investors – called a **cap-intro (capital introduction)** service. Investment banks are often in contact with wealthy family investment offices, private banking offices and institutional investors (**end-investors**) and so can point them in the direction of those hedge funds for which they are prime brokers. A few investment banks also supply fast electronic trading systems to hedge funds so that they can tap into the markets directly and create automated buy and sell strategies.[3]

Private equity (venture capital) investment

This is finance for new and growing companies without a quotation on a stock exchange. It can consist of a mixture of debt and equity, and can be an investment for the bank itself or on behalf of clients of the bank – see *The Financial Times Guide to Financial Markets* (by Glen Arnold) for more.

Securitisation

During the 15 years to the end of 2008 banks (particularly US banks) built an enormous business in re-bundling debt in their structured finance divisions. So, say a bank has recently enticed 1,000 households to borrow money from it for house purchase. It now has the right under the law to receive monthly interest and principal from the households. The traditional thing to do is to hold on to those bank assets until the mortgagees pay off the loan. Banks increasingly thought it better to do something else: 'originate and distribute' debt. Thus once they had the right to the interest, etc., the 1,000 rights on the mortgages are put into a **special purpose vehicle (SPV)** or **special purpose entity (SPE)** (a separate company) which issues bonds to other investors. The investors in the SPV receive regular interest on the long-term bonds they bought, which is paid out of the receipts of monthly mortgage payments by 1,000 households. Thus securitisation involves the pooling and repackaging of relatively small, homogeneous and illiquid financial assets into liquid securities.

Securitisation allows a profit on the difference between the interest on the mortgages and the interest on the bonds. This can happen if the original mortgages pay, say 6%, and the bonds secured on the flow of payments from the mortgagees pay 5%. The extra 1% (less costs) can enable the originator to sell the bonds for a price in excess of the amount it lent to the mortgagees.

The borrower is often unaware that the mortgage is no longer owned by the original lender and everything appears as it did before, with the mortgage company acting as a collecting agent for the buyer of the mortgages. The mortgage company is usually said to be a seller of **asset-backed securities (ABS)** to other institutions (the 'assets' are the claim on interest and capital) and so this form of finance is often called **asset securitisation**. These asset-backed securities may be bonds sold into a market with many players. By creating an SPV there is a separation of the creditworthiness of the assets involved from the general credit of the mortgage company.

The sale of the financial claims can be either 'non-recourse', in which case the buyer of the securities from the mortgage firm or the lender to the SPV (e.g. bondholder) bears the risk of non-payment by the borrowers, or with recourse to the mortgage lender.

Securitisation has even reached the world of rock. Iron Maiden issued a long-dated $30m asset-backed bond securitised on future earnings from royalties. It followed David Bowie's $55m bond securitised on the income from his earlier albums and Rod Stewart's $15.4m securitised loan from Nomura. Tussauds has securitised ticket and merchandise sales, Keele University has securitised the rental income from student accommodation and Arsenal has securitised £260m future ticket sales at the Emirates Stadium.

Securitisation is regarded as beneficial to the financial system, because it permits banks and other financial institutions to focus on those aspects of the lending process where they have a competitive edge. Some have greater competitive advantage in originating loans than in funding them, so they sell the loans they have created, raising cash to originate more loans. Other motives include the need to change the risk profile of the bank's assets (e.g. reduce its exposure to the housing market) or to reduce the need for reserve capital (if the loans are removed from the asset side of the bank's balance sheet it does not need to retain the same quantity of reserves) – the released reserve capital can then be used in more productive ways.

Turmoil

Securitisation was at the heart of the financial turmoil in the noughties. As banks became greedier and keener to originate mortgages and play this game they found they did not have enough of their own money to lend in high volume. They thus turned to the wholesale money markets to raise money. Many of these wholesale loans were only short term – they had to be repaid within days, weeks or months. This was OK if the banks could quickly securitise the newly originated mortgages. But what if everyone suddenly stopped buying securitised bonds? What if you as a bank had borrowed money for 30 days and then lent it out to mortgage holders for 25 years on the expectation of either completing the securitisation (or simply expected to take out another 30 day loan when the first expired to tide you through to a securitisation the next month) and then everyone stopped buying securitised bonds or lending to banks wanting to do securitisations because of fears over the bank's solvency? Answer: financial system disaster. Mortgage-backed bonds/securities, MBS, of SPVs plummeted in value, the asset-backed bond market froze and the business model of lending to households expecting to sell bonds backed with a bunch of mortgages (à la Northern Rock) became untenable as no one would buy the securitised bonds.

As well as playing a major part in originating their own mortgages followed by securitisation, investment banks also assisted others to carry out securitisation, and they traded in the securitised financial instruments and their derivatives. A major driving motive for the rise in securitisation was to get around the prudential regulations for banks to hold high reserves. The more loans a bank has granted in addition to others that are already on the balance sheet the more it has to hold in capital reserves. High capital reserves can lower the return on equity capital (as we saw in Chapter 7). Thus to raise returns banks took the mortgages off their balance sheets by selling them.

Collateralised debt obligations

The **structured finance departments** of investment banks have gone beyond simple securitisation. They have developed some weird – and not so wonderful – instruments such as collateralised debt obligations (CDOs) and structured investment vehicles.

In the years leading up to 2007 the financial markets were not only awash with freshly-minted plain vanilla securitised bonds, with mortgage income being paid into a trust (company or partnership) of an SPV, which then serviced the bond coupons. The bankers also innovated, going one stage further, and then two and then three.

In straightforward securitisations the bonds issued by the SPV are all the same. Each bondholder has an equal share in the returns generated on the underlying loans and will suffer an equal loss in the event of a proportion of the borrowers defaulting. But, thought the innovators, there are bond investors who are willing to take the high risk of, say, the first 5% of borrowers defaulting. They will do this for a high interest rate, say 25% per year. They will then hope that only, say, 4% actually default over the next ten years. Now that the first hit from defaulters has been accepted by the high-risk takers the other bonds that could be sold on that pool of loan obligations have a much lower chance of suffering a loss. If the underlying loans are mortgages then investors can see from the statistical data that it is rare that more than 4% of mortgagees fail to repay. Thus if the first 5% of defaults is to be absorbed by the holders of the high-risk bonds – often called the 'equity tranche' (even though they are bonds) – then there is hardly any chance of the low-risk bondholder suffering any loss through defaults. That is the theory, anyway.

A **collateralised debt obligation** is a bond issued by an SPV set up by a deal structurer, usually an investment bank, where the SPV holds a pool of loans or a pool of debt securities, where the bonds are issued in a number of different classes or tranches, each with their own risk and return characteristics.

Note that while the underlying securities might be mortgages, credit card debts, car loans debts, corporate debt, etc., from the first stage of securitisation, they can also be a collection of asset-backed securitised bonds. Thus, many (most in 2005–07) CDOs were actually securitisations of asset-backed securities.

We will start with an example where the CDO holds a collection of mortgages, rather than ABS. Imagine that Hubris and Grabbit, that well-known investment bank, has granted $1bn of mortgages to families throughout the USA. These are all sub-prime and so have a relatively high chance of default. Therefore it would be difficult to persuade bond investors, most of whom can only invest in AAA-rated bonds to purchase securitised bonds in a plain vanilla asset-backed securitisation. If the overall rate of interest charged to mortgagees is 9% then Hubris and Grabbit could create a CDO vehicle as shown in Figure 11.2.

If it is accepted by potential CDO bondholders that there is a 4% default rate then an equity tranche[4] of CDOs could be created raising $100m for the SPV by selling bonds in it. If the estimates of default prove over time to be spot on, then of the original $1bn, $40m will be lost. The only tranche holders to suffer will be the

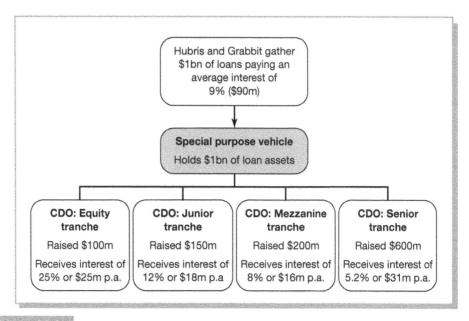

Figure 11.2   An example of a collateralised debt obligation

equity tranche, and they will still have $60m left, plus the accumulated interest. To take this risk let us assume that these investors require 25% per year interest. They might be lucky and only 2% default in which case they accumulate a large sum. On the other hand if, say, 13% of the mortgagees default it will wipe out their investments (apart from the interest they might have already taken), as well as impact on the returns for the next tranche.

This is the **junior tranche**. They have invested $150m on a deal that gives them a fairly high rate of return at 12%. But some of this will be forfeited if the default rate goes above 10% (i.e. the loss taken by equity-tranche holders). Because of the risk of experiencing a default these securitised bonds might be given a credit rating of around BBB– ('investment grade', but only just – see Chapter 20), and so could be bought by a range of financial institutions.

Tranche 3 is the **mezzanine tranche**, paying 8%, and will only suffer losses if the defaults amount to more than $250m (the amounts absorbed by the equity and junior tranche holders). It might gain a single A credit rating. If Tranche 3 raised $200m then the final tranche, the **senior tranche**, will comprise of $600m paying, say, 5.2% per annum and will be granted a AAA rating.

Note that the interest rates charged by the CDO holders to the SPV, when measured on a weighted average basis, is lower than the 9% charged to the house owners. This means that Hubris and Grabbit sell $1bn of loans for a total of $1.05bn, making a profit of $50m.

If you think this is complicated enough, the innovators had hardly warmed up. Some CDOs were structured to have 17 or more different tranches. A CDO squared, CDO^2, was made up of a package of other CDOs (which, in turn, might be made up of a variety of asset-backed bonds). Then there were synthetic CDOs of ABS: these take on credit risk using credit default swaps (see Chapter 22) rather than holding ABS or CDOs.

Banks were greatly encouraged to create CDOs by the capital reserve rules – see Chapters 7 and 25. If they held $1bn of mortgages on their books they were required to hold say $40m (4%) of regulatory capital. If the bank sells 95% of the loans in the form of CDOs, retaining 5% in the form of the equity tranche, then it was required to hold much less equity capital.

Structured investment vehicles

Here is an idea: mortgage-backed securities (MBS) composed of long-term debt obligations, carry higher interest rates than can be obtained by borrowing short term through the money markets. So, thinks a bright banker, why not create billions and billions of dollars-worth of MBS paying, say, 8% per year and then put them into a SPV that is financed by commercial paper, paying, say, 7% per year. The extra 1% can come to us, the bankers, less a few expenses of course. The more MBS we create the more we can make on the difference between the short-term interest rate and the long-term interest rate. So what we need to do is put lots of pressure/incentive on mortgage brokers to generate more mortgages so that the banker's bonus next year can be even greater than last year.[5]

In ancient financial history, that is the 1980s, when bankers were more cautious, these types of vehicles were known as **'conduits'**. In order for them to obtain the very high credit ratings needed to sell commercial paper they had to offer investors belt and braces security. The sponsoring organisation, usually an investment bank, would provide an equity buffer by placing money in the conduit, and would also guarantee a line of credit. In other words, if the pool of mortgages ran into trouble and/or the commercial paper buyers refused to purchase paper for the next three-month period or whatever, the bank would step in and provide money to repay the maturing asset-backed commercial paper (ABCP) so that the legally-separate SPV did not have to sell its assets in a 'fire sale' to repay the short-term money market investors.

Over time, with statistical models saying that the 2000s were a much calmer and safer environment in which to lend on the security of mortgages and ABS, the idea of the conduit grew into the **structured investment vehicle (SIV)**. These too needed high credit ratings to sell commercial paper, but this time the sponsoring bank's guarantee of a line of credit was smaller and outside investors (other than the bank) were brought in to take an equity stake in the SIV. The advantage of these changes was that the investment bank could keep SIVs off their balance sheets. So they had a nice profit earner without the need to hold much regulatory capital. This could lead to great improvements in bank return on equity. Under the rules for capital requirements, because the SIVs raised a proportion of their money other than from the sponsoring bank and because the credit lines offered were less than a year in duration the bank did not have to hold capital reserves for the exposure. The amount of equity capital held within an SIV was typically only 5% or 10% of the assets. Thus they were 10 or 20 times geared.

Of course, you can see the flawed thinking: however many mathematical models you build to calculate past default rates on mortgages, etc., and however many databases you look at to estimate the likelihood of the commercial paper market drying up, you cannot exclude the possibility that the people making decisions will suddenly change behaviour *en masse*. In particular, you need to remember that investors in short-term instruments (**money market** investors) such as commercial paper are looking for very safe investments. If there is even a hint of trouble in the SIVs they will all pull their money at the same time; not just from that SIV, but from the entire sector. If dozens of SIVs are then forced to sell their assets to repay commercial paper as it falls due, then these assets (ABS, CDOs, corporate bonds, Treasury bills, etc.) fall in value, undermining the asset base of banks and other institutions further. SIVs are required to regularly announce the value of their assets – that is to 'mark-to-market' – and so they could not hide and delay reporting losses, they were there for all to see.

One of the remarkable features of this period is the lack of understanding by regulators, governments, credit agencies and the financial Press[6] of what the banks were doing. CDOs and SIVs were only explained to them and to us after the crash. They had grown very big in a very short period of time.

12

The mutuals

In this chapter we will examine a group of organisations that perform important banking functions often without carrying the title 'bank'. Collectively, these mutually-owned, rather than shareholder-owned, institutions form a very significant part of the financial system in many countries. Whereas universal banks have diversified into an amazing array of services the mutuals tend to emphasise the original function of banks; taking and looking after customers' money and lending to them, for the most part without the excessive profiteering and speculating that have been seen in many commercial banks. Mutuals' purpose was and still is to encourage people of limited means to save and allow them to borrow, often for the purpose of buying or building a house or a business. They began to be established in the late 1700s, as industrialisation generated numbers of people who for the first time had money to spare, but who were reluctant to use it, or were not welcomed at traditional banks and were therefore often preyed on by moneylenders.

The idea behind **mutuals** is that each person contributing is a member, one person one vote regardless of the amounts involved, and the organisation is run by its members. The members are usually depositors, or depositors plus borrowers together. With no shareholders to please, they do not need to make great profits. In theory they are able to lend at lower rates and pay higher rates of interest on deposits. Profits are either distributed to members or they are ploughed back into the business. Today there are hundreds of thousands of member-owned financial institutions.

Most mutuals operate for the benefit of local people/their locality and are called by a number of different names: including thrifts, building societies, co-operative banks, savings and loans, savings banks, people's banks, community banks and credit unions. Even with different labels they generally do much the same type of banking, but there are subtle differences in constitution, target members, borrowing purpose, and legal structure from one country to another.

Temptations and vulnerabilities

Mutuals tend to develop a culture of cautious risk-taking because they do not have to maximise profits by buying into the latest financial instruments or stretch their capital bases to conduct high levels of lending. As such they are better positioned to survive a financial crisis. However some have been tempted to take higher risks through overseas expansion, venturing into investment banking territory and plunging into exotic instruments pools, such as US sub-prime mortgage-based instruments (many German mutual banks, for example, were caught out investing in US instruments in 2008).

A general drawback with many mutuals is their vulnerability in times of crisis; because they do not have shareholders to supply extra capital funding, they are more at risk of insolvency. They have to rely on an accumulation of profits and attracting new deposits to rebuild capital, and this can be too slow. For example in 2008–10 European shareholder-owned banks raised over €100bn to buttress their capital by selling new shares. Mutuals on the other hand had limited options. Their main response was to increase the interest rate on deposits to attract funds to lend, which resulted in a profits squeeze because they could not raise lending rates to the same extent. This happened at the same time that the regulators were ratcheting-up the amount of capital reserves they had to hold. As a result many of them were forced into selling themselves or to combine with other mutuals or to accept venture capital money and some found themselves unable to continue. There are moves afoot to remedy the lack of risk-absorbing capital – see Article 12.1.

Origins of the mutuals

The first savings bank was founded in 1810 by the Reverend Henry Duncan. He had a crusade to bring financial independence to the ordinary Scottish people by 'the erection of an economical bank for the savings of the industrious'. This was followed by the Philadelphia Savings Fund Society in the USA in 1816. Building societies, for savings and loans to buy houses had existed since the 1770s (in Birmingham and the North of England). The earliest record of a co-operative dates back to the eighteenth century, but the co-operative movement began in earnest in 1844 with the Rochdale Pioneers, 28 weavers working in cotton mills in Rochdale, who pooled their resources together to buy staple goods at a better price which they were then able to sell at a lower cost to their fellow workers. In Germany credit co-operatives were encouraged by both Franz Hermann Schulze-Delitzsch, who from 1852 began promoting financial co-operatives in urban areas of Germany, and Friedrich Wilhelm Raiffeisen, who developed the financial co-operative idea in rural areas and went on to found the first credit union in 1862.

Article 12.1

Capital future for mutuals

By Jennifer Thompson and Patrick Jenkins

Mutually owned organisations such as building societies and co-operatives have narrower options when it comes to raising capital as they cannot issue equity.

The traditional route for building societies to raise money from investors has been the issuance of permanent interest-bearing shares, known as 'Pibs', a hybrid between stocks and bonds.

However, these are no longer regarded as providing core tier one capital by regulators – a key measure of balance sheet strength. Instead, impending European Union legislation

will pave the way to allow institutions to raise higher quality capital through instruments known as core capital deferred shares. These could potentially be traded on the secondary market while individual institutions will decide on the distribution policy to investors.

Regulators are conscious that they need to tread carefully with mutually and co-operatively owned lenders. The sector is seen by policymakers as an important part of biodiversity in banking and the government has talked enthusiastically about the role it can play in strengthening competition on the high street.

 Source: Thompson, J. and Jenkins, P. (2013) 'Capital future for mutuals', *Financial Times*, 27 February.

Raiffeisen in particular is remembered in many parts of Central and Eastern Europe where co-operative banks are named after him. The mutual movement quickly spread across Germany, and then to Europe and the rest of the world. Today over a billion people are members of a mutual and many of them are members of more than one; if someone banks with a mutual organisation it is quite likely that they will also arrange insurance or pensions with a similar organisation.

The distinction between the different types of mutual organisations is blurred, but what is clear is their significant and beneficial impact on people's lives. According to EU figures, social economy enterprises (this includes mutuals, co-operatives and also charities and voluntary organisations) represent 2 million enterprises (i.e. 10% of all European businesses) and employ over 11 million (about 6% of the working population of the EU). In the USA, there are an estimated 30,000 co-operative enterprises, and over 7,000 credit unions. Financial mutuals often operate in poorer countries where commercial banks find it hard (or unprofitable) to operate.

Various bodies represent the interest of financial mutuals, such as the European Association of Co-operative Banks (EACB) which acts for 4,000 local co-operative banks with 65,000 outlets and 50 million members, and the World Council of Credit Unions (WOCCU) which looks after the interests of over 51,000 credit unions with nearly 200 million members in 100 countries, see Figure 12.1. Notice the strength of the credit union movement in Asia and Africa, where commercial banks have far less influence.

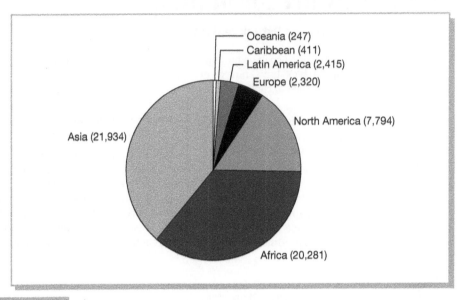

Source: www.woccu.org

Figure 12.1   Number of credit unions worldwide 2012

The International Monetary Fund (IMF) compile numbers for different types of financial institutions in 182 countries – see Figure 12.2. **Microfinance institutions'** primary business model is to take deposits and lend to self-employed or informally employed poor, micro-entrepreneurs and small businesses, usually in developing countries where commercial banks have not found it to be worth their while to set up branches. While some of them are mutual organisations, others are run for profit. 1,954 of these organisations reported to the IMF in 2011 with 25,525 branches. The IMF definition of 'other deposit takers' includes savings and loan associations, building societies, post office giro institutions, **rural banks and agricultural banks** (which are usually community-owned but often assisted by the state, or state-owned; offering bank accounts, loans and money transfers to farmers, etc.), post office savings banks, savings banks and money market funds.

Figure 12.3 gives the ten countries where savings and loan associations, building societies, post office giro institutions, rural, agricultural and savings banks are most prevalent.

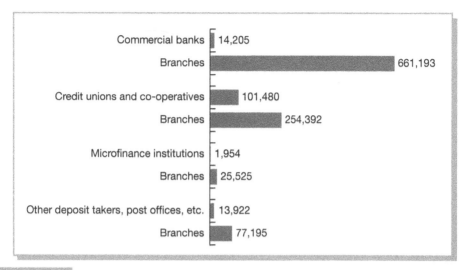

Figure 12.2 Numbers of financial organisations

Source: IMF Financial Access Survey

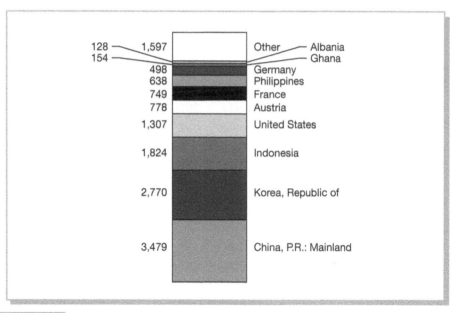

Figure 12.3 Numbers of 'other deposit-taking' institutions

Germany

The two European countries where mutuals are especially influential are Germany and Spain.

In Germany mutuals were principally seen as a good way for thrifty, hard-working nineteenth century families to save up to buy a home or build their business, and they are still a major part of the German banking system today. Each county or federal state (Land) tends to have its own regional **Sparkassen** (savings banks) and **Genossenschaftsbanken** (co-operative banks). Sparkassen use the regional **Landesbanken** as their 'central banks' (there are over 420 Sparkassen and five Landesbanken). The Landesbanken, part-owned by national or regional associations of savings banks are part-owned by regional governments, clear payments for the Sparkassen, assist with their liquidity, help them through rough patches and provide many other services including cross-border transactions as well as lend to the corporate and public sectors.

Where the savings banks are retail banking focused the Landesbanken are wholesale banks. In the strictest sense the Sparkassen are not mutuals because they are owned and controlled by local governments. They were founded by local and regional governments to raise finance for infrastructure projects and make loans to the poor, attracting deposits from local households and firms. They opened up the possibility for ordinary people to create long-term, secure and interest-bearing reserves to cope with the adversities of life (illness, age, etc.). They lend about one-third of all loans to German households and domestic companies.

There are also nearly 1,200 **German credit co-operative banks** (Genossenschaftsbanken) if credit unions are included in the total. These are owned by members of a profession or trade with a total of about 16 million members. The 'central bank' for the cooperatives is DZ Bank, Germany's fourth largest bank, which provides central services and a range of domestic and international corporate banking and investment banking functions, such as insurance products, payment processing and risk management services. It also provides bond trading, export finance, leasing, and structured finance to the co-operatives as well as to small and mid-sized businesses. The German co-operatives account for about 13% of lending to households and German companies and 18% of mortgage lending.

Bausparkassen (building societies) accept deposits and provide finance for people wanting to buy a house. They also provide finance to build houses.

Spain

In Spain there are eight **cajas** (more properly: **cajas de ahoro**, savings banks, **caixa** in some dialects) which account for 40% of the retail assets held by the banking system and more than one-half of mortgage lending. At the time of writing these organisations were in a state of flux as many were technically bankrupt due to bad lending decisions to property developers and home buyers before 2008. As a result they are being forced to merge and/or take government money (through share issues) to prop themselves up. Thus by the time you read this there may be far fewer cajas.

These local savings banks have their roots in the Catholic Church's attempts at providing microfinance for the poor. Originally they were financed by deposits and charitable donations. Prior to the financial crisis they could have been described as quasi-mutual because despite some control being in the hands of depositors and employees, regional politicians and their cronies were able to exert undue influence, especially as the control boards of each caja were partly chosen from local people with no specific experience or knowledge. During the decade up to 2007 the cajas, in competition with the commercial banks, raised vast amounts of money from the bond markets (mostly through securitised bonds) and then lent heavily to property developers, other business organisations and to politically motivated public works projects.

They became very much larger institutions, some of them comparable in size to the commercial banks. The crash in the Spanish property market has been particularly painful (with 1 million empty homes), creating an enormous quantity of bad loans, which were made using funds borrowed on the international markets. The global financial crisis then exacerbated the problem. Before the crisis there were 45 cajas holding in total about half of Spain's financial assets, but with a worrying lack of supervision and regulation. As well as mergers, the government insisted that they reduce their cost bases, particularly by closing surplus branches, reducing lending outside their home regions and refocusing on retail banking and SME (small and medium enterprise) lending. Other post-crisis innovations are the right to sell equity to investors and the restricting of the number of elected politicians and public officials on their management and supervisory boards, with the intention of professionalising the management.

United Kingdom

Mutuals developed in the UK in the 1800s, and took different forms, building societies, friendly societies, credit unions and co-operatives. All operate for the benefit of their members and are authorised by the Financial Conduct Authority (FCA).

Building societies

Within a town or small region **building societies** had a very simple function: households (members) put their savings into them, and when they had saved enough they could borrow to purchase a house (if there was a good prospect of them being able to repay). Once all its members had achieved their goal, the building society would then close down. They were not-for-profit organisations, trying to balance the interests of borrowers seeking low interest rates and savers wanting high interest rates. **Permanent building societies** evolved, which were not self-terminating, but took on new members as the original members obtained their houses and ceased their membership. From 1,723 in 1910, building society numbers have now dwindled to 47 due to mergers, takeovers, failures and **demutualisation** (converting into limited companies with shareholders and floating on the London Stock Exchange).

Deregulation in the 1980s allowed building societies to take on banking functions and banks and other financial institutions to offer mortgages, resulting in building societies and banks offering virtually identical retail services, cheque accounts, unsecured loans, ATMs, loans against commercial assets as well as mortgages. This prompted many building societies to expand and demutualise. The reasons for converting to companies include: the ability to tap shareholders for funds to support the growth or survival of the business; to allow expansion into new areas such as life insurance and corporate lending; pressure from members to receive a windfall by selling their shares; and empire building by directors. In addition, today an increasing proportion of building society funding comes from the wholesale markets rather than retail members, although this rarely exceeds one-third of liabilities.

Of the remaining building societies, Nationwide is by far the largest with over £195bn of assets, nearly six times the size of the second largest, the Yorkshire. Building societies still account for about one-sixth of UK mortgage lending – that is, over £230bn to nearly 3 million borrowers. Many of the best-known building societies have been taken over by and become subsidiaries of commercial banks: Halifax is part of Lloyds as is Cheltenham and Gloucester; and Abbey and Alliance and Leicester are part of Santander.

Friendly societies

Friendly societies have been in existence for many hundreds of years, possibly even going back to Roman times. A group of people contribute to a fund, say £10 per month each, from which benefits (interest accumulates tax free) could be paid out, say after ten years. They may also provide life insurance cover and other services such as funeral expenses savings plans, advice on care and health services, dental and optical costs, legal aid and convalescent home stays.

Before the Welfare State, friendly societies were of tremendous value to the working classes in case of illness or old age. Although the Welfare State removed to a great extent the necessity for a friendly society, about 200 remain. The savings are invested in a range of assets, including quoted shares, gilts, property and commercial mortgages.

Credit unions

Credit unions (CUs) were established during the industrial revolution for the benefit of their members, usually factory workers, enabling them to save and borrow. The FCA now regulates over 600 CUs. Some of the larger ones offer banking services such as current accounts, debit cards and cash withdrawals from ATMs. Life insurance is often included in membership. The affiliations range from taxi drivers to the Toxteth Community. According to the **Association of British Credit Unions**, in 2012 £762m was saved in UK CUs and £604m was out in loans. Membership was restricted to individuals with a common bond i.e. belonging to an association, e.g. church membership or workplace. In January 2012 the law was changed to give credit unions more flexibility over membership and to allow organisations such as community groups and businesses to join. Some credit unions raise investment funds by issuing deferred shares, which can be transferred but not withdrawn and are only repayable in limited circumstances. Deferred shares count towards the capital of a credit union.[1] Some CUs are branching out into mortgages – see Article 12.2.

Article 12.2

Police credit union joins mortgage market

By Kate Allen and Elaine Moore

A police credit union has joined a wave of unorthodox new entrants to the UK mortgage market, in an effort to fill the gap left by the downturn in lending by mainstream banks and building societies. No1 Copperpot, a credit union for police officers and support staff, has become the first such organisation to join the Council of Mortgage Lenders, which represents the industry, a year after offering mortgages to its members. It is one of four credit unions – non-profit financial co-operatives – to have so far launched a mortgage business to meet pent-up demand.

Another credit union to have entered the market is Glasgow CU, the country's largest, with a £43m mortgage book that accounts for more than half its total loans.

About 1m people in the UK save or borrow with a credit union and the government recently relaxed membership rules in an effort to promote them.

➡

Article 12.2   Continued

But there is a limit to how big a role credit unions can play in unblocking Britain's mortgage pipeline. The fact they cannot have a banking licence or borrow money means they can only lend out the funds they have been given as savings. That and their membership-led governance means they are risk-averse.

 Source: Allen, K. and Moore, E. (2012) 'Police credit unions join mortgage market', *Financial Times*, 9 September. © The Financial Times 2012. All rights reserved.

The insider's view   Lending hand

Elinor Bottomley and partner Paul Duke turned to a credit union when they were refused a mortgage with other lenders. The couple, both serving police officers, had a poor credit rating after Mr Duke's previous partner defaulted on the mortgage he had held jointly with her. 'We knew we could afford to pay the mortgage but we also knew that lenders wouldn't take into account our personal circumstances,' Ms Bottomley said. With a mortgage from the police credit union, No1 Copperpot, the couple eventually bought a four-bedroom house in Barnsley with a 10% deposit and a 'very competitive' 25-year loan. Credit unions could have a high level of confidence in clients' creditworthiness because all borrowers [are] existing members.

Source: Allen, K. and Moore, E. (2012) 'Police credit unions join mortgage market', *Financial Times*, 9 September. © The Financial Times 2013. All rights reserved.

Co-operatives

In contrast to much of Europe, where co-operative banking is prevalent, there is only one UK co-operative bank, founded in 1867, which now has 2% of UK bank deposits and over 300 branches (including Britannia, a building society which merged with the Co-op in 2009). The Co-operative Bank is part of The Co-operative Group and offers current accounts, savings accounts, credit cards and loans. The group promotes a strongly ethical stance and was the first UK bank to offer free banking to those in credit. Unfortunately, the Britannia purchase led to the bank's downfall as the new subsidiary came with massive bad loan problems. There is an expectation that this co-operative will convert to being a stockmarket-listed bank so that it can raise money from shareholders.

United States of America

In the USA three types of organisation are collectively referred to as 'thrifts': savings and loan associations, savings banks (mutual savings banks, federal savings associations) and credit unions.

Savings and loan (S&L) associations

Savings and loan associations (**savings associations**)[2] are similar to UK building societies and primarily focused on lending for real estate and house purchase by families. They offer savings accounts and checking (current) accounts. They have been around for over 180 years, and grew rapidly until the crisis of the early 1980s caused by imprudent lending and the restriction of being tied to charging a fixed interest rate while borrowing at a floating rate (on deposits) at a time of rising inflation and interest rates. Up to one-third of S&Ls were broke, and the US government had to step in to manage the assets of failed thrifts. Today over 80% of the finance they raise comes from savings accounts (most of the rest from the wholesale financial markets), while over 90% of their assets are secured by real estate. There are over 700 savings and loan associations with over $1tr of assets. Members (savers and some borrowers) of a savings and loan association are shareholders of the corporation, and so can participate in management and share in the profits.

Savings banks

US savings banks were established in the 1800s by philanthropists to encourage the poor to save. While they do lend for house purchase they are not as heavily concentrated on mortgages as the savings and loan associations; they also lend for automobile purchase, small business lending and personal loans, for example. They are permitted to invest in a greater range of assets, so they hold large amounts of government bonds, money market instruments and corporate bonds.

Credit unions (CUs)

US **credit unions** were established in the early 1900s to help poor people by providing a safe place for their money and allowing them to borrow at reasonable interest rates. Members are individuals belonging to an association, e.g. church membership or workplace – a so-called '**common bond membership**'. The smaller ones are run by volunteers.

The CU member regularly saves money into an account and can then borrow a multiple of the amount. CUs resemble commercial banks in many ways, but there are distinctive legal differences; they are not-for-profit co-operatives with tax exemption status; they return earnings to their membership in the form of reduced rates of interest on loans and increased rates of interest (dividend) on deposits, or they may re-invest earnings into the CU. Employers often assist a CU with office space and items like free electricity. They offer checking accounts, savings accounts, credit cards, money market savings accounts and online banking.

Typical loans made by CUs are $10,000–15,000 with over one-third going for car purchase and one-third for house purchase (often over $200,000 a time). Most CUs have a strong regional base, but a few have become national or international, for example, the Navy Federal Credit Union which has $52bn in assets and 4 million members. Multinational corporations often encourage workplace credit unions; for example, BECU, the Boeing Employees Credit Union set up after the great depression for the benefit of Boeing employees. The USA has over 7,000 credit unions with 94 million members accounting for around 10% of consumer deposits and 15% of consumer loans.

Mutuals in other countries

In France the majority of banks are co-operatives. France's second largest bank, Crédit Agricole S.A., is a coordinating bank for 39 regional banks which own 56% of CA's shares. The other 44% are owned by stockmarket investors and employees. The regional banks are, in turn, majority owned by 2,531 local co-operative banks.[3] The regional banks are independent fully fledged banks offering a wide range of banking services including savings, investments, life insurance, loans, payment instruments and property/casualty insurance products. As well as coordinating the activities of the group, offering central services such as designing the products offered through the regional banks, Crédit Agricole offers the full spectrum of retail banking businesses and related specialised businesses in France and internationally: asset management, insurance, leasing and factoring, consumer finance, corporate and investment banking.

Two of France's other major banks, Banque Populaire and Caisse d'Epargne, also co-operative banks, merged in 2009 to form Groupe BPCE. Crédit Mutuel is another co-operative bank (a federation of cooperatives), serving the north east and the Atlantic coast area of France. Between them, these co-operative banks operate over 12,000 branches, serving over 60 million customers with 22 million co-operative shareholders.

Another major player in French banking is La Banque Postale which uses the 17,082 post office branches to offer banking services. While not strictly a co-operative, it is state-owned, and was established in 2006 to provide banking access to all individuals.

In the Netherlands over 40% of all banking deposits are in co-operatives. Rabobank Nederland is an umbrella organisation that acts for 139 independent agricultural co-operatives with 872 branches, called Rabobanks. Collectively they form the Rabobank Group, the second biggest banking institution in Holland and one of the most successful co-operative banks in the world.

Japan has a thriving co-operative sector which offers banking services to its members. The Shinkin Central Bank is the central financial institution of 271 Shinkin banks, which are cooperatives in the regions serving SMEs and local residents. The Shinkumi Federation Bank is the central bank for 158 Shinkumi banks, which are credit co-operatives, and can only accept deposits from their members (3.8 million of them), while Shinkin banks can accept deposits from anyone.

In Africa there are many areas where access to banking and credit is often poor or non-existent. Micro-finance, the provision of savings and loan facilities in very small amounts, is helping to solve this. Often this is part of a co-operative or credit union scheme, set up for the benefit of local groups or individuals. In some cases innovative projects using mobile phone technology are enabling people to access banking facilities through their mobile phones.

India established a co-operative banking movement towards the end of the nineteenth century. It offered small savings and loan services to the poorest of India's population where no other kind of banking was available. Today there is a network of co-operative banks, with 31 state co-operative banks operating 1,028 offices and with a membership of 234,827; 371 district central co-operative banks operating 13,327 offices and with a membership of 3,146,070; and 93,413 primary agricultural co-operative societies with a membership of 121,224,880 which have made small loans to over 52 million borrowers. These numbers are huge, but because the amounts involved are small, only account for a fraction of Indian banking. There are also 1,645 credit unions with over 20 million members.

Indonesia and Korea both have over 900 credit unions, but the membership differs with Korea's credit unions having three times as many members as Indonesia's, nearly 6 million to just under 2 million. Bangladesh, one of the world's poorest countries, has an astonishing 176,942 branches of credit unions. This underlines the essential purpose of mutual organisations, to provide access to savings and loans to people who have no access to conventional banks for a variety of reasons.

13

Finance houses

Finance houses are very important sources of finance for companies and individuals. They advance credit, usually through factoring, a hire-purchase agreement or a lease, against the security of assets ('**asset finance**' or '**asset-based finance**' (**ABF**)) such as cars or machinery. The asset might also be debts owed by customers. Strictly, these organisations are classified as 'non-bank institutions' but they provide debt finance and they are often owned by the major banks and so are included in this book. Typically they do not take deposits but obtain their funds from the money and bond markets. Some of the largest finance houses are owned by commercial organisations such as General Electric, JCB or Siemens rather than banks.

Factoring

Factoring[1] companies provide three services to firms with outstanding debtors (also called trade receivables – amounts not yet paid by customers), the most important of which is the immediate transfer of cash. At any one time a typical business can have a fifth or more of its annual turnover outstanding in trade debts: a firm with an annual turnover of £5m may have a debtor balance of £1m. These large sums can create cash difficulties which might pressurise an otherwise healthy business.

Finance

For a fee, factors provide a company, often within 24 hours, a high percentage (up to 90%) of the invoice amounts which are due to be paid in say 30, 60 or 90 days' time. When the invoices are due for payment, the payment will be made to the factor, who forwards to the company the remaining balance, less fees. Factoring is increasingly used by companies of all sizes as a way of meeting cash flow needs induced by rising sales and debtor balances. It is usually provided as a continuous cycle, with the factoring company purchasing the invoices of the client as they arise in the normal course of trading over many years.

In the UK about 80% of factoring turnover is handled by the clearing bank subsidiaries, e.g. HSBC Invoice Finance, Lloyds and Royal Bank of Scotland Corporate Banking. However, there are dozens of smaller factoring companies.

Naturally the factor will charge a fee and interest on the money advanced. The cost will vary between clients depending on sales volume, the type of industry and the average value of the invoices. The fee is typically 1% of annual turnover, but there might be survey and audit fees as well. The charge for finance is comparable with overdraft rates (1–3% over base rate). As on an overdraft, the interest is calculated on the daily outstanding balance of the funds transferred to the borrowing firm. Added to this is a service charge that varies between 0.2% and 3% of invoiced sales. This is set at the higher end if there are many small invoices or a lot of customer accounts or the risk of non-payment is high. The sequence involved in factoring is shown in Figure 13.1.

Factors frequently reject clients as unsuitable for their services. The factor looks for 'clean and unencumbered debts' so that it can be reasonably certain of receiving invoice payments. It will also want to understand the company's business and to be satisfied with the competence of its management.

This form of finance has some advantages over bank borrowing. The factor does not impose financial ratio covenants or require fixed (non-current) asset backing. Also the fear of instant withdrawal of a facility (as with an overdraft) is absent as there is usually a notice period. The disadvantages are the raised cost and the unavailability of factoring to companies with many small-value transactions. Also, some managers say it removes a safety margin; instead of spending frugally while waiting for customers to pay, they may be tempted to splurge the advance.

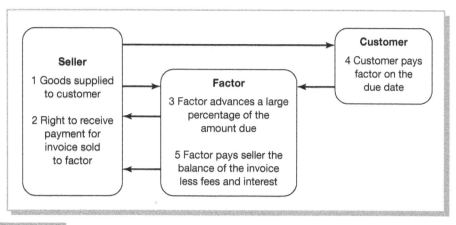

Figure 13.1   **The factoring sequence**

The insider's view   Prestige Pet Products

Natalie Ellis, a 21 year old single mother, set up Prestige Pet Products in 2001. It had limited success until in 2004 she landed a very large order from J. Sainsbury for a range of dog blankets, balls, bowls, etc. "I came out thinking 'Yes I've cracked it'. Then I thought, 'Oh my goodness'." The first order was for 350,000 items and she would need £250,000 to fund production. She could not convince a bank to give her a loan. However, Alex Lawrie, a factoring company agreed to provide finance on the strength of the invoices. Alex Lawrie factored her invoices at 80% and so she had the finance to agree to Sainsbury's 30 day credit terms. She went on to land orders from Asda and Warner Brothers.

Source: Smith, S. (2010) 'Pampered pets help bring in the gravy bones', *Financial Times*, 9 January, p.26. © The Financial Times 2010. All rights reserved.

Sales ledger administration

A second task for factors is total **administration of the sales ledger**. Companies, particularly young and fast-growing ones, often do not want the trouble and expense of setting up a sophisticated system for dealing with the collection of outstanding debts. For a fee (0.75–2.5% of turnover) factors will take over the functions of recording credit sales, checking customers' creditworthiness, sending invoices, chasing late payers and ensuring that debts are paid. Factors are experienced professional payment chasers who know all the tricks of the trade (such as 'the cheque is in the post' excuse) and so can obtain payment earlier. With factoring, sales ledger administration and debt collection generally come as part of the package offered by the finance house, unlike with invoice discounting (see below). However with **confidential invoice factoring** the customer is usually unaware that a factor is the ultimate recipient of the money paid over, as the supplier continues to collect debts, acting as agent for the factor.

Insurance

The third service available from a factor is the **provision of insurance** ('credit protection service') against the possibility that a customer does not pay the amount owed. It is then **'non-recourse'** factoring because the factor cannot ask the client to pay when its customer has failed to meet its obligations. The factoring company underwrites individual credit limits on each customer and will accept the bad debt loss up to the agreed limit. The charge for this service is generally between 0.3% and 0.5% of the value of the invoices.

How credit insurance works

- If an undisputed and credit protected invoice is unpaid for more than 120 days after its due date, or if your customer's business fails, we pay you any outstanding balance due, up to the set value of the credit protection limit.
- There are no lengthy claims procedures and no legal fees for recovery of undisputed credit protected invoices.

Source: www.hsbc.com

Invoice discounting

Firms with an annual turnover under £5m typically use factoring (with sales ledger administration), whereas larger firms tend to use invoice discounting. Here invoices are pledged to the finance house in return for an immediate payment of up to 90% of the face value, but companies maintain control over their sales ledger and credit control processes. The supplying company guarantees to pay to the factor the amount represented on the invoices and is responsible for collecting the debt. Customers are generally totally unaware that the invoices have been discounted. When the due date is reached it is to be hoped that the customer has paid in full. Regardless of whether the customer has paid, the supplying firm is committed to handing over the total invoice amount to the finance house and in return receives the remaining 10% less service fees and interest. Note that even invoice discounting is subject to the specific circumstances of the client agreement and is sometimes made on a non-recourse basis (the selling company does not have to recompense the discounting company if the customer fails to pay).

The finance provider usually only advances money under invoice discounting if the supplier's business is well established and profitable. There must be an effective and professional credit control and sales ledger administration system. Charges are usually lower than for factoring because the sales ledger administration is the responsibility of the supplying company.

Hire purchase

Hire purchase (HP) companies supply goods to companies and individuals in return for a modest (sometimes zero) per cent deposit and regular payments for a set duration. During the term of the agreement, the goods still belong to the HP company, which can take possession if the hirer defaults on the payments. After all payments have been made the hirer becomes the owner, either automatically or on payment of a modest option-to-purchase fee. The payments are made up of a proportion of the interest amount over the term of the agreement and a proportion of the principal sum. Sellers are keen to supply goods on HP, as they receive commission from the finance company, and consumers buying electrical goods or vehicles are familiar with the attempts of sales assistants to also sell an HP agreement so that the customer pays over an extended period. Sometimes the finance is provided by the same organisation, but more often by a separate finance house.

Some examples of goods that may be bought on HP are:

- electrical appliances

- plant and machinery

- vehicles

- computers and office equipment

- furniture and household goods.

Hire purchase is a major source of finance for individuals and businesses and gives some significant advantages compared to bank loans. In fact it is the most common source of finance for UK business purchases up to £100,000. The main advantages are as follows:

- **Small initial outlay.** The firm does not have to find the full purchase price at the outset. A deposit followed by a series of instalments can be less of a cash flow strain. The funds that the company retains by handing over merely a small deposit can be used elsewhere. Set against this are the relatively high interest charges (high relative to the rates at which a large firm or many individuals can borrow) and the additional costs of maintenance and insurance.

- **Easy and quick to arrange usually at point of sale allowing immediate use of the asset.**

- **Certainty.** This is a medium-term source of finance which cannot be withdrawn provided contractual payments are made, unlike an overdraft. On the other hand, the commitment is made for a number of years and it could be costly to terminate the agreement. There are also budgeting advantages to the certainty of a regular cash outflow.

- **HP is often available when other sources of finance are not.** For some firms and individuals the equity markets are unavailable and banks will no longer lend to them, but HP companies will still provide funds as they have the security of the asset to reassure them.

▩ **Fixed-rate finance.** In most cases the payments are fixed throughout the HP period.

▩ **Tax relief.** It is usually possible to claim tax relief on the interest charged on a hire-purchase agreement.

Leasing

Leasing is similar to HP in that an equipment owner (the **lessor**) conveys the right to use the equipment in return for regular rental payments by the equipment user (the **lessee**) over an agreed period of time. The essential difference is that the lessee does not become the owner – the leasing company retains legal title.[2] It is important to distinguish between operating leases and finance leases.

Operating lease

Operating leases commit the lessee to only a short-term contract or one that can be terminated at short notice. These are certainly not expected to last for the entire useful life of the asset and so the finance house has the responsibility of finding an alternative use for the asset when the lessee no longer requires it. Perhaps the asset will be sold in the second-hand market, or it might be leased to another client. Either way the finance house bears the risk of ownership. If the equipment turns out to have become obsolete more quickly than was originally anticipated it is the lessor that loses out. If the equipment is less reliable than expected the owner (the finance house) will have to pay for repairs. Usually, with an operating lease, the lessor retains the obligation for repairs, maintenance and insurance. It is clear why equipment which is subject to rapid obsolescence and frequent breakdown is often leased out on an operating lease. Photocopiers, for example, used by a university department are far better leased so that if they break down the university staff does not have to deal with the problem. In addition the latest model can be quickly installed in the place of an outdated one. The most common form of operating lease is **contract hire**. These leases are often used for a fleet of vehicles. The leasing company takes some responsibility for the management and maintenance of the vehicles and for disposal of the vehicles at the end of the contract hire period (after 12–48 months).

Operating leases are also useful if a business involves a short-term project requiring the use of an asset for a limited period. For example, building firms often use equipment supplied under an operating lease (sometimes called plant hire). Operating leases are not confined to small items of equipment. There is a growing market in leasing aircraft and ships for periods less than the economic life of the asset, thus making these deals operating leases. Many of Boeing's and Airbus's aircraft go to leasing firms.

Finance lease

Under a **finance lease** (also called a **capital lease** or a **full payout lease**) the finance provider expects to recover the full cost (or almost the full cost) of the equipment, plus interest, over the period of the lease. With this type of lease the lessee usually has no right of cancellation or termination. Despite the absence of legal ownership the lessee will have to bear the risks and rewards that normally go with ownership: the lessee will normally be responsible for maintenance, insurance and repairs and suffer the frustrations of demand being below expectations or the equipment becoming obsolete more rapidly than anticipated. Most finance leases contain a primary and a secondary period. It is during the primary period that the lessor receives the capital sum plus interest. In the secondary period the lessee pays a very small 'nominal' rental payment. If the company does not want to continue using the equipment in the secondary period it may be sold second-hand to an unrelated company.

Advantages of leasing

For companies that become lessees the advantages listed for hire purchase also apply: small initial outlay, certainty, available when other finance sources are not, fixed-rate finance and tax relief. There is an additional advantage of operating leases and that is the transfer of obsolescence risk to the finance provider. Article 13.1 discusses the growing importance of asset-based finance.

Article 13.1

Asset-based finance: Follow the money

By Paul Solman

Any chief financial officer in the US will be familiar with asset-based finance (ABF). This type of arrangement is used extensively in US business, from small companies to the largest corporations. Indeed, total credit line commitments by US asset-based financiers amounted to $176.5bn (£113.6bn) in 2011.

Among UK companies, ABF has tended to keep a much lower profile, often seen as the exclusive preserve of smaller companies and entrepreneurs, or even something of a last resort.

Yet the signs are that the pressures created by the recession – and by the banks' clampdown on traditional business loans and overdrafts – are forcing British companies of all sizes to rethink their attitude to ABF such as invoice discounting and asset-based lending.

Article 13.1 Continued

Kate Sharp, chief executive of the Asset Based Finance Association, says: "In the UK, this market has traditionally been an alternative market. Businesses think loan first, overdraft second and ABF something like fifth or sixth. But the fact is that ABF can work for small companies with a very small turnover and it can also work for corporations with a turnover of £400m–£500m."

Ms Sharp says banks' increasing emphasis on risk analysis, especially in the light of the Basel III capital adequacy regulations, could also be prompting them to look again at ABF. "Banks are becoming far more aware of where they lose money, and invoice lending and asset-based products are now recognised as being much less risky for the financier," she says.

One company that has used ABF to help fund rapid growth is Eco Plastics, a Lincolnshire-based recycling group. Its plant sorts and reprocesses plastic – more than 200 tonnes a day – to create rPET (recycled polyethylene terephthalate) for use in making food packaging.

In 2011, Eco Plastics sealed a joint venture with Coca-Cola, that will be worth £250m over the next 10 years, says Jeff Holder, chief financial officer. The company opted for an asset-based lending deal with Close Brothers, the investment bank.

Under this form of ABF, a company borrows money using its assets, such as plant and machinery, as collateral.

"We will have achieved growth of up to about 600 per cent between 2008 and 2012," Mr Holder says. "Our kind of business is obviously asset-rich, and our deal with Close Brothers has enabled us to asset-finance both the equipment and the working capital that we needed to put in place."

He says the company considered loans and overdrafts but those were "not able to factor in the growth that we needed. The asset-based lending approach put together by Close Brothers allowed us to build in growth," he says.

Mr Larkin at Lloyds says: "The asset-based finance market in the UK started with factoring about 40 years ago. The big difference between factoring and invoice discounting is that with factoring, our client's debtors pay us, so they know that our client is using factoring as a form of finance. Invoice discounting is an arrangement between us and our customer, behind the scenes.

"The motivation for businesses has been that they would rather not have the disclosure to their clients about what kind of finance they are using, which is why over the past 20 or 30 years the market has shifted away from factoring towards invoice discounting."

Ms Sharp at the Asset Based Finance Association says: "About 20,000 really small businesses in the UK use factoring. But there are 272 clients with turnover of more than £100m. Asset-based finance really can move through the ranges and can be suitable."

There is obviously still a long way to go before it reaches the kind of level in the US. Businesses need to be re-educated, and that will take some time. But misconceptions and prejudices are changing.

FT *Source*: Solmon, P. (2012) 'Asset-based finance: Follow the money', *Financial Times*, 25 June.

International banking

14

Banking across borders

International banking

Today it is not at all surprising to walk round any large city in the world and find the familiar name of a bank from your own country. The biggest banks are known throughout the world and banking has become a truly international business. **International banking** means banking business conducted across national borders and/or with foreign currencies. This can be retail or wholesale banking, personal or corporate banking, as well as investment banking. The main centres for international banking are the UK and USA, and the most widely used currency is the US dollar. Table 14.1 lists the 20 largest banks in 2012 rated by their total assets.

Internationalisation

Once trading expanded beyond national borders assistance with the associated financial transactions was required, e.g. traders sought reliable methods of payment and deposit without the dangers resulting from carrying large assortments of currency around. Individuals with a surplus of funds began to supply rudimentary credit facilities, lending their money to merchants and traders, and supplying letters of credit and bills of exchange to facilitate trading.

North Italy in the twelfth to fifteenth centuries was home to the most influential banks of the times, often established by Jews as Christians at the time were forbidden to profit from **usury** (the charging of interest, especially high interest, on lending). The banks, based mainly in Venice and Florence and benefiting from handling Papal finances, prospered as Italian merchants achieved successful trading and built up large deposits. Their clients were sometimes Italians, but there were many non-Italians who recognised the need to obtain finance and other banking services beyond the confines of their own nation. However, a mixture of over-zealous lending, greed and defaults by international borrowers combined to bring some of these banks crashing down. Many of the defaulting lenders were

Table 14.1   The 20 largest international banks

	Bank	Country	Total assets ($m)
1	Deutsche Bank	Germany	2,799,977
2	HSBC	UK	2,555,579
3	BNP Paribas	France	2,542,738
4	Industrial and Commercial Bank of China	China	2,456,287
5	Mitsubishi UFJ Financial Group	Japan	2,447,950
6	Crédit Agricole	France	2,431,796
7	Barclays Group	UK	2,417,327
8	Royal Bank of Scotland	UK	2,329,726
9	JPMorgan Chase	United States	2,265,792
10	Bank of America	United States	2,129,046
11	China Construction Bank (CCB)	China	1,949,213
12	Mizuho Financial Group, Inc.	Japan	1,890,219
13	Bank of China	China	1,877,514
14	Citigroup	United States	1,873,878
15	Agricultural Bank of China	China	1,853,313
16	ING Group	Netherlands	1,655,101
17	Banco Santander	Spain	1,619,259
18	Sumitomo Mitsui Financial Group	Japan	1,598,424
19	Société Générale	France	1,528,492
20	UBS	Switzerland	1,508,302

Source: Global Finance www.gfmag.com

European rulers, including English kings, who undertook large loans to pay for wars and then found themselves unable (or unwilling) to repay.

Nineteenth century colonialism and globalisation led to a rapid expansion in international banking, as British, Dutch and other colonialists established bank branches in places as far-flung as Australia and India, while also building a strong presence in the Americas. Towards the end of the century banks from many other countries, e.g. Canada and Japan, also developed international activities. The Americans were relatively slow in getting started because until 1913 they were restrained by law from establishing branches abroad. The rules were relaxed but the US banks did not respond in any significant way until after the Second World War. Even as late as 1960 only eight US banks had overseas branches. But once they got going they grew rapidly, so that now over 50 American banks have branches abroad and some of these institutions have grown to take their place among the dominant banks in many of the financial centres around the globe.

When gold dominated international banking

As financial transactions became increasingly international, exchange rates between countries became ever more crucial. In early times transactions were completed in gold or silver coin, which had intrinsic value worldwide. At the beginning of the twentieth century nearly all countries were on a **gold standard**. That is, in some countries their paper money and coin could be exchanged for gold; other currencies had fixed exchange rates to these currencies, so effectively all were on a gold standard. The major conflicts of the twentieth century made this system an impossibility, as countries used up their gold reserves financing wars, and issued currency without the backing of gold, leading to inflation and instability. It was also found that limiting the money supply in a depression because of a shortage of gold backing just made the economic decline worse.

The UK pound sterling had long been accepted as the international currency, but despite London being the centre for international financial trading, the power of the US dollar gradually made it the frontrunner. This was emphasised at the **Bretton Woods conference** in 1944 when a gold-exchange standard was introduced; the US dollar was set at a value of $35 per ounce of gold and other currencies were valued at a fixed rate against the US dollar. Countries were obliged to keep their currency within 1% of the agreed rates. Figure 14.1 shows gold reserves

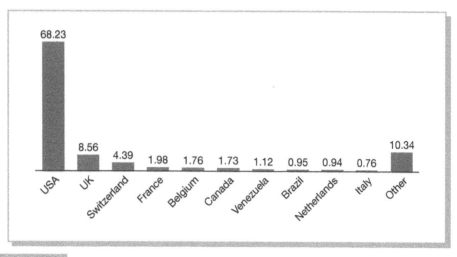

Figure 14.1   **Gold reserves 1950 (percentages)**

Source: World Gold Council

in 1950, when the US dollar was backed up by gold, but other countries' currencies were backed up by the US dollar.

The conference also resulted in the formation of the **International Monetary Fund (IMF)**, an international financial organisation whose aim was, and still is, to 'foster global growth and economic stability'. It mostly does this by lending to countries in trouble, with tough conditions applied. The IMF is funded by contributions from its members, 29 in 1945, 188 at present.

The Bretton Woods agreement lasted for nearly 30 years until the 1970s when inflation, the cost of the Vietnam war and US welfare reforms forced the US to cancel the dollar's convertibility to gold. Since then, most currencies have **floated** against other currencies (moved up and down due to supply and demand variations), with central banks intervening when necessary to buy and sell their own currency to keep its value stable. Figure 14.2 shows gold reserves in 2012, with nearly 20% held by central bodies.

London

London is the largest cross-border lending financial centre with an almost 20% share of worldwide activity. It established this position in the days of Empire. As

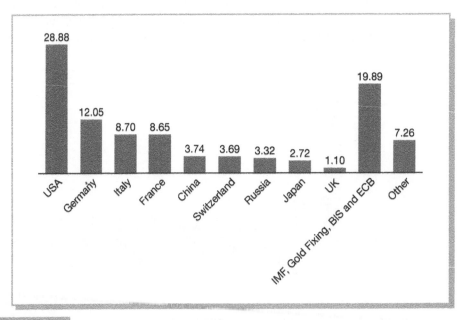

Figure 14.2   **Gold reserves 2012 (percentages)**
Source: World Gold Council

well as being at the centre of the English-speaking trading network it pulled in European bankers. The main attraction for the foreign banks coming to London before 1914 was that it allowed them to participate in the London money markets. Here they could invest surplus cash holdings in interest-bearing instruments that were highly liquid. They could not do this on the same scale in their home financial centres.

Today, having a major presence in London seems to be seen as a prerequisite to be taken seriously as a player in the banking world. London has the advantage of being at the centre of the world time zones; it has great depth and breadth of banking skills and support services (lawyers, accountants, etc.), a strong tradition of rule of law and is the main Eurocurrency, international bond and foreign exchange trading location.

Eurocurrency

In the 1960s and 1970s there was a rapid growth of foreign banks in London due to the take-off of the **Euromarkets** – money held outside the jurisdiction of the regulators and government of the denominating currency, e.g. yen held in Switzerland cannot be controlled by Japanese regulators. US bankers tended to lead here, despite the transactions taking place in financial centres worldwide.

Eurocurrency, short-term wholesale deposits and lending outside the jurisdiction of the authorities of the country of the currency of issue, has a large part to play in the interbank market as well as other lending/borrowing markets. It is very big business with billions being traded every day. The terms **Eurocurrency, Eurodollar, Euroyen, Euroswissfrancs,** etc. have nothing to do with the actual euro currency, which was dreamt up long after the establishment of the Eurocurrency markets.

There is a vast quantity of US dollars (Eurodollars) held in Eurocurrency accounts in London and other places outside the USA which is lent out at Eurocurrency interest rates. This market in international money beyond government control is not confined to European countries; much of the trading takes place in Singapore, the Bahamas and the Cayman Islands.

Today, it is not unusual to find an individual holding a dollar account at a UK bank – a **Eurodeposit** account – which pays interest in dollars linked to general dollar rates. This money can be lent to firms wishing to borrow in Eurodollars prepared to pay interest and capital repayments in dollars. To add an element of confusion, traders in this market often refer to all types of Eurocurrency, from Eurosterling to Euroyen as Eurodollars, and do not reserve the term exclusively for US dollars.

Growth of Eurocurrency markets

Eurocurrency markets came about during the 1950s and 1960s, when substantial amounts of US dollars were deposited in Europe (mainly in London). The American government had set a limit on domestic deposit interest rates, with the result that dollars were pulled abroad where better rates were available.

Stringent US regulations made companies and countries outside the USA wary about depositing their dollars in America, particularly the 'Iron Curtain' countries which worried that their dollars could be seized or frozen for political reasons if they were placed where the rule of the US authorities was in force. Countries earning dollars, especially oil producing countries, looked for banks outside the US where they could deposit their US dollars and earn market rates of interest. In addition, US companies were induced to keep deposits outside the US because of the high tax rates in the US should they move the money there (this was a major consideration for Apple keeping billions outside the US in 2013). So the Eurocurrency market was born, although strictly speaking, the term should be **international market**.

Euro and euros

The title 'Euro' came about because the modern market was started when the former Soviet Union transferred dollars from New York to a French bank at the height of the cold war in 1957. The cable address happened to be EUROBANK. Nowadays, there is daily Eurosecurities business transacted in all of the major financial centres.

Eurocurrency deposits may be fixed for just one day (overnight) or for a longer period such as three months. **'Eurocredit'** is used for the market in medium- and long-term loans in the Euromarkets, with lending rates usually linked to (a few basis points above) the LIBOR rates. Loans longer than six months normally have interest rates that are reset every three or six months depending on the LIBOR rate then prevailing for, say, three-month lending. So a corporate borrower with a two-year loan that starts off paying three-month LIBOR plus 150 bps when three-month LIBOR is 3% pays 4.5%. This is expressed as an annual rate – the borrower will only pay one-quarter of this for three months. If, at the start of the next three months the three-month LIBOR rate has moved to 3.45% the corporate will pay 4.95% (annual rate) for three months.

Benefits of the Eurosecurities markets

Companies large enough to use the Eurosecurities markets are able to put themselves at a competitive advantage *vis-à-vis* smaller firms:

▓ The finance available in these markets can be at a lower cost in both transaction costs and rates of return.

▓ There are fewer rules and regulations such as needing to obtain official authorisation to issue or needing to queue to issue, leading to speed, innovation and lower costs.

▓ There may be the ability to hedge foreign currency movements, e.g. if a firm has assets denominated in a foreign currency it can be advantageous to also have liabilities in that same currency to reduce the adverse impact of exchange-rate movements.

▓ The borrowing needs of some firms are too large for their domestic markets to supply. To avoid being hampered in expansion plans large firms can turn to the international market in finance.

The Eurocurrency market allows countries and corporations to lend and borrow funds worldwide, picking the financial institution which is the most suitable regardless of geographic position. While the world economy is thriving, this works well. However some spectacular problems were highlighted in 2008. For example, Iceland's financial institutions found themselves in trouble after much of their borrowing in the international debt markets suddenly dried up and they were unable to source necessary funding.

The Eurodollar market has become so deep and broad that it now sets interest rates back in the mother country of the dollar. A very large proportion of US domestic commercial loans and commercial paper interest rates are set at a certain number of basis points above US dollar LIBOR rates determined by banks operating out of London.

Banking services in a foreign land

As large companies established themselves in a number of countries they expected that their home country bank would expand with them and provide services when they operated abroad. So, a French company operating in the USA may need banking services from the US-based branch of its French bank. It might need a loan in dollars to build a factory in Chicago, for instance. Or, when goods are sold in dollars it needs its bank to exchange them for euros. Of course, the French manufacturer could use a US bank, but companies often prefer to work with their home bank with which they have a long-term relationship, with mutual trust and an understanding of customs, culture and practices.

Walmart now operates over 10,000 retail units in 27 countries throughout the world, with nearly 6,000 of these units outside the USA. Royal Dutch Shell is a global group of energy and petrochemical companies, operating in over 80 countries, and responsible for 43,000 service stations and more than 30 refineries.

Two very disparate companies, yet what they have in common is the absolute necessity for the ability to send, receive, deposit, withdraw and exchange funds globally. All the cash taken in their retail outlets, in numerous different currencies, has to be deposited in banks, and the proceeds credited eventually to the parent company. International banks facilitate these trades, and countless other types of trades, oiling the wheels of commerce, and ensuring that trade is carried out efficiently and honestly, while at the same time earning considerable fees for these services.

Help offered by banks to corporates

This includes the following services:

- Expansion advice and finance; for example, a new factory complex in a foreign country. Including lending, project finance, leasing, etc.

- Mergers and acquisitions; advising and providing finance if necessary when a company takes the decision to effect a merger with or purchase a company in a foreign country.

- Trade services; trade is often aided by the creditworthiness of the bank when dealing with overseas suppliers/customers.

- Hedging risk; helping companies deal with exchange rate, interest rate and commodity price risk.

- Investment (treasury activity); funds not immediately required can be invested to give the best possible return.

The Corporate Sector Group provides a wide range of banking services via our client relationship managers to some of the world's largest companies. The group is divided into industry/sector-specific teams which are distributed across our offices in Europe, the Middle East, Africa, the Americas and the

Asia-Pacific region. Our established presence across these regions enables us to provide you with the latest industry-specific advice, intelligence and market insight, both from a local and global perspective, while also providing a consistent product offering, coordinated and delivered by a dedicated Relationship Manager in line with each client's banking needs.

In order to meet our clients' investment objectives, clients have access to a wide range of product providers within the bank, each of which specialises in a specific aspect of Global Banking and Markets including: Credit and Lending, Leveraged and Acquisition Finance, Equity Capital Markets, Project and Export Finance, Trade Finance in addition to sales and trading services in nearly every financial instrument, as well as payments and cash management services.

Our clients can also seek the views of the bank's global and regional economists on themes, relating to such topics as the macroeconomic climate, and currency and interest rates.

Source: www.hsbc.com

Correspondent banking

There are many ways to organise overseas banking. A very simple method that does not require the establishment of an office overseas is to employ the services of a **correspondent bank**. Here, a well-established bank in another country is asked to undertake tasks for clients of the foreign bank such as payment transactions, current accounts, custody services and investing funds in financial markets. It may also introduce banking clients to local businesspeople. Correspondent banks are paid a fee by the foreign bank. The foreign bank benefits from the correspondent bank's experience and knowledge without the expense of an overseas base.

Representative office

An operation that requires slightly more commitment to a foreign banking environment is a **representative office**. These are often small, rudimentary affairs that assist the parent bank's customers in a foreign country. They might provide information on the country to clients, help them form banking and business relationships in the country and assist with payments and receipts. Their operations are restricted; they cannot provide core overseas banking business to clients, i.e. no deposits or loans may be undertaken in the foreign country through the office. Representative offices are also used to entice potential new foreign customers, acting as marketing offices for the parent.

Agency office

An **agency office** is a greater commitment than a representative office. Agency offices are able to conduct banking transactions and transfers for their customers, but are usually prohibited from accepting deposits from host country residents. They are not subject to the same full regulatory requirements as the host country banks, such as having **insurance for deposits** (a scheme whereby depositors can get money back from a regulator-run or government-run body if the bank goes bust – see Chapter 25).

Branch banking

A **branch** of the parent bank bears its name and legally acts as part of the overall bank, backed by the parent's credit rating and capital base. Creditors to the branch have a claim on the organisation as a whole, including the parent's assets. Branches often provide as full a range of banking services as the banking regulators in the host country allow. Branches are a very common way for banks to expand, but following the 2008 financial crisis some problems occurred because branches did not maintain capital reserves in the host country (e.g. money could be taken back to the parent and if the parent then fails the depositors (or depositor insurer) may not recover their money). Regulators are therefore now pushing for less branch banking and more subsidiary banking.

Subsidiary banking

A **subsidiary**, set up as a separate legal entity in the host country, will be subject to the same regulations as the host country banks. It has its own capital reserves kept within the country and has to follow the same regulatory procedures as the host country banks. If it ran into trouble then the host country authorities will expect the parent to pump in more capital, but, given the separate company status, the parent may not be obliged to do this and so a subsidiary structure may be safer for the parent. Subsidiaries may be grown from scratch or be formed as a result of an acquisition of a bank(s), as in the case of Santander in the UK, which bought Abbey National in 2004 and Alliance & Leicester together with the retail deposits business of Bradford & Bingley in 2008, acquiring a great number of subsidiary branches. Article 14.1 describes the trend to subsidiaries.

The rogues at the centre of rogue trader scandals often work from an overseas branch office, while the official regulator for that organisation is thousands of miles away in the parent's country. In 2012 JPMorgan's London branch lost around $4bn due to a few individuals making bad bets with derivatives. The UK regulators had limited ability to spot and prevent misbehaviour because the lead regulator was in the USA. The trend toward subsidiary banking has been complicated by the rules allowing branches across the EU – see Article 14.2.

Britain tightens grip on foreign banks

By Brooke Masters

The UK's chief financial watchdog has sharply tightened its grip on overseas banks that want to take deposits in Britain, pressuring them to open locally-regulated subsidiaries with their own access to cash and capital.

The Financial Services Authority is at the forefront of moves by global regulators to force the arms of overseas banks to have separate capital and liquidity to protect depositors and taxpayers from a bank collapse.

Since 2007, the FSA has allowed just four banks to open branches, which rely on their parent for capital, while approving 14 new subsidiaries and six new UK-only banks. Five of the subsidiaries are arms of banks that previously had branches.

US Federal Reserve officials are also talking about imposing tougher capital and liquidity standards on overseas banks and US and UK regulators on Monday will unveil proposals to force their biggest banks to hold capital at the group level so that foreign and domestic subsidiaries could be kept open even if the parent goes bankrupt.

The moves are aimed at protecting depositors and preventing a repeat of the financial crisis, but bankers and industry analysts say the statistics are an early-warning sign that the global market in financial services is fragmenting, potentially driving up lending costs and forcing international banks to pull out of some markets.

In September, the FSA announced plans to force non-European Union banks to use subsidiaries if they are from countries such as the US and Australia that give preference to home depositors in the case of a bankruptcy.

For many banks, though, operating through a subsidiary is more expensive.

Bank watchdog warns on retail branches

By Brooke Masters

The practice of allowing EU banks to take retail deposits across national lines is "dying out" because of repeated bank failures, including the recent problems in Cyprus, the UK's top bank watchdog has predicted.

The EU's single market rules have historically permitted banks to open deposit-taking branches anywhere in the 27-nation bloc without submitting to local regulation. Both supervision and deposit insurance are supposed to be the responsibility of the bank's home country.

But this week, the UK government had to step in for the second time in five years to protect depositors who had put money into UK branches of first Icelandic and now Cypriot banks.

Article 14.2   Continued

That situation is "not sustainable", said Andrew Bailey, chief executive of the new Prudential Regulatory Authority, which oversaw the Tuesday transfer of £270m in deposits away from the UK branch of failed Cyprus bank Laiki. Without the intervention, UK depositors could have lost up to 60 per cent of deposits of more than €100,000 as part of the larger Cypriot bailout.

"Cyprus reminds us that the world is still fragile," Mr Bailey told the Financial Times. "I think the retail deposit-taking model through branches is almost gone...They are dying out."

The UK cannot stop EU banks from opening branches but Mr Bailey's supervisors have been doing all they can to discourage the practice. Last year, the Bank of Cyprus said it was converting its UK branch to a subsidiary because regulators had threatened to force it to write to its depositors to remind them they were not covered by the UK compensation scheme.

That timely conversion meant its depositors were insulated from the Cyprus bailout last week. Under Tuesday's intervention, the Laiki deposits are being moved to the Bank of Cyprus subsidiary where they will receive the same protection.

Mr Bailey said he would "absolutely" be willing to force other EU branches to write letters about deposit insurance to their customers. The debate "highlights another tension between the eurozone and the EU", said Barney Reynolds, partner at Shearman & Sterling. "The EU effectively requires the UK to accept branches of eurozone banks, and yet there is often little effective check in the home states to ensure these banks are non-polluting and prudently managed."

15

UK banking

The UK banking system is unusual in that it offers **'free banking'** to its retail customers, free that is so long as the account is kept in credit. Most other countries make charges for all types of banking services such as money transfers or using an ATM, or simply a monthly service charge for the account. However UK banks make up for this free banking through selling known customers other services, by charging for unauthorised overdrafts, and charging fees for corporate banking.

UK banks have their roots in goldsmith banking dating back to the sixteenth century. When people deposited their gold the goldsmith issued a receipt, and this piece of paper could be traded and used as credit. Private banks (limited to six partners) were established in the industrial areas, the first being founded in 1650 in Nottingham by a cloth merchant called Thomas Smith; eventually part of NatWest. The number of private banks rose to over 800 in the early 1800s, before decreasing as they were taken over by or merged with joint stock banks. **Joint stock companies** (i.e. with shareholders rather than partners), which raised large amounts of capital by selling shares to investors and were therefore able to handle larger transactions, were initially forbidden within a 65-mile radius of London. This restriction was lifted in 1883.

In July 1694 the Bank of England (BoE) received a 12-year Royal Charter which laid down its constitution; there was to be a governor, deputy governor and 24 directors. The Bank was authorised to issue notes up to the value of the amount lent to the government, and also could take deposits. The BoE's paper notes became accepted throughout the country and the extra liquidity introduced into the economy had a strongly beneficial effect on trade and industry, encouraging the UK's dominant position in the world.

The BoE was a shareholder-owned company until 1946, when the government began the process of nationalising major industries and institutions. It took ownership of all BoE shares, compensating existing shareholders with gilts. In 1998 the government gave the BoE's **Monetary Policy Committee** independence to decide on monetary policy, especially the crucially important setting of interest rates, without government interference. It sets the bank base rate to try to control inflation and economic activity. The base rate, in turn, influences interest rates through the economy – see Figure 15.1.

The BoE is still managed by a Court of Directors, consisting now of the governor, three deputy governors and eight directors. It issues bank notes and coins, and acts as a central bank to UK banks and is a lender of last resort in cases of financial crisis, such as taking over Northern Rock when it suffered a bank run due to a loss of confidence in its ability to repay its customers. Following the recent crises, the Bank also owns 39.2% of Lloyds' shares and 82% of RBS.

Some grand old names

UK banks can trace their origins, names and sometimes their distinctive symbols back to the early banks. The symbols were signs which hung outside goldsmiths and early banks at a time when streets were not numbered and the population in general was illiterate. Two of these symbols remain, giving iconic recognition of the brand they represent: the Black Horse of Lloyds and the Spread Eagle of Barclays. The oldest symbol, the Grasshopper of Sir Thomas Gresham, was the symbol of Martins Bank, but was supplanted by Barclays' Eagle when the two banks merged.

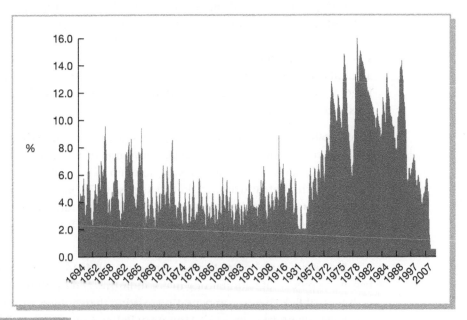

Figure 15.1   The Bank of England bank rate 1694–2013

Banking in the UK is dominated by the 'big four', HSBC, Barclays, Royal Bank of Scotland and Lloyds Banking Group. They have, by dint of strategic mergers and acquisitions, removed their rivals and emerged as giants – see Figure 15.2. In 1990 there were over 16,115 bank branches in the UK; this has now almost halved. The big four banks are responsible for well over 70% of retail banking services in the UK.

Following deregulation in the 1970s and 1980s, banks and building societies were able to offer similar services, resulting in some building societies establishing retail banking divisions. Banks also expanded into the lucrative insurance and pensions sector, sometimes by the takeover of a subsidiary company and sometimes by setting up their own departments. Financial services became more competitive and more risky as banks were able to venture into different kinds of financial trading such as derivatives, with bigger margins but also bigger risks. Many banks were tempted by the prospect of high profits and their employees by the prospect of huge bonuses to indulge in dealings which were not always to the advantage of the banks as a whole nor to their customers.

A fear arising from this continual expansion of the big four is that they have become 'too big to fail', that is the possibility that if they ran into trouble they could cause economic disaster requiring government intervention.

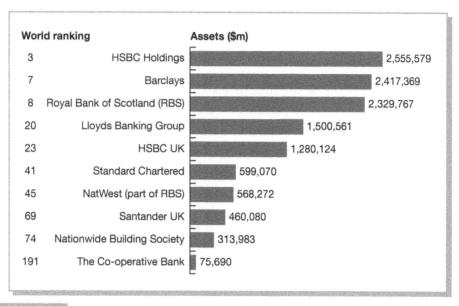

Figure 15.2 **UK banks ranked according to assets in 2012**

Source: thebankerdatabase.com

The big four

HSBC

HSBC, the third largest bank in the world, began life in 1865 in Hong Kong and Shanghai as the Hong Kong and Shanghai Banking Corporation, and opened an office in London in the same year. Its business was originally mainly in the Far East, where it facilitated trading. Having expanded its operations and becoming an influential part of Asian finance, from the 1970s it expanded further afield, acquiring a large US bank, Marine Midland Bank in 1987. Looking to relocate its main base of operations before the 1997 handover of Hong Kong to China by the UK, in 1992 it acquired Midland Bank in the UK, where it established its headquarters, thus achieving its goal of establishing a strong market presence in the USA and Europe.

The Midland Bank, founded in Birmingham, had grown to become one of the UK's leading banks, and formed, along with Westminster, National Provincial, Barclays and Lloyds, the 'big five', the banks which dominated UK retail banking for over 50 years until 1968. (Westminster and National Provincial merged in 1968 and became National Westminster Bank, later NatWest, which was taken over by RBS in 2000.) Nearly all of the acquisitions made by HSBC both in the UK and overseas have become known by the HSBC name, ensuring worldwide recognition. Maintaining its considerable presence in the East, and with over 7,000 branches in 85 countries, its international spread and relative caution about investment banking, enabled it to survive the financial crisis without needing any government assistance. It is the second largest company listed on the London Stock Exchange with a total share value of over £100bn and has secondary stockmarket listings in Hong Kong, New York, Paris and Bermuda. Figures for its UK division and the other UK high street banks are shown in Figure 15.3.

Barclays

In 1690 two London goldsmiths formed a banking partnership. In 1736 the son-in-law of one of them joined the business; his name was James Barclay. From then Barclays Bank expanded, swallowing up dozens of smaller private banks. In 1969 it amalgamated with **Martins Bank**, the earliest English bank, believed to have been founded in 1563 by Sir Thomas Gresham, an adviser to English sovereigns. Martins had progressed in the same way as Barclays, amalgamating with numerous other banks to become a sizeable clearing bank.

In 1966 Barclays was the first bank in the UK to introduce a credit card, the **Barclaycard**, and the following year opened the world's first ATM. In 1987 it was the first UK bank to introduce the now ubiquitous debit card. In 2000 it acquired

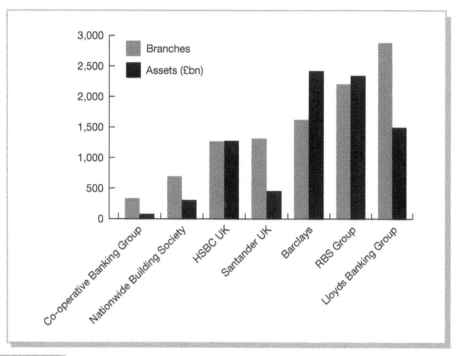

Figure 15.3 **Assets and branches of UK high street banks**

Source: thebankerdatabase.com and bank websites

the **Woolwich Building Society**, which had demutualised in 1997. The banking part of the Woolwich became part of Barclays banking but Barclays retained the name Woolwich for its mortgage division. It has a very large investment banking division (**Barclays Capital** or **Barcap**), boosted when it acquired a large part of Lehman Brothers in 2008. Barclays is very much a global bank. Its main spheres of influence are in Europe, Africa, the Middle East and the Americas and it also has a 55% interest in the South African banking group, **Absa**.

Royal Bank of Scotland

RBS, established in 1727, promptly embarked on many years of fierce rivalry with the Bank of Scotland (established in 1695) which centred on the issue and acceptance of rival banknotes. RBS is famous for having invented that necessity of modern life, the overdraft, when it allowed Mr William Hog, one of its customers, to withdraw more than he had deposited. This practice allowed it to gain customers and to make use of the funds invested by its shareholders. Having failed to force their rival out of business, the two banks came to an agreement in 1751 to accept each other's banknotes. For RBS a familiar history of expansion followed, with acquisitions and the opening of branches, including an office in London in 1874 and further expansion into England and overseas. RBS trained its employees well, and they were in demand all over the world from foreign banks eager to share in the experience and knowledge of a sound banking system.

Meanwhile, in England, following the National Provincial merger with Westminster in 1969, the National Westminster Bank, NatWest, became a giant on the high street with 3,600 branches and numerous overseas offices and subsidiaries. In 2000, after RBS had itself been the subject of failed takeover bids from Lloyds and Standard Chartered, and fought a bitter takeover battle with its old rival BoS, NatWest became the subject of the UK's largest (at the time) banking deal, when RBS paid £21bn for NatWest creating a conglomerate group that was, before the financial crises, the largest bank in the world. The two banking groups successfully merged their IT systems, but the name NatWest remained. Many of RBS's subsidiary companies have retained their own identity, despite being part of the RBS Group, names such as **Coutts, Ulster Bank, Churchill, Green Flag** and **Lombard** among them.

Following the acquisition of the Dutch bank **ABN AMRO** and disastrous investments in 'toxic' financial instruments, in 2008 RBS ran into serious liquidity and solvency problems resulting in the UK government taking a controlling share stake. As a result of the £45bn government aid, EU law dictates that RBS must sell 316 of its branches (RBS branches in England and Wales and NatWest branches in Scotland). A deal with Santander took two years planning, but this has collapsed and the fate of these branches and insurance group is at present unknown. The UK government told RBS in 2013 that it will become a UK-focused commercial bank with a particular expertise in small business lending rather than a universal bank.

Lloyds

Lloyds took over **Halifax Bank of Scotland** in 2009. Lloyds Bank dates back to 1765, TSB (currently part of the Group) to 1810 and Halifax to 1852. The group also includes **Scottish Widows, Cheltenham & Gloucester, Birmingham Midshires, Intelligent Finance, Lex Autolease** and **Black Horse**. It has the greatest presence on UK high streets with nearly 3,000 branches (31% of current accounts), but has a smaller overseas business than the other major banks.

Lloyds Bank has its origins in the Midlands, established by successful industrialists from Birmingham. It expanded rapidly, acquiring over 200 other banks by the time it merged with the TSB in 1995.

The **Trustee Savings Bank (TSB)** began in Scotland when the Reverend Henry Duncan gained local support and set up the first savings bank to enable poor people to save. At a time when banks required a minimum deposit of £10, an account in Duncan's savings bank could be opened with sixpence (2½p). The idea spread through the UK and on to Europe and the USA, with the banks managed by trustees, local respected citizens who gave up their time but carried out their duties with no remuneration. TSBs ran independently, serving a specific geographical area, allowing them better knowledge of their clientele, before they succumbed to the 'bigger is better' theory and joined together, first in 1976 into 16 regional institutions. These all merged into one group which floated on the stock market in 1986, and merged with Lloyds in 1995.

The **Halifax Building Society** grew rapidly to become the largest building society in the UK. Deregulation allowed it to offer retail banking services and in 1997 it demutualised and became a company listed on the London Stock Exchange. In 2001 it merged with the Bank of Scotland to become HBOS.

The Bank of Scotland along with RBS and the **Clydesdale Bank** still, despite all the mergers, retains the right to issue bank notes. In England only the BoE issues bank notes, and four Northern Irish banks also have this right.

The newly-formed Lloyds Bank Group became the UK's largest high-street bank in 2009. Due to the government assistance, under EU regulations the Group must sell off 631 branches totaling 4.3% of UK current accounts; these are now in a separate business 'TSB' within Lloyds, but in 2014 this will be floated on the London Stock Exchange.

The market dominance of the big four makes the government keen to encourage greater competition and to make it easier for customers to switch banks – see Article 15.1.

Article 15.1

Banks face threat of portable accounts

By George Parker and Patrick Jenkins

Banks could be forced to give their customers fully portable accounts – at great expense to the sector – unless they prove they are serious about making it easier for account holders to switch to a rival institution.

Sajid Javid, the Treasury economic secretary, said the banks had one last chance to improve competition on the high street, by ensuring that customers could switch their accounts without fuss within seven days.

Mr Javid said new "seven-day switching" rules, which come into force in September, were an integral part of the government's attempt to improve the culture in banking and to drive down costs for consumers.

But in a sign of the general lack of trust between politicians and the banks, Mr Javid said the banks could be forced to

➡

go much further if the new simplified arrangements did not increase the number of people moving between banks: last year 1.35m people switched.

"If the government looks at it again after a few years and if it doesn't seem to work – or the banks haven't implemented it with full gusto – then we will look at alternatives, that would include bank account portability."

That policy, backed by some Tory MPs, would allow people to keep their own bank account number and simply take it from one bank to another – similar to switching between mobile phone operators but keeping the same number.

Some other major players

Standard Chartered

Standard Chartered is a less well-known name in the UK, but has a very strong presence in Asia, Africa and the Middle East from where 90% of its profits come. It was formed in 1969 by a merger between the Chartered Bank of India, Australia and China and the Standard Bank of British South Africa, both banks established by Scots in the 1800s. Standard Chartered offers wholesale and private banking in the UK and has 1,700 branches in 68 countries, mainly in Africa and the East.

Santander UK

A relative newcomer to the UK, **Santander** became a force in UK retail banking when it completed the acquisitions of three former building societies which had all demutualised, floated on the London Stock Exchange and established as banks. In 2004 it acquired Abbey National, in 2008 Bradford & Bingley, which had encountered serious financial problems and been part nationalised by the UK government, and later in 2008 Alliance & Leicester. Initially each acquisition carried on trading under its own name, but Santander is keen to establish its name globally and by 2010 all had been rebranded 'Santander'.

Nationwide

Nationwide has not followed the demutualistion route, remaining a building society owned by its members with over 700 high street branches. Nationwide is the result of over 100 mergers between building societies, changing its name in 1970 to Nationwide. It is now the largest building society in the world with 15 million members, benefiting from the lack of confidence in the big banks to gain more customers. In the 1990s, Nationwide was the first bank to introduce home and internet banking, something we take for granted now, but revolutionary at the time.

Co-operative bank

The **Co-operative bank,** founded in 1872, now offers a wide range of banking services to its members (see Chapter 12 for more).

Yorkshire and Clydesdale

These two banks are owned by National Australia Bank. **Yorkshire**, with 182 branches operates as a commercial bank operating mostly in the North of England and the Midlands. **Clydesdale** is also a regional commercial bank focused on Scotland (140 branches), but also has a presence in the South of England with its Business & Private Banking Centres.

Other banks

The disquiet caused by banking scandals has led to growing interest in the smaller banks and the formation of some new banks.

Metro Bank opened in 2010 and now has 16 branches in London. It offers commercial banking services and places emphasis on the old idea of service to customers, to the extent of opening seven days a week, emphasising face-to-face contact and welcoming dogs!

The Swedish group, **Handelsbanken**, commenced operations in the UK in 1982 and now has over 100 branches in the UK, all of which are run by 'empowered' local managers making commercial banking loan decisions.

Some retailers have set up banks, e.g. **Tesco, Marks & Spencer, Asda, Sainsbury's** and **Harrods.** These are often in partnership with mainstream banks, but some now have the scale to operate independently. Tesco bank, for example, used to partner RBS but is now on its own, with plans to launch mortgages and current accounts to become a 'full-service bank'.

Danske Bank is the largest bank in Denmark, but it bought some banking operations in Northern Ireland where it has 62 branches.

Aldermore was established in 2009 and deals mainly with SME banking, especially providing loans, something the 'big banks' have been criticised for failing to do. It also provides online savings and mortgages for personal customers.

Virgin Money UK was launched in 2002, but did not get a full banking licence until 2010. In 2012 it took over Northern Rock for £747m and is planning 75 Virgin Money Stores across the UK offering high street banking, but not current accounts yet.

The Post Office now offers current accounts and other banking services from its 12,000 branches.

While the pressure of high capital reserves is being tackled (see Article 15.2), small banks still face formidable obstacles in terms of the investment required in sophisticated computer systems and regulation compliance systems. Furthermore, it currently takes two years for a new bank application process to be completed.

Article 15.2

Capital road eased for new banks

By Brooke Masters

New UK banks will be allowed to operate with lower capital requirements than their established peers, as part of a regulatory push to encourage competition in high street banking.

Lord Turner, head of the City watchdog, told the Banking Standards Commission that the Financial Services Authority had made a "significant shift" in its approach to startups and would allow them to open with core capital equal to just 4.5 per cent of their assets, adjusted for risk.

The lower ratio could help new entrants compete more effectively with banks such as Barclays, Lloyds and RBS. The UK's dominant high street institutions are effectively required to maintain a core capital ratio of between 9 and 10 per cent because of their importance in the banking system.

UK regulators are rethinking their approach, as they seek to stimulate competition and additional lending. While the FSA currently requires new banks to hold more capital than existing banks because they are inexperienced, the new regime will be more focused on ensuring that they can be shut down smoothly if they fail.

The lower capital requirements will include a package of reforms aimed at removing barriers to entry in the banking sector. Regulators are also aiming to accelerate the authorisation process, making it easier for new entrants to raise funds and get started.

New lenders [will have] up to three years to raise their core capital ratio to 7 per cent. They would not be allowed to pay bonuses or dividends until they hit the higher threshold.

The unbanked

The government, determined to try and halve the number of people without access to a bank account, encouraged banks to set up **basic banking accounts**, accessible to people who previously had found it difficult to open a bank account, due to lack of a credit history or a bad credit score. The basic account offers paying-in facilities but not a cheque book or overdraft. Money can be withdrawn at cash machines or post offices and bill payments by direct debit can be set up (some provide a debit card). There are over 8 million of these basic accounts, but there are still a considerable number of people who still do not have or do not want access to banking, see Article 15.3.

Article 15.3

Why do people avoid banks?

By Elaine Moore

More than 1m people in the UK still don't have a bank account, but nobody seems able to agree why this is the case.

Basic current accounts are widely available from high street providers, offering a no-frills service to those on low incomes.

Yet although their take-up has been impressive – halving the number of adults excluded from financial services between 2002–03 and 2007–08 – the government and Europe want more done.

But what?

Nearly 20 providers currently offer a basic bank account in the UK, allowing customers a secure place to deposit money and a way to pay for goods and services easily, but without access to debt products such as a cheque book or overdraft.

To open an account, customers must have proof of identity and address, but this, say campaigners, can be very difficult for individuals who rely on temporary accommodation.

Consumer groups say the problem is information. Many individuals, they say, think they need to pay money in every month to qualify for a current account. Campaigners accuse banks of failing to advertise their (unprofitable) basic account services.

These basic current accounts certainly don't seem to be very popular with banks right now. Lloyds and Royal Bank of Scotland have both introduced restrictions to their services, so that account holders cannot use rival cash machines to withdraw money.

16

European banking

As a result of globalisation modernisation and cross border flows, banking in Europe tends to follow similar methods. The majority of large banks are the product of centuries of mergers and are universal international banks. However, smaller banks still play a crucial role in the economy of their region.

Banking in Europe has a rich and varied history beginning in the north of Italy where merchants with grain from the fertile lands of Lombardy traded very profitably with countries in the East. Loans and credit were given to traders in return for interest payments on the capital supplied. Certain families became exceptionally wealthy and extended their influence abroad, providing finance to many rulers and governments throughout Europe. The world's first modern public chartered bank was the Banco di San Giorgio, founded in 1407 to manage Genoa's public debt and given the right to collect taxes and duties owed to the city. It attracted deposits from all over Europe: Christopher Columbus was a customer. The bank was revived under the same name in 1987 before finally being absorbed into a larger bank, UBI Banca. Italy's grasp on European banking is long gone, its place now taken by the vast conglomerate universal banks of today. Figure 16.1 lists the largest European banks, ranked by their assets.

Germany

Germany is home not only to one of the biggest banks in the world, Deutsche Bank (DB), but also to the oldest surviving bank, Berenberg Bank, founded in 1590 in Hamburg by two Dutch protestants fleeing from enforced Catholicism in the Netherlands. It is still owner-managed and has branches or offices in London, the USA, Europe and China.

Deutsche Bank was founded in 1870 in Berlin; its priority was to finance German overseas trade, replacing the British banks which had so far been the main source of finance for German industry and trade. Seventy-six German bankers became the first shareholders and provided the initial capital. Its first branches were

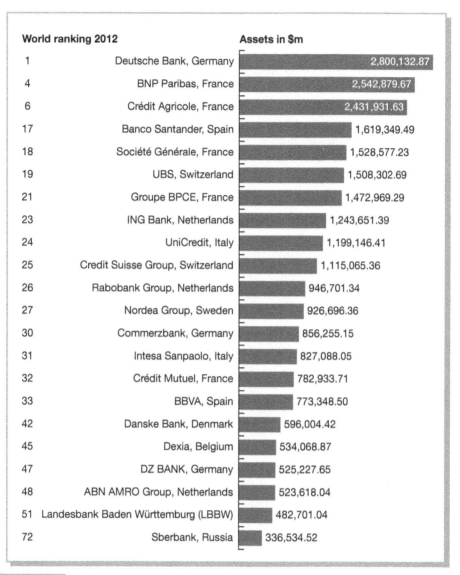

World ranking 2012		Assets in $m
1	Deutsche Bank, Germany	2,800,132.87
4	BNP Paribas, France	2,542,879.67
6	Crédit Agricole, France	2,431,931.63
17	Banco Santander, Spain	1,619,349.49
18	Société Générale, France	1,528,577.23
19	UBS, Switzerland	1,508,302.69
21	Groupe BPCE, France	1,472,969.29
23	ING Bank, Netherlands	1,243,651.39
24	UniCredit, Italy	1,199,146.41
25	Credit Suisse Group, Switzerland	1,115,065.36
26	Rabobank Group, Netherlands	946,701.34
27	Nordea Group, Sweden	926,696.36
30	Commerzbank, Germany	856,255.15
31	Intesa Sanpaolo, Italy	827,088.05
32	Crédit Mutuel, France	782,933.71
33	BBVA, Spain	773,348.50
42	Danske Bank, Denmark	596,004.42
45	Dexia, Belgium	534,068.87
47	DZ BANK, Germany	525,227.65
48	ABN AMRO Group, Netherlands	523,618.04
51	Landesbank Baden Württemburg (LBBW)	482,701.04
72	Sberbank, Russia	336,534.52

Figure 16.1   The top European banks, ranked by assets

Source: The Banker Database

domestic, Bremen and Hamburg, closely followed by Yokohama, Shanghai and London illustrating from the start its emphasis on overseas custom.

German privately-owned (shareholder-owned) banks have always been and still are universal banks, able to engage in investment activities and commerce as well as normal banking business. DB prospered through vast investments in and promotions of industrial and engineering (especially railways) projects in Germany and overseas. It acquired a number of other German banks and built a solid stable base at home as well as making major expansions abroad. This diversity and non-reliance on any one particular source of profit has enabled DB to withstand the effects of two world wars, hyper-inflation, depressions and the recent financial crises which devastated many banks worldwide. It has over 3,000 branches worldwide, two-thirds in Germany, the rest in over 70 countries. Most of its acquisitions have been rebranded Deutsche Bank engendering global recognition of the brand. For much of its existence it has ranked among the top banks in the world.

Commerzbank, another large privately-owned commercial bank, was also established in 1870, in Hamburg, and has grown by dint of various mergers to become the second largest bank in Germany. Its most recent merger in 2008 was with the Dresdner Bank which was founded in 1872. The combined bank, operating as Commerzbank, experienced considerable problems during the financial crisis and was the subject of a €18bn bailout by the German government, since substantially repaid. It operates about 1,200 branches in Germany and 59 branches and offices overseas.

The majority of retail banking in Germany is conducted by co-operative banks and Sparkassen, independent banks serving their local area – see Chapter 12.

France

As a result of various failed financial schemes, the French people developed a deep-rooted mistrust of banks and bankers, and the eighteenth century revolution brought about hyperinflation which forced the closure of most existing banks. Government finances were shambolic, with no settled way of managing them. The French central bank, the Banque de France, was set up as an independent company by Napoleon in 1800 to meet the need for finance for trading and to establish a single issuer of bank notes in Paris. Following this, many local banks were established, some of which issued their own bank notes and were able to call on the Banque de France if necessary, a system that worked well. Banks tended to remain as local banks, dealing with local people and issues; this discouraged the establishment of branch networks and overseas expansion. The Banque de France was given a nationwide monopoly on bank note issue in 1848. Shareholder-owned banks were allowed after 1852 and this is the period during which existing French banks developed and were able to expand into foreign countries. In 1945 commercial banks were nationalised and in 1982 all remaining banks were also nationalised. Privatisation of banks began in 1987 and the denationalisation process was completed in 2002.

BNP Paribas, the largest bank in France, is the result of a succession of mergers, the most significant of which being the 1872 consolidation of the Banque de Paris and the Banque de Crédit et de Dépôt des Pays-Bas which then became Paribas, and the 2000 merger with the Banque Nationale de Paris, one of France's oldest banks dating back to 1848, resulting in its current name of BNP Paribas. Its main areas of operations are in France, Belgium, Luxembourg and Italy, but it has branches all over the world, 7,200 in 80 countries. Some 2,250 of its branches are in France, where it has a strong retail banking sector. It is a universal bank offering all types of financial services to both retail and corporate clients.

During the 1800s it became apparent that small farmers were finding it impossible to get credit resulting in low production and crop failures. Crédit Agricole was founded in 1894 with the creation of local banks by farm union members. These banks were mutual banks, owned by their members and provided credit facilities to revitalise the farming industry. From providing facilities to farmers, Crédit Agricole's network of branches extended their business to rural businesses, mortgages, insurance and other financial services. In 2003 Crédit Agricole took over Crédit Lyonnais, a bank established in Lyon in 1863 which grew to become at one time the largest bank in France. Crédit Lyonnais was rebranded as LCL and under this name operates nearly 2,000 branches throughout France offering a wide range of financial services.

To meet the needs of expanding industry, notably steelmaking and railways, Société Générale (SocGen) was established in 1864 as a limited company, an unusual constitution at the time. It soon established a network of branches and in 1871 opened a branch in London. Along with Crédit Lyonnais it became one of the leading banks in France, and following denationalisation, deregulation and overseas expansion has become one of the leading banks of the world. It has 2,291 branches in France, with another 938 operated by one of its subsidiaries, Crédit du Nord, a banking group of eight banks.

Groupe BPCE is the result of a 2009 merger between the Caisses d'Epargne and the Banque Populaire, two co-operative mutual banking groups with 8,000 branches between them and owned by 8.6 million shareholders. There are 17 Caisses d'Epargne with 4,219 branches and 19 Banques Populaires with 3,336 branches, all operating independently. They provide vital financial services to their localities. The two parts of the BPCE group operate under their own names and maintain their strongly co-operative ethics.

The Dexia Group was formed by the 1996 merger of Belgian and French banking operations specialising in providing local financial services. The new group was headquartered in Brussels and commenced on a series of acquisitions. Then came the crisis of 2008 followed by the sovereign debt crisis of 2010–13. It was forced to seek aid from the governments of France, Luxembourg and Belgium. It has been forced to dispose of numerous overseas and investment business, including the sale of Dexia Bank of Belgium to the Belgian government, and is now concentrating on rebuilding its business and reputation in France, Luxembourg, Belgium and the growing market in Turkey. Dexia's decline is charted in Figure 16.2.

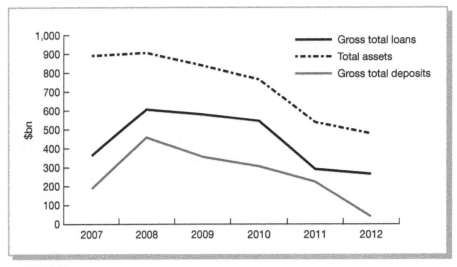

Figure 16.2   Dexia 2007–12

Source: The Banker Database

Spain

Despite the financial problems that have beset Spain, its two largest commercial banks, Santander and BBVA, have weathered the storm well; they are both well-capitalised and have geographic diversity. Some of Spain's other, mainly smaller, banks have experienced major problems due to over-reliance on property investments, and the Spanish government asked for EU financial assistance to help in restructuring its financial sector in 2012. Spain's banking system consists of commercial banks, such as Santander and BBVA, and savings banks, cajas (discussed in Chapter 12).

Banco de España, the Bank of Spain, founded in 1782 to assist with government finances, particularly for war, is the central bank and supervises the Spanish banking system. It was nationalised in 1962, then in 1994 was given independence from government with regard to monetary policy.

Banco Santander, now known worldwide as simply Santander, was founded in the important port and trading centre of Santander in 1857 by 76 businessmen to benefit both local trade and the increasing overseas trade with Latin America. It is now one of the world's largest banks, a multi-national universal bank based in Madrid. It acquired its present position by mergers and acquisitions, and brands nearly all of its subsidiaries with the Santander name. It has over 13,500 branches throughout the world, with a strong presence in eleven countries, particularly in Latin America, where it is the leading retail bank (it operates in over 40 countries).

BBVA's history also dates back to 1857 with the establishment of Banco de Bilbao. BBVA is the result of the 1999 merger between Banco de Bilbao, Banco de Vizcaya and Argentaria. All three financial groups were the result of a variety of previous mergers with Spanish and Latin American banks, nationalisations and privatisations. It has 7,978 branches in 32 countries serving 53 million customers.

Switzerland

Switzerland is renowned worldwide for the efficiency, reliability and discretion (or secrecy) of its banking system. At the time of the eighteenth and nineteenth century explosion in trade and industry, Switzerland, at the heart of Europe, was at the crossroads of important trade routes. This, combined with its strong neutrality and economic and financial stability, instilled confidence that it was a safe haven for money. In times of war, it received deposits from both sides of the conflict, and has gained a reputation, enhanced by films and books, for attracting funds from individuals keen to avoid paying taxes in their own country. Bank secrecy was enshrined in Swiss law in 1934, since when accounts have been numbered and only the bank knows the identity of the account holder. In cases of serious criminal or terrorist behaviour, this secrecy could be removed. Controversially, moves are in process worldwide to remove banking secrecy, encouraged by the USA, concerned at its losses due to tax evasion, and most countries have agreed to share bank data.

Swiss neutrality, independence and stable history played a large part in the 1930 decision to base the Bank for International Settlements (BIS) in Basel. BIS was established to assist central banks to achieve economic and financial stability and to promote international cooperation and standards; it acts as a bank for central banks – see Chapter 24 and 25.

The Swiss National Bank (SNB) is the central bank of Switzerland, responsible for its monetary policy and the issue of currency. The Swiss franc is one of the major currencies of the world and is widely regarded as one of the safest, often bought in times of crisis when other currencies might lose their value.

UBS, the initials originally stood for Union Bank of Switzerland, is the product of a 1998 merger between UBS and the Swiss Bank Corporation, both banks the result of many previous mergers and acquisitions with a history going back to 1854. This merger made it the largest bank in Switzerland. It had a strong presence in the USA and was a major player in the international investment markets, but it is currently withdrawing after failures of management. As well as offering retail and commercial banking services in Switzerland, it operates in 50 countries managing wealth, assets and investments.

Credit Suisse was established in 1856 by Alfred Escher to fund railway construction. Credit Suisse grew and expanded overseas, making a number of mergers and acquisitions. It focuses on wealth management and investment banking, but has also diversified into insurance and other financial services. It now has 46,900 employees in 50 countries.

Much retail banking in Switzerland is carried out through a number of smaller local banks, over 300 banks with 2,500 branches, and through PostFinance, the financial part of the Swiss Post Office which has 3 million customers and over CHF100bn in assets. Online banking is usually free with charges made on the use of other methods. Cheques are little used, and the favoured method of payment is by credit transfer.

The Netherlands

The Netherlands was at the heart of the development of European banking and business and its banks trace their history back to the 1700s. They have been at the forefront of modern technology and online banking is prevalent throughout the country.

ING (Internationale Nederlanden Groep) was formed through a 1991 merger between the insurance company Nationale-Nederlanden and the banking company NMB Postbank Groep when legal restrictions on mergers between insurance companies and banks were removed. ING thus became a universal bank offering all types of financial services in 50 countries. It has been busy selling off various businesses around the world so that it can repay the Dutch government for the €10bn rescue funding following the financial crisis (the EU is insisting on it selling off subsidiaries and splitting its insurance and banking arms). ING Direct in the UK was taken over in 2013 by Barclays.

Rabobank is a universal international bank operating in 47 countries and with nearly 900 branches in the Netherlands and over 700 branches overseas. It is owned by its 139 local co-operative banks, which in turn are owned by their members. Rabobank prides itself on serving local needs, but has also expanded overseas to assist in the provision of finance to agriculture globally.

ABN AMRO was taken over in 2009 by the Dutch government. It was a global bank with branches in many parts of the world and interests in many financial sectors, but doubts existed about its value. It became the target of a bidding war between Barclays and a consortium, RFS, consisting of RBS, Fortis and Santander. RFS won the battle and shared out ABN AMRO's components, but the financial crisis of 2008 caused some assets of ABN AMRO to plummet and RBS and Fortis found themselves unable to raise sufficient capital. RBS was rescued by the UK government. Fortis was taken over by the Dutch government and merged with ABN AMRO. ABN AMRO has retail, commercial and private banking divisions, and maintains its global presence.

Italy

While the names of many European banks are familiar, not many non-Italians would recognise UniCredit, Intesa Sanpaolo, Monte dei Paschi, UBI or Banco Popolare, Italy's five largest banks. After decades of public ownership of most of the banks, the 1990s saw mass privatisations. However when the banks were privatised, a substantial number of their shares were bought by charitable foundations, which used the dividends received to fund social projects as well as cultural and charitable enterprises. These banking foundations are still the largest investors in Italian banks. They are often run by local politicians, but have been accused of unsuitable or even corrupt behaviour. Eighty per cent of Italian banks are limited companies, 16% are co-operatives or mutuals with the remainder made up of foreign banks. Banks in Italy have tended to be smaller with conservative, risk-averse policies, and needed very little government assistance due to the 2008 crisis, with the exception of UniCredit, the Italian bank with most exposure overseas. Consumer credit is also small compared to many other countries.

UniCredit is a vast universal bank, the result of the 1998 merger between a number of Italian banks and the 2005 merger with HypoVereinsbank, a German banking group based in Bavaria. UniCredit's additional acquisitions of banks in Central and Eastern Europe have given it a very strong presence there consolidating its aim of being a single, large European bank, with operations in 22 countries. Some of its acquisitions have been rebranded as UniCredit but some have retained their own name, including HVB. It has nearly 4,000 branches throughout Europe.

Intesa Sanpaolo is the result of a merger between Banca Intesa and Sanpaolo IMI in 2007. It is the largest retail bank in Italy with over 5,000 branches. In Central and Eastern Europe, the Middle East and North Africa it has 1,500 branches and 8.3 million customers in retail and commercial banking.

Retail banking in Italy is largely carried out in branches, although internet banking is becoming more common. Charges are levied for everything, and opening an account can take a considerable length of time. Any credit usually requires a significant down payment.

Northern Europe

Nordea is the largest banking group in the Nordic and Baltic Sea area, offering banking in Sweden, Denmark, Finland and Norway, the Baltic states of Estonia, Latvia and Lithuania, and Poland and Russia. The name Nordea stands for Nordic Ideas. Nordbanken in Sweden, Merita Bank in Finland, Unibank in Denmark and Christiania Bank og Kreditkasse in Norway formed the Nordea Group in 2001 with headquarters in Sweden. The group now operates about 1,400 branches in its nine home countries, with a presence in Europe, the Americas and Asia.

Danske Bank, founded in 1871, is a universal bank based in Copenhagen trading mainly in Northern Europe, Northern Ireland and Ireland. It is the result of a series of mergers between Scandinavian banks. Having ventured into overseas operations in the USA, and Asia, it has decided to concentrate on Northern Europe and has closed its offices in Singapore and Hong Kong and reduced operations in its other overseas branches. The largest retail bank in Sweden is Swedbank with 4 million customers at home and another 3 million or so in the region, followed by Handelsbanken with over 460 branches in Sweden.

Russia

Russia and the countries that until 1991 were part of the USSR have emerged from a banking system that was totally state-run for the benefit of state-owned enterprises and where Gosbank, the State Bank of the USSR, was the only bank. In the 1980s other banks were established, including Sberbank (Savings Bank) to which were transferred the individual savings accounts. Sberbank, privatised in 1991, is the only surviving bank from Soviet times. It is 50% plus one share owned by the Bank of Russia, the Russian central bank. Sberbank has developed and expanded and is now a fully-fledged universal commercial bank, very similar to other such banks and the largest bank in Russia and the CIS (Commonwealth of Independent States). Over a billion Russians bank with Sberbank, which carries out all retail banking services for its customers.

17

Banking in the Americas

United States of America

Banks in the USA have complex histories, involving numerous acquisitions and take-overs, and the breaking up and joining together of various operations. At one time before the Great Depression there were some 30,000 banks in the USA. Thousands failed and many customers and shareholders lost all their money. The Banking Act of 1933 followed a 'bank holiday' of six days through which the government tried to instil calmness to allow banks to recover from the unprecedented volume of withdrawals. Some 4,000 banks never reopened after this period. The 1933 Act, often called the Glass–Steagall Act after the two congressmen who promoted it, required the establishment for depositors of a federal insurance scheme, the Federal Deposit Insurance Corporation (FDIC), the separation of commercial banking from investment banking, forbade the paying of interest on checking (current) accounts and limited the amount of interest that could be paid on other accounts.

The separation of investment from commercial banking led to the splitting up of some of the largest banks, which had to choose which path to follow, and to restrictions in the growth of US banks compared to universal banks in other countries. During the 1980s and 1990s, there was a relaxing of the restrictions placed on US banks, allowing US commercial banks to participate in investment and other financial activities, to establish branches in other states, to become universal banks again and to compete against foreign banks both at home and on the world stage.

The FDIC was established as an independent agency and guaranteed each depositor with an insured organisation up to $2,500, very quickly raised to $5,000; the figure is now $250,000. This restored confidence in banks (only nine banks failed in 1934) and since 1934 not one cent of insured funds has been lost. The FDIC is funded by premiums from financial institutions and investments, and funds stood at $33bn in 2012.

A little more history

1780 saw the first bank established in the USA, in Pennsylvania, to help finance the American War of Independence. This was followed by more local banks, state banks chartered by their local state. Many banks issued their own bank notes. There were serious difficulties in exchanging these notes, as the variety was enormous, and banks were reluctant to accept other banks' notes. Counterfeiting was prolific and substantial sums of money were made by note brokers buying bank notes at a discount and travelling to the issuing bank to redeem them – if they were genuine! The 1863 National Banking Act provided for nationally chartered banks whose bank notes were backed by US government securities. A 10% tax was introduced on state bank notes, resulting in the national bank notes becoming the national currency. With no central bank to help in times of crisis (attempts were made to set up a central bank, but there was great opposition to this from the state banks, which resented possible interference and loss of control) the USA suffered a series of bank crises, bank failures and runs on banks. On two occasions financial meltdown was averted by J. P. Morgan, a very successful financier and banker, and the founder of the current largest bank in the USA measured by assets, JPMorgan

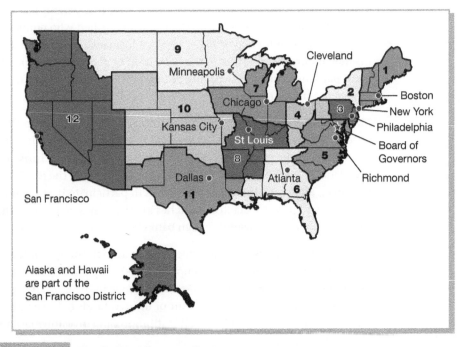

Figure 17.1   **The Federal Reserve System**

Source: The Federal Reserve, www.federalreserve.gov

Chase.[1] There was an obvious, urgent need for a central bank, which could oversee and supervise the thousands of US banks (around 20,000 in 1907).

On 23 December 1913, the Federal Reserve System (the Fed), which serves as the nation's central bank, was created by an act of Congress, which also permitted banks to open foreign branches; the first to do so was Citibank which opened a branch in Buenos Aires. The Fed consists of a seven member Board of Governors with headquarters in Washington, D.C., and 12 Reserve Banks located in major cities throughout the United States (see Figure 17.1). By establishing the regional offices, some of the state banks' opposition was overcome. The Fed System processes some 18 billion cheques (checks) per year using high-speed electronic systems, organises payment through accounts kept by banks with the Fed and acts as a clearing house for automated transactions.

US banks are chartered by a state, the federal government or by the Office of the Comptroller of the Currency. OCC is an independent bureau set up in 1863 and part of the Department of the Treasury, primarily funded by semi-annual assessments levied on banks. Since 1989 all state-chartered banks must insure with the FDIC, which currently insures and supervises for safety and soundness 7,019 institutions and supervises a further 4,415 outside the insured system. From the 1980s, a slackening of laws prohibiting banks operating in other states than their home state encouraged expansion and mergers, resulting in fewer but bigger banks. Figure 17.2 gives details of mergers since 1990. Regulatory supervision is carried out by three different authorities, the Fed, the FDIC and the OCC, so that there is no single body in overall control of financial institutions. Monetary policy is the responsibility of part of the Fed, the Federal Open Market Committee (FOMC).

The big four

The major four banks in the USA are JPMorgan Chase, Bank of America, Citigroup and Wells Fargo, closely followed by Goldman Sachs and Morgan Stanley. They all operate in the USA and overseas, with fingers in all manner of financial pies. All but Wells Fargo are considered to be 'bulge bracket' banks, a group of the leading banks in the world including Barclays, Credit Suisse, Deutsche Bank and UBS. Statistics for the US banks are shown in Figure 17.3.

While the US banks are large, profitable and promote themselves as caring, efficient and the solution to all one's financial needs, in their pursuit of ever bigger profits they have all been involved in an astonishing number of financial controversies and lawsuits. They have been accused of deception, fraud, corruption, racism, money laundering, persuading people to take on unsuitable loans and mortgages, to name but a few. After the financial crisis of 2008, brought about by

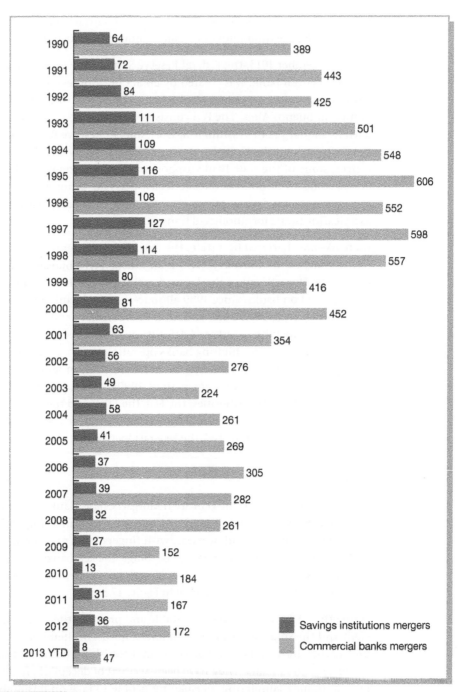

Source: The Federal Reserve, www.federalreserve.gov

Figure 17.2 Merger activity between US banks 1990–2013

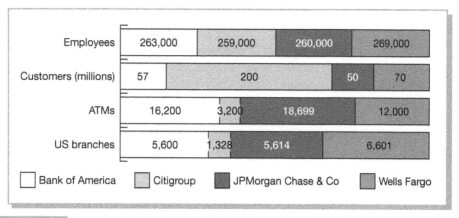

Figure 17.3   **US big four bank statistics**
Source: Bank reports and websites, 2013

the selling of overpriced mortgages to residents who could not afford the high-interest rate repayments, all these banks received government funding to ensure their survival. The size and complexity of large banks has led to serious concern worldwide that they are, or will be, too big to fail.

The insider's view   Ben S. Bernanke

'A too-big-to-fail firm is one whose size, complexity, interconnectedness, and critical functions are such that, should the firm go unexpectedly into liquidation, the rest of the financial system and the economy would face severe adverse consequences. Governments provide support to too-big-to-fail firms in a crisis not out of favouritism or particular concern for the management, owners, or creditors of the firm, but because they recognize that the consequences for the broader economy of allowing a disorderly failure greatly outweigh the costs of avoiding the failure in some way. ... avoiding failure include[s] facilitating a merger, providing credit, or injecting government capital, all of which protect at least some creditors who otherwise would have suffered losses.

In the midst of the crisis, providing support to a too-big-to-fail firm usually represents the best of bad alternatives; without such support there could be substantial damage to the economy.

Source: Chairman of the Board of Governors of the Federal Reserve System, 2 September 2010.

Canada

Canada is in the enviable position of having the soundest banks in the world due to tighter regulation and a natural resources led economic boom, according to the World Economic Forum, which has placed Canada at number one for the past five years – see Table 17.1 for the 2012 figures. The results need to be interpreted with care given that a serious crisis in US or UK banking could easily threaten world stability, whereas a similar crisis in say Malta or Panama would be unfortunate but not world-threatening. Notwithstanding this ringing endorsement, Canada's banks received bailouts totalling $114bn from their own central bank, the Bank of Canada, the Canada Mortgage and Housing Corporation (CMHC) and the US Fed in 2008–10. Canada's government argues that this was not a true bailout, it was a liquidity problem, not a solvency problem, but it all happened very quietly – perhaps a question of semantics.

Table 17.1   **2012 World Economic Forum Global Competitiveness Survey**

	Bank Soundness Survey				Bank Soundness Survey	
	Country	Value out of 7			Country	Value out of 7
1	Canada	6.79556774		14	Brazil	6.20517387
2	South Africa	6.66075928		15	Mauritius	6.15520426
3	New Zealand	6.64827473		16	Saudi Arabia	6.12946268
4	Panama	6.61547747		17	Israel	6.11925372
5	Australia	6.53855997		18	Luxembourg	6.07803599
6	Finland	6.50667913		19	Sweden	6.05135321
7	Hong Kong	6.50308054		20	Peru	6.02972369
8	Singapore	6.48704420		26	Switzerland	5.93924080
9	Norway	6.41151334		54	France	5.44991186
10	Barbados	6.37762737		63	Japan	5.35390223
11	Chile	6.35292999		75	Germany	5.05010005
12	Lebanon	6.24297171		80	United States	4.98145979
13	Malta	6.23094571		97	United Kingdom	4.62483138

Source: World Economic Forum

According to the Canadian Bankers Association (CBA), there are 70 banks in Canada with 6,205 branches, of which just over 2,000 are based in small towns and the countryside. The country's largest bank by assets is the Royal Bank of Canada (RBC). Founded in 1864 in Halifax, Nova Scotia as the Merchants Bank of Halifax, it adopted its current name in 1901 and eventually became not only

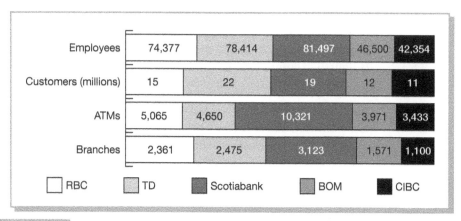

Figure 17.4　**Canadian five bank statistics**
Source: Bank reports and websites

the largest bank, but also the largest company, in Canada. It is a universal bank, offering all types of financial services to its 15 million clients at home and overseas. Initially its main area of expansion was South and Central America and the Caribbean, where it became influential. However, as countries in these areas developed, RBC's influence decreased and some of its branches were nationalised. In 2011 RBC sold its US RBC branches to PNC Financial Services Group, an up-and-coming US financial services conglomerate. RBC no longer has any US branches, but it offers banking to Canadian citizens in the USA via the internet, telephone banking and PNC's network of ATMs.

The other large Canadian banks are Toronto-Dominion Bank (TD Bank Group) founded in 1855, Scotiabank (Bank of Nova Scotia) founded in 1832, Bank of Montreal (BOM) founded in 1817 and Canadian Imperial Bank of Commerce (CIBC) founded in 1867 – see Figure 17.4. TD Group and BOM focus most of their operations in North America, while Scotiabank and CIBC also maintain a strong presence in the Caribbean. Canadian banks are very keen to promote cross-border banking, to make it easier for US and Canadian citizens to travel and shop in either country. In contrast to the USA, many banking services are free in Canada.

South America and the Caribbean

Brazil is a member of the BRICS group of emerging economies set to develop strongly and increasingly influence the world economy, Brazil, Russia, India, China and South Africa. According to the IMF, there are about 1,600 deposit-taking institutions in Brazil, of which 160 are banks. The majority are privately-owned, nine are state-owned and there are some foreign-owned or foreign-controlled. Brazil's banks are rated fourteenth on the WEF table for soundness. The Brazilian banking system is very profitable, has a strong capital base, and its limited exposure to cross-border funding and foreign-exchange risks made it less susceptible to the crisis of 2008 – see Figure 17.5 for the largest banks.

The central bank is Banco Central do Brasil (BCB) which was created in 1964. It is part of the National Financial System (SFN), supervises banking and sets monetary policy through its Monetary Policy Committee (COPOM).

Banco do Brasil and Caixa Econômica Federal are both state-owned banks. Banco do Brasil was founded in 1808 and is one of the oldest banks in the world. At one time, between 1821 and 1964, it acted as the country's central bank, issuing currency as well as being a commercial bank. Although it is controlled by the government, its shares trade on the São Paulo stock exchange. Caixa Econômica Federal was founded in 1861. Both banks have their headquarters in the national capital, Brasilia.

Itaú Unibanco Holding, the result of a 2008 merger between two large Brazilian banks, Itaú and Unibanco, and Banco Bradesco are large, private universal banks. Itaú Unibanco is the largest universal bank in Latin America. Both banks have thousands of branches and offices throughout this area and the rest of the world.

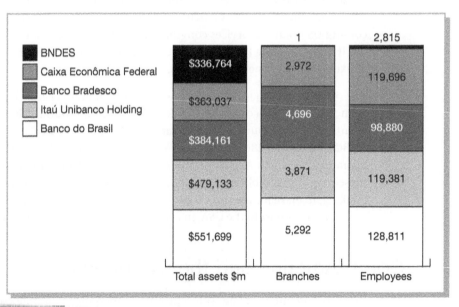

Figure 17.5 Statistics for the five largest Brazilian banks

Source: Banco Central do Brasil, www.bcb.gov.br

The Banco Nacional de Desenvolvimento Econômico e Social (BNDES), the National Bank for Economic and Social Development, is a development bank with supervisory duties. It and the other development banks, which are all state-controlled, play a large part in supplying the funding for public projects and its funds are lent on for private projects by the other four big banks.

Until 1997 foreign banks were not allowed to operate in Brazil. Since this restriction was lifted the major world banks have expanded into Brazil, among them HSBC, Santander, Citibank, JPMorgan Chase, Credit Suisse and Deutsche Bank, all of them now rated in the top 50 banks in Brazil. This is the picture throughout South America, Central America and the Caribbean; some local banks have expanded and thrived, but the big universal banks have gained footholds and are ever increasing their influence.

In Argentina the largest bank is the state-owned Banco de la Nación Argentina, but in world terms this is a small bank with assets of $37,534m. The Argentinean financial crisis of 2002 led foreign banks to leave the country, but they have since returned to some degree.

Apart from Brazil, Mexico has the largest banking sector in this area, with a thriving financial market. In 1997 it allowed foreign banks to acquire Mexican banks and set up their own banks, which they did with gusto. In 1991 only 1% of Mexico's banks were owned by foreigners; in 2013 that figure is a remarkable 74%. As might be expected from such a close neighbour of the USA, Mexico was drawn into the sub-prime mortgage crisis of 2008. However the soundness of its banking system has enabled it to make a good recovery, but there must be some concern due to the predominance of foreign ownership of its banks. Out of the eight largest banks in Mexico only two, Grupo Financiero Banorte and Banco Inbursa, are Mexican, the rest are part of global conglomerates BBVA (Spain), Citigroup (US), Santander (Spain), HSBC (UK), Scotiabank (Canada) and Deutsche Bank (Germany). Spain's influence in Mexico is extensive.

Grupo Financiero Banorte has roots dating back to 1899. It was nationalised, along with all Mexican banks, in 1982, and, when they were all reprivatised in 1991–92, was bought from the government in 1992 by a group of wealthy investors. It is now a prosperous universal bank. Banco Inbursa is a universal bank offering all types of financial services. It is 71% owned by one man, the Mexican billionaire, Carlos Slim, who according to Forbes is the richest man in the world.

18

Banking in Asia and Australasia

Over the past three decades the sophistication and size of the financial systems of Asia and Australasia have grown tremendously. From almost a standing start, now 31 of the world's largest 100 banks are from this region; with China alone having 13 in the top 100, and one-fifth in the top 20. In many cases the sector is dominated by state-controlled banks, which has led to some fairly inefficient lending as money is allocated based on political judgements of the economic need, or simply political need. However, there is a gradual movement toward more commercial banking.

China

While China's banks are increasingly behaving more like western banks it has to be said that they remain largely in the control of the Communist party. The largest four banks listed in Figure 18.1 are majority state-owned (57–83% of the shares), but under a 1995 law they are supposed to act in a commercial fashion. At times they are less commercial than obedient to the Party's bidding (board directors are generally appointed by central government). They lend mostly to state-owned enterprises for example, many of which are loss making. While the State owns the majority of the shares they are listed on the Hong Kong, Shanghai and Shenzhen stock exchanges for the minority shareholders to trade. The fifth bank, making up the so-called 'big five', Bank of Communications, used to be wholly state-owned but now the government holds only a minority of the shares.

Three major banks remain wholly state-owned:

- Agricultural Development Bank of China – serving rural customers, including village enterprises:

- China Development Bank – traditionally for large infrastructure projects, but has begun to diversify in its transition into a commercial bank;

- Export-Import Bank of China (Exim) – financial services to promote exports, particularly of high-tech products, and facilitate the import of technology.

As well as the big state-controlled commercial banks there are dozens of smaller commercial banks, and some of the largest are shown in Figure 18.1. 'City commercial banks', e.g. Shanghai Pudong Development Bank, emerged from urban credit co-operatives in the 1990s. The local authority/state is usually the largest shareholder but other Chinese banks, corporations, foreign banks, employees and private investors may also hold shares. They tend to focus on financing local projects and infrastructure, but are increasingly willing to lend to businesses in other regions. There are more than 140 city commercial banks and over 3,000 small credit co-operatives and rural financial institutions.

There are a handful of 'private' commercial banks, e.g. China Minsheng, with the majority of the shares owned by non-governmental entities. Even here the senior officers are members of the Communist Party.

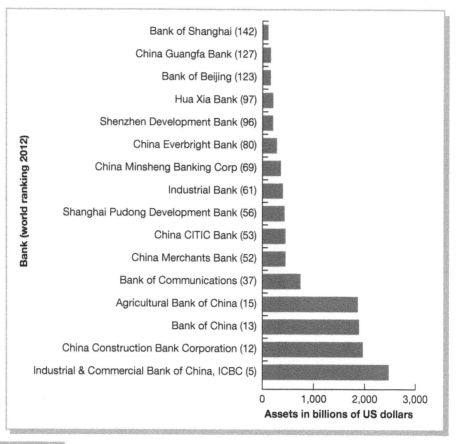

Figure 18.1 The top Chinese banks, ranked by assets

Source: The Banker Database

China's banks are more traditional in the sense of focusing on intermediation between depositors and borrowers with very little of the money they use coming from the debt markets and investment banking activities are constrained. Foreign banks have not made much progress, but they are trying hard, with a presence in hundreds of locations.

'Underground banks' operate illegally, but are nevertheless increasingly significant. For example a fund manager may set up an investment fund that looks and feels much like a bank, with money deposited and commercial and personal loans made. Higher returns are available as well as concealment from government and the offer of a loan that would not be available through legal banks (at a high interest rate). In some areas most businesses and households have loans with them. The authorities are very concerned about these 'shadow banks' with their potential to cause bubbles in property and other assets, wreaking havoc when they burst (see Chapter 26).

The People's Bank of China is the central bank. It is on the path to reforming the Chinese financial system, but the legal segment remains very tightly controlled and subject to political influence, with accumulating non-performing loans. The illegal segment is out of the authorities' control and very big relative to the size of the economy. On top of that local authorities have encouraged vast amounts of borrowing by organisations they control engaged in infrastructure, welfare and other projects financed by the banks they control – an accident waiting to happen?

Australia and New Zealand

For a country of only 23 million people Australia has a banking sector that punches above its weight, with four of the world's leading banks, assisted by a stable English-speaking infrastructure (e.g. legal, accounting) and a resource-blessed economy. These four (see Figure 18.2) dominate a sophisticated system which, while being reasonably competitive, is not one that policymakers want further concentrated.

The building society, mutual bank and credit union sectors are strong, but even the largest are tiddlers alongside the big four. Foreign banks were virtually barred from Australia until the 1980s, but a gradual opening up has permitted dozens of subsidiaries: however, only a handful, e.g. HSBC and Citibank, have fully fledged retail operations. Overseas banks tend to focus more on investment banking.

New Zealand has five commercial banks (ANZ, ASB, Bank of New Zealand, Kiwibank and Westpac) and a trustee savings bank (a mutual).

The central banks are the Reserve Bank of Australia and the Reserve Bank of New Zealand.

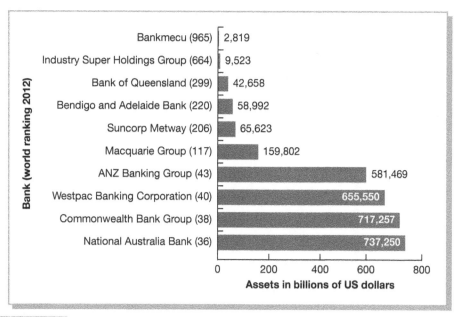

Figure 18.2 The top Australian/New Zealand banks, ranked by assets
Source: The Banker Database

Taiwan, South Korea and Hong Kong

Taiwan has a lot of relatively small banks in a crowded market which leads to intense competition and insufficient economies of scale, leading to none being ranked in the world top 100. Approximately one-half of bank assets are with state-owned banks such as the Bank of Taiwan – see Figure 18.3. Land Bank of Taiwan is another wholly state-owned bank; it is designated as a specialised bank for handling real estate and agricultural credit. The oddly named Taiwan Cooperative Bank is actually a stockmarket listed bank, as is Mega International Commercial Bank. The First Commercial Bank is a subsidiary of First Financial Group, which is listed. Large overseas competitors, such as Standard Chartered and Citigroup have bought Taiwanese banks, helping to consolidate the sector. The central bank is the Central Bank of the Republic of China (Taiwan).

South Korea has some reasonably large banks, but none has the scale to compete with the might of the US and European global players in other countries. The centralising government of the 1960s nationalised all banks, then denationalised in the 1980s, but the government still maintained a high level of control over their management. Most of the loans granted went to the industrial conglomerates,

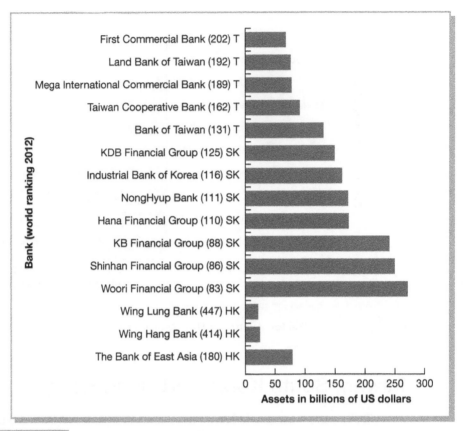

Figure 18.3   The top banks in Taiwan, South Korea and Hong Kong, ranked by assets

Source: The Banker Database

called **chaebol**, which led to much poor lending and corruption. All were privatised by 1997, but the financial crisis of that year wiped out their value. IMF-directed reforms led to a sharp increase in foreign ownership of Korean banks and the entry of foreign banks' subsidiaries and branches.

Between 1998 and 2000 eight major banks were nationalised (owning over one-half of bank assets) and many others went bust. The authorities thought Korea over-banked and so insisted on mergers designed to create 'mega' universal banks: Woori was the result of merging four large banks. It is stockmarket listed, but the government still owns 57% of the shares, which it hopes to sell. The welcome for foreigners has been so great that few banks are domestically owned. The majority of the shares in KB (Kookmin), Shinhan and Hana (KEB), for example, are owned by foreigners. The Bank of Korea is the central bank.

Hong Kong can lay claim to being the original home of one of the biggest banks in the world, HSBC, originally Hong Kong and Shanghai Bank. Despite HSBC shares being listed on the Hong Stock Exchange, because it is so international and its head office is now London it does not register in the statistics for Hong Kong. This small but economically open enclave is home to many other global titans because of its status as an international financial centre; 70 of the world's 100 largest banks have operations in Hong Kong.

The financial markets operate with a high degree of liquidity and under effective and transparent regulations which meet international standards, with a strong emphasis on the rule of law and fair markets. There are no barriers of access to the market by foreign businesses and no restrictions on capital flows into and out of Hong Kong resulting in strong international money, bonds, equities, derivatives and foreign exchange markets. The Hong Kong Monetary Authority is the central bank.

Japan

Japan is home to some of the largest banks in the world – see Figure 18.4. It has a dozen, major, internationally-oriented banks and more than 100 regional banks. Japan Postal Bank has a major banking presence through 24,000 post offices. In the early 1990s the five largest banks in the world were Japanese as they rapidly expanded abroad, particularly into wholesale and investment banking. They had been buoyed by a land and sharemarket bubble back home. However the subsequent long period of economic stagnation and resulting accumulation of bad debt at home, overseas financial crises and poor management of acquisitions means that they have to a large extent drawn back from foreign adventures and are now much less prominent around the globe.

Tokyo remains one of the top ten financial centres, with over 50 foreign banks, operating mainly wholesale and investment banking. But many of the international universal banks are reducing their presence there, partly in response to the 2008 financial crisis (pulling back to the home country) and partly due to the lack of dynamism in the Japanese economy and slowdown in financial deals. More open and less difficult Singapore and Hong Kong are taking Tokyo's crown as the regional centre. The Bank of Japan is the central bank.

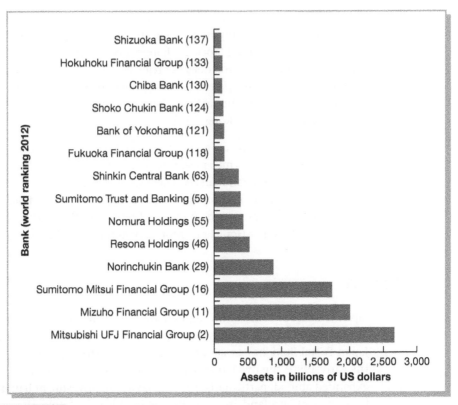

Figure 18.4   The top Japanese banks, ranked by assets

Source: The Banker Database

South Asia

The Indian banking system has long been dominated by lumbering and undercapitalised state-owned banks, previously accounting for 90% of assets and branches, and now four-fifths of the same. There are 26 nationalised 'public sector banks', the majority owned by the government (minimum 51% of the shares). For example, the State Bank, Canara, the Punjab National, the Bank of Baroda and the Bank of India are listed on the Indian Stock Market but are mostly state-owned – see Figure 18.5. There are also over 80 state-controlled 'regional rural banks' which provide low-cost loans to rural people.

Since 1990 barriers to entry have been lowered and new banks have emerged, e.g. ICICI and HDFC are private banks. Also foreign banks such as Standard Chartered, Citibank and HSBC expanded with subsidiaries and branches across India, in spite of heavy-handed restrictions. They mainly cater to investors, businesses and

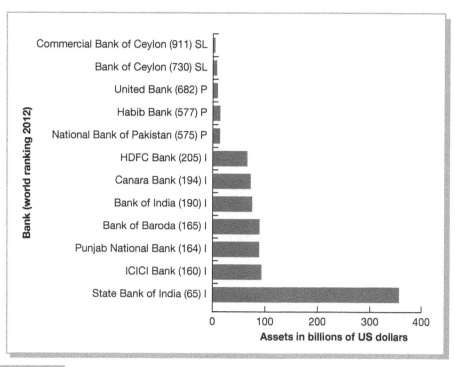

Figure 18.5   The top banks in Sri Lanka, Pakistan and India, ranked by assets

Source: The Banker Database

wealthy consumers in the cities. The private and foreign banks brought new technology and competitive vigour, forcing the state banks to improve their offer. It
was said that India's banks were used to the 4–6–4 method (borrow at 4%; lend at
6%; go home at 4). Even the mighty State Bank of India, the largest commercial
bank with 18,000 branches (60% owned by the government but traded on the
stock market) had to up its game considerably to avoid being overtaken by ICICI
and other private banks in the 2000s.

Private Indian banks now control about 16% and foreign banks 5% of bank
assets. The central bank, the Reserve Bank of India (RBI), is permitting foreign
ownership of a greater percentage of the shares of Indian's private banks (26%
of votes), but this remains a country far from being completely open and fully
commercial. For example, given that 40% of the population do not have access
to even basic banking RBI insists that one-quarter of new branches be opened in
rural areas. Also branches each need a licence and banks are required to direct
much of their lending to particular sectors such as agriculture. There are also
over 80 co-operatives lending to small borrowers and businesses. For reference

when examining India: the lakh unit is equal to 100,000 rupees and the crore unit is equal to 10,000,000 rupees.

During the period 1971–90 the Pakistani banking system came under state control – all were nationalised, resulting in poor service and corruption. A handful of banks are still state owned, e.g. the National Bank of Pakistan. But since 1990 there have been moves towards encouraging conventional market-based systems of financial intermediation, including privately owned banks, e.g. Habib and United. Because the majority of banks are of this type, professionalism and service are now much more to the fore. There are also six Islamic Banks, accounting for about 6% of assets, obedient to Shariah law in their conduct, including interest-free lending – see Chapter 19. Microfinance organisations also have an impact at the smallest scale with people below the poverty line. There are merely seven foreign banks, with Standard Chartered particularly prominent. The State Bank of Pakistan is the central bank.

In Sri Lanka there are about 16 local banks, a dozen foreign banks and three savings banks. The sector is dominated by the public-sector banks with about one-half of assets. It is a relatively concentrated market with the six largest banks accounting for two-thirds of assets. Foreign banks are relatively small at about one-eighth of assets.

Bangladesh's banks are so small that the biggest is ranked 868 in the world by assets. Commercial banks dominate the system, but state, Islamic and foreign banks and micro-finance organisations (e.g. Grameen) are also present.

South East Asia

Singapore is one of the five most advanced financial centres in the world. It provides a base for all the global banks (over 100), but has relatively small home-grown banks (six of them) – not surprising given a population of only 5 million. Its attractions as a financial centre serving the world include liberation from government interference, strong rule of law, political/economic stability, low tax, and concentration of skills including accounting and legal. The Monetary Authority of Singapore is the central banking and financial regulator.

In Malaysia a conventional banking system sits alongside a number of Islamic banks. It also has almost as many foreign-controlled banks as Malaysian-controlled banks. Islamic banks account for approximately one-fifth of domestic banking, and the country is an international hub for this fast-growing area. The three Malaysian banks in Figure 18.6 each have both conventional arms and Islamic arms. Bank Negara Malaysia is the central bank of Malaysia.

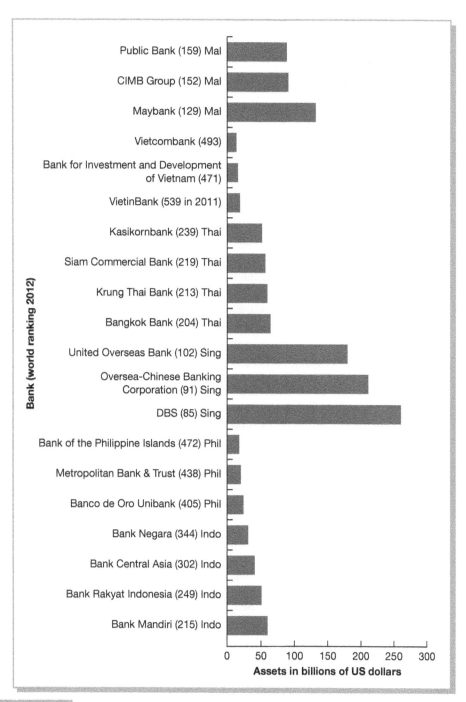

Figure 18.6   The top banks in South East Asia, ranked by assets

Source: The Banker Database

There are over 100 commercial banks in Indonesia, mostly private (e.g. Bank Central Asia), but four are state owned, Bank Negara, Bank Mandiri, Bank Rakyat Indonesia and PT Bank Tabungan Negara (Persero). There are also 26 government regional banks. The 30 dominating public sector banks (the top three have one-third of the assets) are regarded as inefficient, holding back the financial system and economic development. There are a handful of purely Islamic commercial banks but most of the other banks also have Islamic banking units. A dozen or so foreign banks are allowed to operate, but are faced with onerous regulation. Bank Indonesia is the central bank.

The 1997–98 Asian financial crisis and poor lending practices led to a legacy of non-performing loans, inadequate capital and government share stakes in Thai banks. The government's Financial Sector Reform Master Plan, introduced in 2004 and revamped in 2013, provides tax breaks for banks that merge and encouragement for new entrants to promote economies of scale and scope and greater competition. Nevertheless the government still controls large equity stakes in some leading banks. Publically listed banks are Kasikorn, Bangkok, Krung Thai (with a majority of shares owned by government) and Siam. About 15 global banks also operate in Thailand, mostly with just one branch due to restrictions, although they can now apply to open up to 20: these are mostly wholesale operations. The Bank of Thailand is the central bank.

The Philippines currently has 19 universal banks and a similar number of commercial banks, but there is central bank encouragement toward mergers to strengthen the sector in terms of capital, scale and managerial ability. It also has hundreds of mutuals, including rural and co-operative banks focused on providing people such as farmers and merchants in rural communities with deposit, loan and payment facilities. Banco de Oro Unibank, Metropolitan and Bank of the Philippine Islands are privately owned banks, but there are large government-owned players, e.g. Development Bank of the Philippines (economic development focused) and Land Bank of the Philippines (countryside development). About 15 foreign banks have taken the plunge to compete with the locals; it is one of a few countries where foreign banks can take a majority of the shares in a domestic bank. The Bangko Sentral ng Pilipinas (BSP) is the central bank.

Vietnam has moved toward a more market-oriented economy since 1992. It now has a mixture of state-owned, shareholder-owned and foreign banks (with irritating restrictions), but the dominant forces are state-owned commercial banks such as Vietcombank, Bank for Investment and Development and VietinBank which are expected to provide loans to state-owned corporations as well as act as conventional banks. The Bank of Vietnam is the central bank.

19

Banking in the Middle East and Africa

This region of the world contains a high proportion of young and relatively small banks. However, the potential for future growth is enormous coming from both the oil-fuelled modernistic sophistication of the Gulf States as they reach out around the world to the rapidly growing and newly-banked middle classes of Africa hungry for accounts, loans and payment services.

Islamic banking

Islamic banking has had its greatest impact in this part of the world and so we start with a description of that. Under Islamic Sharia (*šarì ah*) law the payment of riba[1] (interest) is prohibited and the receiver of finance must not bear all the risk of failure. Also investment in alcohol, tobacco, pornography or gambling is not allowed. However, Islam does encourage entrepreneurial activity and the sharing of risk through equity shares. Thus a bank can create profit-sharing products to offer customers. 'Depositors' can be offered a percentage of the bank's profits rather than a set interest rate. 'Borrowers' repay the bank an amount that is related to the profit produced by the project for which the loan was made.

Examples   **Profit-sharing products**

Musharakah. A joint enterprise is established by the bank and borrower. Both contribute capital plus management and labour (although some parties, e.g. banks, contribute little other than capital). Profit or loss is shared in pre-agreed proportions – there is a prohibition against a fixed lump sum for any party. All partners have unlimited liability. The share of the financier is divided into a number of units and the client purchases the units one by one periodically, thus increasing his own share until all the units are purchased to make him the sole owner of the property, or the

▶

commercial enterprise, as the case may be. Thus for a house purchase the property is purchased by the bank with clients contributing perhaps 10% of the purchase price. The customer purchases the bank's share gradually, until he is made sole owner after a specified period, usually 25 years. Over the financing period, the bank's share is rented to the customer; the rent can be varied to allow for a floating rate (which may, in some countries, be linked to bank base rate).

Ijara (leasing). Example: a house (or aircraft, say) is bought by the bank and rented to the 'mortgage holder'. The house title may or may not be transferred when the contract ends.

Murabaha. Example: a bank buys a house (car, or other property) and sells it to the customer at a fixed price – more than the bank paid – permitting the customer to pay in monthly instalments (or a lump sum). When the final instalment is paid the house is transferred to the customer.

From its inception in 1975, when the Islamic Development Bank and the Dubai Islamic Bank (the first commercial Islamic bank) were established to operate in strict accordance with Sharia law, Islamic banking has made significant progress worldwide, and it is estimated that there is over $1,500bn of Islamic finance (about 1% of world bank assets), mostly from banks, but also some Islamic bonds. Growth has been driven by the rising consciousness of Islamic principles over the past 40 years and the rising wealth of Muslim oil states. Over 600 banks and financial institutions offer services according to Sharia law. They are most heavily concentrated in the Arabian Gulf countries, Malaysia, Pakistan and Iran. But many conventional banks also offer Sharia products, e.g. HSBC and Lloyds have Islamic loans available. What is regarded as Sharia compliant in one part of the world may not be considered by Islamic scholars to be acceptable in another. Malaysia, for example, tends to be more liberal than Saudi Arabia. The UK has introduced tax,[2] legislative and regulatory changes to encourage Islamic financial services in the City and around the country at the retail level. This has been successful, attracting over $30bn of funds to London, making it one of the top ten centres. The London Shard building was partly financed with Sharia-compliant funds.

Remarkably, Islamic banking has been slow to establish in North Africa compared with other Muslim countries, but it is growing rapidly following the 'Arab Spring' of 2011–12. It is not only the African countries with Muslims in the majority that have adopted Islamic banking, e.g. South Africa, with 2–3% of its population Muslim has Sharia-compliant accounts and facilities.

The Middle East

Figure 19.1 shows the Middle Eastern banks featuring in the world top 500 by assets. Iran is the country with the most significant Islamic finance activity. By some estimates it has over one-third of all Islamic finance assets and the largest Islamic banks in the world. All banking has to be interest-free and the system is dominated by the State and its controlled banks. Even the 19 private banks suffer state-interference because most are at least part owned by companies affiliated to those with political backing or state-run organisations, such as the Revolutionary Guards. There is very little investment banking-type activity. It is thought that international sanctions, cronyism, undercapitalisation, poor regulation and general inefficiency have so damaged the banks that many are technically insolvent.

The six-member Gulf Cooperation Council (GCC) area is quite mixed. While Dubai suffered greatly from the property bust after the global financial crisis, with its banks needing to be rescued by the State, and banks in Kuwait and Bahrain came close to failing (also linked to over-exuberant property lending), banks in Oman, Qatar and the rest of the UAE were built on firm foundations. It helps that they get backing from wealthy states (particularly Abu Dhabi and Qatar) as well as a more cautious approach to lending for speculative ventures. Kuwait, with its vast oil wealth, now has a strong banking sector with very high capital adequacy ratios and high liquidity.

In the region generally, while most or all banks provide Sharia-compliant products, and some banks provide only these products, conventional banking seems to be offered side-by-side with Islamic banking, usually by the same bank. Both Kuwait and Bahrain have a particularly high ratio of Islamic banking activity. Bahrain has both a vibrant retail banking sector and wholesale sector providing off-shore wholesale and investment banking services to the whole region. In Kuwait the banking sector is highly concentrated with a high proportion of assets in just two banks. This is similar to Oman where the big two, Bank Muscat and the National Bank of Oman, have half the market, and Qatar where Qatar National Bank, Commercial Bank of Qatar, and Doha Bank have 70%. The presence of foreign banks in the region is generally limited by laws prohibiting controlling shareholdings.

Islamic banking has become an important aspect of the Saudi banking industry. Large proportions of the shares of leading banks are in the hands of the State despite being listed on stock exchanges. The three largest, National Commercial Bank, Samba Financial Group, and Al Rajhi Bank, have roughly half the banking market. Saudi's banks remain among the most profitable and well-capitalised in the region. The financial regulator, Saudi Arabian Monetary Agency (SAMA), is

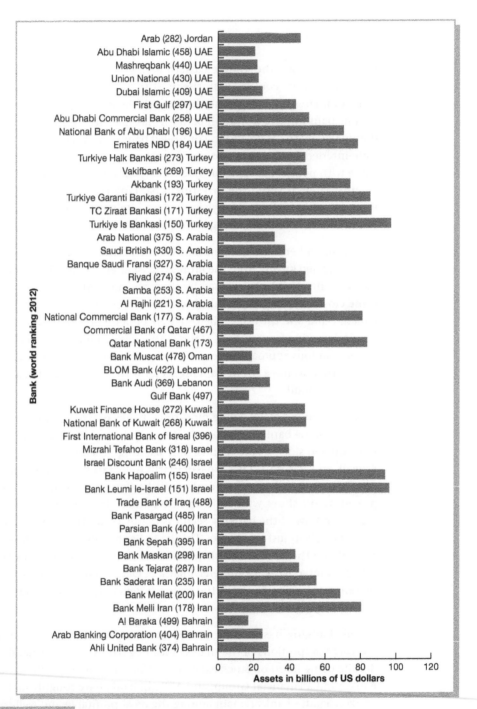

Figure 19.1   The top Middle Eastern banks, ranked by assets

Source: The Banker Database

gradually liberalising the sector and has licensed a number of other GCC banks and foreign banks to establish their presence in the Saudi market.

Before 1980 Turkey was a highly controlled economy. Following a crisis it deregulated and liberalised financial markets which increased the number of banks operating in the market, partly through the establishment of new banks, and partly through the arrival of foreign banks. Turkey is very open to overseas banks buying up Turkish banks, and attracted by the recent fast economic growth foreigners have been buying a lot, as well as establishing their own branches. The banking sector is mostly private sector commercial banks operating as universal banks. Many of the private banks are owned by wealthy families and/or industrial groups. While the private banks are strong, the three state-owned banks still have about one-third of the nation's branches and assets. Interest-free (Sharia-compliant) banking is only now being established in Turkey, a secular republic.

Israel has a very concentrated banking system with the largest two banks controlling about 60% of assets, and the five largest 95%. There are merely four foreign banks. A crisis in the 1980s led to the nationalisation of most banks. Since then shares in the banks have been sold and the banks floated on the Israeli Stock Exchange but the State usually continues to hold a substantial stake. In 2005 banks were forced to divest most non-banking activities, such as insurance and pensions services. The banks focus on traditional domestic banking business, with relatively little overseas activity. Thus there is a reliance on deposit funding and a lack of complex asset and securitised markets. There is strong and intrusive bank supervision by the Bank of Israel.

Lebanon has a relatively large banking sector because this economically-free, competitive and open country offers itself as a financial service centre to the world. There are virtually no restrictions on foreign exchange or capital movement into or out of the country. Lebanon's banking system is regarded as safe and strong with good liquidity and capital buffers. Depositors provide most of their funds, with much coming from the Lebanese diaspora.

Jordan's banks are regarded as sound with a cautious approach, e.g. loan to deposit ratios are low. Their main source of funding is deposits and they have high liquidity and capital buffers. Jordan's largest bank, the stockmarket-listed Arab Bank, dominates the banking system, accounting for one-quarter of the total banking assets. It is the most international of the banks in the Arab world with operations in 30 countries, mostly in Europe, the Middle East and North Africa. Jordan would like to become a hub for Islamic banking, but this sector still only accounts for 6% of banking assets.

Africa

All the African banks in the world top 1,000 are shown in Figure 19.2. Clearly the banking system is underdeveloped compared with other continents. The only significant advanced financial centre on the continent is in South Africa. Nigeria has many banks, but none in the top 400. Morocco and Egypt are the relatively large players in the African context north of the Sahara.

The recent fast economic growth and the potential of both a rapidly expanding middle class, mineral wealth and increasingly competitive manufacturing and agriculture has raised expectations of a flourishing of banking over the next two decades. In preparation many banks are opening branches at a rapid rate. There remains much untapped potential; vast swathes of the continent remain unbanked, e.g. Senegal and Tanzania have very few branches. In Africa only about one-quarter of adults have accounts at financial institutions, and only 3% have credit cards. However, in South Africa over 50% have bank accounts and in Mauritius it is 80%, so the potential for catch-up is plain.

The financial crises in Europe, Japan and in America have caused many of the global players to pull in their horns, leaving local African banks with the opportunity to expand into other African countries. The South African banks, in particular, have the skills, knowledge and scale of operation to confidently expand across the continent. Standard and FirstRand are growing their retail offering outside of South Africa significantly. Absa, another of South Africa's 'big four', is expanding across Africa, but is not shown in Figure 19.2 because it is a subsidiary of Barclays. The Kenyan banks (Kenya Commercial Bank (KCB), Equity Bank, Cooperative Bank, NIC Bank, Diamond Trust Bank (DTB), and Fina Bank) have crossed the border into the larger East and Central African region. Nigeria's banks continue their spread across West Africa.

The Ecobank Group has the largest branch network of any bank in sub-Saharan Africa, with a presence in 33 countries and 1,251 branches across the continent. It grew by acquisition and organically. The acquisition of Oceanic bank in Nigeria makes it one of the top five banks in the country. Following the acquisition of Trust Bank, it is now the largest bank in Ghana. It started in West Africa and then moved to Central Africa, then Eastern Africa and now into Southern Africa. Although headquartered in Togo, it does not belong to any one country.

The Moroccan banks Attijariwafa and Banque Centrale Populaire, already operating in a number of other African countries are currently on a path of rapid expansion into the rest of the African continent. Tunisia is going through a period of transition after the 2011 overthrow of the ruling family. However, for now the

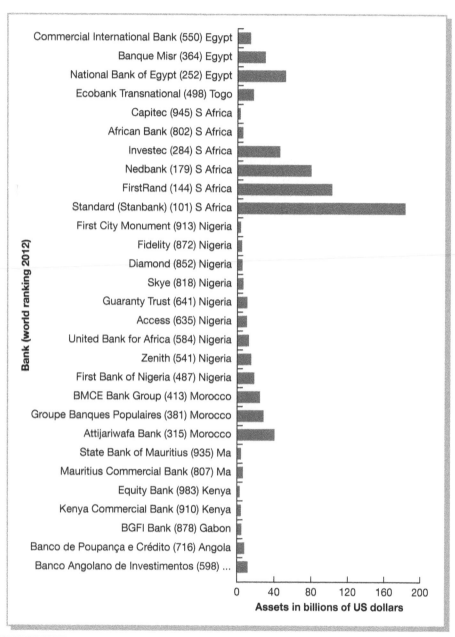

Figure 19.2   **The top African banks, ranked by assets**

Source: The Banker Database

highest proportion of lending is linked to the government and the dominant banks are state-owned and stodgy.

Africa boasts a remarkable breakthrough of technological adoption: Safaricom of Kenya pioneered banking by mobile phone. Now Africa has 500 million mobile phone users and in Kenya alone there are 19 million or so M-bank subscribers (see Chapter 4). Now many African mobile companies, often in partnership with banks, offer this service.

Where the international giants, such as Citi, still triumph is in areas of investment banking such as helping governments raise funds through bond issues on international markets, offering large-scale corporate sophisticated services. Standard Chartered has the benefit of both long-term experience in retail and corporate banking on the ground through branch networks in many African countries (it operates in 17 countries) and access to global capital markets should an African corporate grow to such a size.

Despite Egypt having a relatively old and large banking system, still only one in ten adults has a bank account. In the nineties, as part of Egypt's economic and financial reform programme, the banking sector was liberalised, including privatisation of many banks. This openness has recently led to a number of Egyptian banks being taken over by banks from the Gulf and elsewhere and the number has almost halved to 39. The sector is still dominated by three major state-owned banks, National Bank of Egypt, Banque Misr and Banque du Caire. Following the 2011 overthrow of Mubarak the banking sector suffered high delinquencies, a flight of foreign capital and a miserly attitude toward lending to small and medium-sized businesses while favouring large borrowers, in a fit of risk aversion. It was not as though in normal times the flow of funds through the banking system to the small borrowers was healthy; the loan-to-deposit ratio of the typical Egyptian bank is not only below the world average but is significantly less than for banks in the region. This inefficiency has prompted the growth of a large shadow banking system, an unregulated hidden flow of money from savers to borrowers. Sharia-compliant banking accounts form only about 3–4% of assets. The proportion is even less in much of the rest of North Africa.

part 3

Instruments and markets

20

Debt markets

Banks are dominant participants in the debt markets. Not only do they borrow money from there but they place surplus cash in debt instruments to earn a return every day. They also act as brokers for clients wishing to buy and sell debt securities, and deal as market makers providing a place for others to conduct trades. They engage in proprietary trading to try to make a return from price movements of debt securities.

The debt markets are vast with a very wide range of different instruments and this chapter provides a brief introduction to the main markets and instruments. Many of the instruments are covered in earlier chapters and so will not be described again here.[1] A distinction before we start: the term money markets is used for debt deals of one year or less, and bond markets for more than one year.

The markets in short-term money

When governments or corporations find themselves in need of short-term funds they may sell an **instrument (security)** which carries the promise to pay, say £10m in 30 days from now. The purchaser of that promise will not pay the full £10m because they want to receive an effective interest rate for lending. So they might pay, say £9.9m. Thus the security is sold for less than **face value (par or nominal value)**. The **discount** is the difference between face value and purchase price. The **yield**, the rate of interest gained by the holder, occurs when the instrument reaches maturity and the face value is paid by the issuer to the holder. Having said this, not all money market securities are issued at a discount to face value. Certificates of deposit and interbank deposits (both described in earlier chapters) are issued at their face value, and redeemed at a higher value.

Secondary market

Many money market instruments are **negotiable,** i.e. they can be resold on the secondary market. So, staying with the example, after 20 days the original purchaser could sell this promise to pay £10m in a further ten days for, say £9.96m. Thus a profit can be made by trading on the secondary market before the redemption date – in this case £60,000.

However, it must be noted that a loss may be incurred. If the original purchaser (lender) can only attract buyers at a price of £9.87m then it makes a £30,000 loss. This low price may occur if interest rates on similar financial instruments with ten days to maturity are now yielding a higher rate of return because investors have become more wary and demand higher rates of return to compensate for higher risk – a lot can change in the financial markets in 20 days. Any potential secondary market purchaser would be silly to pay a price higher (receive a lower yield) than the going market rate for this particular issue – i.e. the potential buyer has an opportunity cost (the return on the best alternative use of its investment money) and so the best the original purchaser can get, if it has to sell, is £9.87m. If it can avoid selling for another ten days then it will receive the full £10m from the borrower.

The discount and rate of return (yield) earned is dependent on the risk level and the **maturity** of the instrument. The maturity is the length of time between issue of the instrument (start of borrowing) and the time it is redeemed (money due is paid), or the length of time between when a security is priced or purchased in the secondary market and the date of redemption.

Participants

Money markets are used by banks, governments, corporations and institutions for borrowing and lending all over the world. Pension funds and insurance companies also maintain a proportion of their investment funds in liquid, low-risk form to meet unpredictable cash outflows, e.g. following a hurricane. These markets are also used by central banks to influence interest rates charged throughout the economy – see Chapter 24.

Money market instruments are traded over the telephone and then the deal is completed electronically by brokers and traders operating from the trading rooms of the big banks and specialist trading houses. These market makers maintain an inventory of securities and advertise prices at which they will sell and buy. By providing these middle-man services they assist the players in the market to quickly find a counterparty willing to trade, thus enhancing liquidity. They are said to be traders in **STIR (short-term interest rate) products.**

Some of the trades are simply private deals with legal obligations to be enforced by each side, but some are conducted through a central clearing house with each party responsible for reporting the deal to the clearing house, which settles the deal by debiting the account of the buyer and crediting the account of the seller. The clearing house then holds the security on behalf of the buyer. The risk of a counterparty reneging on the deal (counterparty risk) is reduced by trading through a clearing house, because the clearing house also acts as a **central counterparty**, effectively becoming the buyer to every seller and seller to every buyer.

Money market funds

Private individuals with small investment funds can participate in money market transactions by investing in **money market funds**. These are administered by financial institutions, e.g. banks, which benefit from economies of scale by investing in a portfolio of money market securities (e.g. repos issued by banks). The process is that the individual buys *shares* in the money market fund. Investors earn a return, technically a dividend, but in effect an interest rate. Corporations may also deposit surplus cash in money market funds to obtain good rates of interest through professional management of the fund. They can also gain access to their money by withdrawing it from the fund on a 'same-day' access basis. It is also possible to put in place a **sweep facility** so that money exceeding a certain balance is automatically transferred at the end of each day from a bank account to a money market account (paying more interest), and vice versa.

Treasury bills

Banks place a high proportion of their money in **Treasury bills (T-bills or Treasury notes)**, which are issued by government agencies to raise money for the State. They are negotiable securities, easily traded in the secondary market to release cash. Securities issued by reputable governments are regarded as risk-free investing because these institutions are able to raise income from taxes or by creating money, and there is minimal likelihood of default. This only applies if the country has a reputation for good financial management. Greece had a troublesome 2011–12 when investors doubted the soundness of its government finances and pushed up the interest rates the government had to pay.

UK Treasury bills

UK Treasury bills are issued at weekly tenders by the **Debt Management Office (DMO)** with a **face value** or **par value** of £100 and are sold at a **discount to par** with a maturity date of one month (28 days), three months (91 days), six months (182 days) or 12 months. They are sold by competitive tender to a small group of banks (around 28), which can sell them on in turn to other investors. The buyer (minimum £500,000) may redeem the bill at maturity or trade it in an active secondary market. The T-bill markets are both deep (many buyers and sellers) and liquid, so there is little risk that a holder cannot sell when necessary with low transaction costs. During the time he or she has held the bill, he or she has made a **yield** or **investment return**, the difference between the price paid and the maturity value (or sale price in the secondary market), and this yield is calculated as an annual percentage (even when only held for a few days) which can then be compared with other types of investment. The **bond equivalent yield (BEY)** (also known as **coupon equivalent rate** or **equivalent bond yield**) is the yield quoted in newspapers and it allows comparison between different types of securities by working out the **annualised** return on the price paid for an investment.

Example   **Bond equivalent yield (BEY)**

A six-month T-bill with a par value of £100 is currently trading at £98.50

$$\frac{\text{(Face value} - \text{Purchase price)}}{\text{Purchase value}} \times 100$$

$$\frac{100 - 98.50}{98.50} \times 100 = 1.522843\%$$

But this does not represent the true annual discount rate, because the maturity of the bill is only six months, so the annual rate is calculated by multiplying by 365/182 days, i.e. around 2, for each half year.

To calculate the BEY on the Treasury bill sold for £98.50, a discount of £1.50:

$$\frac{\text{Face value} - \text{Purchase price}}{\text{Purchase price}} \times \frac{\text{Days in year}}{\text{Days to maturity}} \times 100$$

$$\frac{100 - 98.50}{98.50} \times \frac{365}{182} \times 100 = 3.054053\%$$

The inverse relation between bill prices and interest rates

An investor buying a money market instrument with a maturity of six months expects the security to offer the same rate of return as other instruments with similar risk and time to maturity. If two weeks later interest rates on five and one-half month instruments being issued at that time suddenly shoot up there are now securities being issued that offer any buyer a much higher rate of return to maturity. In the secondary market potential buyers are unwilling to pay the price they did only a few days ago because the high price equals a low effective interest rate. Because there are alternative investments offering much higher interest rates, the discount on the bill will grow larger as the price people are willing to pay falls, until the rate of return is the same as other instruments in the market. Thus we see the inverse relation between prices of money market securities in the secondary market and the effective interest rate to maturity: a rise in bill prices means interest rates fall, a fall in bill prices equals interest rate rises.

Bonds

A bond is a long-term contract in which the bondholder lends money to a company, government or some other organisation. In return the company or government, etc., promises to make predetermined payments (usually regular) in the future which may consist of interest and a capital sum at the end of the bond's life. They come in all shapes and sizes, from Zambian government bonds to Chinese company bonds. The time to maturity for bonds is generally between five and 30 years although a number of firms have issued bonds with a longer maturity date. IBM and Reliance of India have issued 100-year bonds as have Coca-Cola and Walt Disney (Disney's was known as the 'Sleeping Beauty bond'). There are even some 1,000-year bonds in existence; Canadian Pacific Corporation is paying a dividend of 4% on a 1,000-year bond issued in 1883.

Bonds are often referred to collectively as **fixed-interest securities**. While this is an accurate description for many bonds, others do not offer *regular* interest payments that are *fixed* amounts. Nevertheless they are all lumped together as fixed-interest to contrast these types of loan instrument with equities (shares) that do not carry a promise of a return.

Bonds with up to three years left until they mature and pay their principal amount are generally known as **ultra-shorts,** but the boundary lines are often blurry. **Shorts** are up to seven years (but some say five years is the cut-off); **medium-dated** bonds generally have maturities of between seven and 15 years; **longs** are bonds with maturities of over 15 years. It should be noted that a bond is classified according to the time remaining to maturity, not the maturity when it was issued, so a 30-year bond which has only four years left until it matures is a short.

The volume of bonds issued throughout the world is vast, over $90tr, roughly two-thirds domestic bonds (denominated in the issuer's local currency and offered to local residents) and one-third issued outside of the domestic markets on the international bond markets. For comparison, the annual output (GDP) of the UK for one year is about £1.4tr.

Government bond markets

Most governments issue bonds to raise money when their tax receipts are less than their expenditure; these are known as **sovereign bonds**. When the British government does not raise enough in taxes it makes up a large part of the difference by selling bonds called **gilts** because in the old days you would receive a very attractive certificate with gold-leaf edges (**gilt-edged securities**). While the risk of non-receipt of interest and capital is minute if you buy and hold gilts to the maturity date, you can lose money buying and selling gilts from year to year (or month to month) in the secondary market before they mature. There have been many occasions when, if you purchased at the start of the year and sold to another investor in the secondary market at the end of the year, even after receiving interest, you would have lost 5% or more. On the other hand there were many years when you would have made large gains.

The UK government issues gilts via the UK **Debt Management Office (DMO)**. On 7 October 2013, the total amount of gilts in issue was £1328.88bn. This was rising at a rapid rate as the UK government spent around £100bn more than it raised in taxes – approximately 7% of gross national product. Gilts are sold with a **nominal** (**face** or **par** or **maturity**) value of £100. This is not necessarily what you would pay. The nominal value signifies what the government will pay *you* (the bondholder) when the bond reaches its maturity or **redemption date** at the end of, say, five, 10 or 25 years. You might pay £100, £99, £100.50, or some other sum for it, depending on the coupon offered and the general level of interest rates in the markets.

The **coupon** (sometimes called the **dividend**) is the stated annual rate of return on the nominal value of the bond. It is a percentage figure shown immediately before the name of each gilt – see Table 20.1. So, the '4% Treasury Gilt 2022' pays out £4.00 each year for every £100 nominal. Then in the year 2022 the nominal value of £100 is paid to the holder when the gilt is redeemed. The coupons are paid twice yearly in two equal instalments (£2 each) on set dates.

Between the six-months coupon payments the interest **accrues** on a daily basis. If you buy a gilt you are entitled to the accrued interest since the last coupon. You will receive this when the next coupon is paid. That is, you buy the gilt **cum-dividend**. But in the few days before the payment of the next coupon there is not enough time to change the register of ownership should it be sold before

Table 20.1   Gilts in issue 15 May 2013

Conventional Gilts	ISIN Code	Redemption Date	First Issue Date	Dividend Dates	Current/Next Ex-dividend Date	Total Amount in Issue (£m) nominal
Ultra-short						
8% Treasury Stock 2013	GB0008921883	27-Sep-2013	01-Apr-1993	27 Mar/Sep	18-Sep-2013	8,679
2$\frac{1}{4}$% Treasury Gilt 2014	GB00B3KJDW09	07-Mar-2014	20-Mar-2009	7 Mar/Sep	29-Aug-2013	35,104
5% Treasury Stock 2014	GB0031829509	07-Sep-2014	25-Jul-2002	7 Mar/Sep	29-Aug-2013	40,579
2$\frac{3}{4}$% Treasury Gilt 2015	GB00B4LFZR36	22-Jan-2015	04-Nov-2009	22 Jan/Jul	11-Jul-2013	28,813
4$\frac{3}{4}$% Treasury Stock 2015	GB0033280339	07-Sep-2015	26-Sep-2003	7 Mar/Sep	29-Aug-2013	36,129
8% Treasury Stock 2015	GB0008881541	07-Dec-2015	26-Jan-1995	7 Jun/Dec	29-May-2013	10,357
2% Treasury Gilt 2016	GB00B3QCG246	22-Jan-2016	03-Nov-2010	22 Jan/Jul	11-Jul-2013	32,037
Short						
4% Treasury Gilt 2016	GB00B0V3WX43	07-Sep-2016	02-Mar-2006	7 Mar/Sep	29-Aug-2013	34,648
1$\frac{3}{4}$% Treasury Gilt 2017	GB00B3Z3K594	22-Jan-2017	19-Aug-2011	22 Jan/Jul	11-Jul-2013	27,014
8$\frac{3}{4}$% Treasury Stock 2017	GB0008931148	25-Aug-2017	30-Apr-1992	25 Feb/Aug	15-Aug-2013	10,879
1% Treasury Gilt 2017	GB00B7F9S958	07-Sep-2017	08-Mar-2012	7 Mar/Sep	29-Aug-2013	31,269
5% Treasury Gilt 2018	GB00B1VWPC84	07-Mar-2018	25-May-2007	7 Mar/Sep	29-Aug-2013	34,398
1$\frac{1}{4}$% Treasury Gilt 2018	GB00B8KP6M44	22-Jul-2018	15-Feb-2013	22 Jan/Jul	11-Jul-2013	14,024
4$\frac{1}{2}$% Treasury Gilt 2019	GB00B39R3F84	07-Mar-2019	26-Sep-2008	7 Mar/Sep	29-Aug-2013	35,485
3$\frac{3}{4}$% Treasury Gilt 2019	GB00B4YRFP41	07-Sep-2019	08-Jul-2009	7 Mar/Sep	29-Aug-2013	28,057
4$\frac{3}{4}$% Treasury Stock 2020	GB00B058DQ55	07-Mar-2020	29-Mar-2005	7 Mar/Sep	29-Aug-2013	32,517
Medium						
3$\frac{3}{4}$% Treasury Gilt 2020	GB00B582JV65	07-Sep-2020	10-Jun-2010	7 Mar/Sep	29-Aug-2013	23,997
8% Treasury Stock 2021	GB0009997999	07-Jun-2021	29-Feb-1996	7 Jun/Dec	29-May-2013	23,499
3$\frac{3}{4}$% Treasury Gilt 2021	GB00B4RMG977	07-Sep-2021	18-Mar-2011	7 Mar/Sep	29-Aug-2013	27,709
4% Treasury Gilt 2022	GB00B3KJDQ49	07-Mar-2022	27-Feb-2009	7 Mar/Sep	29-Aug-2013	37,045
1$\frac{3}{4}$% Treasury Gilt 2022	GB00B7L9SL19	07-Sep-2022	22-Jun-2012	7 Mar/Sep	29-Aug-2013	28,360

Source: UK Debt Management Office website. Contains public sector information licensed under the Open Government Licence v2.0. www.dmo.gov.uk/index.aspx?page=Gilts/Gilts_In_Issue

the sending out of the money. Thus the bond switches to being **ex-dividend**. If you buy a gilt during the ex-dividend period the person you bought from would receive the accrued interest from the issuer – this would be reflected in the price you pay.

Prices and returns

The coupons showing on different gilts can have a wide range from 1% to 12%. These were (roughly) the rates of interest that the government had to offer at the time of issue. The wide variety reflects how interest rates have fluctuated during the past 80 or more years. These original percentages are not the rates of return offered on the gilt to a buyer in the secondary market today. So, if we take an undated gilt (no redemption date – goes on paying coupons ad infinitum) offering a coupon of 2.5% on the *nominal value* we may find that investors are buying and selling this bond that offers £2.50 per year at a price of £50, not at its nominal value of £100. This gilt offers an investor today a yield of 5%: £2.50/£50. Thus we see some bonds trading above and, as in this case, below the nominal value of £100 in the secondary market. By means of this variation in the price of the bond, investors are able to receive the current going rate of return for that type of investment.

Yield

There are two types of yield on dated gilts (and on other bonds with a fixed redemption date). The case of a Treasury 10% with five years to maturity currently selling in the secondary market at £120 will serve to illustrate the two different types. From the name of the gilt we glean that it pays a coupon of £10 per year (10% of the nominal value of £100). For £120 investors can buy this gilt from other investors on the secondary market to receive a **current yield** (also known as the **flat yield, income yield, simple yield, interest yield, annual yield** and **running yield**) of 8.33%.

$$\text{Current yield} = \frac{\text{Gross (before tax) interest coupon}}{\text{Market price}} \times 100$$

$$= \frac{£10}{£120} \times 100 = 8.33\%$$

This is not the true rate of return available to the investor because we have failed to take into account the capital loss over the next five years. The investor pays

£120 but will receive only the nominal value of £100 at maturity. If this £20 loss is apportioned over the five years it works out at £4 per year. The capital loss as a percentage of what the investor pays (£120) is £4/£120 × 100 = 3.33% per year. This loss to redemption has to be subtracted from the annual interest yield to give an approximation to the **yield to maturity (YTM)** or **redemption yield**. This is also called the **gross redemption yield** ('gross' meaning that it ignores taxation on the bond: we do not know the bond holder's tax status and therefore cannot allow for tax deducted on the interest or capital received on the bond).

> Approximation to yield to maturity: 8.33% – 3.33% = 5%

While this example tries to convey the essence of YTM calculations, it over-simplifies and really we should carry out a compound interest-type calculation to get a precise figure.[2]

Bond prices and redemption yields move in opposite directions. Take the case of our five-year gilt purchased for £120 offering a coupon of 10% with a (approximate) redemption yield (YTM) of 5%. If general interest rates rise to 6% because of an increase in inflation expectations, investors will no longer be interested in buying this gilt for £120, because at this price it yields only 5%. Demand will fall resulting in a price reduction until the bond yields 6%. A rise in yield goes hand in hand with a fall in price.

Corporate bonds

Corporate bonds offer a higher rate of return than well-respected government bonds but, as you might expect, this comes with a greater degree of risk of default.[3] Many corporate bonds are sufficiently negotiable (tradable) to be **listed** on the London Stock Exchange and other exchanges in Europe, Asia or the Americas, but the majority of trading occurs in the **over-the-counter** (OTC) market directly between an investor and a bond dealer. Access to a secondary market means that the investor who originally provided the firm with money does not have to hold on to the bond until the maturity date. However, because so many investors buy and then hold to maturity rather than trade in and out, corporate bonds generally have very thin secondary markets compared with shares or money market instruments. For example, there are 30,000 different investment-grade corporate bonds trading in the USA, but only 20 trade more than 10 times per day.

Corporate bonds have generally been the province of investing institutions, such as banks, pension and insurance funds. Private investors tended not to hold them, mainly due to the large amounts of cash involved – occasionally £1,000 minimum, but more often £50,000. The par value of one bond at, say, £50,000, €50,000 or $50,000 is said to have a 50,000 minimum 'lot' or 'piece'.

Infinite variation

Corporate bonds come in a variety of forms. The most common is the type with regular (usually semi-annual or annual) fixed coupons and a specified redemption date. These are known as **straight, plain vanilla** or **bullet** bonds. Other corporate bonds are a variation on this. Some pay coupons every three months, some do not pay a fixed coupon but one which varies depending on the level of short-term interest rates such as LIBOR (**floating rate** or **variable-rate bonds**) and some have interest rates linked to the rate of inflation. In fact, the potential for variety and innovation is almost infinite. Bonds issued in the past few years have linked the interest rates paid or the principal payments to a wide variety of economic events, such as a rise in the price of silver, exchange-rate movements, stock market indices – even to the occurrence of an earthquake. These bonds were generally designed to let companies adjust their interest payments to manageable levels in the event of the firm being adversely affected by the changing of some economic variable. Sampdoria, the Italian football club, issued a €3.5m bond that paid a higher rate of return if the club won promotion to the 'Serie A' division, 2.5% if it stayed in Serie B, 7% if it moved to Serie A and if the club rose to the top four in Serie A the coupon would rise to 14%.

Debentures and loan stocks

In the UK and a few other countries the most secure type of bond is called a **debenture,** secured by either a fixed or a floating charge against the firm's assets. Debentures secured on property may be referred to as **mortgage debentures.** With a floating-charge debenture the company has a high degree of freedom to use its assets as it wishes, such as sell them or rent them out, until it commits a default which 'crystallises' the floating charge. If this happens a **receiver** will be appointed with powers to dispose of assets and to distribute the proceeds to the creditors. Even though floating-charge debenture holders can force a **liquidation,** fixed-charge (specific-asset-assigned) debenture holders rank above floating-charge debenture holders in the pay out after insolvency.

The terms bond, debenture and **loan stock** are often used interchangeably and the dividing line between debentures and loan stock is a fuzzy one. As a general rule debentures are secured and loan stock is unsecured but there are examples that do not fit this classification. If liquidation occurs the unsecured

loan stockholders rank beneath the debenture holders and some other categories of creditors such as the tax authorities. In the USA, Canada and some other
countries the definitions are somewhat different and this can be confusing. In
these places a debenture is a long-term unsecured bond and so the holders become
general creditors who can only claim assets not otherwise pledged. In the USA the
secured form of bond is referred to as the **mortgage bond** and unsecured shorter-
dated issues (less than 10 years) are called **notes.**

Deep-discounted bonds and zero-coupon bonds

Bonds sold well below the par value are called **deep-discounted bonds**, the most
extreme form of which is the **zero-coupon bond**. The investor makes a capital
gain by holding the bond instead of receiving coupons. For example, a company
may issue a bond at a price of £60 which is redeemable at £100 in eight years.
These bonds are particularly useful for borrowers with low cash flows in the near
term, for example firms engaged in a major property development that will not
mature for many years.

Credit rating

Firms often pay to have their bonds and short-term debt rated by specialist **credit-
rating organisations**. The **debt rating** depends on the likelihood of payments
of interest and/or capital not being paid (that is, default) and in some cases on
the extent to which the lender is protected in the event of a default by the loan
contract (the **recoverability of debt**).[4] Government bonds from the leading
economies have an insignificant risk of default whereas unsecured subordinated
corporate loan stock has a much higher risk.

A top rating (AAA or 'triple A' for long term bonds and P-1, A-1+ and F1+ for
short-term borrowing) indicates very high quality, where the capacity to repay
interest and principal is extremely strong. Single A indicates a strong capacity to
pay interest and capital but there is some degree of susceptibility to impairment as
economic events unfold. BBB indicates adequate debt service capacity but vulnerability to adverse economic conditions or changing circumstances. B- and C-rated
debt have predominantly speculative characteristics. The lowest is D which indicates the firm is in default. Ratings of BBB- (or Baa3 for Moody's) or above are
regarded as **investment grade** – this is important because many institutional investors are permitted to invest only in investment grade bonds. Bonds rated below
investment grade are called **high-yield (or junk) bonds** – see Table 20.2. The difference in yield between the different grades in the investment grade group can be as
little as 30 basis points (0.3%), but this can rise at times of financial trauma.

Table 20.2   Credit rating systems

Moody's		Standard & Poor's		Fitch Ratings			
Long-term debt	Short-term debt	Long-term debt	Short-term debt	Long-term debt	Short-term debt		
Aaa	P-1	AAA	A-1+	AAA	F1+	Prime	Investment grade securities
Aa1		AA+		AA+		High grade	
Aa2		AA		AA			
Aa3		AA–		AA-			
A1		A+	A-1	A+	F1	Upper medium grade	
A2		A		A			
A3	P-2	A–	A-2	A–	F2		
Baa1		BBB+		BBB+		Lower medium grade	
Baa2	P-3	BBB	A-3	BBB	F3		
Baa3		BBB–		BBB–			
Ba1	Not Prime	BB+	B	BB+	B	Somewhat speculative	Non-investment grade, high-yield or 'junk' securities
Ba2		BB		BB		Speculative	
Ba3		BB–		BB–			
B1		B+		B+		Highly speculative	
B2		B		B			
B3		B–		B–			
Caa		CCC+	C	CCC	C		
Ca		CCC				Extremely speculative	
C		CCC–				May be close to default with little prospect for recovery	
/		D	D	DDD	D	In default	
/				DD			
/				D			

The agencies consider a wide range of quantitative and qualitative factors in determining the rating for a bond. The quantitative factors include the ratio of assets to liabilities of the company, cash flow generation and the amount of debt outstanding. The qualitative factors include the competitive position of the company, quality of management and vulnerability to the economic cycle. A company can issue bonds with different ratings: one may be raised because it is **higher ranking** in the capital structure, meaning that if the firm runs into trouble and has difficulty paying its debts the holders of this bond will be paid before the holders of lower-ranking bonds. Another difference may be that one bond is secured on specific assets.

The rating agencies also provide **issuer ratings** to firms and other organisations, which are assessments of the creditworthiness of the whole entity rather than a particular bond. A key measure in the bond markets is the **spread**, which is the number of basis points a bond is yielding above a benchmark rate, usually the government bond yield to maturity for that currency and period to redemption.

Bond default rates

Table 20.3 shows the proportion of bonds that have defaulted 1, 2, 3, 4, 5 and 10 years after issue over the period 1990–2012. Notice the large differences in default rates between the ratings. After five years only 0.19% of AA bonds defaulted, whereas 10.52% of B bonds defaulted. When examining data on default rates it is important to appreciate that default is a wide-ranging term, and could refer to any number of events from a missed payment to bankruptcy. For some of these events all is lost from the investor's perspective. For other events a very high percentage, if not all, of the interest and principal is recovered. The average recovery rate rule-of-thumb of around 40 cents on the dollar seems to have held over time with – in approximate terms – defaulted senior-secured debt returning over 60% and subordinated bonds under 30%.

Table 20.3   Fitch Global Corporate Finance Average Cumulative Default Rates 1990–2012

Rating	1 year	2 years	3 years	4 years	5 years	10 years
	%	%	%	%	%	%
'AAA'	0	0	0	0	0	0
'AA'	0.03	0.03	0.07	0.13	0.19	0.19
'A'	0.08	0.24	0.41	0.57	0.76	1.93
'BBB'	0.20	0.68	1.23	1.84	2.45	4.73
'BB'	1.05	2.80	4.46	5.97	6.91	11.55
'B'	2.02	4.79	7.24	9.50	10.52	11.60
'CCC to C'	24.88	31.87	35.59	38.32	36.84	43.75
Investment grade	0.12	0.36	0.64	0.92	1.22	2.29
High yield (Speculative grade)	2.99	5.53	7.66	9.51	10.25	14.14
All Industrials	0.74	1.45	2.08	2.63	2.95	4.14

Source: Fitch Ratings Global Corporate Finance 2012 Transition and Default Study, http://www.fitchratings.com/web_content/nrsro/nav/NRSRO_Exhibit-1.pdf

High-yield (junk) bonds

High-yield or junk bonds are debt instruments offering a high return with a high risk. They may be either unsecured or secured but rank behind senior loans and bonds, having credit ratings below BBB–. This type of debt generally offers interest rates two to nine percentage points more than that on senior debt and frequently gives the lenders some right to a share in equity values should the firm perform well. It is a kind of hybrid finance, ranking for payment below straight debt but above equity – it is thus described alternatively as **subordinated, intermediate** or **low grade.** One of the major attractions of this form of finance for the investor is that it often comes with equity warrants or share options attached (see Chapter 22) which can be used to obtain shares in the firm – this is known as an '**equity kicker**'. These may be triggered by an event taking place such as the firm joining the stock market.

Convertible bonds

Convertible bonds (or **convertible loan stocks**) carry a rate of interest in the same way as ordinary bonds, but they also give the holder the **right to exchange** the bonds at some stage in the future into ordinary shares according to some pre-arranged formula.[5] The owner of these bonds is not obliged to exercise this right of conversion and so the bonds may continue until redemption as an interest-bearing instrument. Conversion of these bonds into shares may have the effect of diluting the value of individual shares: there is an increase in the number of shares as more are created, but not necessarily any increase in the profits/value of the company. Usually the **conversion price** is 10–30% greater than the share price at the date of the bond issuance. So, if a £100 bond offered the right to convert to 40 ordinary shares the conversion price would be £2.50 (that is £100 ÷ 40) which, given the market price of the shares of, say, £2.20, would be a **conversion premium** of 30p divided by £2.20, which equals 13.6%.

Covered bonds

Covered bonds are similar to securitised asset based bonds (see Chapter 11) in that a specific group of assets (e.g. mortgage receivables) are used to back up the claims of the bondholders – they have the assets acting as collateral. However, there is one crucial difference compared with asset-backed securities (ABS) bonds which gives an extra layer of protection for investors. These assets and bonds are kept on the balance sheet of the issuing bank, which means that if the pool of assets runs into trouble investors in the covered bonds can call on the originating bank to pay up – the risk is not transferred. If an underlying loan goes bad (e.g. the mortgagee stops paying) the originating bank has to replace that loan with another. Furthermore, if it is the originating bank that runs into trouble the investors in the covered bonds have the security of the ring-fenced assets separate from the parent. So long as the issuing institution remains solvent the cash flows to the covered bondholders are independent of the performance of the assets. Because of their high level of backing, covered bonds are given high credit ratings (usually AAA), and are therefore a relatively low cost way for financial institutions to raise money. Typical maturity ranges are 2–10 years. They are common in Europe, where they originated (in Prussia in the eighteenth century), now making up to one-third of bank debt securities. Germany has a particularly large covered bond (**Pfandbriefe**) market at around €1,000bn outstanding. Spain and France have over €100bn outstanding.

Foreign bonds

A **foreign bond** is a bond denominated in the currency of the country where it is issued when the issuer is a non-resident. For example, in Japan bonds issued by non-Japanese companies denominated in yen are foreign bonds. They are known as Samurai bonds and the interest and capital payments will be in yen. Other foreign bonds from around the world issued by non-domestic entities in the domestic market include Yankee bonds (US), Bulldog bonds (UK), Rembrandt bonds (the Netherlands), Matador bonds (Spain), Panda bonds (China), Kangaroo bonds (Australia) and Maple bonds (Canada). Foreign bonds are regulated by the domestic authority of the country where the bond is issued. These rules can be demanding and an encumbrance to companies needing to act quickly and at low cost. The regulatory authorities have also been criticised for stifling innovation in the financial markets. The growth of the less restricted Eurobond market has put the once dominant foreign bond market in the shade.

Eurobonds (international bonds)

Eurobonds were in existence decades before Europe thought of creating the euro; the first Eurobond issue was in 1963 on the Luxembourg Stock Exchange, with the $15m issue by Autostrade, the Italian motorway company. The term 'Euro' in Eurobond does not even mean European. They are bonds sold outside the jurisdiction of the country of the currency in which the bond is denominated. So, for example, the UK financial regulators have little influence over Eurobonds issued in Luxembourg and denominated in sterling (known as **Eurosterling bonds**), even though the transactions (e.g. interest and capital payments) are in sterling. The Autostrade issue, although denominated in US dollars, was not subject to US regulations because it was issued outside the USA.

Eurobonds are medium to long-term instruments with standard maturities of three, five, seven and ten years, but there are long maturities of 15 to 30 years driven by pension and insurance fund demand for long-dated assets. They are not subject to the rules and regulations which are imposed on foreign bonds, such as the requirement to issue a detailed prospectus.[6] More importantly they are not subject to an **interest-withholding tax**. In many countries the majority of domestic bonds are subject to a withholding tax by which basic rate income tax is deducted before the investor receives interest. Interest on Eurobonds is paid gross without any tax deducted – which has attractions to investors keen on delaying, avoiding or evading tax.

Moreover, Eurobonds are normally **bearer bonds,** which means that the holders do not have to disclose their identity – all that is required to receive interest and capital is for the holder to have possession of the bond. Eurobond holders can be anonymous, making it possible for them to avoid paying tax in their own country. In contrast, domestic bonds are usually **registered**, which means that companies and governments are able to identify the owners. Despite the absence of official regulation, the **International Capital Market Association (ICMA)**, a self-regulatory body, imposes some restrictions, rules and standardised procedures on Eurobond issue and trading.

Issuing Eurobonds

With Eurobonds, and other large bond issues, a bank (**lead manager** or **book runner** or **lead underwriter**) or group of banks acting for the issuer invite a large number of other banks or other investors to buy some of the bonds. The managing group of banks may enlist a number of smaller institutions to use their extensive contacts to sell the bonds (the **selling group** or **syndicate**).[7] Eurobonds are traded on the secondary market through intermediaries acting as market makers. Most Eurobonds are listed on the London, Dublin or Luxembourg stock exchanges but the market is primarily an over-the-counter one; that is, most transactions take place outside a recognised exchange. Most deals are conducted using the telephone, computers, telex and fax, but there are a number of electronic platforms for trading Eurobonds. The extent to which electronic platforms will replace telephone dealing is as yet unclear. It is not possible to go to a central source for price information. Most issues rarely trade. Those that do are generally private transactions between investor and bond dealer and there is no obligation to inform the public about the deal.

21

Futures markets

Derivatives – forwards, futures, options, swaps, etc. – are the subject of this and the next two chapters. Derivatives have become increasingly important financial instruments over the past 30 years. These powerful tools can be exploited to either reduce risk or to go in search of high returns. Naturally, exceptionally high returns come with exceptionally high risk. So traders, bankers and corporate managers using derivatives for this purpose need to understand the risk to which they are exposing their company. Banks are usually at the centre of derivatives trading, dealing on behalf of clients, as market makers, as facilitators in a brokerage or adviser role, or trading on their own account.

What is a derivative?

A **derivative instrument** is an asset whose performance is based on (derived from) the behaviour of the value of an underlying asset (usually referred to simply as the 'underlying'). The most common **underlyings** include commodities, shares, bonds, share indices, currencies and interest rates. Derivatives are contracts which give the right, and sometimes the obligation, to buy or sell a quantity of the underlying, or benefit in another way from a rise or fall in the value of the underlying. It is the legal *right* that becomes an asset, with its own value, and it is the right that is purchased or sold.

The derivatives markets have received an enormous amount of attention from the press in recent years. This is hardly surprising as spectacular losses have been made and a number of companies brought to the point of collapse through the employment of derivative instruments. Some examples of the unfortunate use of derivatives are:

- Barings, Britain's oldest merchant bank, which lost over £800m on Nikkei Index (the Japanese share index) contracts on the Singapore and Osaka derivatives exchanges, leading to the bank's demise in 1995;

- Long-Term Capital Management, which attempted to exploit the 'mispricing' of bond financial instruments, by making use of option pricing theory. In 1998 the firm collapsed and the Federal Reserve Bank of New York cajoled 14 banks and brokerage houses to put up $3.6bn to save LTCM and thereby prevent a financial system breakdown;

- financial institutions that were destroyed in 2008 because they bought derivatives whose values depended on US mortgage borrowers continuing to pay their mortgages:

- UBS lost over $2bn in 2011 due to a rogue trader making bets on stockmarket movements through derivatives.

A long history

Derivative instruments have been employed for more than 2,000 years. Olive growers in ancient Greece unwilling to accept the risk of a low price for their crop when harvested months later would enter into **forward agreements** whereby a price was agreed for delivery at a specific time. This reduced uncertainty for both the grower and the purchaser of the olives. In the Middle Ages forward contracts were traded in a kind of secondary market, particularly for wheat in Europe. In the seventeenth century a futures market was established in Osaka's rice market in Japan and tulip bulb options were traded in Amsterdam. Commodity futures trading really began to take off in the nineteenth century with the Chicago Board of Trade regulating the trading of grains and other futures and options, and the London Metal Exchange dominating metal trading.

So derivatives are not new. What is different today is the size and importance of the derivatives markets. We have witnessed an explosive growth of volumes of trade, variety of derivatives products, and the number and range of users and uses. In the 30 years to 2013 the face value of outstanding derivatives contracts rose dramatically to stand at about $600tr ($600,000,000,000,000).

Forwards

Imagine you are responsible for purchasing potatoes to make crisps. In the free market for potatoes the price rises or falls depending on the balance between buyers and sellers. These movements can be dramatic. Obviously, you would like to acquire potatoes at a price which is as low as possible, while the potato producer wishes to sell for a price that is as high as possible. However, both parties may have a similar interest in reducing uncertainty. This will assist both to plan production and budget effectively. One way in which this could be done is to reach an agreement with the producer(s) to purchase a quantity of potatoes at a price agreed today to be delivered at a specified time in the future. Crisp producers buy up to 80% of their potatoes up to two years forward. Once the forward agreements have been signed and sealed the crisp manufacturer may later be somewhat regretful if the spot price (price for immediate delivery) subsequently falls below the price agreed months earlier. Unlike option contracts, forwards commit both parties to complete the deal. However, the manufacturer is obviously content to live with this potential for regret in order to remove the risk associated with such an important raw material.

> A **forward contract** is an agreement between two parties to undertake an exchange at an agreed future date at a price agreed now.

The party buying at the future date is said to be taking a *long position*. The counter-party which will deliver at the future date is said to be taking a *short position*.

There are forward markets in a wide range of commodities but the most important forward markets today are for foreign exchange, in which hundreds of billions of dollars of currency are traded every working day – see Chapter 23.

Forward contracts are tailor-made to meet the requirements of the parties. This gives flexibility on the amounts and delivery dates. Forwards are not traded on an exchange but are **over-the-counter instruments** – private agreements outside the regulation of an exchange. This makes them different from futures, which are standardised contracts traded on exchanges. A forward agreement exposes the counterparties to the risk of default – the failure by the other to deliver on the agreement. The risk grows in proportion to the extent by which the spot price diverges from the forward price pushing up the incentive to renege.

Futures

Futures contracts are in many ways similar to forward contracts. They are agreements between two parties to undertake a transaction at an agreed price on a specified future date. However, they differ from forwards in some important respects. Futures contracts are exchange-based instruments traded on a regulated exchange. The buyer and the seller of a contract do not transact with each other directly. The clearing house becomes the formal counterparty to every transaction. This reduces the risk of non-compliance with the contract significantly for the buyer or seller of a future, as it is highly unlikely that the clearing house will be unable to fulfil its obligation.

Example — **A simple future**

Imagine a farmer wishes to lock in a price for his wheat, which will be harvested in six months. You agree to purchase the wheat from the farmer six months hence at a price of £60 per tonne. You are hoping that by the time the wheat is delivered the price has risen and you can sell at a profit. The farmer is worried that all he has from you is the promise to pay £60 per tonne in six months, and if the market price falls you will walk away from the deal. To reassure him you are asked to put money into what the farmer calls a margin account. He asks and you agree to place £6 for each tonne you have agreed to buy. If you fail to complete the bargain the farmer will be able to draw on the money from the margin account and then sell the wheat as it is harvested at the going rate for immediate ('spot') delivery. So, as far as the farmer is concerned, the price of wheat for delivery at harvest time could fall to £54 and he is still going to get £60 for each tonne: £6 from what you paid into the margin account and £54 from selling at the spot price.

But what if the price falls below £54? The farmer is exposed to risk – something he had tried to avoid by entering a futures deal. It is for this reason that the farmer asks you to top up your margin account on a daily basis so that there is always a buffer. He sets a maintenance margin level of £6 per tonne. This means you have to maintain at least £6 per tonne in the margin account. So, if the day after you buy the future, the harvest-time price in the futures market falls to £57 you have only £3 per tonne left in the margin account as a buffer for the farmer. You agreed to buy at £60 but the going rate is only £57. To bring the margin account up to a £6 buffer you will be required to put in another £3 per tonne. If the price the next day falls to £50 you will be required to put up another £7 per tonne. You agreed to buy at £60, so with the market price at £50 you have put a total of £6 + £3 + £7 = £16 into the margin account. By putting in top-ups as the price moves against you, you will always ensure there is at least £6 per tonne, providing security for the farmer. Even if you go bankrupt or simply renege on the deal he will receive at least £60 per tonne, either from the spot market or from a combination of a lower market price plus money from the margin account. As the price fell to £50 you have a £10 per tonne incentive to walk away from the deal except for the fact that you have put £16 into an account that the farmer can draw on should you be so stupid or unfortunate. If the price is £50 per tonne at expiry of the contract and you have put £16 in the margin account you are entitled to the spare £6 per tonne of margin.

It is in the margin account that we have the source of multiple losses in the futures markets. Say your life savings amount to £10 and you are convinced there will be a drought and shortage of wheat following the next harvest. In your view the price will rise to £95 per tonne. So, to cash in on your forecast you agree to buy a future for one tonne of wheat. You have agreed with the farmer that in six months you will pay £60 for the wheat, which you expect to then sell for £95. (The farmer is obviously less convinced than you that prices are destined to rise.)

To gain this right (and obligation) to buy at £60 you need only have £6 for the initial margin. The other £4 might be useful to meet day-to-day margin calls should the wheat price fall from £60 (temporarily, in your view). If the price does rise to £95 you will make a £35 profit, having laid out only £6 (plus some other cash temporarily). This is a very high return of 583% over six months. But what if the price at harvest time is £40? You have agreed to pay £60, therefore the loss of £20 wipes out your savings and you are made bankrupt. You lose over three times your initial margin. That is the downside to the gearing effect of futures.

This example demonstrates the essential features of futures market trading, but in reality participants in the market do not transact directly with each other, but go through a regulated exchange. Your opposite number, called a counterparty, is not a farmer but an organisation that acts as counterparty to all futures traders, buyers or sellers, called the central counterparty at the clearing house. In the example we have assumed that the maintenance margin level is set at the same level as the initial margin. In reality it is often set at 70 to 80% of the initial margin level.

An exchange provides standardised legal agreements traded in highly liquid markets. The contracts cannot be tailor-made, e.g. for 77 tonnes of wheat or coffee delivered in 37 days from now. The fact that the agreements are standardised allows a wide market appeal because buyers and sellers know what is being traded: the contracts are for a specific quality of the underlying, in specific amounts with specific delivery dates.

For example, for sugar traded on NYSE Liffe one contract is for a specified grade of sugar and each contract is for a standard 50 tonnes with fixed delivery days in late August, October, December, March and May. It is important to remember that it is the contracts themselves that are a form of security bought and sold in the market. Thus a December future priced at $282.5 per tonne is a derivative of sugar and is not the same thing as sugar. To buy this future is to enter into an agreement with rights and obligations. It is these that are being bought and sold and not the commodity. When exercise of the contract takes place then the physical amount of sugar is bought or sold.[1] However, as with most derivatives, usually futures positions are cancelled by an offsetting transaction before exercise.

Marking to market and margins

With the clearing house being the formal counterparty for every buyer or seller of a futures contract, an enormous potential for credit risk is imposed on the organisation given the volume of futures traded and the size of the underlying they represent. (NYSE Liffe, for example, has an average daily volume of around 5 million contracts worth hundreds of billions of pounds/dollars.) If only a small fraction of market participants fail to deliver this could run into hundreds of millions of pounds/dollars. To protect itself the clearing house operates a margining system by which the futures buyer or seller has to provide, usually in cash, an initial margin. The amount required depends on the futures market, the level of volatility of the underlying and the potential for default; however it is likely to be in the region of 0.1–15% of the value of the underlying. The initial margin is not a 'down payment' for the underlying: the funds do not flow to a buyer or seller of the underlying but stay with the clearing house. It is merely a way of guaranteeing that the buyer or seller will pay up should the price of the underlying move against them. It is refunded when the futures position is closed (if the market has not moved adversely).

The clearing house also operates a system of daily **marking to market**. At the end of every trading day the counterparty's profits or losses created as a result of that day's price change are calculated. Any counterparty that made a loss has his or her member's margin account debited. The following morning the losing counterparty must inject more cash to cover the loss if the amount in the account has fallen below a threshold level (the maintenance margin). An inability to pay a daily loss causes default and the contract is closed, thus protecting the clearing house from the possibility that the counterparty might accumulate further daily losses without providing cash to cover them. The margin account of the counterparty that makes a daily gain is credited. This may be withdrawn the next day. The daily credits and debits to members' margin accounts are known as the **variation margin**.

Example **Margins**

Imagine a buyer and seller of a future on Monday with an underlying value of £50,000 are each required to provide an initial margin of 10%, or £5,000. The buyer will make profits if the price rises while the seller will make profits if the price falls. In the following table it is assumed that counterparties have to keep all of the initial margin permanently as a buffer.[2] (In reality this may be relaxed by an exchange.)

At the end of Tuesday the buyer of the contract has £1,000 debited from his or her member's account. This will have to be paid over the following day or the exchange will automatically close the member's position and crystallise the loss. If the buyer does provide the variation margin and the position is kept open until Friday the account will have an accumulated credit of £5,000. The buyer has the right to buy at £50,000 but can sell at £55,000. If the buyer and the seller closed their positions on Friday the buyer would be entitled to receive the initial margin plus the accumulated profit, £5,000 + £5,000 = £10,000, whereas the seller would receive nothing (£5,000 initial margin minus losses of £5,000).

Example of initial margin, variation margin and marking to market

£		Day			
	Monday	*Tuesday*	*Wednesday*	*Thursday*	*Friday*
Future daily closing price	50,000	49,000	44,000	50,000	55,000
Buyer's position					
Initial margin	5,000				
Variation margin (+ credited) (– debited)	0	–1,000	–5,000	+6,000	+5,000
Accumulated profit (loss)	0	(1,000)	(6,000)	0	5,000
Seller's position					
Initial margin	5,000				
Variation margin (+ credited) (– debited)	0	+1,000	+5,000	–6,000	–5,000
Accumulated profit (loss)	0	1,000	6,000	0	(5,000)

▶

This example illustrates the effect of leverage in futures contracts. The initial margin payments are small relative to the value of the underlying. When the underlying changes by a small percentage the effect is magnified for the future, and large percentage gains and losses are made on the amount committed to the transaction:

$$\text{Underlying change (Monday–Friday)} \quad \frac{55,000 - 50,000}{50,000} \times 100 = 10\%$$

$$\text{Percentage return to buyer of future} \quad \frac{5,000}{5,000} \times 100 = 100\%$$

$$\text{Percentage return to seller of future} \quad \frac{-5,000}{5000} \times 100 = -100\%$$

To lose all the money committed to a financial transaction may seem disappointing but it is as nothing compared with the losses that can be made on futures. It is possible to lose a multiple of the amount set down as an initial margin. For example, if the future rose to £70,000 the seller would have to provide a £20,000 variation margin – four times the amount committed in the first place.

Settlement

Historically the futures markets developed on the basis of the **physical delivery** of the underlying. So if you had contracted to buy 40,000 pounds of lean hogs you would receive the meat as settlement. However in most futures markets today only a small proportion of contracts result in physical delivery. The majority are **closed out** before the expiry of the contract and all that changes hands is cash, either as a profit or as a loss. Speculators certainly do not want to end up with five tonnes of coffee or 15,000 pounds of orange juice and so will **reverse their trade** before the contract expires, e.g. if they originally bought a futures for 50 tonnes of white sugar they later sell a future for 50 tonnes of white sugar.

Hedgers, say confectionery manufacturers, may sometimes take delivery from the exchange but in most cases will have established purchasing channels for sugar, cocoa, etc. In these cases they may use the futures markets not as a way of obtaining goods but as a way of offsetting the risk of the prices of goods moving adversely. So a confectionery manufacturer may still plan to buy, say, sugar, at the spot price from its longstanding supplier in six months and simultaneously, to hedge the risk of the price rising, will buy six-month futures in sugar. This position will then be closed before expiry. If the price of the underlying has risen the manufacturer pays more to the supplier but has a compensating gain on the future. If the price falls the supplier is paid less and so a gain is made here, but, under a perfect hedge, the future has lost an equal value.

As the futures markets developed it became clear that most participants did not want the complications of physical delivery and this led to the development of futures contracts where **cash settlement** takes place. This permitted a wider range of futures contracts to be created. Futures contracts based on intangible commodities such as a share index or a rate of interest are now extremely important financial instruments. With these no physical delivery takes place and if the contract is held to the maturity date one party will hand over cash to the other (via the clearing house system).

Equity index futures

Equity index futures are an example of a cash settlement market. The underlyings here are collections of shares, for example 225 Japanese shares for the Nikkei 225. Hedgers and speculators do not want 225 different shares to be delivered say one month from now. They are quite content to receive or hand over the profit or loss made by buying and then selling (or the other way around) a future of the index.

The equity index futures table (see Figure 21.1) from ft.com shows futures in indices from stock markets around the world. These are notional futures contracts. If not closed out before expiry (by the holder of a future doing the reverse transaction to their first – so if they bought the future first, selling will close the position) they are settled in cash based on the average level of the relevant index (say the FTSE 100) between stated times on the last day of the contract.

Figure 21.1 is a very much cut-down version of the futures available to traders. As well as the May and June delivery futures shown, NYSE Liffe for example also offers traders the possibility of buying or selling futures that 'deliver' in June, September, December and March. Delivery dates are the third Friday of the month.

Figure 21.1 shows the first price traded at the beginning of the current day (Open), the **settlement price** used to mark to market (usually the last traded price), the change from the previous day's settlement price, the highest and lowest prices during the day's trading, the estimated number of contracts traded that day (Est. vol.) and the total number of open contracts (these are trading contracts opened over the last few months that have not yet been closed by an equal and opposite futures transaction). Each point on the UK's FTSE 100 share index future is worth £10, by convention. So if the future rises from 5634.50 to 5684.50 and you bought a future at 5634.50 you have made 50 × £10 = £500 if you were to now sell at 5684.50.

EQUITY INDEX FUTURES

May 17		Open	Sett	Change	High	Low	Est. vol.	Open int.
DJIA	JUN3	15275.00	15315.00	+103.00	15330.00	15260.00	63	12,466
DJ Euro Stoxx‡	JUN3	2783.00	2806.00	+15.00	2824.00	2779.00	1,092,120	2,776,738
S&P 500	JUN3	1649.00	1663.00	+14.90	1665.50	1648.60	5,896	182,318
Mini S&P 500	JUN3	1649.50	1663.00	+15.00	1665.75	1648.25	1,913,168	3,169,768
Nasdaq 100	JUN3	3001.50	3022.75	+24.50	3027.00	2999.00	66	8,794
Mini Nasdaq	JUN3	3001.00	3022.75	+24.50	3028.25	2998.00	187,547	417,474
CAC 40	MAY3	3963.50	4000.70	+21.20	4009.00	3962.00	13,558	109,685
DAX	JUN3	8354.50	8394.50	+30.00	8477.50	8327.00	109,829	173,866
AEX	MAY3	364.35	368.05	+2.95	368.10	364.05	8,776	34,351
MIB 30	JUN3	17200.00	17354.00	+67.00	17400.00	17200.00	21,707	57,926
IBEX 35	MAY3	8528.00	8565.70	+27.50	8588.00	8517.00	7,626	20,643
SMI	JUN3	8216.00	8259.00	+9.00	8335.00	8199.00	22,717	154,111
FTSE 100	JUN3	6654.00	6697.50	+40.00	6730.00	6645.00	85,593	667,901
Hang Seng	MAY3	22977.00	22973.00	–	23009.00	22949.00	1,757	114,476
Nikkei 225†	JUN3	15200.00	15190.0	+120.00	15340.00	15140.00	36,133	462,092
Topix	JUN3	1257.50	1257.50	+10.00	1269.00	1253.00	4,074	677,840
KOSPI 200	JUN3	257.60	259.35	–	261.00	257.50	189,871	116,075

North American Latest. Contracts shown are among the 25 most traded based on estimates of average volumes in 2004. CBOT volume, high & low for pit & electronic trading at settlement.
Previous day's Open Interest. †Osaka contract. ‡Eurex contract

Figure 21.1 Equity index futures table from www.ft.com for close of trading on 17 May 2013

Source: Financial Times, www.ft.com, 17 May 2013

Example   Hedging with a share index future

It is 17 May 2013 and the FTSE 100 is at 6723. A bank wishes to hedge a £13,000,000 equity fund against a decline in the market. A June FTSE 100 future is available at 6697.50 – see Figure 21.1. The investor retains the shares in the portfolio and *sells* 194 index futures contracts. Each futures contract is worth £66,975 (6697.50 points × £10). So 194 contracts are needed to cover £13,000,000 (£13,000,000 ÷ (£10 × 6697.5) = 194).[3]

Outcome on the third Friday of June

For the sake of argument assume that the index falls by 10% from 6723 to 6051, leaving the portfolio value at £11,700,000 (assuming the portfolio moves exactly in line with the FTSE 100 index). The closing of the futures position offsets this £1,300,000 loss by now buying 194 futures at 6051 to close the position producing a profit[4] of:

Able to sell at 6697.50 × 194 × £10 =   £12,993,150

Able to buy at 6051 × 194 × £10 =   −£11,738,940

£1,254,210

These contracts are cash settled so £1,254,210 will be received. Furthermore, the investor receives back the margin laid down, less broker's fees.

Note that this was not a **perfect hedge** as less than £13m was covered by the derivative due to only being able to obtain cover in £66,975 increments (and the 10% fall was from 6723 not 6697.50).

Over-the-counter (OTC) and exchange-traded derivatives

As well as OTC contracts allowing perfect hedging and permitting hedges of more unusual underlyings because they are tailor-made, they also permit contracts of very long maturities, e.g. a decade. Companies with a longstanding relationship with a bank can often arrange OTC derivative deals with it, without the need to find any specific margin or deposit. The bank is willing to accept the counterparty risk of its customer reneging on the deal because it regards this possibility as very low risk, given its historical knowledge of the firm. However, due to the fear of counterparty risk, OTC participants with less than high-quality reputations may not be able to transact in OTC derivatives.

Forward contracts are difficult to cancel, as agreement from each counterparty is needed, and a penalty may be charged. Also client firms often find it difficult to reverse a hedge once the agreement has been made: it is difficult to find a counterparty willing to do exactly the opposite transaction to your first position. The low level of regulation of OTC markets can result in loss of transparency (e.g. what deals have taken place) and price dissemination (private deals are not usually made public). Finally, OTC transactions may not be settled promptly at the agreed time – whereas the clearing house on an exchange will insist on prompt settlement.

On the other hand exchange-traded derivative standardisation may be restrictive, e.g. standardised terms for quality of the underlying, quantity, delivery dates. Small companies, with say a £100,000 share portfolio to hedge or a €400,000 loan to hedge, find the standard quantities cumbersome.

In the wake of the financial crisis governments and regulators are trying to move as much of the derivatives trades as possible away from opaque OTC markets where there is counterparty risk to exchanges, or at least electronic trading platforms, where they will be processed through clearing houses with central counterparty functions. Also there will be more open reporting of trades – at least to regulators.

Short-term interest rate futures

Trillions of pounds, dollars and euros of trading takes place every year in the **short-term interest rate futures** markets. These are notional fixed-term deposits, usually for three-month periods starting at a specific time in the future. The buyer of one contract is buying the (theoretical) right to deposit money at a particular rate of interest for three months.

So if the current time is May you could arrange a futures contract for you to 'deposit' and 'receive interest' on, say £1m, with the deposit starting next July and ending in October. The rate of interest you will 'receive' over the three months is agreed in May. (This is a notional receipt of interest, as these contracts are cash settled rather than actual deposits being made and interest received – an example is given later.) So you now own the right to deposit £1m and receive x% interest for three months (at least in notional terms).

Short-term interest rate futures will be illustrated using the three-month sterling market, that is, deposits of pounds receiving notional interest for three months starting at some point in the future. Note, however, that there are many other three-month deposits you could make. For example, you could 'deposit' euros for three months, the interest rate on which is calculated with reference to 'Euribor 3m'. Other three-month deposits, often for money held outside the jurisdiction of the currency's country of origin, include Swiss francs deposited in London (Euroswiss), Eurodollars and Euroyens – see Figure 21.2.

The unit of trading for a three-month sterling time deposit is £500,000. Cash delivery by closing out the futures position is the means of settlement, so the buyer would not actually require the seller of the future to accept the £500,000 on deposit for three months at the interest rate indicated by the futures price. Although the term 'delivery' no longer has significance for the underlying it does define the date and time of the expiry of the contract. This occurs in late September, December, March and June and the nearest two consecutive months.

Short-term interest contracts are quoted on an index basis rather than on the basis of the interest rate itself. The price is defined as:

$$P = 100 - i$$

where:

P = price index;

i = the future interest rate in percentage terms.

Thus, on 17 May 2013 the settlement price for a July three-month sterling future was 99.52, which implies an interest rate of 100 – 99.52 = 0.48% for the period July to October – see Figure 21.2. Similarly the March 2014 quote (on 17 May 2013) would imply an interest rate of 100 – 99.51 = 0.49% for the three months March to June 2014.

In both cases the implied interest rate refers to a rate applicable for a notional deposit of £500,000 for three months on expiry of the contract – the July futures contract expires in July (i.e. the right to 'deposit' in July through to October expires in July) and the March 2014 future expires in March 2014. The 0.48% rate

INTEREST RATES – FUTURES

May 17		Open	Sett	Change	High	Low	Est. vol.	Open int.
Euribor 3m*	Jul	99.82	99.82	+0.01	99.82	99.82	11	750
Euribor 3m*	Oct	0.00	99.82	-	0.00	0.00	-	-
Euribor 3m*	Dec	99.82	99.83	+0.01	99.84	99.88	68,570	488,593
Euribor 3m*	MAR4	99.79	99.82	+0.02	99.83	99.79	72,081	389,097
Euroswiss 3m*	Jun	99.99	99.99	-	100.00	99.99	6,784	77,554
Euroswiss 3m*	Sep	100.02	100.02	-	100.03	100.02	7,119	81,802
Euroswiss 3m*	Dec	100.04	100.04	+0.01	100.05	100.03	8,403	81,596
Sterling 3m*	Jul	0.00	99.52	−0.01	0.00	0.00	-	-
Sterling 3m*	Sep	99.50	99.52	+0.01	99.52	99.50	32,425	322,095
Sterling 3m*	Dec	99.50	99.52	+0.01	99.52	99.49	50,471	299,908
Sterling 3m*	MAR4	99.49	99.51	+0.01	99.51	99.49	70,300	302,014
Eurodollar 3m†	Jul	99.720	99.72	−0.005	99.720	99.715	223	11,252
Eurodollar 3m†	Oct	0.000	99.69	−0.010	0.000	0.000	-	2,561
Eurodollar 3m†	Dec	99.680	99.67	−0.015	99.685	99.660	197,003	822,139
Eurodollar 3m†	MAR4	99.660	99.64	−0.015	99.660	99.635	214,326	766,116
Fed Fnds 30d‡	MAY3	0.000	99.88	-	0.000	0.000	-	46,846
Fed Fnds 30d‡	Jun	0.000	99.88	+0.01	0.000	0.000	-	45,104
Fed Fnds 30d‡	Jul	0.000	99.88	-	0.000	0.000	-	30,694
Euroyen 3m‡‡	Jul	0.000	99.775	+0.005	0.000	0.000	-	-
Euroyen 3m‡‡	Sep	99.770	99.775	+0.005	99.775	99.765	8,934	175,678
Euroyen 3m‡‡	Dec	99.765	99.770	+0.005	99.770	99.765	2,733	79,000
Euroyen 3m‡‡	MAR4	99.750	99.750	-	99.755	99.745	3,525	62,227

Contracts are based on volumes traded in 2004   Sources: Based on data from*NYSE LIFFE. †CME. ‡‡TIFFE

Figure 21.2   Interest rates – futures

Source: Financial Times, www.ft.com, 17 May 2013

for three-month money starting from July 2013 is the *annual* rate of interest even though the deal is for a deposit of only one-quarter of a year.

The price of 99.52 is not a price in the usual sense – it does not mean £99.52. It is used to maintain the standard inverse relationship between prices and interest rates. For example, if traders in this market one week later, on 24 May 2013, adjusted supply and demand conditions because they expect generally raised interest rates by July, they would push up the interest rates for three-month deposits starting in July 2013 to, say, 1.0%. Then the price of the future would fall to 99.00. Thus, a rise in interest rates for a three-month deposit of money results in a fall in the price of the contract – analogous to the inverse relationship between interest rates offered on long-term bonds and the price of those bonds.

In relation to short-term interest rate futures it is this inverse change in capital value when interest rates change that it is of crucial importance to grasp. Understanding this is more important than trying to envisage deposits of £500,000 being placed sometime in the future.

Example   **Hedging three-month deposits**

An example of these derivatives in use may help with gaining an understanding of their hedging qualities. Imagine the treasurer of a large company anticipates the receipt of £100m in late September 2013, 4 months hence. She expects that the money will be needed for production purposes in January 2014 but for the three months following late September it can be placed on deposit. There is a risk that interest rates will fall between now (May 2013) and September 2013 from their present level of 0.48% per annum for three-month deposits starting in late September.

The treasurer does not want to take a passive approach and simply wait for the inflow of money and deposit it at whatever rate is then prevailing without taking some steps to ensure a good return.

To achieve certainty in September 2013 the treasurer buys, in May 2013, September 2013 expiry three-month sterling interest rate futures at a price of 99.52. Each future has a notional value of £500,000 and therefore she has to buy 200 to hedge the £100m inflow.

Suppose in September 2013 that three-month interest rates have fallen to 0.39%. Following the actual receipt of the £100m the treasurer can place it on deposit and receive a return over the next three months of £100m $\times$ 0.0039 $\times \frac{3}{12}$ = £97,500. This is significantly less than if September 2013 three-month deposit interest rates had remained at 0.48% throughout the 10-month waiting period.

Return at 0.48% ($£100m \times 0.0048 \times \frac{3}{12}$)	£120,000
Return at 0.39% ($£100m \times 0.0039 \times \frac{3}{12}$)	£97,500
Loss	£22,500

However, the caution of the treasurer pays off because the futures have risen in value as the interest rates have fallen.

The 200 futures contracts were bought at 99.52. With interest rates at 0.39% for three-month deposits starting in September the futures in September have a value of 100 − 0.39 = 99.61. The treasurer in September can close the futures position by selling the futures for 99.61. Thus, a purchase was made in May 2013 at 99.52 and a sale in September 2013 at 99.61, therefore the gain that is made amounts to 99.61 − 99.52 = 0.09.

This is where a **tick** needs to be introduced. A tick is the minimum price movement on a future. On a three-month sterling interest rate contract a tick is a movement of 0.01% on a trading unit of £500,000.

One-hundredth of 1% of £500,000 is equal to £50, but this is not the value of one tick. A further complication is that the price of a future is based on annual interest rates whereas the contract is for three months. Therefore £50/4 = £12.50 is the value of a tick movement in a three-month sterling interest rate futures contract. In this case we have a gain of 9 ticks with an overall value of 9 × £12.50 = £112.50 per contract, or £22,500 for 200 contracts. The profit on the futures exactly offsets the loss of anticipated interest when the £100m is put on deposit for three months in September.

Note that the deal struck in May was not to enter into a contract to actually deposit £100m with the counterparty on the NYSE Liffe market. The £100m is deposited in September with any one of hundreds of banks with no connection to the futures contract that the treasurer entered into. The actual deposit and the notional deposit (on NYSE Liffe) are two separate transactions. However, the transactions are cleverly arranged so that the value movements on these two exactly offset each other. All that is received from NYSE Liffe is the tick difference, based on the price change between buying and selling prices of the futures contracts − no interest is received.

Forward rate agreements (FRAs)

FRAs are useful devices for hedging future interest rate risk. They are agreements about the future level of interest rates. The rate of interest at some point in the future is compared with the level agreed when the FRA was established and compensation is paid by one party to the other based on the difference.

Example

A company needs to borrow £6m in six months' time for a period of a year. It arranges this with Bank X at a variable rate of interest. The current rate of interest is 7%. (For the sake of argument assume that this is the LIBOR rate for borrowing starting in six months and lasting one year, and that this company can borrow at LIBOR.) The company is concerned that by the time the loan is drawn down interest rates will be higher than 7%, increasing the cost of borrowing.

The company enters into a separate agreement with another bank (Y) – an FRA. It 'purchases' an FRA at an interest rate of 7%. This is to take effect six months from now and relates to a 12-month loan. Bank Y will not lend any money to the company but it has committed itself to paying compensation should interest rates (LIBOR) rise above 7%.

Suppose that in six months, spot one-year interest rates are 8.5%. The company will be obliged to pay Bank X this rate: £6m × 0.085 = £510,000; this is £90,000 more than if the interest rates were 7%.[5] However, the FRA with Bank Y entitles the company to claim compensation equal to the difference between the rate agreed in the FRA and the spot rate. This is (0.085 − 0.07) × £6m = £90,000. So any increase in interest cost above 7% is exactly matched by a compensating payment provided by the counterparty to the FRA. However, if rates fall below 7% the company makes payments to Bank Y. For example, if the spot rate in six months is 5% the company benefits because of the lower rate charged by Bank X, but suffers an equal offsetting compensation payment to Bank Y of (0.07 − 0.05) × £6m = £120,000. The company has generated certainty over the effective interest cost of borrowing in the future. Whichever way the interest rates move it will pay £420,000.

This example is a gross simplification. In reality FRAs are generally agreed for three-month periods. So this company could have four separate FRAs for the year. It would agree different rates for each three-month period. If three-month LIBOR turns out to be higher than the agreed rate, Bank Y will pay the difference to the company. If it is lower the company pays Bank Y the difference. The 'sale' of an FRA protects against a fall in interest rates. For example, if £10m is expected to be available for putting into a one-year bank deposit in three months from now the company could lock into a rate now by selling an FRA to a bank. Suppose the agreed rate is 6.5% and the spot rate in three months is 6%, then the depositor will receive 6% from the bank into which the money is placed plus ½% from the FRA counterparty bank.

These two examples are described as 6 against 18 (or 6 × 18) and 3 against 15 (or 3 × 15). The first is a 12-month contract starting in six months, the second is a 12-month contract starting in three months. Typically sums of £5m–£100m are hedged in single deals in this market. Companies do not need to have an underlying lending or borrowing transaction – they could enter into an FRA in isolation and make or receive compensating payments only.

Banks enter FRAs between themselves as well as transacting with corporates. FRAs can be arranged in highly liquid markets in all the major currencies – the market has so much activity that the rates offered are displayed on computer screens by banks and brokers. Deals are agreed either over the telephone or over a dealing system such as Reuters.

Derivatives users

There are three types of user of the derivatives markets: hedgers, speculators and arbitrageurs.

Hedgers

To **hedge** is to enter into transactions which protect a business or assets against changes in some underlying. The instruments bought as a hedge tend to have the opposite-value movements to the underlying. Financial and commodity markets are used to transfer risk from an individual or corporation to another more willing and/or able to bear that risk.

Consider a firm which discovers a rich deposit of platinum in Kenya. The management are afraid to develop the site because they are uncertain about the revenues that will actually be realised. Some of the sources of uncertainty are that: (a) the price of platinum could fall, (b) the floating-rate loan taken out to develop the site could become expensive if interest rates rise and (c) the value of the currencies could move adversely. The senior managers have more or less decided that they will apply the firm's funds to a less risky venture. A recent graduate steps forward and suggests that this would be a pity, saying: 'The company is passing up a great opportunity, and Kenya and the world economy will be poorer as a result. Besides, the company does not have to bear all of these risks given the sophistication of modern financial markets. The risks can be hedged, to limit the downside. For example, the platinum could be sold on the forwards or the futures market, which will provide a firm price. The interest-rate risk can be reduced by using an FRA or the interest futures markets. Other possibilities here include a "cap" or a swap arrangement into a fixed-rate loan (these are discussed in the next chapter).

The currency risk can be controlled by using currency forwards or options (discussed in Chapter 23).' The board decides to press ahead with development of the mine and thus show that derivatives can be used to promote economic well-being by transferring risk.

Speculators

Speculators take a position in financial instruments and other assets with a view to obtaining a profit on changes in price. Speculators accept high risk in anticipation of high reward. The gearing effect of derivatives makes speculation in these instruments particularly profitable, or particularly ruinous. Speculators are also attracted to derivatives markets because they are often more liquid than the underlying markets. In addition the speculator is able to sell before buying (to 'short' the market) in order to profit from a fall. More complex trading strategies are also possible.

The term 'speculator' in popular parlance is often used in a somewhat critical fashion. This is generally unwarranted. Speculators are needed by financial markets to help create trading liquidity. Many people argue that prices are more, not less, likely to be stable as a result of speculative activity. Usually speculators have dissimilar views regarding future market movements and this provides two-way liquidity which allows other market participants, such as hedgers, to carry out a transaction quickly without moving the price. Imagine if only hedgers with an underlying were permitted to buy or sell derivatives. Very few trades would take place each day. If a firm wished to make a large hedge this would be noticed in the market and the price of the derivative would be greatly affected. Speculators also provide a kind of insurance for hedgers – they accept risk in return for a premium.

Speculators are also quick to spot new opportunities and to shift capital to new areas of economic output. For example, if a speculator foresees a massive rise in the demand for cobalt because of its use in mobile phones they will start to buy futures in the commodity, pushing up the price. This will alert the mining companies to go in search of more cobalt deposits around the world and pump money into those countries that have it, such as the Congo. The speculator has to examine the underlying economic messages emanating from the world economy and respond to them in a truthful manner – dumping the currency of a badly run country or selling bonds in banks, for example.

Arbitrageurs

The act of **arbitrage** is to exploit price differences on the same instrument or similar assets. The arbitrageur buys at the lower price and immediately resells at the higher price. So, for example, traders arbitrage share index futures. These often trade on two different markets. Theoretically the price should be identical on both, but in reality this is not always the case, and it is possible simultaneously to buy the future in one market and sell the future in the other and thereby make a risk-free profit. An arbitrageur waits for these opportunities to exploit a market inefficiency. Arbitrageurs can help to ensure pricing efficiency – their acts of buying or selling tend to reduce pricing anomalies.

22

Swaps and options

Swaps, options, caps and floors are used by banks in great volume every working day. This chapter outlines these important derivatives.

Swaps allow you to exchange a series of future cash payment obligations. For example, you could have a seven-year loan agreement whereby you pay a series of interest amounts based on whatever the six-month LIBOR is at the time. Obviously, the concern you have is that LIBOR might jump to a much higher level at some point in the seven years, which might jeopardise your firm. One solution is to agree with a counterparty for it to pay you LIBOR every six months if you pay its fixed interest rate obligations – an interest rate swap.

Credit default swaps, invented only in the 1990s, allow you to pass on the risk of a borrower defaulting on a debt deal to other participants in the financial markets, in return for a fee (premium). These are instruments that can be used to reduce risk or to speculate.

The last chapter showed how derivatives can be used to fix a future outcome. So, if you are currently vulnerable to rises in the price of the underlying you can arrange an offsetting future agreement that has the opposite value movements to your current exposure. The problem with futures, forwards and FRAs is that they do not allow you to benefit from a favourable movement in the underlying. Options, on the other hand, do. With an option you can choose at a later date whether or not you would like to proceed with the deal or not.

As well as interest swaps, credit default swaps and options this chapter examines caps, which permit a limit to be set on interest paid, and floors, which can be used to set a minimum interest to be received.

Interest rate swaps

An **interest rate swap** is where one company arranges with a counterparty to exchange interest rate payments (where the notional principal for each is identical). For example, the first company may be paying fixed rate interest but prefers to pay floating rates. The second company may be paying floating rates of interest, which go up and down with LIBOR, but would benefit from a switch to a fixed obligation. Imagine that firm S has a £200m ten-year loan paying a fixed rate of interest of 8%, and firm T has a £200m ten-year loan on which interest is reset every six months with reference to LIBOR, at LIBOR plus 2%. Under a swap arrangement S would agree to pay T's floating rate interest on each due date over the next ten years, and T would be obligated to pay S's 8% interest.

One motive for entering into a swap arrangement is to reduce or eliminate exposure to rises in interest rates. Over the short run, futures and FRAs could be used to hedge interest rate exposure. However, for longer-term loans (more than two years) swaps are usually more suitable because they can run for the entire lifetime of the loan. So if a treasurer of a company with a large floating rate loan forecasts that interest rates will rise over the next four years, he or she could arrange to swap interest payments with a fixed rate interest payer for those four years. Another reason for using swaps is to take advantage of market imperfections. Sometimes the interest rate risk premium charged in the fixed rate borrowing market differs from that in the floating rate market for a particular borrower – see the Example.

Example **Swaps**

Take the two companies, Cat plc and Dog plc, both of which want to borrow £150m for eight years. Cat would like to borrow on a fixed rate basis because this would better match its asset position. Dog prefers to borrow at floating rates because of optimism about future interest rate falls. The treasurers of each firm have obtained quotations from banks operating in the markets for both fixed and floating rate eight-year debt. Cat could obtain fixed rate borrowing at 10% and floating rate at LIBOR +2%. Dog is able to borrow at 8% fixed and LIBOR +1% floating:

	Fixed	Floating
Cat can borrow at	10%	LIBOR +2%
Dog can borrow at	8%	LIBOR +1%

▶

In the absence of a swap market Cat would probably borrow at 10% and Dog would pay LIBOR +1%. However, with a swap arrangement both firms can achieve lower interest rates.

Notice that because of Dog's higher credit rating it can borrow at a lower rate than Cat in both the fixed and the floating rate market – it has an absolute advantage in both. However the risk premium charged in the two markets is not consistent. Cat has to pay an extra 1% in the floating rate market, but an extra 2% in the fixed rate market. Cat has an absolute disadvantage for both, but has a comparative advantage in the floating rate market.

To achieve lower interest rates each company should borrow in the market where it has comparative advantage and then swap interest obligations. So Cat borrows floating rate funds, paying LIBOR +2%, and Dog borrows fixed rate debt, paying 8%.

Then they agree to swap interest payments at rates which lead to benefits for both companies in terms of: (a) achieving the most appropriate interest pattern (fixed or floating), and (b) the interest rate that is payable, which is lower than if Cat had borrowed at fixed and Dog had borrowed at floating rates. One way of achieving this is to arrange the swap on the following basis (see Figure 22.1):

- Cat pays to Dog fixed interest of 9.5%;
- Dog pays to Cat LIBOR +2%.

Cat pays LIBOR +2% to a bank but also receives LIBOR +2% from Dog and so these two cancel out. Cat also pays 9.5% fixed to Dog. This is 50 basis points (bps) lower than if Cat had borrowed at a fixed rate directly from the bank. On £150m this is worth £750,000 per year.

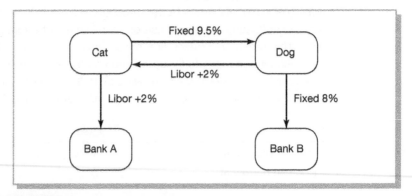

Figure 22.1   **An interest rate swap**

Cat:

Pays	LIBOR +2%
Receives	LIBOR +2%
Pays	Fixed 9.5%
Net payment	Fixed 9.5%

Dog takes on the obligation of paying a bank fixed interest at 8% while receiving 9.5% fixed from Cat on the regular payment days. The net effect is 1.5% receivable less the LIBOR +2% payment to Cat – a floating rate liability of LIBOR +0.5%.

Dog:

Pays	Fixed 8%
Receives	Fixed 9.5%
Pays	LIBOR +2%
Net payment	LIBOR +0.5%

Again there is a saving of 50 bps or £750,000 pa. The net annual £1.5m saving is before transaction costs.

Under a swap arrangement the principal amount (in this case £150m) is usually never swapped and Cat retains the obligation to pay the principal to Bank A. Neither of the lending banks is involved in the swap and may not be aware that it has taken place. The swap focuses entirely on the three-monthly or six-monthly interest payments.

Banks are at the centre of the swaps market

Prior to the widespread development of a highly liquid swap market each counterparty incurred considerable expense in making the contracts watertight. Even then, the risk of one of the counterparties failing to fulfil its obligations was a potential problem. Today intermediaries (usually banks) take counterparty positions in swaps and this reduces risk and avoids the necessity for one corporation to search for another with a corresponding swap preference. The intermediary generally finds an opposite counterparty for the swap later. Furthermore, standardised contracts reduce the time and effort needed to arrange a swap and have permitted the development of a thriving secondary market, and this has assisted liquidity. This more developed approach, with a bank intermediary offering rates to swap fixed to floating, or floating to fixed is illustrated in the following example.

Swaps with an intermediary bank

Expori, a French property developer, has agreed to buy and develop a shopping centre in England. It needs to borrow £80m for six years. The company treasurer asked banks what they would charge for a term loan. The quotes are for both floating (LIBOR-related) rates and fixed rates. She has also looked into the possibilities of issuing a floating rate bond with the interest re-fixed to LIBOR at six-month intervals and the issuance of a fixed interest rate bond. She has concluded that all the fixed rates offered are excessively high – each quote is over 4%. The best floating rate offer is a reasonable 6-M (six month) LIBOR + 200 bps, but Expori's directors insist that, because the company already has too much exposure to a rise in interest rates, such a large loan should not add to the company's interest rate exposure. The treasurer's solution is to borrow £80m at floating rate and then contact one of the banks offering swap rates to swap into a fixed rate. It is 20 May 2013 and an idea of the swap rates available are shown in the FT table displayed in Figure 22.2 – in reality you need to contact brokers and individual banks.

For this illustration we are most interested in the pound sterling columns (£ Stlg). Two prices are given for each contract period. The ask rate is the interest you pay under the swap if you were to pay the fixed rate and receive from the bank the LIBOR rate set for each of the six months over the term of the agreement. The bid rate is the fixed rate you would receive from the bank in return for you paying LIBOR to it. The banks in these markets expect to conclude numerous deals both paying fixed and receiving fixed rates, and they make a few basis points of profit between the two.

Expori must ensure that any deal it makes with a bank in the swap market matches the underlying floating rate loan transaction it has concluded with another bank – e.g. length of time to maturity and dates of resetting interest rates ('rollover dates'). The deal it wants to make in the swap market is to pay fixed rate and receive floating rate. Looking along the six year row we see that the fixed rate payable is 1.29% pa if Expori is a top-ranking company. However it is not regarded as 'top ranking' in terms of default risk. Because as a counterparty it is less safe than one of the many banks that can obtain the rates shown in Figure 22.2 it will have to pay slightly more. In this case we find that Expori contacted the swap dealing banks and discovered that it will have to pay: 1.4% pa rather than 1.29%. This will be paid semi-annually – roughly one-half of 1.4% for six

INTEREST RATES – SWAPS

May 20	Euro-€		£ Stlg		SwFr		US$		Yen	
	Bid	Ask	Bid	Ask	Bid	Ask	Bid	Ask	Bid	Ask
1 year	0.28	0.32	0.48	0.51	0.04	0.10	0.30	0.33	0.22	0.28
2 year	0.35	0.39	0.61	0.65	0.05	0.13	0.37	0.40	0.25	0.31
3 year	0.45	0.49	0.71	0.75	0.13	0.21	0.51	0.54	0.32	0.38
4 year	0.60	0.64	0.85	0.90	0.24	0.32	0.72	0.75	0.42	0.48
5 year	0.78	0.82	1.04	1.09	0.38	0.46	0.97	1.00	0.52	0.58
6 year	0.96	1.00	1.24	1.29	0.53	0.61	1.23	1.26	0.62	0.68
7 year	1.14	1.18	1.44	1.49	0.68	0.76	1.47	1.50	0.71	0.77
8 year	1.30	1.34	1.64	1.69	0.82	0.90	1.69	1.72	0.80	0.86
9 year	1.46	1.50	1.83	1.88	0.94	1.02	1.88	1.91	0.89	0.95
10 year	1.59	1.63	2.00	2.05	1.05	1.13	2.05	2.08	0.97	1.03
12 year	1.82	1.86	2.26	2.33	1.21	1.31	2.33	2.36	1.14	1.22
15 year	2.06	2.10	2.53	2.62	1.38	1.48	2.61	2.64	1.39	1.47
20 year	2.24	2.28	2.79	2.92	1.50	1.60	2.85	2.88	1.70	1.78
25 year	2.30	2.34	2.95	3.08	1.54	1.64	2.97	3.00	1.86	1.94
30 year	2.33	2.37	3.02	3.15	1.56	1.66	3.04	3.07	1.93	2.01

Bid and Ask rates as of close of London Business. £ and Yen quoted on a semi-annual actual/365 basis against 6 month Libor with exception of the 1 Year GBP rate which is quoted against actual 3M Libor. Euro/Swiss Franc quoted on an annual bond 30/360 basis against 6 month Euribor/Libor.

Source: Based on data from ICAP plc.

Figure 22.2 Interest rates – swaps

months. In return Expori will receive 6-M LIBOR, which will be reset for each six month period depending on market rates at the time.

Thus, on each of the six-monthly rollover dates the LIBOR rate will be deducted from the agreed fixed rate of 1.4% and the difference paid by one party to the other. For example, if six months after the agreement LIBOR is at 1.00% (expressed as an annual rate) at the 11 a.m. London fixing, Expori owes 1.4% to the bank (which needs adjusting down for the six-month period) while the bank owes Expori 1.00% (0.5% for six months). Rather than make two payments, only the difference changes hands, 0.4% (half that for six months) – see Figure 22.3.

Expori is now receiving LIBOR to offset the payment of LIBOR it makes to the bank that lent it £80m. However, it has to pay 200 bps more than this to the lending bank as well as the fixed rate of 1.4% pa, thus it has fixed its interest at 3.4% for the six-year life of the loan. This is better than the 4% offered as a direct fixed rate loan to the company.

▶

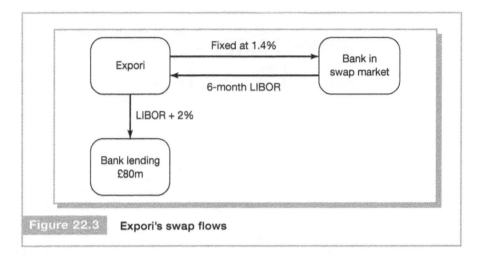

Figure 22.3   Expori's swap flows

The relationship between FRAs and interest rate swaps

If a corporation buys (or sells) a sequence of LIBOR-based FRAs stretching over, say, two years, in which each of the three-month periods making up that two years is covered by an FRA then we have an arrangement similar to a two-year swap. The company has made a series of commitments to pay or receive differences between the FRA agreed rate and the prevailing spot rate at three-monthly intervals.

For example, Colston plc has a £100m two-year floating rate loan. Interest is set at 3-M LIBOR. So, every three months, whatever the rate that London banks are charging for three-month loans to each other is to be charged to Colston. Thus the company is vulnerable to interest rate rises. The current time is June 20X1 and spot LIBOR is set at 5.09%. This is the annualised rate that Colston will pay for the next three months. To lock in a rate for the next rollover date, i.e. in September, the company could buy (in June) an FRA set at LIBOR for the three months starting in September and ending in December (a 3 × 6 forward rate agreement). This FRA is priced at 5.71%. The amount covered can be exactly £100m because FRA arrangements are flexible to suit the client, being an over-the-counter market. The £100m is known as the **notional amount**.

The FRA buyer (Colston) has technically agreed to deliver to the FRA seller 5.71%. In return the FRA seller will pay Colston whatever is the spot rate for LIBOR in September. Of course, it would be inefficient to have these two payments made when only one payment, the difference between the two rates, is needed. If LIBOR is 5.71% in September no payment is made by either side. However, if LIBOR in September resets at 6.2% Colston will receive a settlement cash flow of 0.49%, or 49 bps, on £100m for the three-month period. Thus a payment of £122,500 is received (£100m × 0.0049 × 3/12) from the FRA seller.[1]

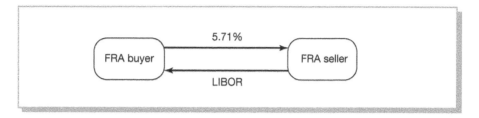

If, however, the spot LIBOR in September is 5.5%, Colston will pay a settlement cash flow of 21 bps: £100m × 0.0021 × 3/12 = £52,500.

FRAs are priced **at-the-money**, i.e. the current rate in the market for future LIBOR. In the case of Colston in June this is 5.71% for the September three-month FRA. The participants in this market consider that the market rate has zero initial value to both parties. However, as market rates change the contract gains value for one or other of the contractors.

Colston has locked in the interest rate it will pay for the three months September to December, but what about the other months of the two-year loan commitment? It could enter a series of FRAs for each of the remaining rollover dates. The rates that would be set are shown in Table 22.1.

Table 22.1   **FRA prices for the next two years**

Time	Libor rate quoted in June 20X1 for three-month periods starting at various dates over next two years
June 20X1 (Spot)	5.09
Sept. 20X1	5.71
Dec. 20X1	6.05
Mar. 20X2	6.42
June 20X2	6.70
Sept. 20X2	6.98
Dec. 20X2	7.06
Mar. 20X3	7.18

By executing seven FRAs at these rates Colston would pay its lender 5.09% (annualised rate) for the first three months. Thereafter, regardless of how LIBOR moves the effective cost of the loan is 5.71% for the second three months, 6.05% for the third, and so on. Each one of these FRA deals is like a mini swap, with Colston committed to delivering the rate shown in Figure 22.4 and the FRA seller committed to delivering LIBOR to Colston. Or, rather, net payments on the difference between the FRA rate and LIBOR are made. Figure 22.4 illustrates the first four payments.

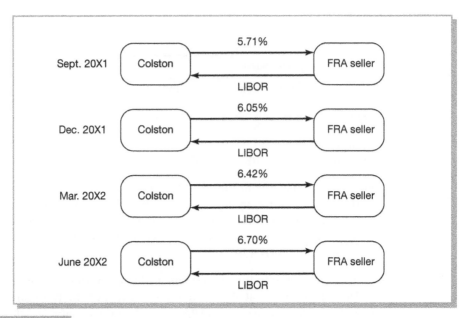

Figure 22.4   Colston's first four FRA payments

Using FRAs in this way Colston knows how much it has to pay out over the next two years and so is not vulnerable to unexpected changes in LIBOR. But note that the interest rates are different from one three-month period to another. An alternative open to Colston is to buy a contract with the same rate payable in each of the eight quarters. This rate would be an approximate average of the FRA rates stretching over the two years. This is called a swap. A rough average of the eight LIBOR rates payable in Table 22.1 is 6.39%. The interest rate swap arrangement is shown in Figure 22.5. For each three-month period Colston pays the counterparty

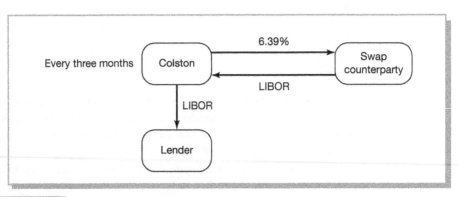

Figure 22.5   Colston's pay outs and receipts under a swap

the swap rate (6.39%) and receives LIBOR. If interest rates rise above 6.39% Colston would benefit from the swap arrangement because it receives payments from the swap counterparty, which amount to the difference between 6.39% and LIBOR. This enables Colston to accept any increase in LIBOR with equanimity, as the effective cost of the loan is constant at 6.39% regardless of how much is paid to the lender.

Credit default swap

Until the early 1990s once a lender to a company had assumed the risk of loss through default or a similar **credit event** (failure of the borrower to abide by the agreement) there was little that they could do except wait to see if the borrower paid all the interest and principal on time. In other words, the lender retained all the credit risk and could not pass any of it on to others more willing to bear it. Today, however, we have an enormous market in the selling and buying of protection against default.

Under a **credit default swap (CDS)** the seller of protection receives a regular fee (usually every three months over a period of years) from the buyer of protection (BP), and in return promises to make a pay off should the underlying specified **reference entity** (e.g. BP) default on its obligations with regard to a **reference obligation**, i.e. a specific bond or loan. Thus the payment from the buyer of credit protection is a regular amount but the payment the other way, from protection seller to buyer, is a contingent payment depending on whether there is a credit event – see Figure 22.6.

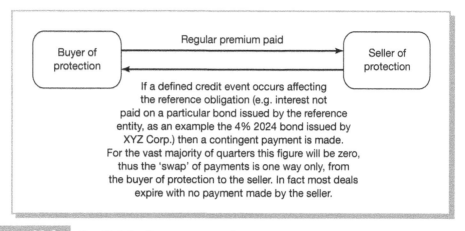

Credit default swap payments

A credit default swap

A pension fund manager has bought £20m (nominal value) of bonds from a software company, Appsoft. He is concerned that at some point over the five-year life of the bonds the company will fail to meet its obligations – there will be a credit event. Even though this is unlikely the manager needs to make absolutely sure that he is protected on the downside. He thus consults one of the organisations that provide CDS prices (e.g. www.markit.com) to gain an idea of the amount he would have to pay for five years of protection. The prices on this website only give a general indication because they report only deals struck by one dealer some time in the previous day. To obtain a more precise cost he will need to contact dealers.

The quote he is given is 160 basis points as the 'spread' expressed as a percentage of the notional principal per year. Thus for £20m of cover he will pay an annual amount of £20m x 0.016 = £320,000. However, in this market it is normal for this payment to be split up into four quarterly amounts payable on 20 March, 20 June, 20 September and 20 December. Thus the quarterly payments will be £80,000.

The cash flows between the pension fund and the CDS dealer (market maker) are shown on the left half of Figure 22.7. The pension fund manager makes quarterly payments and in return the CDS dealer pays an amount contingent on a credit event occurring. In most cases the CDS dealer never pays anything to the pension fund because the reference entity (e.g. Appsoft) abides by its bond/loan

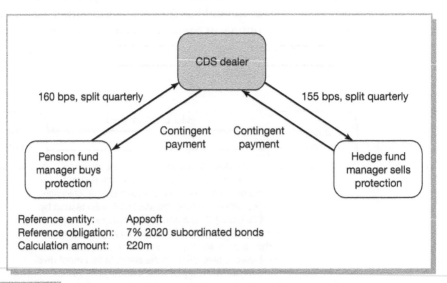

Reference entity: Appsoft
Reference obligation: 7% 2020 subordinated bonds
Calculation amount: £20m

Figure 22.7   **Credit default swap arrangement: five-year Appsoft with 155/160 bid/offer**

agreements. Thus CDS arrangements are very similar to standard insurance and, in fact, many insurance companies have entered this market as protection sellers. The major difference between CDS protection and standard insurance is that with insurance you have to own the asset and suffer the loss to receive a pay out. With a CDS you can buy 'protection' and receive a pay out from the dealer regardless of whether you own the asset. So another fund may never own bonds in Appsoft, but can speculate in the CDS market; e.g. make regular quarterly payments to the dealer in the hope that Appsoft commits a default and the dealer is forced to make a large pay out.

The right side of Figure 22.7 shows the payments between the dealer and a hedge fund manager who will take on the credit event risk in return for a quarterly payment. Thus the dealer ends up both buying protection and selling protection. But notice that he has made a margin between the two. Protection is sold for 160 basis points and bought for 155 basis points.

Settlement and credit events

CDSs can be **physically settled** which means that when a credit event occurs the protection buyer will deliver debt assets of the reference entity to the protection seller. In return the protection seller pays their par value (£20m for Appsoft). The bonds or loans delivered do not have to be the specified reference obligation, but they cannot be subordinated (higher risk) to it. Appsoft might have issued some other bonds which the pension fund manager chooses to deliver instead of the bond acting as the reference obligation. Once the settlement process is triggered the CDS quarterly premiums paid by the protection buyer cease.

Some CDSs are **cash settled**, that is a credit event triggers a cash payment. To figure out how much is to be paid we first need to find the recovery value on the debt, that is the current market value of the instrument now that it has defaulted. A default does not usually result in the debt becoming completely worthless; a typical recovery rate on a defaulted bond is around 40% of its par value, but this varies tremendously. For some defaulted bonds there may be an active secondary market which will fix the current price, for others it is necessary to conduct an auction process in which dealers submit prices at which they would buy and sell the reference entity's debt obligations. In the case of Lehman Brothers in an October 2008 auction, the price was set at 8.625 through billions of dollars-worth of actual trades, which means that dealers were still willing to pay 8.625% of the par value of Lehman's bonds to hold them even though they were in default. The protection sellers therefore had to make up the remainder of the par value as a cash payment to the CDS holders, i.e. 91.375% of the par value was paid out.

When Metro-Goldwyn-Mayer defaulted in 2009 the bonds were valued at 58.5% of par and so 41.5% was paid out.

So far we have skipped over what we mean by a credit event.

What do we mean by a credit event?

The following are the main categories:

- **Insolvency of the entity** (but not for governments).
- **Failure to pay.** Principal and/or interest not paid.
- **Debt restructuring.** When companies have difficulty paying their debts they negotiate with their lenders to vary the terms of the debt in their favour – e.g. an extension of maturity, interest deferral, principal forgiveness, swapping debt for shares in the firm – resulting in a poorer deal for the lenders. These restructurings are often defined as defaults, but some CDS agreements specifically exclude this type of event due to the lack of clarity on whether a particular restructuring is really a default.
- **Obligation acceleration.** This refers to technical defaults such as violation of a bond covenant, but these are rarely included.
- **Repudiation/moratorium.** Government borrower renounces its debt obligations and refuses to pay, e.g. disclaims or disaffirms the validity of a debt claim.

Other swaps

Currency swap

With a straight currency swap a borrower takes up a loan offer in a currency, say euros. However, the borrower prefers to have money and exposure to sterling-based borrowing. It arranges a swap with a swap dealer (usually a bank) whereby the borrower agrees to immediately swap the euros received for sterling. It also agrees to pay periodic interest in sterling. The dealer in return will pay regular euro interest (the borrower can satisfy its euro creditor). The final element of the swap occurs at the maturity of the loan. The borrower now swaps back the sterling principal amount to the swap dealer in return for the euros. The borrower can then use these euros to pay off the debt. The currency swap might be motivated by potentially lower overall interest rates and/or hedging of interest rate positions and/or hedging of foreign exchange risk. Note that, unlike interest rate swaps, currency swaps involve the exchange of principal.

Commodity price swap

Each counterparty agrees to make regular payments to the other where one of the payments is determined by the varying price of a commodity or an index of commodities. Thus an airline vulnerable to a rise in the price of oil, might agree to pay regular fixed amounts to a swap dealer over several years in return for the swap dealer paying on the same dates a sum based on an oil price index. So if the price of oil rises the airline will pay more in the oil marketplace, but will receive more from the swap dealer than it pays the swap dealer.

Equity swaps

An investor agrees to receive the percentage return on a share market index (or a company's shares) such as the FTSE 100 over a number of months. In return the investor pays the swap dealer the return on another underlying, e.g. LIBOR, S&P500 or a fixed sum of money.

Real estate swaps

One counterparty pays a rate of return linked to the level of an index of property prices, while the other pays another return, say LIBOR.

Options

An **option** is a contract giving one party the right, but not the obligation, to buy or sell a financial instrument, commodity or some other underlying asset at a given price, at or before a specified date. The purchaser of the option can either exercise the right or let it lapse – the choice is theirs.

A very simple option would be where a firm pays the owner of land a non-returnable **premium** (say £10,000) for an option to buy the land at an agreed price because the firm is considering the development of a retail park within the next five years. The property developer may pay a number of option premiums to owners of land in different parts of the country. If planning permission is eventually granted on a particular plot the option to purchase may be **exercised**. In other words, the developer pays the price agreed with the land owner at the time that the option contract was arranged, say £1,000,000, to purchase the land. Options on other plots may be **allowed to lapse** and will have no value. By using an option the property developer has 'kept the options open' with regard to which site to buy and develop and, indeed, whether to enter the retail park business at all.

Options can also be **traded**. Perhaps the option to buy could be sold to another company keener to develop a particular site than the original option purchaser. It may be sold for much more than the original £10,000 option premium, even before planning permission has been granted. Once planning permission has been granted the greenfield site may be worth £1.5m. If there is an option to buy at £1m the option right has an **intrinsic value** of £0.5m, representing a 4,900% return on £10,000. From this we can see the gearing effect of options: very large sums can be gained in a short period of time for a small initial cash outlay.

Share options

A **share call option** gives the purchaser a right, but not the obligation, to *buy* a fixed number of shares at a specified price at some time in the future. In the case of traded options on NYSE Liffe, one option contract relates to a quantity of 1,000 shares. The seller of the option, who receives the premium, is referred to as the **writer**. The writer of a call option is obligated to sell the agreed quantity of shares at the agreed price some time in the future. **American-style options** can be exercised by the buyer at any time up to the expiry date, whereas **European-style options** can only be exercised on a predetermined future date. Just to confuse everybody, the distinction has nothing to do with geography: most options traded in Europe are American-style options.

Call option holder (call option buyer)

Now let us examine the call options available on an underlying share – AstraZeneca on 20 May 2013. There are a number of different options available for this share, many of which are not reported in the table presented in the *Financial Times*.[2] A section of this table is reproduced as Table 22.2. These are American-style options.

Table 22.2   **Call options on AstraZeneca shares, 20 May 2013**

	Call option prices (premiums) pence		
Exercise price	June	July	Aug
3300p	114.5	132.5	149
3400p	50.5	72	87.5
Share price on 20 May 2013 = 3390.5p			

Source: www.ft.com.

So, what do the figures mean? If you wished to obtain the right to buy 1,000 shares on or before late July 2013,[3] at an **exercise price** of 3400p, you would pay a premium of £720 (1,000 × 72p). If you wished to keep your option to purchase open for another month you could select the August call. But this right to insist that the writer sells the shares at the fixed price of 3400p on or before a date in late August will cost another £155 (the total premium payable on one option contract = £875). This extra £155 represents additional *time* **value**. Time value arises because of the potential for the market price of the underlying to change in a way that creates intrinsic value.

The intrinsic value of an option is the pay off that would be received if the underlying were at its current level when the option expires. In this case, there is currently no intrinsic value because the right to buy is at 3400p whereas the share price is 3390.5p. However, if you look at a call option with an exercise price of 3300p then the right to buy at £33 has intrinsic value because if you purchased at 3300p by exercising the option, thereby obtaining 1,000 shares, you could immediately sell at 3390.5p in the share market: intrinsic value equals 90.5p per share, or £905 for 1,000 shares. The longer the time over which the option is exercisable the greater the chance that the price will move to give intrinsic value – this explains the higher premiums on more distant expiry options. Time value is the amount by which the option premium exceeds the intrinsic value.

The two-exercise price (also called **strike price**) levels presented in Table 22.2 illustrate an **in-the-money option** (the 3300 call option) and an **out-of-the-money option** (the 3400 call option). The underlying share price is above the strike price of 3300 and so this call option has an intrinsic value of 90.5p and is therefore in-the-money. The right to buy at 3400p is out-of-the-money because the share price is below the option exercise price and therefore has no intrinsic value. The holder of a 3400p option would not exercise this right to buy at 3400p because the shares can be bought on the stock exchange for 3390.5p.

To emphasise the key points: the option premiums vary in proportion to the length of time over which the option is exercisable (e.g. they are higher for an August option than for a July option). Also, call options with lower exercise prices will have higher premiums.

Example   Options

Suppose that you are confident that AstraZeneca shares are going to rise significantly over the next three months to 3600p and you purchase an August 3300 call at 149 pence.[4] The cost of this right to purchase 1,000 shares is £1,490 (149p × 1,000 shares). If the share rises as expected then you could exercise the right to purchase the shares for a total of £33,000 and then sell these in the market for £36,000. A profit of £3,000 less £1,490 = £1,510 is made before transaction costs (the brokers' fees, etc. would be in the region of £20–£50). This represents a 101% rise before costs (£1,510/£1490).

▶

However, the future is uncertain and the share price may not rise as expected. Let us consider two other possibilities. First, the share price may remain at 3390.5p throughout the life of the option. Secondly, the stock market may have a severe downturn and AstraZeneca shares may fall to 2900p. These possibilities are shown in Table 22.3.

Table 22.3 Profit (loss) on the AstraZeneca August 3300 call following purchase on 15.5.13

	Assumed share prices in August at expiry date		
	3600p	3390.5p	2900p
Cost of purchasing shares by exercising the option	£33,000	£33,000	£33,000
Value of shares bought	£36,000	£33,905	£29,000
Profit from exercise of option and sale of shares in the market	£3,000	£905	Not exercised
Less option premium paid	*£1490*	*£1490*	*£1490*
Profit (loss) before transaction costs	£1,510	(£585)	(£1490)
Percentage return over 3 months	101%	–39%	–100%

In the case of a standstill in the share price the option gradually loses its time value over the three months until, at expiry, only the intrinsic value of 90.5p per share remains. The fall in the share price to 2900p illustrates one of the advantages of purchasing options over some other derivatives: the holder has a right to abandon the option and is not forced to buy the underlying share at the option exercise price – this saves £4,000. It would have added insult to injury to have to buy at £33,000 and sell at £29,000 after having already lost £1,490 on the premium for the purchase of the option.

Call option writers

If the market price is less than the exercise price (3300p) in August the option will not be exercised and the call writer profits to the extent of the option premium (149p per share). A market price greater than the exercise price will result in the option being exercised and the writer will be forced to deliver 1,000 shares for a price of 3300p. This may mean buying shares on the stock market to supply to the option holder. As the share price rises this becomes increasingly onerous and losses mount.

Note that in the sophisticated traded option markets of today very few option positions are held to expiry. In most cases the option holder sells the option in the market to make a cash profit or loss. Option writers often cancel out their exposure before expiry, e.g. they could purchase an option to buy the same quantity of shares at the same price and expiry date.

Liffe share options

The *Financial Times* lists over 50 companies' shares in which options are traded – see Figure 22.8, which shows some option prices for 20 May 2013, including that of AstraZeneca. This table is a cut down version of the data available at **https://globalderivatives.nyx.com/en/nyse-liffe** where over 570 company options are traded through the day (also a wider variety of strike prices are shown).

Put options

A **put option** gives the holder the right, but not the obligation, to sell a specific quantity of shares on or before a specified date at a fixed exercise price. Imagine you are pessimistic about the prospects for Sainsbury, the supermarket chain, on 20 May 2013. You could purchase, for a premium of 11.5p per share (£115 in total), the right to sell 1,000 shares in or before late August 2013 at 370p (see Figure 22.8). If a fall in price subsequently takes place, to, say, 340p, you can insist on exercising the right to sell at 370p. The writer of the put option is obliged to purchase shares at 370p while being aware that the put holder is able to buy shares at 340p on the stock exchange. The option holder makes a profit of 370 – 340 – 11.5 = 18.5p per share (£185), a 161% return (before costs of £20–£40).

For the put option holder, if the market price exceeds the exercise price, it will not be wise to exercise as shares can be sold for a higher price on the London Stock Exchange. Therefore the maximum loss, equal to the premium paid, is incurred. The option writer gains the premium if the share price remains above the exercise price, but may incur a large loss if the market price falls significantly.

Caps

An **interest rate cap** is a contract giving the purchaser the right effectively to set a maximum level for interest rates payable. Compensation is paid to the purchaser of a cap if interest rates rise above an agreed level. This is a hedging technique used to cover interest rate risk on longer-term borrowing (usually two to five years). Under these arrangements a company borrowing money can benefit from interest rate falls but can place a limit to the amount paid should interest rates rise.

EQUITY OPTIONS

Option	Calls Jun	Jul	Aug	Puts Jun	Jul	Aug
AstraZeneca (*3390.5) 3300	114.5	132.5	149	22.5	39.5	79
3400	50.5	72	87.5	58.5	79	126
Aviva (*339.4) 330	13.75	17.25	20.25	4.25	7.5	10.5
340	7.75	11.5	14.25	8	11.75	14.5
BAE Systems (*413) 410	12.75	16.25	20.25	9.5	13	16.75
420	7.75	11.5	15.25	14.75	18.25	21.75
Barclays (*326.2) 320	13.25	17.25	20.25	7	10.75	14.25
330	8	12	15	11.5	15.5	19
BG Group (*1232) 1200	52.5	65	74.5	20	32	46.5
1250	26	38.5	49.5	43.5	56	72.5
BHP Billiton (*1925) 1850	103	123.5	-	27	47.5	-
1900	71	93	110	45	66.5	83
BP (*472.550) 470	10.25	13.75	16.25	7.5	10.75	17
480	5.5	8.75	11.5	12.75	15.75	22.5
BAT (*3772) 3800	61.5	92.5	117.5	87.5	117.5	141
3900	27	54	76	153.5	179	199.5
BT Group (*322.2) 310	16.75	19.25	21.5	4.25	7	12.5
320	10	13.25	15.75	7.75	11	17.25
Diageo (*2045) 2000	64	78	87.5	18	31.5	54.5
2050	34.5	-	-	39	-	-
GlaxoSmKl (*1721.5) 1650	80.5	90	96	8.5	17.5	30.5
1700	44.5	56	63	22	33	50.5
HSBC (*769.9) 760	17.25	23.5	28.75	13.5	19.5	24.75
780	8.5	13.75	19.5	24.75	30	35.5
ICA (*282.6) 280	13.25	17.25	20.75	10.5	14.5	17.75
290	9	12.75	16.16.25	25	20	23.25
Kingfisher (*330.5) 330	9	12	14	8.25	11.25	13.25
340	4.5	7.75	10	14	17	19.25

Option	Calls Jun	Jul	Aug	Puts Jun	Jul	Aug
Land Sec Gp (*994) 1000	12.75	18	22	23.25	29.5	34.75
1100	-	0.5	1.75	112.25	112.5	114
Legal & Gen (*185.6) 180	7.75	9.25	10.75	2	3.5	5
185	4.5	6	7.75	3.75	5.25	6.75
Lloyds Bkg (*62.2) 60	3.5	4.25	5	1.25	2	2.75
62	2.5	-	-	2.25	-	-
Man Group (*131.9) 130	7.25	9.75	11.75	5.5	7.75	9.75
135	5	7.5	-	8.25	10.5	-
Marks & S (*440.5) 440	10.75	14.5	16.75	20	24.25	26.5
450	7.5	10.75	13.75	27.25	30.75	33.5
Morrison (Wm) (*263.9) 280	11.75	13.5	15	2.25	3.75	5.25
300	1.75	3.5	5	12.25	14	15.25
Natl Grid (*647.5) 820	29.5	30.5	32	14	19.25	23.75
840	14.75	16.5	19.25	25.75	30.75	35
Rio Tinto (*2903.5) 2900	107.5	147.5	177	102.5	141.5	200.5
3000	64	103	131	159.5	197	258
Royal Bk Scot (*351.9) 360	10.5	15.75	19.5	18.5	23.5	27.25
380	4.75	8.75	12.25	32.75	36.75	40
RI Dch Shell 'B' (*2304.5) 2300	38	52.5	62	32.5	46	72
2400	6	14.5	22.5	100.5	108.5	139
RSA Ins Gp (*115.9) 115	2.75	3.25	4.25	1.75	2.25	3.25
120	1	1.25	2	5	5.25	6
Sainsbury (*377.2) 370	14.75	17.25	19.25	7.25	9.75	11.5
380	9.25	12	14.25	12	14.5	16.75
Shire (*2006) 2000	107	125	144.5	20.5	37.5	56
2100	47.5	67.5	89.5	60.5	80	101
Std Chartd (*1626) 1650	35	52	63.5	57.5	73.5	98.5
1700	18.5	33.5	42.5	92	106.5	129.5

Option	Calls Jun	Sep	Dec	Puts Jun	Sep	Dec
Tesco (*383.1) 380	9.75	12.5	14.75	6.5	9.25	11.25
390	5.25	8.25	10	12.25	14.5	16.5
Vodafone (*197.6) 200	3.5	4.5	5.75	11.25	13	14.25
205	2	3	4.25	15.5	16.75	18
Xstrata (*334.950) 328	12.5	16.5	23	12	16	25
344	6	10	-	22	25.5	-
3iGroup (*357) 360	6.5	12.75	18.5	13.25	20.75	27.25
370	3	-	-	20.25	-	-
Carnival (*2410) 2300	117.5	-	-	22	-	-
2370	70	-	-	45.5	-	-
Compass (*898) 900	18.25	22.75	28.25	20	30.75	36.75
920	10	14.25	19.75	31.75	43	48.5
Experian (*1268) 1200	74.75	92.5	110.75	9.5	34	51.25
1250	39	-	-	27	-	-
Imp Tobacco (*2334) 2300	67.5	-	-	32.5	-	-
2400	25.5	66	98.5	90.5	159.5	191
IntContHotels (*1962) 1900	86	128.5	163	23.5	74.5	110
1950	54.5	-	-	41.5	-	-
ITV (*130.7) 126	6	-	4.75	1.25	-	-
135	1.75	-	-	6	9	11
Lon Stk Exchg (*1426) 1450	30.25	43.75	-	53.75	-	-
1500	15.25	-	62	88.5	134.75	160
Next (*4675) 4600	124	199.5	-	47	189.5	-
4700	69.5	146	-	93	238	-
Pearson (*1220) 1150	74.75	94	-	4.25	29.25	-
1200	36.25	62.25	78.75	15.75	49.5	66.75

Option	Calls Jun	Sep	Dec	Puts Jun	Sep	Dec
Reckitt Benck (*4770) 4800	87	127	157.5	115	153.5	221
5000	27	56.5	80.5	255.5	282.5	325.5
Reed Elsevier (*767.5) 740	34.25	-	-	-	6.5	-
760	20.5	36.25	49	12.75	33	45.75
Rentokil Init (*93.7) 88	6.25	7.75	9.25	0.5	2.25	3.75
92	3.25	-	3.25	-	1.5	-
Rolls-Royce (*1197) 1150	62.5	-	81.75	-	15	-
1200	29.75	62.75	81.75	32.25	64	88.25
SAB Miller (*3586) 3500	137.5	144	190	-	50	248.5
3600	77.5	-	-	90	188.5	-
Sage Group (*368.1) 360	12	20.25	27	3.75	11.5	17.75
370	6.5	-	-	8.25	-	-
Sm & Nephew (*788.5) 760	34.75	51.25	59.75	5.75	21.5	34.5
780	20.5	-	-	-11.75	-	-
SSE (*1646) 1600	60	75	84.5	13.5	59.5	77
1650	28.5	-	-	31.5	-	-
Standard Life (*415.4) 405	18.75	-	-	8.25	-	-
410	15.5	-	-	10	-	-
Unilever (*2853) 2800	79.5	99	113.5	25.5	44	70
2900	27.5	44.5	61	73	89.5	121
Utd Utilities (*784.5) 780	29.5	40	-	-35.75	52	-
800	18.75	30	41	47	62.25	90.25
Whitbread (*2837) 2700	152	-	160.5	-14	-	-
2800	80.5	131.5	160.5	88.5	90	140.5
Woseley (*3473) 3400	122.5	201.5	237.5	48	123	187.5
3500	72.5	-	-	98	-	-
WPP (*1165) 1150	35.5	-	-	-35.75	-	-
1200	15.25	46.5	66	68.5	99.25	127.75

Source: Euronext.liffe

*Underlying security price. Premiums shown are based on settlement prices. May 20 Total contracts, Equity and Index options: 500115 Calls: 119290 Puts: 71785

Figure 22.8   Equity options table displayed in the *Financial Times* (or available at www.ft.com)

Example   **Interest rate cap**

Oakham plc wishes to borrow £20m for five years. It arranges this with Bank A at a variable rate based on LIBOR plus 1.5%. The interest rate is reset every quarter based on three-month LIBOR. Currently this stands at an annualised rate of 3%. The firm is concerned that over a five-year period the interest rate could rise to a dangerous extent.

Oakham buys an interest rate cap set at LIBOR of 4.5% from Bank B. For the sake of argument we will assume that this costs 2.3% of the principal amount, or £20m × 0.023 = £460,000 payable immediately to the cap seller. If over the subsequent five years LIBOR rises above 4.5% in any three-month period Oakham will receive sufficient compensation from the cap seller to offset exactly any extra interest above 4.5%. So if for the whole of the third year LIBOR rose to 5.5% Oakham would pay interest at 5.5% plus 1.5% to Bank A but would also receive 1% compensation from the cap seller (a quarter every three months), thus capping the interest payable. If interest rates fall Oakham benefits by paying Bank A less.

The premium (£460,000) payable up front covers the buyer for the entire five years, with no further payment due.

Caps are usually arranged for amounts of £5m or more, but can be for underlyings of only $1m – but when they are this low it may be difficult to obtain competing cost quotes from the banks. It is up to the client to select the strike rate and whether the rollover frequency (when LIBOR is compared with the strike) will be, say, three months or six months. They are available in all the main currencies.

The size of the cap premium[5] depends on the difference between current interest rates and the level at which the cap becomes effective; the length of time covered; and the expected volatility of interest rates. The cap seller does not need to assess the creditworthiness of the purchaser because it receives payment of the premium in advance. Thus a cap is particularly suitable for highly geared firms, such as leveraged buyouts.

Floors and collars

Buyers of interest rate caps are sometimes keen to reduce the large cash payment at the outset. They can do this by simultaneously selling a **floor**, which results in a counterparty paying a premium. With a floor, if the interest rate falls below an agreed level, the seller (the **floor writer**) makes compensatory payments to the floor buyer. These payments are determined by the difference between the prevailing rates and the floor rate. The combination of selling a floor at a low strike rate and buying a cap at a higher strike rate is called a **collar**.

Example   Interest rate floor and collar

Returning to Oakham, the treasurer could buy a cap set at 4.5% LIBOR for a premium of £460,000 and sell a floor at 2% LIBOR receiving, say, £200,000. In any three-month period over the five-year life of the loan, if LIBOR rose above 4.5% the cap seller would pay compensation to Oakham; if LIBOR fell below 2% Oakham would save on the amount paid to Bank A but will have to make payments to the floor buyer, thus restricting the benefits from falls in LIBOR. Oakham, for a net premium of £260,000, has ensured that its effective interest payments will not diverge from the range 2% + 1.5% = 3.5% at the lower end, to 4.5% + 1.5% = 6% at the upper end, i.e. it has used a collar.

23

Foreign exchange markets

Foreign exchange (**forex** or **FX**) markets developed thousands of years ago in response to the growth of international trade. Today most of that trading is carried out by the FX departments of major banks, and it is a colossal amount each day – around $4,000bn. Actual import and export trading forms a tiny percentage of this figure. World exports are about $16,000bn per year, equating to a mere $44bn per day, about 1% of the amount traded on the FX markets.

This chapter looks at the foreign exchange markets from a number of angles. First, there is a description of the different types of FX markets, from simple spot 'immediate' delivery of one currency for another (immediate means within two days), to options which allow exchange of currency at a future date. Also examined are the ways in which FX prices are quoted, with a particular emphasis on understanding the tables in the *Financial Times*. Another important angle is the impact of shifts in FX rates on businesses and the ways in which banks can help reduce the risks.

The foreign exchange markets

On the most basic level, foreign exchange markets are markets in which one currency is exchanged for another, at a rate usually determined by market supply and demand. For example, if there is a lot of demand from the UK for US dollars, then the buying actions of market players will lead to pressure for the price of each US dollar to rise and conversely the price of each UK pound will fall.

FX trading takes place round the globe 24 hours a day. It is largely **OTC (over the counter)** where the trades are carried out between two parties directly without going through a regulated exchange.

We can see that there are many different FX markets – see Figure 23.1. In other words, there are many different types of foreign exchange deals available:

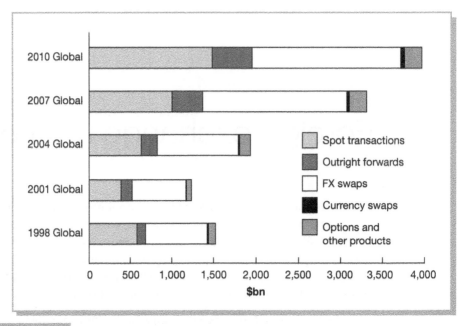

Figure 23.1   Global daily FX turnover in April

Source: Triennial Central Bank Survey: Report on global foreign exchange market activity in 2010, Bank for International Settlements, www.bis.org

Spot transaction

This is a single outright transaction involving the exchange of two currencies at a rate agreed on the date of the contract for delivery within two business days.[1]

Forward

This is a transaction involving the exchange of two currencies at a rate agreed on the date of the contract for delivery at some time in the future (more than two business days later). These contracts are negotiated and agreed between the two parties without going through a regulated exchange. Later in the chapter we look at the use of forward markets by corporations to fix the exchange rate for a transaction they will undertake months, or even years, from now. This brings a high degree of certainty about the rate of exchange at which they will be able to transact. **Foreign currency futures** are very similar to forwards except that they are traded on a regulated exchange, with standard contract sizes and maturity dates: e.g. £62,500 for next November at an agreed rate. Because the range of currencies, dates and contract sizes is so restricted the FX futures market is tiny compared with forwards.

Foreign exchange swap (FX swap)

A single deal with two parts to it. First, there is the actual exchange of two currencies on a specific date at a rate agreed at the time of the conclusion of the contract – this is usually a spot exchange but it can be a forward. Secondly, there is a reverse exchange of the same two currencies at a date further in the future at a rate agreed at the time of the contract. The rates of exchange are usually different in the two parts. These FX swaps take place all the time between professional players based in banks as they try to balance out their currency positions, reduce their risk exposure or speculate to gain higher returns.

Example   **An FX swap**

Your bank has £1bn invested in short-term sterling denominated securities. You know that in two weeks you will need the £1bn, but think that you can benefit from investing in US dollars in the meantime. However, you cannot take any risk from exchange rate movements.

Solution: In two days you swap pounds for dollars at an agreed exchange rate agreed today (a spot transaction). Also today you agree to swap the dollars back into pounds in two weeks at a rate of exchange agreed today. The dollars received at spot can be invested in interest-bearing assets, in say the Eurodollar market for two weeks. If you are correct you will have locked-in a higher return than if you left the money in sterling.

In effect you have borrowed dollars and lent sterling for two weeks to allow investment without fear of shifts in exchange rates.

Currency swap

This is a contract which commits two counterparties to exchange streams of interest payments in different currencies for an agreed period of time and to exchange principal amounts in different currencies at a pre-agreed exchange rate at maturity. These are the swaps discussed in Chapter 22 being linked to long-term loans with interest payments to be made: they should not be confused with FX swaps. A **currency swaption** is an option to enter into a currency swap contract.

Currency option

This is an option contract that gives the right to buy or sell a currency with another currency at a specified exchange rate during a specified period – illustrated later.

Places and currencies

Although over one-third of all FX trading takes place in London (see Figure 23.2), with London carrying out twice as much trade as its nearest rival, the USA, the actual currency that dominates is the US dollar, which acts as a counterparty in over 85% of all trading on one side of the trade (see Figure 23.3). The US dollar has become the currency that is accepted and used worldwide due to the size, strength and stability of the US economy. The currencies most commonly traded are: USD, the US dollar ($); EUR, the euro (€); JPY, the Japanese yen (¥); GBP, the UK pound (£); AUD, the Australian dollar (A$); CAD, the Canadian dollar (C$); and CHF, the Swiss franc (SFr).

Trading is constant, taking place on a 24-hour basis, with the high concentration of activity moving with the sun from one major financial centre to another. Most trading occurs when both the European and New York markets are open – this is when it is afternoon in Frankfurt, Zurich and London and morning on the east coast of the Americas. Later the bulk of the trade passes to San Francisco and Los Angeles, followed by Sydney, Tokyo, Hong Kong and Singapore. There are at least 40 other trading centres around the world in addition to these main ones.

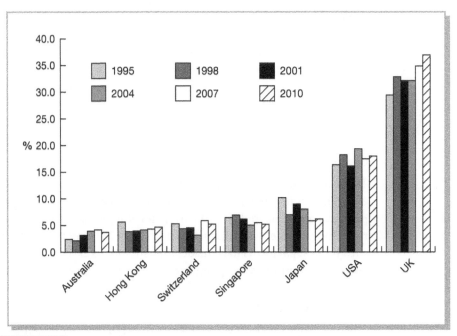

Figure 23.2 **Percentages of global foreign exchange market turnover by country, daily averages in April**

Source: Triennial Central Bank Survey: Report on global foreign exchange market activity in 2010, Bank for International Settlements, www.bis.org

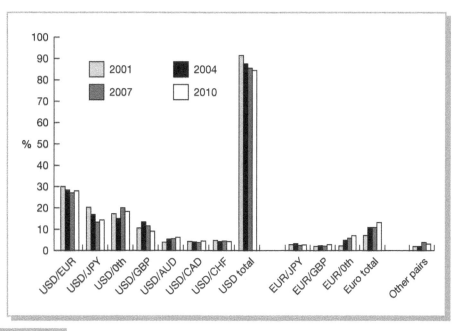

Figure 23.3   **Percentages of global foreign exchange market turnover by currency pair, daily averages in April**

Source: Triennial Central Bank Survey: Report on global foreign exchange market activity in 2010, Bank for International Settlements, www.bis.org

FX trading

In contrast to equity trading, where most countries tend to have one major exchange and trading is tightly regulated, trading on the foreign exchange market does not have a focal position where all trading is supervised and data are collected and displayed. Trading is carried out wherever a trader is and can access a computer screen or a mobile phone screen. Many trading platforms now offer an app for the new generation of mobile phones and tablet computers giving traders full access to all their facilities and data, enabling them to download data and carry out trading wherever they are. Some of the trades are on regulated exchanges but most are not. Anyone with the requisite knowledge can take part in FX trading, and regulation is lax for the most part. Having said that, the vast majority of trading is done by major international banks and their subsidiaries, with reputations to lose, so there is a high degree of self-regulation.

Most banks carry out proprietary trading, i.e. they trade in the hope of making profits on behalf of the bank itself. The banks are in the process of concentrating their dealers in three or four regional hubs. These typically include London as well as New York and a site in Asia, where Tokyo, Hong Kong and Singapore are keen to establish their dominance.

When a non-bank organisation needs an FX deal it mostly trades with a bank, but there are exchanges for some types of dealing. The main difference between FX trading via banks and FX trading carried out on exchanges such as the Chicago Mercantile Exchange (CME) is that exchange trading tends to deal in standard amounts and maturities. The amounts and maturities of these contracts are fixed and inflexible, so they may be less suitable for company use, where the company might need to hedge specific amounts for a specific time, and would therefore be better served using the flexibility offered by a bank. Dealing through an exchange facilitates clearing and settlement and exchange-traded currency instruments are liquid.

The buyers and sellers of foreign currencies are shown in Figure 23.4.

There are various ways in which deals are done. First, there is the traditional approach of the two dealers talking on the telephone and agreeing to trade. One of the dealers here may be a non-bank customer such as a manufacturing firm. If the customer approaches the bank without going through an intermediary

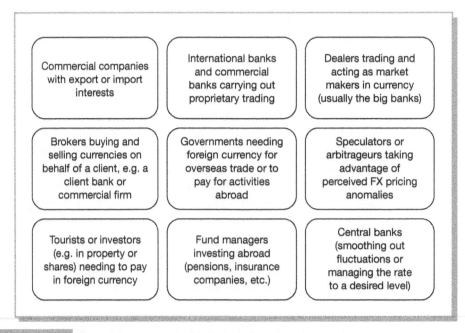

Figure 23.4   Buyers and sellers of foreign currencies

these are **customer direct trades**. However, a broker will frequently act on behalf of a customer to deal with banks in the FX markets – if conducted over the telephone these are **voice broker** trades. The trades between banks, referred to as **inter-dealer direct trades**, can be either via direct telephone communication or direct electronic dealing systems. Increasingly deals are conducted over electronic dealing systems. Banks are the main users of these systems, but there are special systems set up for customers. Some of these are run by a single bank as a **proprietary platform**. Others are managed by a group of banks – **multibank dealing systems**, e.g. FXall, Currenex, FX Connect, Globalink and eSpeed.

The electronic platforms have allowed smaller banks to access better prices and provide them with the opportunity to deal alongside the large banks on a more even basis because of the transparency of the systems. Rapid price dissemination from electronic systems has, to a great extent, levelled the playing field, whereas in the old days only the large banks could 'see' the market prices through their telephone contacts.

Exchange rates

> An exchange rate is the price of one currency (**the base currency**) expressed in terms of another (**the secondary, counter or quote currency**).

Therefore if the exchange rate between the US dollar and the pound is US$1.51 = £1.00 this means that £1.00 will cost US$1.51. Taking the reciprocal, US$1.00 will cost 66.23 pence. The standardised forms of expression are:

US$/£: 1.51	or	US$1.51/£	or	USD1.51/£

Exchange rates are expressed in terms of the number of units of the first currency per single unit of the second currency. Most currencies are quoted to four decimal places and the smallest variation used in trading is a **pip** which is one ten thousandth of one unit of currency (e.g. $1), or 0.0001. So for the US$/£ exchange rate on 24 May 2013 the rate was quoted in the *Financial Times* as:

US$1.5139/£

However, this is still not accurate enough because currency exchange rates are not generally expressed in terms of a single 'middle rate' as above, but are given as a rate at which you can buy the first currency (bid rate) and a rate at which you can sell the first currency (offer rate). This is called the **spread** and it enables market makers (traders) to make a profit on buying and selling currencies. In the case of the US$/£ exchange rate the market rates on 24 May 2013 were:

US$1.5139/£ 'middle rate'

	bid rate	offer rate
	↓	↓
US$/£	1.5137	1.5141
	↑	↑
	You can buy dollars from a bank or broker at this rate.	You can sell dollars to a bank or a broker at this rate.
	The difference (the spread) between bid and offer is 4 pips	

So if you wished to purchase US$1m the cost would be:

$$\frac{\$1,000,000}{1.5137} = £660,633$$

However, if you wished to sell US$1m you would receive:

$$\frac{\$1,000,000}{1.5141} = £660,458$$

The foreign exchange dealers are transacting with numerous buyers and sellers every day and they make a profit on the difference between the bid price and offer price (the bid/offer spread). In the above example if a dealer sold US$1m and bought US$1m with a bid/offer spread of 0.04 of a cent, a profit of £660,633 – £660,458 = £175 is made.

The FT table

The *Financial Times* displays some of the FX rates – see Figure 23.5, which relates to dealings on 24 May 2013.

The prices shown under the pound columns are the middle price of the foreign currency in terms of £1 in London at 4 p.m. So, for instance, the mid-price of £1 for immediate delivery is 1.5644 Australian dollars. For the US dollar columns the prices for the pound and euro are the number of dollars per currency unit, either per pound or per euro. However, for other currencies the rate shown is the number

May 24	Currency	DOLLAR Closing Mid	DOLLAR Day's Change	EURO Closing Mid	EURO Day's Change	POUND Closing Mid	POUND Day's Change		Currency	DOLLAR Closing Mid	DOLLAR Day's Change	EURO Closing Mid	EURO Day's Change	POUND Closing Mid	POUND Day's Change
Argentina	(Peso)	5.2685	0.0080	6.8125	0.0253	7.9760	0.0515	Poland	(Zloty)	3.2449	-0.0134	4.1957	-0.0081	4.9123	0.0042
Australia	(A$)	1.0333	0.0029	1.3361	0.0067	1.5644	0.0121	Romania	(New Leu)	3.3661	-0.0094	4.3525	-0.0025	5.0959	0.0111
Bahrain	(Dinar)	0.3770	-	0.4875	0.0011	0.5708	0.0029	Russia	(Rouble)	31.3290	-0.0760	40.5100	-0.0088	47.4290	0.1206
Bolivia	(Boliviano)	6.9100	-	8.9350	0.0197	10.4611	0.0519	Saudi Arabia	(SR)	3.7502	-	4.8492	0.0107	5.6774	0.0281
Brazil	(R$)	2.0489	-0.0061	2.6493	-0.0021	3.1018	0.0061	Singapore	(S$)	1.2644	-0.0008	1.6349	0.0026	1.9141	0.0083
Canada	(C$)	1.0325	-0.0018	1.3350	0.0006	1.5630	0.0050	South Africa	(R)	9.5588	-0.0112	12.3600	0.0129	14.4710	0.0549
Chile	(Peso)	488.250	-0.6000	631.332	0.6173	739.162	2.7580	South Korea	(Won)	1127.25	-1.3250	1457.59	1.5032	1706.54	6.4583
China	(Yuan)	6.1316	-0.0024	7.9285	0.0144	9.2827	0.4424	Sweden	(SKr)	6.6452	-0.0203	8.5925	-0.0072	10.0601	0.0193
Colombia	(Peso)	1868.61	4.4300	2416.20	11.0411	2828.88	20.6879	Switzerland	(SFr)	0.9608	-0.0087	1.2424	-0.0086	1.4546	-0.0060
Costa Rica	(Colon)	499.775	0.7200	646.235	2.3531	756.611	4.8330	Taiwan	(T$)	29.9095	-0.0560	38.6745	0.0130	45.2800	0.1399
Czech Rep.	(Koruna)	20.0530	-0.2074	25.9295	-0.2105	30.3582	-0.1621	Thailand	(Bt)	29.9300	-	38.7010	0.0853	45.3110	0.2244
Denmark	(DKr)	5.7641	-0.0134	7.4532	-0.0009	8.7262	0.0230	Tunisia	(Dinar)	1.6540	-0.0035	2.1387	0.0002	2.5039	0.0071
Egypt	(Egypt £)	6.9820	-		9.0280	0.0198	10.5700	0.0524	Turkey	(Lira)	1.8463	-0.0048	2.3874	-0.0009	2.7951	0.0066
Hong Kong	(HK$)	7.7635	0.0001	10.0385	0.0222	11.7531	0.0584	UAE	(Dirham)	3.6730	-	4.7494	0.0105	5.5606	0.0275
Hungary	(Forint)	223.530	-2.3617	289.035	-2.4100	338.402	-1.8813	UK (0.6605)*	(£)	1.5139	0.0075	0.8541	-0.0023	-	-
India	(Rs)	55.6050	-0.0350	71.9001	0.1133	84.1804	0.3643	One Month		1.5136		0.8544		-	-
Indonesia	(Rupiah)	9772.50	-	12636.3	29.1417	14794.6	74.8002	Three Month		1.5131		0.8551	0.0000	-	-
Iran	(Rial)	12278.5	-	15876.7	34.9937	18588.4	92.0887	One Year		1.5117	-0.0001	0.8579	-0.0001	-	-
Israel	(Shk)	3.7010	-0.0032	4.7856	0.0064	5.6029	0.0228	Ukraine	(Hrywnja)	8.1460	0.0010	10.5332	0.0245	12.3323	0.0626
Japan	(Y)	101.185	-0.2500	130.837	-0.0342	153.184	0.3822	Uruguay	(Peso)	19.0150	-	24.5874	0.0541	28.7869	0.1427
One Month		101.171	-0.0004	130.840	-0.0014	153.131	-0.0001	USA	($)	-	-	1.2931	0.0029	1.5139	0.0075
Three Month		101.135	-0.0002	130.845	-0.0020	153.022	-0.0010	One Month		-	-	1.2933	-	1.5136	-
One Year		100.849	-0.0025	130.791	-0.0282	152.453	-0.0209	Three Month		-	-	1.2938	-	1.5131	-
Kenya	(Shilling)	86.3000	-0.0500	109.004	0.1757	127.622	0.5569	One Year		-	-	1.2969	-0.0002	1.5117	-0.0001
Kuwait	(Dinar)	0.2867	-	0.3707	0.0008	0.4340	0.0021	Venezuela (Bolivar Fuerte)		6.2921	-	8.1360	0.0180	9.5256	0.0472
Malaysia	(M$)	3.0345	-	3.9238	0.0087	4.5940	0.0228	Vietnam	(Dong)	21000.0	-	27154.1	59.8485	31791.9	157.500
Mexico	(New Peso)	12.4990	0.0073	16.1619	0.0450	18.9222	0.1046								
New Zealand	(NZ$)	1.2345	0.0012	1.5963	0.0051	1.8689	0.0111	Euro (0.7734)*	(Euro)	1.2931	0.0029	-	-	1.1708	0.0032
Nigeria	(Naira)	158.000	-0.3000	204.302	0.0632	239.196	0.7331	One Month		1.2933	-	-	-	1.1704	0.0000
Norway	(NKr)	5.8329	-0.0155	7.5422	-0.0033	8.8304	0.0205	Three Month		1.2938	-	-	-	1.1695	-
Pakistan	(Rupee)	98.2850	-0.1400	127.087	0.0995	148.794	0.5262	One Year		1.2969	-0.0002	-	-	1.1656	0.0001
Peru	(New Sol)	2.6735	0.0020	3.4570	0.0102	4.0474	0.0231								
Philippines	(Peso)	41.600	-0.0750	53.7909	0.0218	62.9783	0.1990	SDR	—	0.6691	-0.0011	0.8652	0.0005	1.0129	0.0034

Rates are derived from WM/Reuters at 4pm (London time). * The closing mid-point rates for the Euro and £ against the $ are shown in brackets. The other figures in the dollar column of both the Euro and sterling rows are in the reciprocal form in line with market convention. Currency redenominated by 1000. Some values are rounded by the F.T. The exchange rates printed in this table are also available on the internet at **http://www.ft.com/marketsdata**

Euro Locking Rates: Austrian Schilling 13.7603, Belgium/Luxembourg Franc 40.3399, Cypriot Pound 0.585274. Finnish Markka 5.94572. French Franc 6.55957, German Mark 1.95583, Greek Drachma 340.75, Irish Punt 0.787564, Italian Lira 1936.27, Maltese Lire 0.4293, Netherlands Guilder 2.20371, Portuguese Escudo 200.482, Slovenia Tolar 239.64, Spanish Peseta 166.386.

Figure 23.5   **Currency rates from the Financial Times, 24 May 2013**

Source: The WM Company/Reuters

of units of the other currency per US$1 – for example, 1.0325 Canadian dollars per US dollar. For the euro columns the rate shown is the number of units of the other currency per euro, e.g. the spot mid-rate against the pound is 85.41p per euro.

While the most common currencies often have forward rates quoted, there are many currencies for which forward quotes are difficult to obtain, so-called **exotic currencies.** These are currencies for which there is little trading demand to support international business, etc. On the other hand, spot markets exist for most of the world's currencies.

The first forward price (middle price) is given as the 'one-month' rate. Looking at the sterling and US$ rates you could commit yourself to the sale of a quantity of dollars for delivery in one month at a rate that is fixed at about US$1.5136 per pound. In this case you will need fewer USDs to buy £1 in one month's time compared with the spot rate of exchange, therefore the dollar is at a **premium** on the one-month forward rate. (If it was more the dollar one-month forward rate would be at a **discount**.)

The *Financial Times* table (see Figure 23.5 again) lists quotations of up to one year for the four strongest currencies, the dollar, euro, yen and pound, but, as this is an over-the-counter market it is possible to go as far forward in time as required – provided a counterparty can be found. The table displays standard periods of time for forward rates, one month, three months and one year. These are instantly available and are frequently traded. However, forward rates are not confined to these particular days in the future. It is possible to obtain rates for any day in the future, say, 74 or 36 days hence for any amount of currency, but these would require a specific quotation from a bank.

FX volatility and its effects

You might wonder what the significance of fluctuating FX rates is. If you go on holiday to Europe, you might get more or less euro for your pound or dollar than last year – usually a fairly minor boost or inconvenience. But for companies trading millions or billions internationally, even small differences in exchange rates can have major consequences. If a UK firm holds dollars or assets denominated in dollars and the value of the dollar rises against the pound, then the dollars and dollar assets are worth more in pounds and an FX profit is made. Conversely, should the pound rise relative to the dollar, dollars and dollar assets are worth less compared to the pound and an FX loss will be incurred. These potential gains or losses can be very large.

For example, between December 2007 and February 2009 the dollar appreciated by just over a third against the pound, so anyone who sold pounds for dollars in December 2007 and kept them would have made a 33% profit on changing them back into pounds in 2009 – see Figure 23.6. If the money had also been put to work earning interest more could have been realised.

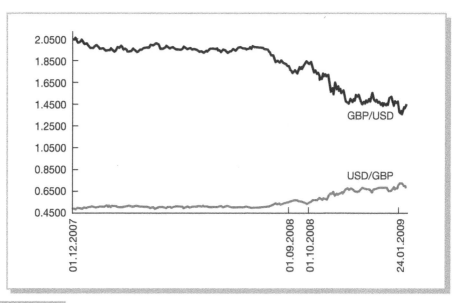

Figure 23.6 The exchange rate rates of the US dollar and GB pound

Source: © 2013 OANDA Corporation. Used with permission. (www.oanda.com)

Example **Loss on FX**

On 24 July 2008 two UK companies, GBX and GBA, each agreed to purchase $10,000 of goods from US company USY. GBX paid the $10,000 in July 2008 but GBA was permitted to delay payment until January 2009, expecting to exchange pounds for dollars then.

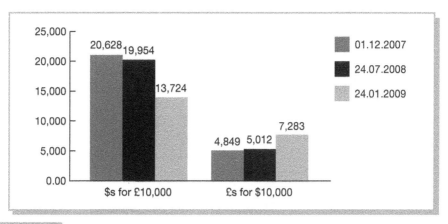

Figure 23.7 The relative value of 10,000 USD and GBP

> At the time of purchase, the goods would have cost £5,012 if the pounds were exchanged at the prevailing spot rate. However due to GBP/USD rates changing, when 24 January came, company GBA had to pay £7,283 to obtain $10,000, so GBA made a substantial FX loss compared to GBA who obtained the dollars in July 2008 – see Figure 23.7.

Apart from the problems fluctuating exchange rates cause for importers there are at least four other major issues:

1 **Income to be received from abroad.** If a UK firm has exported goods to Canada on six months' credit terms, payable in Canadian dollars (C$), it is uncertain how many pounds it will actually receive because the Canadian currency could change in value compared to the pound in the intervening period.

2 **The valuation of foreign assets and liabilities.** In today's globalised marketplace many firms own assets abroad, or have foreign subsidiaries. The value of any of these assets or liabilities in domestic currency terms can change simply because of FX movements.

3 **The long-term viability of operations in particular countries.** UK company Burberry is benefiting from the weakness of sterling to gain custom from Chinese consumers. Thus we see that the long-term future returns of subsidiaries located in some countries can be enhanced by a favourable FX change. On the other hand, firms can be destroyed if they are operating in the wrong currency at the wrong time.

4 **The acceptability, or otherwise, of an overseas investment project.** When evaluating the value-creating potential of major new investments a firm must be aware that the likely future currency changes can have a significant effect on estimated value generated from the venture.

Dealing with exchange rate risk

How then do banks assist companies to deal with all this volatility? There are various ways of ameliorating the risk of currency fluctuations. Some of them are outlined below in the context of an exporter selling goods on credit – banks earn a considerable amount of money facilitating these trades. We will use the example of a UK company exporting £1m of goods to a US firm when the spot rate of exchange is $1.5139/£. The American firm is given three months to pay the invoice amount of $1,513,900, and naturally the spot rate in three months is unknown at the time of the shipment of goods. What can the firm do?

Covering in the forward market

If the pound strengthens against the dollar to $1.80/£, the UK exporter will make a currency loss by waiting three months and exchanging the dollars received into sterling. The exporter will receive only £841,056:

$$\frac{\$1,513,900}{1.80} = £841,056$$

which is a loss of £158,944 compared with if FX rates had been static.

If sterling weakens to $1.40/£ a currency gain is made. The pounds received in three months at this spot rate will be:

$$\frac{\$1,513,900}{1.40} = £1,081,357$$

which is a currency-shift gain of £81,357. Some managers are content to take a 'win-some-lose-some' attitude to their overseas transactions, but many are so fearful of the impact of adverse movements that they hedge their positions. In this case, rather than run the risk of a possible loss on the currency side of the deal, the exporter decides to cover in the forward market. Under this arrangement the exporter promises to sell $1,513,900 against the pound to a bank in three months (the agreement is made at the start for delivery of currency three months later). The three-month forward rate available is $1.5131/£. This forward contract means that the exporter will receive £1,000,529 regardless of the way in which the spot exchange rate moves over the three months:

$$\frac{\$1,513,900}{1.5131} = £1,000,529$$

After three months the following transactions take place.

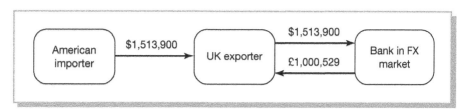

From the outset the exporter knew the amount to be received, assuming away counterparty risk. It might, with hindsight, have been better not to use the forward market but to exchange the USD at a spot rate of, say, $1.4000/£. This would have resulted in a larger income for the firm. But when the export took place there was uncertainty about what the spot rate would be three months later. If the exporter had waited to exchange the currency until later and the spot rate turned out to be $1.8000/£ it would have made less. Covering in the forward market is a form of insurance which leads to greater certainty – and certainty has a value. For many companies it is of vital importance that they have this certainty about income and expenditure; they cannot afford to leave things and hope they will turn out satisfactorily.

Money market hedge

Money market hedging involves borrowing in the money markets. For example, the exporter could, at the time of the export, borrow in dollars on the money markets for a three-month period. The amount borrowed, plus three months' interest, will be equal to the amount to be received from the importer ($1,513,900).

If the interest rate charged over three months is 8% annualised, 2% for three months, then the appropriate size of the loan is:

$$\$1,513,900 = \$? \times (1 + 0.02)$$

Rearranging the equation:

$$\$? = \frac{\$1,513,900}{1.02} = \$1,484,216$$

Thus the exporter has created a liability (borrowed funds) which matches the asset (debt owed by the American firm). The borrowed dollars are then converted to sterling on the spot market for the exporter to receive £980,392 immediately:

$$\frac{\$1,484,216}{1.5139} = \pounds980,392$$

The exporter has removed FX risk because it now holds cash in sterling three months before the debt was originally due, taking a small loss of £19,608, but this could be offset by three months' interest. Three months later $1.5139m is received from the importer and this exactly matches the outstanding debt:

Amount borrowed + Interest = Debt owed at end of period

$1,484,216 + ($1,484,216 × 0.02) = $1,513,900

The five steps in the money market hedge are as follows:

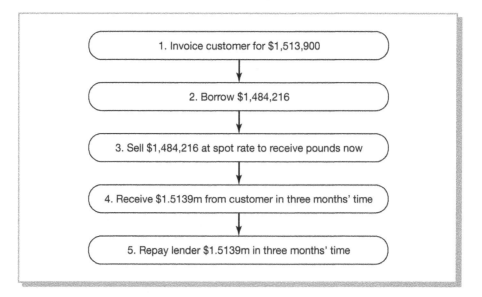

1. Invoice customer for $1,513,900

2. Borrow $1,484,216

3. Sell $1,484,216 at spot rate to receive pounds now

4. Receive $1.5139m from customer in three months' time

5. Repay lender $1.5139m in three months' time

An importer could also use a money market hedge. A Swiss company importing Japanese cars for payment in yen in three months could borrow in Swiss francs now and convert the funds at the spot rate into yen. This money is deposited to earn interest, with the result that after three months the principal plus interest equals the invoice amount.

Currency option hedge

A **currency option** is a contract giving the buyer (that is, the holder) the right, but not the obligation, to buy or sell a specific amount of currency at a specific exchange rate (the strike price), on or before a specified future date.

A call option gives the right to buy a particular currency.

A put option gives the right to sell a particular currency.

The option writer (usually a bank) guarantees, if the option buyer chooses to exercise the right, to exchange the currency at the predetermined rate. Because the writer is accepting risk the buyer must pay a premium to the writer – normally within two business days of the option purchase. (For more details on options see Chapter 22.)

Table 23.1 shows currency options premiums for the currency rates between the pound and the dollar.

Table 23.1   GBP/USD options for 'delivery' in August as quoted in May

Strike price	Premium
15000 Call	4.07 cents
15000 Put	1.80 cents
15100 Call	3.41 cents
15100 Put	2.15 cents
15200 Call	2.83 cents
15200 Put	2.57 cents

For the GBP/USD call options the purchaser has the right but not the obligation to purchase pounds for dollars. Potential call option buyers have a number of possible rates of exchange open to them beyond the strike prices of $1.5000/£ to $1.5200/£ shown in Table 23.1. The premiums payable are quoted as US dollars per pound. One contract is for £62,500,[2] and only whole numbers of contracts on the exchange may be purchased. If you purchased a 15000 call option for expiry in August you would pay a premium of 4.07 US cents per UK pound (the total premium payable would be $0.0407 × 62,500 = $2,543.75) giving you the right to buy pounds with dollars in August at a rate of $1.50/£. Note that a less favourable exchange rate, e.g. 15200 ($1.52/£) commands a lower premium, only 2.83 cents per pound in the contract.

The purchase of a put option gives you the right but not the obligation to sell pounds and receive dollars. Again the quantity of an exchange-traded contract is £62,500.

The crucial advantage an option has over a forward is the absence of an obligation to buy or sell. It is the option buyer's decision whether to insist on exchange at the strike rate or to let the option lapse.

Imagine that the UK exporting firm hedges by buying a three-month sterling call option giving the right but not the obligation to deliver dollars to a bank in exchange for pounds with a strike price of $1.51/£. A premium will need to be paid up front. According to Table 23.1 this will be 3.41 cents per pound. On the regulated exchanges we can only trade in multiples of £62,500 so we need £1,000,000 ÷ £62,500 = 16 contracts. Thus the premium to have the right but not the obligation to exchange dollars for pounds at any point up to late August, is $0.0341 × 62,500 × 16 = $34,100. This is payable two business days after the option deal is struck.

Three months later

The dollars are delivered by the importer on the due date. Should the option at $1.51/£ be exercised? Let us consider two scenarios.

Scenario 1

The dollar has strengthened against the pound to $1.4/£. If the company exercises the right to exchange at $1.51/£ the UK firm will receive:

$$\frac{\$1,513,900}{1.51} = £1,002,583$$

If the company lets the option lapse – 'abandons it' – and exchanges the dollars in the spot market, the amount received will be:

$$\frac{\$1,513,900}{1.4} = £1,081,357$$

an extra £78,774.

Clearly in this case the best course of action would be to abandon the option, and exchange at the spot rate.

Scenario 2

Now assume that the dollar has weakened against sterling to $1.70/£. If the treasurer confirms that the exporter wishes to exercise the $1.51/£ option the treasurer will arrange delivery of $1,513,900 to the bank and will receive £1,002,583 in return:

$$\frac{\$1,513,900}{1.51} = £1,002,583$$

If the option is abandoned and the $1.5139m is sold in the spot FX market, the amount received will be:

$$\frac{\$1,513,900}{1.70} = £890,529$$

This is unattractive and so the option will be exercised.

With the option, the worst that could happen is that the exporter receives £1,002,583 less the premium. However the upside potential is unconstrained.

part

4

Central banking and regulation

24

Monetary policy

If interest rates are held at a level that is too low then inflation will start to take off. This can be disruptive to businesses in addition to destroying the savings of people. It is especially problematic if inflation is high and fluctuating. The resulting uncertainty about future price levels is likely to inhibit economic growth or, at the very least, penalise those who are not protected against inflation. Unpredictability makes planning very difficult.

On the other hand, if interest rates are set at an excessively high level this will inhibit business activity, cause people to put off buying houses and reduce spending in the shops, leading to a recession with massive job losses. Clearly a society needs an organisation whose task it is to select the appropriate interest rate for the economic conditions it faces: neither too high nor too low. That organisation is the central bank.[1] This **monetary policy** function is examined in this chapter, but there are many other tasks for central banks; these are considered in the next chapter.

Monetary base

When the amount of money spent rises faster than the quantity of goods and services produced in the economy the result is likely to be raised inflation. To understand how a central bank controls money supply and interest rates you need to appreciate that it acts as banker to the banks (including other depository institutions, e.g. building societies). As well as accepting deposits from them it has special powers because it can insist that each bank leaves a certain proportion of the amount it has received as deposits from its customers (households, small businesses, etc.) at the central bank. If a bank's reserves at the central bank fall below the minimum required then it has to top this up.[2,3]

Furthermore, banks and other depository institutions (henceforth 'banks') like to maintain an additional buffer beyond the required reserves at the central bank. This extra safety margin of money is called excess reserves. This is an amount that makes a bank feel comfortable about the prospect of a sudden outflow of cash – say dozens of large depositors withdraw billions over a period of a week (see Chapter 7). The target amount of the excess reserves may, in fact, be largely dictated by the banking regulator (which is usually the central bank) and may be strongly influenced by international agreements on the appropriate amounts, e.g. Basel III – see 'Bank supervision' in the next chapter.

The central bank has a liability – it accepts deposits from banks. Another liability of a central bank is what you see written on notes (or coins) that you have in your wallet or purse. The central bank 'promises to pay the bearer on demand the sum of...' or some similarly worded promise.[4] Thus a typical commercial bank will hold some of its assets in the form of reserves either at the central bank or in the form of vault cash in hand. As well as the money held in the banks an economy will have **currency in circulation**, that is outside of banks. The combination of the two is the monetary base:

Monetary base = Currency in circulation	+ Reserves	
Reserves = Required reserves	+ Vault cash (excess reserves)	

It is changes in these accounts that determine the size of a nation's money supply (everything else being held constant). If there is an increase either in the currency in circulation or reserves there will be an increase in the money supply. An increase in reserves, either cash deposited by a bank at the central bank or vault cash, leads to an increase in the level of deposits and thus contributes to the money supply. Central banks conduct monetary policy by changing the country's monetary base.

A central bank might insist that, say, 10% of the amount deposited by customers be held as the **required reserve ratio**.[5] The reserve accounts[6] held by banks at the central bank are used to settle accounts between depository institutions when cheques and electronic payments are cleared. A bank may also hold, say, another 5–10% of the amount deposited by customers as excess reserves. It is important to note that the sole supplier of reserves – notes and coins and balances at the central bank as liabilities of the central bank – is the central bank.

The monetary base described above is often referred to as M0, which is a very extreme form of **narrow money**, i.e. defining what money is in a very narrow way. Banks can use this base to create **broad money**, which is a multiple of the monetary base. The definitions of broad money vary from country to country, but generally include money that is held in the form of a current (checking) account or deposit account, and some money market instruments. These broad money aggregates often have names such as M3 or M4. You can see why it is difficult to define money because banks can 'create money' (see the following example).

> **Example**   **Money creation – the credit multiplier[7]**
>
> Assume that all banks in a monetary system are required to keep 20% of deposits as reserves. Bank A has $100m of deposits from customers. Because it is sticking to the reserve requirement (both required by the central bank and its own prudential reserves policy) it lends out only $80m and keeps $20m as cash or in its account with the central bank (assume no vault cash for simplicity).
>
> **Bank A's opening balance sheet**
>
> | ASSETS | | LIABILITIES | |
> |---|---|---|---|
> | Reserves | $20m | Deposits | $100m |
> | Loans | $80m | | |
>
> Now if deposits in Bank A are increased by $5m the position changes. Deposits rise to $105m and reserves rise to $25m as the additional $5m is initially held as reserves at the central bank.
>
> **Bank A: An increase in deposits – intermediate period**
>
> | ASSETS | | LIABILITIES | |
> |---|---|---|---|
> | Reserve | $25m | Deposits | $105m |
> | Loans | $80m | | |
>
> This means that the reserve ratio has risen to $25m ÷ $105m = 23.8%. The bank earns no or little interest from reserves,[8] so it will wish to reduce the reserve ratio to 20% by lending out the extra. The next balance sheet shows the amount of lending that leaves a 20% reserve ratio, $84m.
>
> **Bank A: Lending out just enough to attain minimum reserve ratio**
>
> | ASSETS | | LIABILITIES | |
> |---|---|---|---|
> | Reserves | $21m | Deposits | $105m |
> | Loans | $84m | | |
>
> Now let us bring in more banks. In lending an additional $4m Bank A will have an impact on the rest of the banking system. If the $4m is lent to a company and, initially at least, that company deposits the money in Bank B, then at the central bank, Bank A's account will be debited (reserves go down) and Bank B's account will be credited (reserves increase). Bank B will lend out 80% of the amount, or $3.2m, keeping $800,000 in reserves to maintain its 20% ratio of reserves to deposits. The $3.2m lent finds its way to Bank C which, again holds 20% as reserves and lends the rest ... and so on. At each stage 80% of the deposit is lent out increasing the deposits of other banks, encouraging them to lend.

▶

The effect on the banking system of an injection of $5m of money, under a reserve ratio of 20%

	Change in deposits, $m	Change in loans, $m	Change in reserves, $m
Bank A	5.00	4.00	1.00
Bank B	4.00	3.20	0.80
Bank C	3.20	2.56	0.64
Bank D	2.56	2.05	0.51
Bank E	2.05	1.64	0.41
Bank F	....	....	....
Bank G	....	....	....
Bank...			
Total of all banks	25	20	5

The credit multiplier is a reciprocal of the reserve ratio, which in this case = 1 ÷ 0.20 = 5. Following an injection of $5m into the financial system the whole process ends when an additional $25m of deposits have been created; equilibrium has been reached again. Broad money grows by $25m. (The model is a simplification for illustrative purposes. In reality, there might be leakages from the system due to money flowing abroad, or people holding cash or buying government bonds rather than placing it in bank deposits.)

Remember: the creator of the monetary base is the central bank because it has a monopoly on the issuance of currency. If it has control over this then it can strongly influence the broader money supply (including deposits at banks) through the reserves requirements. So, once the system has settled down from the injection of a new deposit then it will be fairly stable – little money creation or removal.

Let us think about where the initial deposit put into Bank A might have come from. If it came from a customer who withdrew it from another bank then the example is null and void because while Bank A benefits from the $5m deposit the other bank, Bank X, sees a reduction in its reserves at the central bank by an equal amount. It can now lend less than it could before because it has to rebuild its reserves. Thus the stimulus effect of Bank A's deposit is exactly offset by the removal of money from the system by Bank X. If, however, the $5m came from the central bank purchasing Treasury bills from an investor who then put the newly created cash received into his account with Bank A then we have new money coming into the system and we can expect something like the credit multiplier effect shown above. The central bank is the only player here who can create money out of thin air and pump it into the system if the system is at equilibrium.

Thus, despite commercial banks' ability to create money on the way to equilibrium, there is a limit to the amount that the system as a whole can go up to because for every dollar, pound, euro, etc. created there has to be a fraction held as a cash reserve. It is the central bank that controls the total volume of monetary base (reserves at the central bank plus cash in circulation and at deposit-taking institutions) and so the broader aggregates of money have an upper limit. Small changes in the monetary base can have a large impact on the amount of broad money in the system and so we often refer to the monetary base as **high-powered money**. It is the monetary base that central banks target to influence money supply, interest rates, inflation and economic output.[9]

Central banks have three major tools they use to increase or decrease the money supply and interest rates:

▩ open market operations;

▩ discount rate changes;

▩ reserve requirement ratio changes.

Open market operations

This is the most important tool of monetary policy in most countries today. **Open market operations** means the buying and selling of government securities (Treasury bills and bonds) in the normal trading markets on a day-to-day basis. In purchasing government securities the central bank creates money to hand it over to those selling. It issues currency notes (as in your wallet/purse) or it writes a cheque in the name of the owner. When the cheque is drawn on, the central bank just creates an amount of credit for itself to satisfy the buyer – money from thin air. When the central bank sells some of its stock of previously market-bought government securities the purchasers draw on their money in the banking system which leads to a lowering of reserves.

To illustrate the creation of money by a central bank we can take Bank A's balance sheet from the example box earlier. The starting position is:

Bank A: Lending out just enough to attain the minimum reserve ratio

ASSETS		LIABILITIES	
Reserves	$21m	Deposits	$105m
Loans	$84m		

The central bank wants to inject money into the financial system and lower interest rates. It offers to buy billions of dollars of government securities. One of the customers of Bank A sells $6m of securities to the central bank. The central bank sends money to the customer of Bank A who deposits the newly created money (an electronic record rather than cash) in Bank A.[10] Bank A adds this $6m to its reserve account at the central bank. Now Bank A's balance sheet looks like this.

Bank A: Balance sheet after an injection of $6m

ASSETS		LIABILITIES	
Reserves	$27m	Deposits	$111m
Loans	$84m		

Bank A has a very high reserve level relative to its deposits, $27m ÷ $111m = 24.3%. The managers will want to employ the surplus money above that needed to maintain the target reserve ratio (20%) to earn higher interest by lending it, thus new money flows into the financial system. If the central bank wanted to drain money from the system through open-market operations it would sell government securities to investors which reduces the amount held by banks in their reserve accounts at the central bank or reduces vault cash. This would curb lending and raise interest rates.

Central banks tend to use Treasury securities to conduct open-market operations because the secondary market in these securities is very liquid, there is a large volume of these securities held by dealers and investors, meaning that the market can absorb a large number of buy and sell transactions. The main method used is a repurchase agreement – **a repo** – in which the central bank may purchase securities with a prior agreement to sell them back to the counterparty after say, 24 hours, seven days or 14 days[11] if it wants to inject money into the system. The difference between the buying and selling price provides the effective interest rate. If the central bank wanted to drain money it would engage in a **reverse repo** (there is more on repos in Chapter 9). An alternative, used in many countries, is to lend or borrow in the interbank market (see Chapter 6) to add or subtract reserves and influence rates of interest charged.[12]

Repos and reverse repos are, by their nature, temporary interventions because the opposite transaction takes place on maturity, a few days after the first buy or sell. There are times when the central bank wants to effect a more permanent change in the money supply. Then it can go for an outright transaction, a purchase or a sale, that is not destined to be reversed in a few days.

Incentives for individual banks to move to their target reserves

Apart from simply obeying the central bank, what are the incentives for individual banks to move to the target reserve levels? Banks that maintain reserve balances close, on average, to their target usually receive interest on their balances at the target rate of interest. In the UK this is the Official Bank Rate, currently 0.5% pa. But they are charged interest if their reserves balance is on average either excessively over or under their monthly target. Thus, they have a strong incentive to comply with the reserve targets.

Banks trade surplus reserves with each other. Banks always have an incentive to lend – even if only for 24 hours – if they find themselves with too many reserves. On the other hand, each day there will be dozens of other banks that find themselves temporarily below the reserve level they need, and so they willingly borrow in the market. However, there are occasions when a bank finds it difficult to borrow from other banks in the repo or other money markets to top up their reserves. Then the central bank will lend to it, if it has high-quality collateral, such as government bonds and T-bills, to offer in repo deals. It simply creates additional reserves and adds them to its account at the central bank.

In the UK this is called a **standing lending facility**, and is available to banks on demand, but there is a catch: it carries a penalty interest rate. The repos created here are charged an extra 1% above the official Bank Rate.[13] This penalty is a strong incentive for UK banks to keep within the limit for reserves either by having cash of their own or having access to the repo market at the normal rate. This will engender caution in lending if a bank is getting anywhere near the limit, thus broad money supply is influenced.

The supply and demand of reserves

The main target for central banks is usually the overnight (24-hour) interest rate on loans of reserves from one bank to another. In the USA this is the federal funds rate, in the eurozone it is the overnight repo rate in euros, and in the UK it is the overnight sterling repo rate. Switzerland opts for the Swiss franc LIBOR target rate. Soon after the official rate changes (typically the same day) banks adjust their standard lending rates ('base rate' in the UK) usually by the exact amount of the policy changes. This is transmitted through money market rate changes, repos, interbank lending, etc. (the impact on longer-term interest rates can go either way when the short-term rates are changed depending on what the market perceives the future will bring in terms of inflation and additional rises or falls in the overnight interest rate).

If we take the banking system as a whole, the demand for reserves falls as interest rates rise. That is, the quantity of reserves demanded by banks (holding all else constant) reduces if banks have a higher opportunity cost of keeping money in the form of reserves. They would rather lend it out to achieve higher interest rates. This becomes more and more of a lost opportunity as rates in the short-term interest rate markets rise. Bankers increasingly start to think that they can economise on the vault cash buffer if interest rates are high and so lend these out more at the overnight repo rate, say. Thus, the demand curve for reserves, D, slopes downward in Figure 24.1.

The central bank usually has a continuous programme of lending into the general repo market and so there is a large quantity of money borrowed by the banks from the central bank at any one time – that is, via the general repo market rather than at the penalty rate under the standing lending facility. It is through the adjustment to the amount of lent reserves outstanding that the central bank controls interest rates. The supply curve for reserves, S, shown dashed, is the amount of reserves borrowed from the central bank supplied through its open market operations – fixed at that point in time. Equilibrium occurs where the demand for reserves equals the quantity supplied. This occurs at an interest rate of A, providing the short-term interest rate in the market.

Now imagine that the central bank wishes to increase the supply of money and lower interest rates. It does this by increasing its purchases of government securities, providing a greater quantity of reserves. This pushes the supply curve in

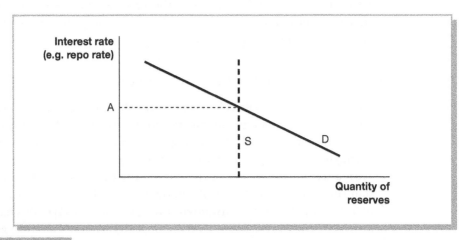

Figure 24.1   The demand and supply of reserves

Figure 24.2 from S1 to S2, and moves the equilibrium interest rate from A to B. Obviously, if the central bank reduced its reserves outstanding to the banking system by selling additional securities the supply curve would move to the left and interest rates would rise.

So far we have discussed dynamic open market operations. That is, where the central bank takes the initiative to change the level of reserves and the monetary base within a reasonably static banking environment. However, many times the environment is not static because there are a number of factors changing demand for borrowed reserves, e.g. greater or lesser banker confidence in the economy and thus the potential for low-risk lending. Thus, it intervenes – a **defensive open market operation** – to offset the other factors influencing reserves.

When the central bank wants to change short-term interest rates it can often do so merely by announcing its new target rate and threatening to undertake open-market operations to achieve it rather than actually intervening. The money market participants know that if they do not immediately move to the new rate they will find difficulties. For example, if the central bank shifts to target an interest rate lower than previously (i.e. it will lend on the repo market at a new lower rate) then any bank wanting to borrow will be foolish to borrow at a higher rate. Conversely, if the central bank announces a new higher target rate any bank wanting to lend will be foolish to accept a lower rate than the central bank's target, because it stands ready to trade at its stated rate. India targets the repo rate – see Article 24.1.

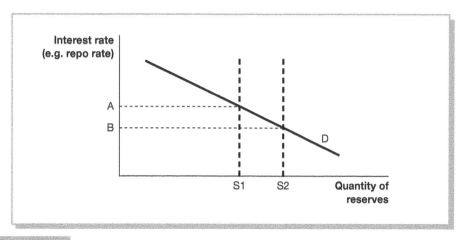

Figure 24.2   An open market increase in the supply of reserves

Article 24.1

India cuts interest rate to revive growth

By Amy Kazmin

India's central bank has lowered a key interest rate by 0.25% as it seeks to revive an economy that has slowed to the same pace as during the global financial crisis.

The Reserve Bank of India cut its key repo rate to 7.5%, as concerns about India's faltering economy outweigh worries about persistently high inflation.

But in its outlook, the central bank warned that the "headroom for further easing remains quite limited", with inflation expected to remain stuck at levels that are "not conducive for sustained economic growth".

The RBI also left the cash reserve ratio unchanged, disappointing many who had expected a slight reduction.

India's economy grew just 4.5% from October to December, the slowest pace in 15 quarters – sharply down from the near double-digit growth rates recorded earlier in the decade.

Indian businesses have been complaining that high interest rates, coupled with policy gridlock on such issues as land acquisition polices, are constraining economic expansion.

Discount rate changes

There is an option for banks to borrow additional reserves from the central bank – this is **discount window borrowing**.[14] In the case of the BoE's discount window facility, rather than cash being borrowed, the more usual form of borrowing is UK government bonds, gilts, which are lent for up to 30 days (or 364 days for an additional fee). The BoE hands over the gilts and receives in return less liquid collateral in a repo-type deal. These less liquid securities are much more risky than sovereign bonds, e.g. the collateral put up could be securitised bonds or a portfolio of corporate bonds.

Once it is in receipt of the gilts the borrowing bank then obtains cash by lending them in the market – another repo. While the discount window deals are available every day, each one needs specific approval of the BoE (unlike with its standing lending facility). The discount window borrowing is designed only to address short-term liquidity shocks and the fees are set to ram home the extraordinary nature of this type of help with reserves. The BoE states that 'the fees are set to be unattractive in "normal" market conditions so that participants use the facility as back up rather than a regular source of liquidity'.

Discount window borrowing can allow an increase in reserves in the financial system and therefore an increase in the money supply. When the discount loans are repaid the total amount of reserves, the monetary base and the money supply will fall.

If the interest premium charged in discount lending falls then an increasing number of banks will borrow at the discount rate. If the premium rises then few banks will borrow this way. Thus banks rein-in their lending to customers for fear of having to borrow themselves at punitive interest rates. The discount rate acts as a back-stop for the open market target interest rate. The money market rate will not rise above the discount rate, so long as the central bank remains willing to supply unlimited funds at the discount rate.

If we introduce the possibility of large volumes of supply of money (reserves) from the central bank at a high interest rate then we have the up-side-down L-shaped supply curve shown in Figure 24.3. If the demand curve D1 is the relevant demand schedule then the horizontal portion of the supply curve – banks borrowing from the central bank at the discount rate – does not come into play. Banks will continue to borrow and lend in the money markets but not from the central bank,[15] and the equilibrium interest rate remains at A. This is the case most of the time: changes in the discount rate have no direct effect on the market interest rate.

Now, consider the case where there has been a shock to the system and banks increase their demand for reserves all the way along the curve – the demand curve has shifted to the right, from D1 to D2. Indeed it has shifted so much that banks now borrow from the central bank at the discount rate to top up their reserves – see the demand curve D2 intersecting the supply curve at the discount rate at point M in Figure 24.4. Now, if the central bank moves the discount rate up or

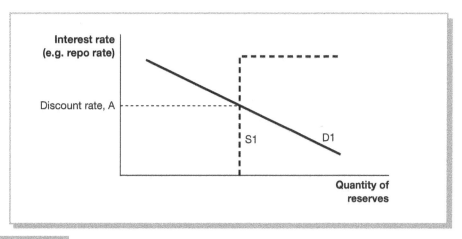

Figure 24.3 Discount rate lending availability changes the supply curve

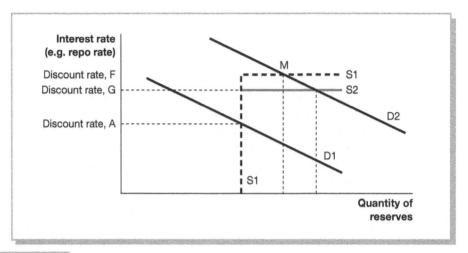

Figure 24.4   Discount window lending

down the point of intersection with the demand curve shifts and thus the market interest rates change. If the central bank wanted to lower interest rates it could move the discount rate from, say F to G, leading to increased borrowing from the central bank and an increased money supply.

A few decades ago adjusting the discount rate was the main way in which many central banks effected monetary policy, but the problem with this approach became increasingly apparent. It is difficult to predict the quantity of discount rate borrowing that will occur if the discount rate is raised or lowered, and so it is difficult to accurately change the money supply. Today changes in the discount rate are used to signal to the market that the central bank would like to see higher or lower interest rates: a raising indicates that tighter monetary conditions are required with higher interest rates throughout; lowering it indicates that looser, more expansionary, monetary conditions are seen as necessary. Discount rate borrowing is used by generally sound banks in normal market conditions on a short-term basis, typically overnight, at a rate above the normal open market target rate. But, given the higher interest rate it is used sparingly. Companies in real trouble, unable to borrow in the money markets and experiencing severe liquidity problems, may have to pay a very high fee to borrow from the central bank.

Reserve requirement ratio changes

The power to change the reserve requirement ratio is a further tool used by central banks to control a nation's money supply. A decrease in the reserve requirement ratio means that banks do not need to hold as much money at the central bank, and so they are able to lend out a greater percentage of their deposits, thus increasing the supply of money. The new loans result in consumption or investment in the economy, which raises inflows into other banks in the financial system and the credit multiplier effect takes hold, as shown in the first Example box in this chapter. The process of borrowing and depositing in the banking system continues until deposits have grown sufficiently such that the new reserve amounts permit just the right amount of deposits – the target reserve ratio is reached.

The main drawback to using changes in the reserve ratio is that it is difficult to make many frequent small adjustments because to do so would be disruptive to the banking system (e.g. a sudden rise can cause liquidity problems for banks with low excess reserves). Open market operations, on the other hand, can be used every day to cope with fluctuations in aggregate monetary conditions. Article 24.2 discusses the raising of reserves in China to bear down on inflation.

Article 24.2

Beijing tightens bank lending reins

By Jamil Anderlini

China's central bank stepped up its efforts to rein in inflation by ordering domestic banks to increase the level of deposits they hold in reserve.

The People's Bank of China said it would raise the reserve requirement ratio by half a percentage point. This would force most large institutions in China to hold a record 20% of their deposits in reserve at the central bank.

Economists said the increase in the reserve ratio would lock up as much as Rmb370bn ($56bn) in funds that banks would otherwise have been able to lend.

The increase is designed to reduce liquidity in the system and curb inflation, which has remained stubbornly high in recent months.

The central bank has now raised the reserve requirements for banks nine times since the start of last year and has lifted benchmark deposit and lending interest rates three times since October.

Small and medium-sized Chinese banks will have to keep as much as 18% of their deposits on reserve.

The central bank has recently introduced a "differentiated reserve management" system that allows it to punish institutions that lend too much by imposing even higher reserve ratios on transgressors.

FT *Source*: Anderlini, J. (2011) 'Beijing tightens bank lending reins', *Financial Times*, 18 March.

How monetary policy affects the economy

The actions of the central bank are designed to have significant impact on the key economic variables. These relationships are shown in Figure 24.5. If the central bank believes that the economy needs to expand at a faster rate (while not unleashing high inflation) then it can follow the lightly-tinted route (selecting the most appropriate monetary tool). Lower interest rates encourage consumers to borrow and businesses to invest. If, however, it looks as though it is already expanding too fast to achieve the required inflation rate the central bank can rein it in by following the darker-tinted route in which interest rates rise, money supply falls and people and businesses spend less.

We have not yet discussed the impact of interest rate changes on the exchange rate. This is a complicated area, but generally the rule is: if interest rates are falling relative to those in foreign countries the currency drops relative to those other currencies because international investors, looking for high returns, place their money elsewhere by selling the assets in the currency with the low interest rate and buying another currency to invest in that country. However, this superficially neat relationship is complicated by anticipated inflation rates and a host of other factors impinging on exchange rates.

Some central banks have specific goals for inflation. For example, the European Central Bank (ECB) has a stated aim of a rate below, but close to, 2% over the medium term, whereas the Bank of England (BoE) is required to achieve 2%, but anything within the 1% to 3% range is regarded as acceptable in the short run so long as there is a plan to move to nearer 2%. Those central banks that have a specific target as well as those who do not, other than 'low and stable inflation', also take into account the impact of their actions on the other major macroeconomic variables. There are a number of other elements they consider:

- **High employment and steady economic growth.** Not only does unemployment often cause pain to those families affected by it, but the economy wastes resources in idleness, lowering long-term well-being. Having said that, it makes sense to allow some unemployment as people are happily searching for the right position for them. So, while they are searching they are classified as unemployed. Many people who have taken time out to attend college, raise a family or to go travelling may re-enter the jobs market but not find an appropriate job quickly and so they are classified as unemployed. Matching people to suitable posts does not happen instantaneously, thus there will always be some amount of **frictional unemployment**. Another type is **structural unemployment**. This is where the skills people have do not match what the market needs or the location of people does not match the needs of employers. For example, coal miners have been laid off and find it difficult to obtain new positions when their skill-set and location of their family homes are not suited to the newer industries. If the central bank tries to stimulate the economy through lower interest rates to such an extent that

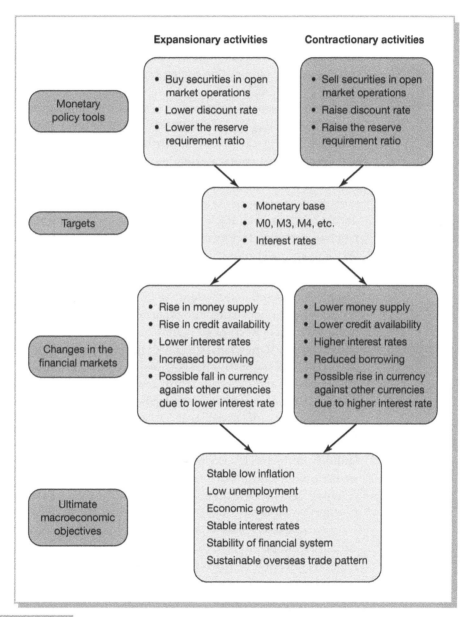

Figure 24.5 The flow through from monetary policy to the economy

frictional and structural unemployment is reduced below its natural rate then inflation is likely to rise as output fails to keep up with the new quantities of money flooding the economy. Thus, we tolerate, even welcome, some unemployment. The best that policymakers can hope for is that the economy reaches its **natural rate of unemployment**, i.e. a level of **non-accelerating inflation rate of unemployment (NAIRU)**. To achieve long-run reductions in unemployment below the current NAIRU policymakers need to work on the supply-side efficiency of the economy, e.g. raise skill levels, create a more pro-business, pro-innovation environment and culture, lower labour market rigidities inhibiting corporations from hiring and people from moving, and lower taxes to encourage investment by firms. The difficulty for our economic leaders is estimating the level of NAIRU. Is it at 4% unemployment or 6%? If a better job-finding service were launched would NAIRU decline significantly? It is around these issues that economists, central bankers and politicians debate.

- **Interest rate stability.** People and businesses are harmed by volatility in interest rates because of the additional uncertainty it introduces to their decision making, resulting in forward-planning problems. Thus house purchase decisions, factory investment decisions or bond market purchase decisions are made more hesitantly in a fluctuating interest rate economy, leading to lower economic output.

- **Stability of the financial system.** An important function of the financial system is to channel savings into productive use. These mechanisms can be disrupted if financial crises are permitted to occur. Just ask the Cypriots, Greeks and Portuguese if they value stability of the financial system. Instability can cause economic output drops, high unemployment, asset price crashes (e.g. houses) and austerity measures cutting wages and pensions. While monetary policy is one tool to promote stability, there are many more measures that the central bank (or other designated regulators) can take. (These are discussed in Chapter 25.)

- **Stability in the foreign exchange markets.** The economies of nation states are increasingly integrated into the world economy with ever larger volumes of imports, exports and overseas investment. The value of a currency relative to others can have profound effects on the producers in that economy, e.g. a rising currency may make exporting more difficult. Also, fluctuations in the currency make planning difficult. Thus central banks are cognisant of the impact of interest rate changes on the level and stability of the exchange rate.

Over a run of years the goal of price stability does not conflict with the other goals. For example, higher inflation does not produce lower unemployment so there is no long-term trade-off between these two goals. There might be a trade-off in the short run. So, lowering interest rates may encourage consumer spending, house purchase and corporate investment, and the taking on of more workers. But once the economy has reached its productive capacity limit additional demand from the lower rates is likely to push up wages and prices, rather than output. The alarmed authorities then need to take firm action (e.g. much higher interest rates) to squeeze demand out of the economy, causing painfully higher levels of unemployment. All in all, it is better if price stability at a low inflation rate is pursued from year to year, rather than having to make corrections after explosions or slumps in demand. Stability promotes economic growth.

Having said this, it is important to avoid focussing excessively on inflation in the short term and thereby forcing economic growth to fluctuate too much. For example, for a number of months in 2010–12 UK inflation was above the 3% limit. Mervyn King, the Governor of the BoE, explained that it would be wrong to raise interest rates to counteract this, because he believed that the high inflation rate was merely temporary, and to raise rates while the UK economy is in recession could be very damaging. He, thus, temporarily prioritised growth over immediate inflation, while keeping a watchful stance on anticipated inflation a year or so down the line – see Article 24.3.

Article 24.3

BoE sees inflation staying above target

By Claire Jones in London

Among the traditionally conservative central bankers of London's Threadneedle Street, a revolution is happening. For the first time since gaining independence in 1997, the Bank of England's policy makers admitted this month that inflation is likely to stick above its 2% target for the next two years. If the new forecasts are right, then inflation will exceed the target for almost all of the eight years between 2008 and 2015. What's more, the Monetary Policy Committee said it had no intention of trying to tighten monetary policy in order to hit the target.

On Wednesday, it emerged Sir Mervyn King, the outgoing governor, had joined the ranks of the BoE's top brass calling for more government bond buying. From the man credited with masterminding the UK's switch to inflation targeting, Sir Mervyn's apparently sanguine attitude to a persistently high inflation rate is remarkable.

Simon Hayes, UK economist at Barclays, said: "When I'm asked to say where I think inflation will be in five years' time, now I'd say that it's more likely to be nearer to 2.5% than 2%. In the past, I would've said that it would fall to target."

This switch to a far more flexible approach to fighting inflation, which allows central banks to prioritise boosting growth over stamping out price pressures, is not confined to British shores.

With a strong recovery continuing to elude all of the major advanced economies, both the

Article 24.3 Continued

Federal Reserve and the Bank of Japan have in recent months signalled that they will do more to support their economies.

But neither the US and Japan, nor the major eurozone economies, such as Germany, has experienced inflation as high as in the UK in recent years.

The Bank's relaxed attitude to fighting inflation is beginning to spook investors. Investors' concerns, however, are not matched by the person in the street. The people surveyed by the BoE for its quarterly poll of households' price expectations continue to think that inflation will be around the 3% mark in five years' time.

Well-anchored household inflation expectations, coupled with high unemployment and lower rates of union membership, make the sort of wage-price spiral seen in the 1970s unlikely.

Michael Saunders, economist at Citi [said] "The credibility of the 2% inflation target is low. But that's an inevitable consequence of a more sensible economic policy. What the experience of the past few years shows is the need to move from a fixed target to a band of between 1% and 3%."

Many financial systems have a hierarchy of objectives whereby price stability is set as the primary objective. Then, so long as that is achieved the other objectives can be aimed at. The Federal Reserve is supposed to balance out full employment and stable low inflation (2%). It stated in 2012 that when there was a conflict it would balance the two, focusing on whichever was furthest from a satisfactory level. It backed this up by saying that interest rates will not be raised until unemployment falls to 6.5% of the workforce. The 'Forward guidance' on interest rates is thought to help reduce both short- and long-term interest rates.

The independence of central banks

An important question for a government to decide is the degree of freedom it gives its central bank to conduct monetary policy. Is it to be conducted by the central bank's own experts or should elected politicians have the ultimate say on whether interest rates should rise or fall?

There are two types of independence:

1 **Instrument independence.** The central bank can decide when and how to use monetary policy instruments without political interference.

2 **Goal independence.** The central bank decides the goals of monetary policy.

Instrument independence is common, but goal independence is rare. The US Federal Reserve has both types of independence – politicians do not control the Board of Governors nor the purse strings of the Fed (although they can influence the appointment of some board members). The European Central Bank has an extraordinary degree of independence. The member country governments of the eurosystem are not permitted to instruct the ECB. The Maastricht Treaty, which established the monetary union, states that the long-term goal of the ECB is price stability, but did not specify what that meant, leaving that up to the Executive Board members to decide the target inflation rate. And, of course the ECB has control over the tools it uses. Furthermore, whereas the US system can be changed by new legislation (if the politicians change the law they can establish control over the Fed), this is more difficult in the eurozone, because the eurosystem's charter can only be altered by a revision of the Maastricht Treaty, which requires consent of *all* the signatory countries. In 1997 the Bank of England was given a high degree of instrument independence to decide when and how to raise or lower interest rates (prior to that the Chancellor of the Exchequer had ultimate control). However, the government can in extreme economic circumstances overrule the BoE for a limited period. The inflation goal is still established by the Chancellor.

The advantages of independence

▓ **Political control can lead to higher inflation**. It is argued that politicians often have a short-term perspective driven by the need to impress voters before the next election. This may mean sacrificing a stable price level to achieve immediate improvements in unemployment, growth or house mortgage rates. The populace, also often short-sighted, sees the immediate improvement, but does not grasp the long-term damage wrought when inflation takes off in the low interest rate environment. It is only a year or so later that people suffer the effects of economic instability and the need to bring down inflation. A politically insulated central bank is more likely to take decisions which are beneficial over the long run, even if they cause a little pain now. Thus, instead of politically motivated booms just before elections and busts after them we see a more stable pattern of growth and inflation.

▓ **Reduced temptation to support government spending.** The central bank regularly buys and sells bonds and Treasury bills previously issued by the government to influence the interest rates banks are charging each other when borrowing to top up their reserves. It is another step to start buying government instruments direct when the government wishes to expand its spending. In buying them the central bank will create new money which the government will put into the economy when it, say, buys new bridges or pays out more in social security. This can be dangerously inflationary. It is what Zimbabwe did in the 2000s – resulting in inflation of millions of per cent per year.

- **Politicians lack expertise.** Central bank employees have much more skill in this area than the average politician, or even the above-average politician.

The disadvantages of independence

- **Undemocratic.** The central bank makes important decisions that affect everyone and yet it is in the control of people who are not accountable at the ballot box. Politicians control fiscal policy (government spending and taxation), but perhaps they should also control monetary policy so that the two can be better co-ordinated. But would such consolidating of the levers of economic power really bring about a better result?

- **Central banks fail from time to time.** In the early 1930s central banks failed to put money into the financial system at crucial moments. They also failed to analyse and act upon the build-up to the 2008 crisis, in particular the excessive borrowing and rise in asset (e.g. house) prices. Many think they failed in 2012–13 by pumping too much money into the system. Are these failures of independence? Were there wiser political voices outside the central banks anticipating problems and calling for robust countervailing action? I cannot speak for the 1930s politicians, but my memory of 2006 and 2013 is not peppered with smart politicians' warnings of doom.

Some academic research has investigated the correlation between independence and inflation performance and concluded that more independence leads to lower inflation without lower real economic performance (unemployment or output).

Quantitative easing

In extreme circumstances a central bank may find that interest rates have been reduced to the lowest level they could go, and yet still economic activity does not pick up. People are so shocked by the crisis – increased chance of unemployment, lower house prices, lower business profits – that they cut down their consumption and investment regardless of being able to borrow at very low interest rates. This happened in 2009–13. Annualised, short-term interest rates in eurozone countries were less than 1%, in the UK they were 0.5% and in the USA they were between 0 and 0.25%. Clearly low, short-term interest rates were not enough to get the economy moving, even with the additional boost of government deficit spending to the extent that up to one-eighth of all spending was from government borrowing.

In response another policy tool was devised: **quantitative easing**. This involves the central bank electronically creating money ('printing money', but without any more bank notes) which is then used to buy assets from investors in the market. Thus pension funds, insurance companies, non-financial firms, banks, etc. can sell assets, mostly long-term government bonds (but can include mortgage-backed securities and corporate bonds), and their bank accounts are credited with newly created money. This raises bank reserves, allowing more lending in the economy. Furthermore, the increased demand for government bonds raises their prices and lowers interest rates along the yield curve – so the influence is on interest rates for medium- and long-term bonds. Also, it is hoped that the new cash will be used to invest in other assets such as shares pushing up equity issuance, prices and lowering required returns on these assets, thus stimulating investment in companies. Lower interest rates on government borrowing can lower taxation.

In the UK the BoE bought so many bonds in 2009–13 that it now owns about one-third of all gilts, pushing 10-year yields at times to only 1.5%. Between 2008 and 2013 the Fed bought over $3tr bonds (mostly mortgage-backed and government). At the time of writing it is committed to buying $85bn each month (approximately 0.5% of GDP), but is increasingly anxious about the consequences of ceasing: interest rates might re-bound dramatically and devastatingly; and inflation might take off at some point given all the extra cash floating about (optimists argue that the central bank can just sell the bonds to suck cash out of the system, others are not so sure). Japan launched the most audacious quantitative easing plan in 2013: $1.4tr in less than one year. Many suspect that bubbles are being created in bond and other asset markets.

Funding for Lending scheme

Another way of boosting the amount of money, or at least stopping it falling further, in the banks and the economy is to entice banks to lend to households and small and medium-sized enterprises (SMEs) by offering banks access to exceptionally cheap finance on condition that they maintain or increase lending to these groups. The UK Funding for Lending scheme (2012) is designed to do this:

▦ The BoE lends UK Treasury bills to banks for up to four years, for a fee (as low as 0.25%). Banks will provide collateral in the form of collections of loans to businesses and households and other assets to BoE to secure this borrowing.

▦ When the loans from the BoE mature the collateral will be swapped back again.

▦ In the meantime, banks can use the T- Bills they access in the scheme to borrow money at rates close to the expected path of the Bank Rate by issuing, say, a repo: in 2013, 0.5%.

- Taking that rate together with the fee paid to the BoE gives the overall cost of around 0.75%. All banks have to do for that is maintain the same level of lending year on year.

Such low borrowing rates for banks and building societies brought mortgage rates down substantially and increased lending. However, SME lending stagnated, so an extra incentive for SME lending was introduced from April 2013: for every £1 of net lending to SMEs in 2014, banks will be able to draw £5 from the scheme. And to encourage banks to lend to SMEs sooner rather than later, every £1 of net lending to SMEs during the remainder of 2013 will be worth £10 of initial borrowing allowance in 2014.

25

Central banking: other functions

A modern society could not function efficiently without the services provided by a central bank. These organisations not only improve the well-being of the banking sector, but, through their oversight of the entire financial system make life better for all of us. Deciding on interest rates is one important activity (as described in the last chapter), but there are many others.

Banks are organisations with high levels of borrowing. That is, the deposits put into them plus the money borrowed from the wholesale financial markets is many times the amount put in by shareholders. Most of the money raised from depositors, wholesale lenders and shareholders is lent out. There are two constant dangers in this. One is that a large proportion of depositors or other lenders insist on withdrawing their cash in the immediate future when the assets held by the bank (e.g. business loans) cannot be liquidated quickly to satisfy these demands. The second is that the assets of the bank decline while the liabilities remain the same or increase, resulting eventually in insolvency as assets are no longer greater than liabilities. Central banks are usually the regulators that investigate whether banks are being properly managed so that neither liquidity risk nor solvency risk is high.

In addition to the crucial functions of monetary policy and bank supervision for safety and soundness, central banks help a society in a number of other ways. For example, they usually manage, or at least oversee, the payment systems such as cheque clearing. They also help establish special schemes to guarantee that a depositor will receive at least a minimum sum should the bank become insolvent. This helps create confidence in the banking system.

Another useful service to bolster confidence in the system is that of lender of last resort; if the usual sources of funds for a bank are no longer forthcoming with money, then the central bank will stand ready to supply funds to see the bank through a difficult period. Central banks also act as bankers for the government and may assist with management of the government's debt. And they may hold a nation's reserves of gold and foreign currency, and take some part in managing the currency's exchange rate.

Note that this chapter describes the wide variety of responsibilities that a nation *may* choose to allocate to the purview of the central bank. However, many countries decide to establish alternative organisations to undertake some of the tasks described here while leaving the central bank to concentrate on a few of them.

Safety and soundness of the financial system

The collapse of many banks into insolvency between 2008 and 2013 is a reminder of the vulnerability of these institutions. The mere fear of a bank collapse can lead to recession/depression as a damaging wave of lowered confidence in financial institutions sweeps through economies. A hundred and fifty years ago banks would fail on a regular basis, but today we have a number of mechanisms to reassure people and businesses that their money is safe within the banking system. Many of these mechanisms were found wanting in the recent financial crisis and so policymakers are currently looking for fixes for these, but nevertheless the modern system is generally far safer than it was.

Depositor insurance

Bank runs occur when depositors fear that because a bank holds in cash or near-cash only a fraction of the total deposits, then if say 20% of depositors want to take their money in cash the bank would not be able to pay and could be declared bust. Most of the time people are sanguine about this problem because they know that on a typical day the amount of net withdrawals (i.e. money taken from the bank minus money put into accounts at that bank) is a miniscule proportion of total deposits. This all relies on psychology: people have to have a great deal of confidence that the bank will be able to pay out when they want their money back. The trouble arises when something disturbs that confidence. When news spread that Northern Rock, a building society turned bank, might be unable to repay depositors the panicked depositors queued around the blocks of towns and cities up and down the country to withdraw their money.

Losing one bank to a run, caused either by rational or irrational fear and rumour is bad enough, but the problem stretches further than that because the bank subject to a run is likely to have lent other banks money or have other interbank transactions outstanding, e.g. it is due to pay large sums on derivatives deals. Once it feels under pressure from its depositors it might withdraw money it holds with other banks to raise some cash, causing one or two of them to have liquidity problems.

They might then collapse leading to yet more banks (who have lent to these banks or hold deposits from these banks) coming under pressure. And so a domino effect might flow through the banking system.

One way to reduce the risk of bank runs (and to make the system fairer for the innocent depositors) is for the government or some regulatory body to step in and say it will guarantee that depositors will be repaid even if the bank cannot do so. In the case of Northern Rock the UK government guaranteed all deposits without a limit on how much they would pay out to any one depositor. This was an extreme situation; normally a limit is set. Thus in the eurozone scheme the limit is €100,000 per depositor. It is thought that people with large deposits are sophisticated enough to look after themselves, to be able to assess the bank's true financial status, and so should avoid high-risk banks, or at least demand a premium return for the additional risk. This toughness does have a drawback, e.g. in 2013 depositors started to run from Cypriot banks because the governments of the eurozone when asked to contribute money to a bailout insisted that any depositor with more than €100,000 sacrifice most of it, i.e. write it off. Some Cypriot banks were saved from having all deposits withdrawn by the introduction of limits on withdrawals (€300 per day) and prohibitions against transferring money abroad (the larger depositors tended to be Russian).

In the USA the insurer of deposits is not the Fed, but the **Federal Deposit Insurance Corporation (FDIC)**, which pays out up to $250,000 per depositor per insured bank. In the UK, the **Financial Services Compensation Scheme** (outside of BoE) pays out full compensation up to the maximum of £85,000 per person per firm, which covers the vast majority of depositors.

Lender of last resort

Another safety net for banks and their depositors is the **lender of last resort** function of the central bank: to prevent a bank failure leading on to other bank failures the central bank will step in to provide reserves when no one else will lend to the banks. Following the September 11 2001 World Trade Center attack many cheques were stuck on grounded aircraft and so a number of banks missed an inflow of money for a few days, thus their reserves declined. Furthermore bank customers increased their demand for cash. The Federal Reserve kept the banking system going by adding $38bn through repurchase agreements to the banks that needed money to restore their reserve level. It also increased its discount window lending by 200-fold to $45bn. The terrorists did not bring down the financial system.

In 2008 the sub-prime crisis produced a fear among the banks. They did not know the extent of another bank's exposure to the sub-prime mortgage instrument risk. In response they held onto cash and refused to lend it to other banks. The ECB and the Fed therefore provided very large volumes of short-term funds to the banks so that they could maintain reserve levels and not run out of cash.

Note that the lender of last resort function is not there all the time – it is for when the central bank judge sees an emergency. Also, not every bank will be bailed out – many will be left to fail depending on the route they took to get to a poor liquidity or solvency position (e.g. possibly down to fecklessness or bad luck) or on whether the bank's failure will cause systemic collapse of the banking industry.

It is necessary to have both the lender of last resort role and deposit insurance schemes because insurance tends to only cover about 1% of the outstanding deposits – there are many financial deals, usually between banks, which dwarf retail deposits. These financial and corporate institutions need reassurance that the central bank will not permit a failure due to a bank running short of reserves – a liquidity crisis.

An extreme form of support for a bank is for the government to nationalise it, as happened with Northern Rock in 2008 and Anglo Irish Bank in 2009. While not fully nationalised, 82% of Royal Bank of Scotland's shares and 33% of Lloyds Bank shares are now owned by the UK taxpayer.

Too big to fail

The danger with having a lender of last resort facility available to banks is that it might encourage banks to take high risk. If their bets are successful then the managers and their shareholders reap the reward. If they fail they are bailed out by the central bank or government. This is a **moral hazard** problem – encouraging bad behaviour. The problem for the rest of society is not too great when it comes to small banks, whose failure would not cause knock-on failures of other banks or financial institutions. The authorities often let these go bust and impose pain on the managers (lose jobs), shareholders (lose all value in their shares) and bondholders (bonds become worthless), to encourage other banks to believe that they will not be saved regardless of incompetence or recklessness.

The problem arises with the large banks, who have numerous interbank and other borrowings and derivative transactions, that could pose a threat to the entire system should they fail; because if they go under then many of their counterparties might lose so much in the fallout (liquidity-wise or solvency-wise) that they fail too. These are the banks that pose a **systemic risk.** Rather than size being the criteria we should really focus on degree of importance and significance of the bank dubbed 'too important to fail'. The phrase 'too big to fail' has stuck with the media, but increasingly policymakers are using **'Sifi, systemically important financial institutions'** or, for the internationally important, **Global Sifis (GSifis).**

The regulators frequently face a difficult decision. For example, in 2008 Bear Stearns was saved because it was seen as necessary to step in and stop its failure from wrecking the system. Then along comes the failing Lehman Brothers asking for help. Rightly or wrongly the authorities felt that Lehman could be allowed to go without money from the central bank or government being pumped in to save it. Many now believe that this was an error, that Lehman posed a very high systemic risk which went unrecognised until it was too late.

Currently, governments and regulators are grappling with the problem presented of having so many banks that are too big to fail. Should we break them into smaller units so that each individual unit can go bust without any systemic/domino effect? Should we tax them more because of the costs they impose on society? Should we impose very high capital reserve ratios and liquidity reserve ratios (and make them even higher for the most risky activities) to reduce the likelihood of liquidation? Should we introduce **living wills**, whereby banks have to report regularly to the authorities on how they would put into effect an orderly winding down of the business as well as how they would plan for recovery in a crisis?[1] See Article 25.1.

Article 25.1

When global banks fail, resolve them globally

By Martin Gruenberg and Paul Tucker

During the financial crisis governments provided taxpayer support for banks, steadying the global financial system and helping to avoid a repeat of the Depression. Those bank rescues exposed governments and taxpayers to losses. And in the long term they will have made banking riskier if managers and creditors conclude that bailout is part of the fabric of the system.

To avoid that fate, the "too big to fail" problem must be cured. We believe it can be and that serious progress is being made. Evidence can be seen in the joint paper released by our organisations, which outlines a resolution strategy for large and complex financial companies.

Alongside higher capital and liquidity requirements, the best chance of a durable solution will come from a process for resolving the largest international banks – so-called global systemically important financial institutions (GSifis) – in an orderly way when they fail. The failures of GSifis that confronted the US and UK in 2008 were unprecedented in scale, complexity and interconnectedness. They also outstripped the capabilities of the legal frameworks in place.

In the US, the Federal Deposit Insurance Corporation only had the power to put insured institutions into receivership; it could not wind down failing bank holding companies or other non-bank financial companies whose activities posed a systemic risk. With no bank resolution powers, the UK authorities' options were even more limited when the crisis broke in 2007.

Since then, both the US and the UK have enacted significant legislative reforms that are the basis of new resolution frameworks. In the US, the Dodd–Frank act provides the FDIC

➡

Article 25.1   Continued

with the power to resolve failed GSifis through an orderly liquidation process. In the UK, the 2009 Banking act will be supplemented by the planned EU recovery and resolution directive.

Over the past year, the FDIC and the Bank of England, in conjunction with the prudential regulators in our jurisdictions, have been working to develop contingency plans for the failure of globally systemic banks that have core operations in both the US and UK. Of the world's 28 GSifis, 12 are headquartered in the US or UK. Because many of these institutions have operations that are concentrated in our two jurisdictions, we have a shared interest in ensuring that, when such a business fails, it can be resolved at no cost to taxpayers and without placing the financial system at risk. Importantly, a shared strategy will help us to avoid working at cross purposes or being blind to each other's plans.

Our joint paper outlines a strategy we believe can accomplish our objectives. Under the plan, the resolution authority will take control of the parent of the GSifi group, apportion losses to the company's shareholders and unsecured debtholders and remove senior management. In all likelihood, the organisation's shareholders would lose all value.

The unsecured debtholders can expect that their claims would be written down to reflect any losses that shareholders could not cover. Sound subsidiaries (domestic and foreign) would be kept open and operating, thereby limiting contagion effects and cross-border complications. In both countries, whether during execution of the resolution or thereafter, restructuring measures may be taken, especially in the parts of the business responsible for the group's distress. Those businesses could be shrunk, broken into smaller entities, or certain operations could be liquidated or closed. A portion of the surviving unsecured debt would be converted into equity, where needed, to provide capital to support the process.

The writers are chairman of the FDIC and deputy governor for financial stability at the Bank of England, respectively.

Bank supervision

It is important that an authority investigates and approves the appointment of those who operate banks and continues monitoring and surveillance to ensure they are operated well. This is **bank supervision** or **prudential supervision**. Banks can be powerful money-grabbing tools in the hands of crooks. They can also be a temptation to over-ambitious entrepreneurs who may see a large pot of (depositors) money that could be used to invest in speculative ventures. Thus, the authorities (often central banks) license or charter all banks (and other deposit-taking institutions) to ensure that they are run by fit and proper persons. In this way any proposal for a new bank is scrutinised, as are the controllers of the bank. The regulator then requires regular reports and makes regular visits to the banks to ensure that there is compliance with the safety rules. This usually includes aspects shown in Figure 25.1.

	Examples of questions considered
C Capital adequacy	Does it have sufficient equity capital for the amount of lending it is doing? Is management prepared to obtain additional capital?
A Asset quality	Are the assets held too risky? Is there good diversification? Are there sound processes/systems for controlling risk (e.g. are staff abiding by prudent policies and have limits of the risk exposure that they can create)? Is there sufficient provision for bad debts (the bank examiner can force a write-off)?
M Management	Is the quality of its management good? Honest and competent at identifying, measuring, monitoring and controlling risk? Are there adequate controls and internal information flows? Are there good controls to prevent fraud?
E Earnings	Are bank profits stable at a reasonably high level? Is the source of earnings high quality?
L Liquidity	Does the bank hold sufficient reserves? Are there plenty of assets that can be converted to cash quickly without serious loss of value? Does the bank have good access to money market loans?
S Sensitivity to market risk	Are management processes good for coping with interest rate risk, exchange rate risk, equity market risk and commodity risk? Is the bank particularly sensitive to these risks?

Figure 25.1 The CAMELS method of bank inspection

The central bank may also consider whether consumers are sufficiently well protected against unfair selling, bad advice, poor quality products, as well as discrimination (e.g. racial). They may also look at whether the bank's electronic systems are safe against cyber attack, e.g. criminal hacking into accounts and stealing money. If, on examination, a bank performs badly on any of the CAMELS or other factors the regulator will order it to correct its behaviour. In extreme cases the bank will be closed.

Capital and liquidity adequacy

Banks know that they would be foolish to lend out all the money they take. It makes sense to have self-imposed rules on what proportion to keep in cash and what proportion to keep in short-term securities (e.g. money-market instruments) that could fairly quickly be turned into cash. However, banks are foolish from time to time, tempted away from the rational path, and therefore need externally imposed rules to prevent them from stepping over the line that takes them into imprudent territory. Holding cash and short-term lending is usually less profitable than long-term lending and so ambitious bankers, looking to boost profits, sometimes transfer more of their resources to long-term lending, leaving only a small buffer of cash or near-cash to meet immediate extraordinary cash outflows should, say, large numbers of depositors insist on a return of their money. In other words, they take an excessively high liquidity risk.

The other major risk is solvency risk. This is less to do with running out of cash in the immediate future and more to do with allowing the capital base of the bank to diminish to such an extent that the assets of the bank (loans to customers, etc.) are barely greater than the liabilities (e.g. deposits). In such a situation it would not take too many bad debt write-offs as customers go bust, for example, for the bank to find that it cannot repay all its depositors and other creditors. Other events that could reduce assets below liabilities include a collapse in value of the bank's complex securities holdings, fraud or the failure of a subsidiary. This happened to the UK's Co-operative Bank in 2013; its Britannia subsidiary had an extraordinarily high level of bad debt leading to very thin capital protection for the Co-op.

Obviously lowering both liquidity risk and solvency risk is important to the wellbeing of the financial system. I remember an impassioned debate in 2008 as one bank after another called on their central banks for funds. The managers would declare that the only issue facing them was a short-term decline in cash balances: they had grown used to drawing loans from the money market on a daily basis and suddenly these were now closed. At first the central banks agreed and supplied the needed cash. There were sceptical voices in the press saying that the loss of bank assets, as households found they could not repay their mortgages and as corporate loans turned sour (particularly those lent to property developers) and as 'sophisticated' financial assets became worthless, meant that the buffer of capital was diminishing by the day, to the point where many banks were heading toward negative equity territory. We witnessed a rapid morphing from a liquidity crisis into a bank solvency crisis. As the economy spiralled downward it became plain for all to see that there was going to be such a volume of loan impairments and financial instrument counterparty defaults that banks desperately needed more equity capital injected into them to widen the gap between assets and liabilities to a safe level.

A safe reserve level

The questions regulators have grappled with for many decades are: what is a safe level for capital reserves? And, what is a safe level for liquidity reserves? If we look at capital reserves first we can start our thinking by recognising that some assets held by a bank have little or no risk of default. Obviously, as cash has no risk of default there is no need to keep a capital buffer for this asset. Some types of loans made by banks, e.g. lending to the German, UK or US governments, have some degree of risk of default but this is very small. On the other hand, lending to a manufacturer usually has a fairly high level of default. It is clear that we need different amounts of capital depending on the asset category. Thus, the total of all unsecured corporate loans a bank holds might need to backed up with, say, 8% of their balance sheet value composed of capital, whereas the loans to local government lending need to be backed up with only, say, 1.6% of their value in the form of capital.

This line of thought is leading us to the concept of **risk-weighted assets**. Thus if the 'normal' capital proportion put aside is 8% for loans such as unsecured corporate debt this is given a weighting of 100%, i.e. it is not reduced from the full 8%. So a £10m loan needs the bank to have £800,000 of capital – of course, the bank will also source money from depositors, etc. to lend the £10m. A total of £10bn of loans needs £800m. The weight for mortgages might be 50%, which means that if the bank holds £5bn of mortgages it has to back that with capital of £200m ($0.08 \times 0.50 \times £5bn$). The holding of government bills might require only 20% of the full capital safety reserve – the risk-weighting is 20%. Thus, a collection of £3bn of bills will require $£3bn \times 0.20 \times 0.08 = £48m$.

Another way of looking at this is to first reduce the asset values by their risk-weighting and then take 8% of the risk-weighted value – see Table 25.1.

Table 25.1	A bank's capital risk weighting		
Assets	Full balance sheet value (£m)	Risk weighting (%)	Risk weighted value (£m)
Cash	100	0	0
T-bills	3,000	20	600
Mortgages	5,000	50	2,500
Unsecured loans	10,000	100	10,000
Total	**18,100**		**13,100**

Total capital required: £13,100m × 0.08 = £1,048m. Thus, bank assets must exceed bank liabilities by £1,048m to withstand the possibility of a substantial proportion becoming bad loans.

Basel I

Capital reserve levels are not just national affairs, because banking is international. The 'banker to the central banks' is the **Bank for International Settlements** based in Basel, Switzerland. The central bankers gathered together in the 1980s to discuss setting minimum solvency standards applicable to any bank from a member country of the Basel committee. Now the 'Basel rules' have been adopted in more than 100 countries.

To understand the Basel rules you need to first deal with a point of difficulty I have so far skipped over: defining what we mean by capital. The Basel I committee split capital into two, tier 1 and tier 2:

Tier 1:

- Equity capital placed in the bank by shareholders when they purchase shares or from accumulated retained profits.
- Non-cumulative perpetual preference shares. Because they do not form a payable liability, should the bank have a run of bad luck – they do not have to be redeemed, nor do dividends have to be paid – so they can act as a buffer against a drop in asset values.
- Minority interests in subsidiaries whose accounts are consolidated in the group accounts (less goodwill and other intangible assets).

One half of capital had to be tier 1 (4% of risk-weighted assets), but the other 4% could be tier 2.

Tier 2:

Tier 2 consisted of various balance-sheet elements that might also act as a (less-effective) buffer such as subordinated debt that did not have to repaid for at least five years (being subordinated, on liquidation, depositors and other creditors would be paid first).

Banks regarded as being undercapitalised under the Basel rules may be seized by national authorities in a worst case. It is more likely that the country's regulator will insist on guiding them back to health, which could include rights issues to raise more equity capital, asset sales, subsidiary sales and the sacking of executives.

Basel II

In the late 1990s regulators and bankers concluded that the Basel I rules were too simplistic because they took broad categories of loan and insisted that the same risk weight apply to each. Thus, when any bank from a developed country borrowed the debt was to be regarded as having the same risk-weighting (i.e. 20%) as for all other developed country banks, regardless of whether it was a US bank or from a more risky country. The risk-weighting for this type of loan was much lower than lending to multinational corporations whose loans were often given a 100% weight, and yet most observers would agree that many multinationals are safer borrowers than some banks in some developed countries. Another bone of contention was that Basel I did not properly differentiate between a loan to a company with an AAA credit rating and one to a company with a much lower rating – they all carried the same weight. This led to a form of **regulatory arbitrage** (dancing round the rules to present a safe image) in which, within a category (same risk-weight), banks mostly lend to the riskiest clients because this paid the highest interest without requiring any more capital than a low-risk, low interest rate loan.

Basel II was launched in the mid-2000s and made much greater use of credit ratings of both government debt and corporate debt to decide weightings. Thus, AAA debt would get a zero weighting, whereas grades of B– or less would get a 150% weighting. It went further, and recognised that a high proportion of bank assets did not have credit ratings and so banks were permitted to use **internal ratings** devised from their own models to risk-weight assets (subject to monitoring by their national central banks). Also Basel II took account of market risk (the risk that financial market assets, such as securitised bonds, can decrease in price on the markets) and operational risk (the way the bank is run can lead to calamity, e.g. a rogue trader destroys the bank, or there are other operational dangers, e.g. another 9/11 attack could damage a bank's access to finance). Banks were also required to disclose some other risks, such as concentration risk (too many eggs in one basket) and liquidity risk.

In addition, there are a number of off-balance-sheet assets (and liabilities) for which capital needs to be assigned. Thus, the holding of positions in derivatives, or positions in the foreign exchange market or commodity market, of commercial letters of credit and bank guarantees create the possibility of loss and so could erode capital. Under Basel II these items were risk-weighted and added to the on-balance-sheet assets.

Unfortunately Basel II was not a success. Surprise, surprise, once the banks were able to use their own valuation and risk models to influence the regulatory capital level the amount they held fell. Well, you see, bankers were so smart that they had diversified away much of the risk, or they had bought insurance so that if a loan went bad the insurer paid up. Lower risk, therefore lower risk-weighting. Perfect. Except they forgot[2] to account for the possibilities of asset returns all going down together (so much for diversification) or for the insurers/derivative counterparties going bust and not paying out.

Basel III

Basel II was rapidly overtaken by events: the financial crisis revealed that many banks had not been cautious enough in setting their capital and liquidity reserves. The regulatory framework simply did not work. The rules were complicated, carefully calculated from detailed formulae, but as with so much in finance, the answers were precisely wrong rather than roughly right. Only five days before Lehman went bust it had a Tier 1 capital ratio of 11%. There was far too much optimism, far too much faith in the reported market value of assets, and far too little recognition of the possibility that the new-fangled financial instruments can both lose value overnight and that, when they do so, many banks experience knock-on effects and they all collapse together in an enmeshed mass. Banks had moved so far away from simple deposit taking to lending into weird and dangerous securities that it was difficult for the regulators to keep up. Banks would deliberately structure an obligation so that it could be granted a low risk-weighting, even though the bankers knew that the real exposure was high. For example, if you took a group of mortgages that had a risk weighting of 50% and converted them into securitised bonds with an AAA rating you could sell them to other investors taking them off the balance sheet. You could then replace the asset by buying other bank's AAA-rated mortgage-backed bonds and you no longer need to hold much capital reserve for them. Risk just seemed to disappear from the system. There is more on the crisis in Chapter 16 of *The Financial Times Guide to Financial Markets* by Glen Arnold.

Basel III is being rolled-out. This is much tougher. First, the definition of what can be called capital has been narrowed down to exclude virtually everything other than money put in by bank shareholders or kept in the bank on behalf of shareholders from retained earnings. This is called **core tier 1** or **common equity tier 1** and leaves out preference shares, unsecured bonds, etc.

Secondly, instead of tier 1 being 4% of risk-weighted assets and tier 2 being 4% of risk-weighted assets we have the requirement that core tier 1 is effectively raised to 7%, from the previous typical level of 2%.[3] The picture is a little more complicated than that – as shown in Figure 25.2.

The capital reserve levels shown in Figure 25.2 are to be required in normal times. In a financial crisis regulators expect the buffer to be partially used up – thus it might fall to the minimum 4.5% level. These new rules are to be phased in over the period until the end of 2018. For the years 2013–2015 the minimum (simply to operate as a bank) is to be gradually raised to 4.5% of risk-weighted assets. In the three years after January 2016 the conservation buffer will be phased in on top of the minimum until the full 7% is reached. This seems a leisurely timetable, but many central banks have already signalled that they expect their banks to achieve the targets much faster than this. Article 25.2 shows that many leading banks have already reached the 2019 minimums.

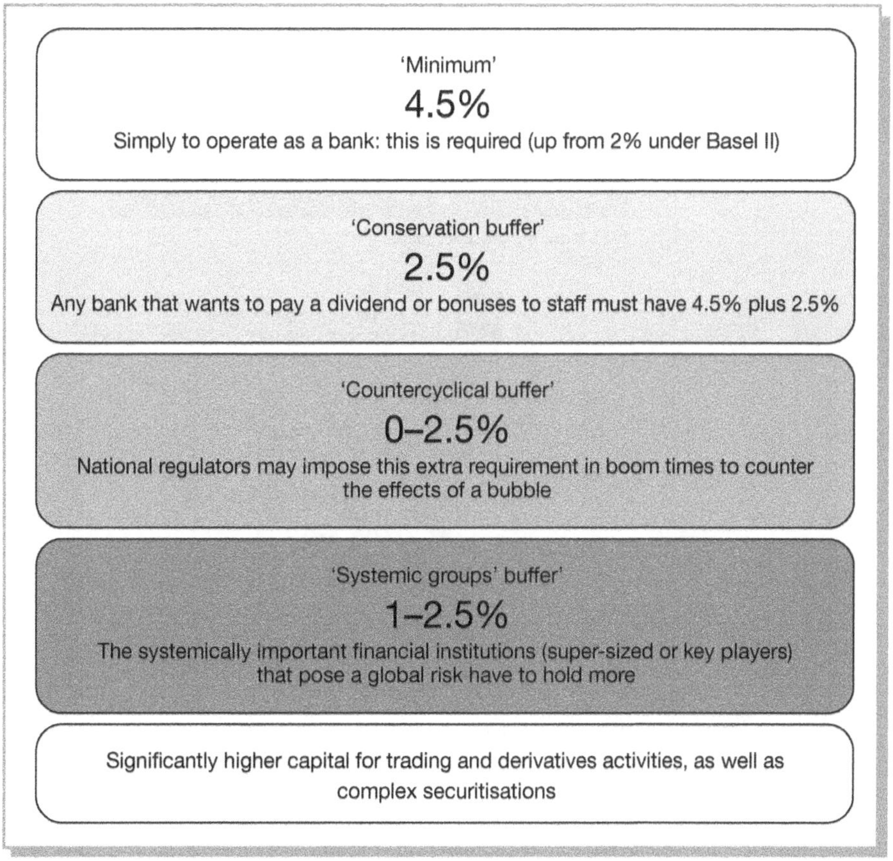

'Minimum'

4.5%

Simply to operate as a bank: this is required (up from 2% under Basel II)

'Conservation buffer'

2.5%

Any bank that wants to pay a dividend or bonuses to staff must have 4.5% plus 2.5%

'Countercyclical buffer'

0–2.5%

National regulators may impose this extra requirement in boom times to counter the effects of a bubble

'Systemic groups' buffer'

1–2.5%

The systemically important financial institutions (super-sized or key players) that pose a global risk have to hold more

Significantly higher capital for trading and derivatives activities, as well as complex securitisations

Figure 25.2 Basel III core tier 1 capital to be held by banks as a percentage of risk-weighted assets

Europe's banks turn to capital raising to meet Basel III

By Patrick Jenkins and Daniel Schäfer

After a dearth of equity raising from banks over the past year or so, cash calls all of a sudden seem to be the fashion of the day. Deutsche Bank recently completed a €2.96bn accelerated issue of new shares, fellow German lender Commerzbank in March said it would raise €2.5bn and Greek banks are on the road to raise as much as they can from commercial investors to plug a €21.7bn equity shortfall. Is this the start of a rush to boost capital levels and get ahead of the incoming Basel III regulations?

Certainly, there is a fresh focus on complying with more demanding Basel III capital rules.

Over the past few weeks, most large banks have published "fully loaded" Basel III capital ratios, reflecting the market pressure on lenders to comply early with regulations that formally phase in gradually between now and 2019.

Huw van Steenis, analyst at Morgan Stanley, says there is now a "magnetic pull" towards a 10% core tier one ratio. The number is seen as safely above the 9.5% that the Basel III rule

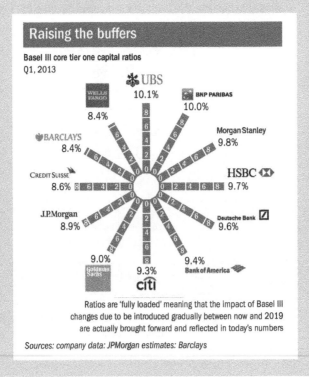

Raising the buffers

Basel III core tier one capital ratios
Q1, 2013

UBS 10.1%
BNP PARIBAS 10.0%
WELLS FARGO 8.4%
Morgan Stanley 9.8%
BARCLAYS 8.4%
CREDIT SUISSE 8.6%
HSBC 9.7%
J.P.Morgan 8.9%
Deutsche Bank 9.6%
9.0%
Goldman Sachs
citi 9.3%
9.4% Bank of America

Ratios are 'fully loaded' meaning that the impact of Basel III changes due to be introduced gradually between now and 2019 are actually brought forward and reflected in today's numbers

Sources: company data: JPMorgan estimates: Barclays

Article 25.3 Continued

book demands for the largest global banks before they are allowed to distribute dividends.

"There is a growing appreciation that you need to be close to or above 10% before you can pay a much higher dividend," Mr van Steenis says.

Some analysts, however, believe that the push by Europe's banks towards that panacea could yet be undermined by more fundamental flaws in their balance sheets. Regulators are increasingly questioning the validity of core tier one ratios, which relate equity to risk weighted assets, amid concerns about the consistency of risk weightings across banks and countries.

Simon Samuels, banks analyst at Barclays, says: "Just as some of the banks are strengthening their core tier one ratios, based on RWAs, the prize might slip away from them. Regulators [will] either raise risk weightings and/or give more emphasis to nominal [without adjustment for risk] balance sheets."

Some countries have stated that they will go much further than the Basel committee recommendations. Switzerland, with bank assets many times greater than national GDP, is insisting that UBS and Credit Suisse expand conservation buffers from 2.5% to 8.5%. However, three percentage points of that may be in the form of a new type of capital called **contingent convertible (CoCo)** instruments. These behave like bonds, paying a coupon, but convert to equity if a bank's capital ratio falls below a predetermined level. Alternatively contingent capital can become worth nothing (the bank does not have to repay) if the risk-adjusted capital falls below say 7%. Barclays has issued these **total-loss bonds** – see Article 25.3.

Article 25.3

Barclays bond a key test for cocos market

By Mary Watkins

Big, bold and with the ability to wipe out holders if it hits the trigger, Barclays' contingent capital bond issue last week drew a whopping $17bn order book from investors.

Yet just over a week after the launch of the first high-trigger total-loss bond by a bank and with investors muttering over the bond's weak performance since issuance, the question is whether the $3bn issue will encourage more banks to follow the Barclays format.

More than 500 fund managers, insurers, private banks and other investors took part in the Barclays issue, attracted by the 7.625% interest rate on the 10-year bonds.

Article 25.3   Continued

The Barclays deal is seen as a key test for a nascent market that many agree has to grow if financial institutions are to meet new regulations governing how much capital banks must hold in crisis situations.

Banks have long been expected to meet those regulatory targets by issuing variations of contingent convertible bonds, dubbed cocos, which developed after the 2007–08 crisis as a way for banks such as Lloyds and RBS to boost capital. But until recently, lack of regulatory clarity in Europe has hampered issuance.

But some analysts and investors remain sceptical about certain aspects of the high-trigger total loss structure adopted by Barclays.

In contrast to most of the cocos issued since 2009 that convert to equity once a pre-agreed financial trigger is breached, the Barclays notes write down to zero should the lender's common equity tier-1 ratio fall below 7%.

Some investors question whether the yield on the Barclays issue is adequate to compensate for the tail [extreme event] risk.

More importantly, they say the issue upsets the normal hierarchy of the capital structure as bondholders would be left with nothing should the bank hit the trigger, even as the bank remained a going concern.

"The fact that as bondholders you could find you are written off completely while shareholders still have a hold is a bit of an issue," says Steve Hussey, of AllianceBernstein.

The Swiss are also insisting on a 6% systemic groups' buffer, rather than 1–2.5%. That is a total of 19% of risk-weighted assets as a capital buffer! The Swiss National Bank can also impose a counter-cyclical buffer of up to 2.5% as well should the economy start to grow too quickly or bubbles develop in say the housing market.[4] UK regulators have signalled that UK banks will also be subject to higher capital ratios than under Basel III, which banks have already responded to – see Figure 25.3.

Basel III on leverage ratio

Banks are very clever at manipulating the categorisation of their assets so that they fall into a lower risk-weighted group.[5] This may result in a bank with an apparently high level of capital relative to risk-weighted assets still being very vulnerable to adverse events. Many experienced bankers and regulators have therefore called for a much simpler gauge of capital reserves: leave out the complication of the risk weighting and simply measure capital as a percentage of total assets – the **leverage ratio**. In 2013 while many leading European banks had Basel III capital at around 9–11% of risk-weighted assets, the figure fell to only 2–4% before risk-weighting.

The Basel III rules insist that the leverage ratio be used as a 'backstop measure' to reinforce the risk-weighted approach, but they are slow about implementation. From 2015 banks are to 'report' leverage ratios. They have a further three years to comply with a minimum leverage ratio of 3% (about the same as for the largest

US banks prior to the 2008 crisis). Even this modest requirement is meeting much resistance, with powerful bank lobbying and politicians having their say. Some regulators in the UK and USA think that at least 4% is needed. Figure 25.4 shows that UK banks' leverage ratios got down to very low levels in the 2000s.

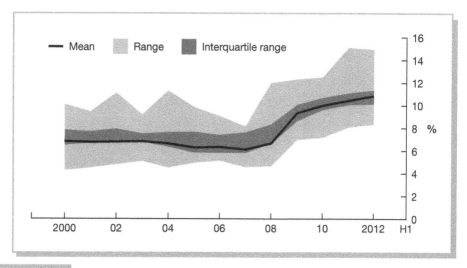

Figure 25.3   **Major UK banks' average core tier 1 capital ratios as a percentage of their risk-weighted assets**

Source: Bank of England (2013) 'The Financial Policy Committee's powers to supplement capital requirements: A Draft Policy Statement'

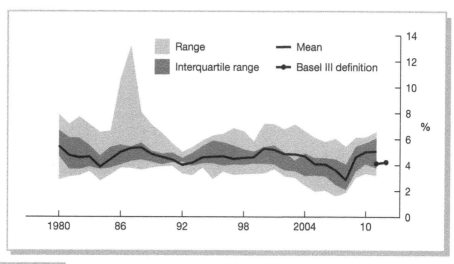

Figure 25.4   **UK banks' leverage ratios**

Source: Bank of England (2013) 'The Financial Policy Committee's powers to supplement capital requirements: A Draft Policy Statement'

Article 25.4 describes the leverage ratio debate.

Article 25.4

Fed weighs tighter cap on bank leverage

By Tom Braithwaite and Shahien Nasiripour

Federal Reserve officials are weighing a stricter cap on bank leverage, a move that would respond to increasing demands to constrain the riskiness of large lenders.

Fed officials have discussed increasing the amount of equity capital banks are required to hold, setting the bar higher than the 3% of assets level agreed internationally.

The move is being considered amid growing scepticism about the Basel III capital accords, which impose higher capital requirements on banks around the world but allow them to vary the amount depending on the riskiness of individual assets. Officials are concerned that some banks are gaming the system.

However, critics of a higher leverage ratio argue that it is a blunt tool that makes no distinction between safe securities, such as US Treasuries, and risky assets

such as leveraged loans, and could result in banks taking on more risk.

In Congress, a proposal to impose a 15% leverage ratio on the largest banks has secured bipartisan support. Analysts calculate it would require the likes of JPMorgan Chase and Bank of America to forego dividends for years to retain a total of $1.2tn of equity.

Few regulators want to go so far, with many believing it would harm the financial sector and curb lending. Any increase would also reduce profitability.

Tom Hoenig, vice-chairman of the Federal Deposit Insurance Corporation, has said 10% would be a "reasonable" leverage ratio. A policy group, whose members include Paul Volcker, former Fed chairman, and Sheila Bair, the previous head of the FDIC, has urged the Fed to set a leverage ratio of 8%.

In the UK, Andy Haldane, executive director for financial stability at the Bank of England, has advocated a leverage ratio of 4–7%.

A majority of officials at both the FDIC board and the Office of the Comptroller of the Currency, another bank regulator, are also in favour of going further, according to people familiar with discussions.

Jeb Hensarling, House financial services committee chairman, said he favoured simpler rules governing capital, as opposed to the current risk-weighting scheme which benefits larger banking groups with significant trading operations that rely on internal models. "Balance sheets are going to have to become far less opaque in order to reinstate market discipline," he said.

Basel III on liquidity risk

Basel III also deals with liquidity – the ability to pay out cash on deposit with-drawals and other outflows of cash while satisfying loan commitments and other obligations. Liquidity management consists of two parts:

1 **Asset management.** Making sure there is enough cash and near-cash available at any one time.

2 **Liability management.** Obtaining liquid resources quickly and avoiding excessive outflows of cash to repay creditors in the near term. For example, the bank maintains access to the money markets and obtains additional funds for liquidity by borrowing there if required – it only needs to offer a slightly higher interest rate than others to obtain billions almost instantly. That is the theory at least, but we now have less faith in this method than bankers did before 2008 because all of a sudden no one was lending in these markets. The other aspect of liability management is not to have a high proportion of liabilities maturing in the next few months or years. Thus, long-term bond issues are to be favoured with a spread of maturities over many years.

The Basel III rules insist that banks maintain a high **liquidity coverage ratio**, that is enough cash and near cash to survive a 30-day market crisis, a 'stressed funding scenario', as specified by supervisors.[6] What is envisaged is something on the same scale as the Lehman induced crisis – a complete freeze in the money markets so the bank cannot access borrowed cash, a loss of deposits and a credit rating down-grade. However, because many banks lobbied their governments hard saying that they could not reach this level of liquidity quickly without significantly reduc-ing lending, the full implementation of this new rule has been delayed until 2019. Until January 2015 it is 'observational', regulators speak for monitoring as banks work their way up to the standard to see if there are serious unintended consequences. No political leader wanted to take the slightest chance of reduced lending at a time when we were trying to recover from recession. Between 2015 and 2019 the coverage will rise from 60% to 100%.

The other liquidity risk-reducing measure is known as the **net stable fund-ing rule**. It seeks to reduce banks' dependence on short-term funding. Another Northern Rock fiasco is what the regulators are trying to avoid: the bank borrowed on the short-term money market to lend long-term for mortgages, and then the short-term market froze. The new rule forcing a greater proportion of long-term borrowing will not apply until 2018 because of the current weakness of the banks in some countries.

The current direction of travel is much more focused on **macro-prudential regulation** than previously. That is, trying to reduce systemic risks rather than assuming that a sound system can be built by focusing only on supervising individual banks (**micro-prudential regulation**). One aspect of this is to prevent bubbles building up in the financial system (e.g. irrational optimism about the increasing value of a group of assets such as houses). Hence the extra capital added in boom times (a **counter-cyclical regulatory capital** regime). Another aspect is to prevent contagion across the system: measures here include high capital ratios for all banks at all times and inspections to ensure limited exposure to any one counterparty bank going bust. However central banks will have a difficult time explaining to lenders, borrowers and politicians that we should have greater constraints on bank lending when times are good. Politicians are likely to ask why is the central bank slowing things down when clearly we are not in a bubble (they never see them beforehand), merely booming as a result of their brilliant and beneficent policies that have led us to a new era of faster growth?

Other activities of central banks

Banker to the government and national debt management

Central banks usually act as their government's banker. They hold the government's bank account and provide services such as deposit holding. As taxes go in the account balance rises, but as the government pays private contractors its account at the central bank will be debited, while the commercial banker to the contractor will see an uplift in its central bank account.

It may also administer the **national debt** (the cumulative outstanding borrowings of a government), raising money by selling Treasury bills and bonds. Increasingly this task is undertaken by a separate organisation; in the UK by the Debt Management Office. This can amount to a very large sum of money. Japan's gross national debt is over 240% of annual GDP, for example. For the UK the figure is heading towards 90%; Italy and Belgium are already over 100%.

Currency issue

Central banks control the issue of bank notes and often control the issue of coins.[7] Notes are issued to commercial banks as they demand them, but in return their reserves at the central bank are surrendered. It is important that the central bank has a monopoly over deciding the size of the issue because excess amounts can result in high inflation, while too little can inhibit the economy. In the past, if the economy grew in nominal terms by 6% the central bank would generally issue a further 6% of notes to keep up with the needs of commerce. However, in recent times this relationship has become more complicated as we increasingly use electronic funds transfer rather than cash. In addition to increasing the volume of notes the central bank stands ready to replace banknotes that are wearing out.

Smooth functioning of the payments system

A central bank may run some or all of the payment systems in an economy, such as cheque clearing and those for electronic transactions. Those systems they do not run they may oversee as a regulator.

Currency reserve control

Countries find it prudent to hold a reserve of gold and foreign currencies at their central banks. This can be useful as rainy day money and for intervening in the foreign exchange markets, e.g. using the foreign currency to buy the home currency thereby increasing demand for it and raising its exchange rate. Even countries that permit a floating exchange rate may want to smooth out sharp day-to-day fluctuations.

Co-ordination with other central banks and international bodies

We have already discussed one form of international co-operation (on solvency and liquidity rules) under the auspices of the Bank for International Settlements (BIS) at Basel. The BIS also acts as a kind of banker to the central banks. It helps in the transfer of money from one central bank to another and keeps a proportion of the central banks' reserves. Central banks also work with the International Monetary Fund. For example, they worked together on the bailout of Cyprus in 2013. Another international economic and financial point of discussion and co-ordination is the regular G20 meetings – gatherings of finance ministers, presidents and prime ministers of the 20 leading economies. Central bankers have a significant input in terms of preparing for the meetings and then may help with the process of implementing agreements.

Bank of England

The Bank of England (BoE – the 'Old Lady of Threadneedle Street') is over 300 years old. Despite its name it is the central bank for the whole of the UK. It was originally mainly used as the government's bank which raised borrowed money for its master. In Victorian times it was granted a monopoly on the issue of new banknotes and was used to rescue individual banks and the banking system. It also managed the nation's foreign currency and gold reserves.

The bank is overseen by the Court of Directors, which consists of a governor, three deputy governors and eight non-executive directors, who decide BoE strategy and objectives, budget and senior appointments. The BoE is responsible for the overall stability of the banking system as a whole, which will involve:

- stability of the monetary system – setting interest rates and dealing with day-to-day fluctuations in liquidity;

- payment systems oversight and strengthening to reduce systemic risk;

- macro-prudential regulation of the financial system as whole;

- authorisation and micro-prudential supervision of banks and other deposit-taking institutions – safety and soundness of individual banks;

- note issuance;

- lender of last resort in selected instances – some banks will be allowed to fail;

- managing the UK's gold and currency reserves and intervening in the foreign exchange markets.

Monetary policy is decided by the **Monetary Policy Committee (MPC)** which consists of the governor, two deputy governors, the Bank's chief economist and director for markets and four outside experts. These experts are drawn from the academic community as well as the world of business (particularly banks). Also, they can and have been non-UK citizens, with expertise being the over-riding consideration. The MPC meets each month to decide on the short-term interest rate target. The BoE staff then engage in open-market operations in the money market to move the market rates to the desired target.

European Central Bank

The European Central Bank (ECB), given responsibility for monetary policy in 1999, is part of the **European System of Central Banks, ESCB (Eurosystem).** The National Central Banks (NCBs) were not discarded, but remain important parts of the regulatory system. The ECB and the ESCB control monetary policy for those countries that are members of the **euro area**, the eurozone. The governors of each of the 17 National Central Banks each have a vote on the Governing Council which makes decisions on monetary policy. Each of the NCBs became independent of both the European Commission and the governments of the individual states when the ESCB was established, if they were not already independent.

The ECB, based in Frankfurt, has an executive board consisting of the president, the vice-president and four other members, who are appointed by a committee of heads of state for eight years. These six people are also voting members of the Governing Council. The Governing Council of 23 meets each month to decide monetary policy and announces the target short-term interest rate (the **refinancing rate**).

Monetary operations are not centralised at the ECB, but are conducted by the individual National Central Banks. In open market operations (the predominant one is called **main refinancing operations (MRO)**), banks and other credit institutions submit bids to borrow and the central banks decide which bids to accept – the unattractively priced offers will not be accepted. This is usually in the repo market or secured loans market. For standing-facility lending (marginal-lending facility) the national central banks will lend, against collateral, overnight loans at say 50, 75 or 100 basis points over the target financing rate, thus providing a ceiling rate in the markets. Banks may also deposit money with the ECB and usually receive interest say 75 or 100 bps below the target financing rate (**deposit facility**), but currently this is 0% with target repo rates at 0.5%.

As well as monetary policy, including the issuance of banknotes, the ECB (in partnership with the NCBs) is responsible for the conduct of foreign exchange operations and holds and manages the official reserves (gold and currency) of the eurozone countries. It also promotes the smooth working of payment systems. Prudential supervision of financial institutions is a responsibility of the NCBs, as are payment mechanisms and the stability of their national financial systems.

The US Federal Reserve

The Americans have a heightened fear of centralised power, and as a consequence emphasise the need for checks and balances in society. One manifestation of their mistrust was the failure of the nineteenth century experiments with establishing central banks because the public mistrusted such a nationwide system, especially if it could be manipulated by Wall Street money men. Thus for much of the nineteenth and the early part of the twentieth century there was no central bank to act as lender of the last resort should banks' reserves get uncomfortably low. As a result there were regular runs on banks and hundreds of bank collapses. The 1907 crisis brought so many bank failures and massive losses to depositors that a consensus was finally reached to create a central bank, which was established in 1913.

However, the Federal Reserve is unlike other central banks because it was structured in such a way as to disperse power to the regions of the country and to disperse power among a number of individuals so that neither Wall Street nor politicians could manipulate it. There are 12 Federal Reserve banks, one for each region of the country. These are overseen by directors who are mostly drawn from the private sector banks and corporates in that region, so that they reflect the American citizenry. These regional Federal Reserve banks supervise the financial institutions in their area (the New York one is the busiest on this score, with so many universal banks to watch over). They also make discount rate loans to banks in their area; issue new currency; clear cheques; supervise the safety and soundness of banks in their area with regard to applications for a bank to expand or merge; and investigate and report on local business conditions.

In addition to the 12 regional Federal Reserve banks there is a Board of Governors of the Federal Reserve System based in Washington which has seven members called governors (usually economists), including the chairman, currently Ben Bernanke. These are appointed by the President of the United States and confirmed by the Senate, but for terms much longer than those of the President or members of congress at 14 years, to reduce the chance of political control of a governor.

Monetary policy through the use of open market operations is decided by the **Federal Open Market Committee (FOMC)** whose voting members include the seven governors of the Federal Reserve Board plus the presidents of the New York Fed and four other regional Feds.[8] Thus, there is input from the regions. Note that the Board has the majority of the votes. The FOMC meets about every six weeks to decide the general stance on open market operations (setting the target federal funds rate, which is the interest rate banks charge each other to lend their balances at the Federal Reserve overnight), but the actual day-to-day interventions in the money markets are conducted by the trading desk at the Federal Reserve Bank of New York. The manager of this desk reports back to the FOMC members daily.

The Board sets reserve requirements (averaged over a maintenance period) and shares the responsibility with the regional Reserve banks for discount rate policy. The Fed now pays interest on reserves (in 2013: 0.25%). The Board plays a key role in assuring the smooth functioning and continued development of the nation's payments system. The Board approves bank mergers and applications for new activities, and regulates the permissible activities of domestic and foreign banks in the USA. However, the safety and soundness of the US financial system is entrusted to a number of different government agencies alongside the Fed, e.g. the **Federal Deposit Insurance Corporation (FDIC)** insures deposits, and identifies, monitors and addresses risks to the financial system. Other organisations include the **Office of the Comptroller of the Currency** (charters, regulates and supervises all national banks and federal savings associations), the **Office of Thrift Supervision** (regulator of federal and many state-chartered thrifts), and the **Securities and Exchange Commission (SEC)** (oversees stockbrokers, funds, stock trading, stock exchanges and financial disclosures by publicly traded corporations). State regulators oversee state-chartered banks, savings institutions, and credit unions as well as all insurance companies.

Finally, the Chairman and his team have some other duties:

▦ advising the nation's president on economic policy;

▦ representing the country in international negotiations on economic matters.

26

Regulation

Bank customers place a great deal of trust in the employees of the various departments of banks when they hand over their money or follow their advice. Naturally, in most cases clients do not understand in any great detail where their money goes. They accept a promise that it will be returned to them, or at least that, if it is put at risk in order to generate a return, the managers will be careful, thoughtful and skilled in applying their savings to investment.

The lack of customer control and lack of customer information once the money is handed over leaves depositors, etc. exposed to a number of human failings. There is the danger of incompetence that either through ignorance or laziness bankers waste their clients' money, possibly losing it all. There is also the danger of outright fraud and other criminal acts that siphon money from the innocent to the crooked.

The banking industry recognised long ago that it is in its own best interest to establish minimum standards of behaviour. If the users of financial services fear that malpractice is prevalent they will not allow their funds to flow through the system and the financial sector will shrink. These minimum standards need some sort of enforcement mechanism beyond a gentleman's agreement that all participants will behave ethically. Crooks and incompetents would love to join an industry where the majority of providers act with probity, because they can free-ride on the industry's reputation. Thus we need regulation. This may be provided by the industry itself with the back-up of statutory laws or could be provided by the government in some form.[1]

This chapter firstly explains why, despite its high cost, we have bank regulation, and then discusses the dangers that arise in a regulated system. The main tasks and activities required of regulators is outlined followed by an examination of one of the most sophisticated regulatory structures in the world, the UK's. We then look at the additional regulatory rules imposed at the European Union level and at the global level.

Why regulate banks?

Bank regulation is expensive. It costs hundreds of millions, even billions, to pay for regulators to carry out their tasks in a modern economy. There are further billions to be paid by the banks in **compliance costs**, i.e. putting in place systems and training to ensure that staff behave according to the rules. These additional costs are likely to be passed on to clients. Then there are the potential losses because new organisations that are keen to provide a financial service are put off entering the industry by the costs and time of obtaining a licence from the regulator and the subsequent monitoring – perhaps society loses much innovatory and competitive fizz as a result. So, given the costs, a fundamental question is: why do we bother with regulation? This section presents some ideas to answer that question.

Safety and soundness

Consumers are frequently unable to assess the safety and soundness of a bank or the products it provides. They simply do not have the time or the expertise to evaluate whether the organisation is taking too much risk with their money. An example here is the flood of money that went into Icelandic banks in the mid-2000s. Large numbers of savers from all over Europe were attracted by the high interest rates offered on deposit accounts. Little did they know that the accumulated bank deposits were lent out to high-risk ventures with only small amounts being retained as a safety buffer. The managers of these banks were tempted by the higher interest rates they could charge on the more risky lending, producing large, short-term (apparent) profits and therefore large bonuses. Regulators are supposed to conduct prudential bank regulation (discussed in Chapters 7 and 25) to protect consumers from unsound bank policies and actions. They clearly failed in the case of the Icelandic banks, so after their collapse the authorities (governments in this case) were forced to guarantee all deposits, which is an expensive way to protect depositors. They are now much keener on ensuring banks are managed for safety and soundness.

Capital reserves and liquidity reserves were discussed in detail earlier (in Chapters 7 and 25) and so, despite this being a very important element in financial regulation, we will not discuss it any further here. Another element of safety and soundness for banks is that they do not have too many eggs in one (or a few) basket, say an excessive proportion of lending to one sector (e.g. property developers) – called concentration risk.

Safety and soundness concerns arise not only in the relationship between financial service providers and consumers, they also arise in the trading that takes place between financial intermediaries, e.g. interbank lending and borrowing, trading in the foreign exchange market or derivatives trading all involve a degree of risk that the counterparty you have made a deal with fails to fulfil its part of the bargain.

Conflicts of interest

Conflicts of interest arise when a person or institution has a number of objectives (interests) and is free to choose which receives the most emphasis, when one of them might have the potential to corrupt the motivation to act. The choice made may not be one that would suit the consumer because it might be tainted by the self-interest of the financial service provider. But the consumer is unable to see the extent of the bias.

Conflicts of interest can lead to the misuse of information, the providing of false information, the providing of biased or selective information, or the concealing of information.

- **Misuse.** An example of the misuse of information is **spinning** by an investment bank organising an initial public offering (IPO) of a company's shares that it thinks will rise substantially. It allocates blocks of shares to a few select clients such as directors of companies that may give the bank a mandate to assist in raising capital (e.g. an IPO) in the future. These selected executives will make a killing in the week or two following the flotation. They will then repay the investment bank by directing their company to pay fat fees for a new bond or equity issue. This might be a lot more expensive for the company than if it shopped around for an arranger of funding. Thus the cost of raising capital is inflated and bankers take home large bonuses.

- **False.** An example of false information dissemination arose in the case of **payment protection insurance (PPI)**. This is insurance cover for loan repayments should the borrower die, become ill or disabled, lose a job or face other circumstances that may prevent him or her from earning income to service the debt. When a loan is taken out borrowers were often subject to pressurised sales techniques to also take out this insurance for an additional fee. In the 2000s UK sales staff received bonuses based on volume of PPI sold. Customers frequently received false information, e.g. that the policy paid out if a self-employed person lost their income or that the loan would not be granted if they did not also take out PPI. (The banks have admitted that they mis-sold and are now paying back billions.) False information was also given to LIBOR compilers (see Chapter 6).

- **Biased.** An example of biased information arises in a badly organised investment bank which while issuing research reports and advising investors on good bond purchases also arranges a bond issue by a client company.

A great deal of effort goes into understanding the company when arranging a bond issue, and the information generated may be useful to the research team supplying analysis to investors. However, the issuing firm would like to sell the bonds at as high a price as possible and so would like the researchers to be optimistic. If the fee received for organising the bond is sufficiently large then the investment bank may (if not properly controlled) select the information it releases to boost the potential sales level. These banks are supposed to have high 'Chinese walls' separating different departments to prevent these conflicts of interest, but it is surprising how positive many of them are about the equity or debt securities of their client companies (it is difficult to find negative comments).

▓ **Concealment.** An example of the concealment of information is when a bank has a loan outstanding to a company that it suspects is running into serious financial difficulties. Bank officers have access to this information but the bond issue department is nevertheless encouraged to sell bonds in the company without telling investors about the company's likelihood of distress. The loan is paid off and the bank earns a fee for selling the bonds.

Many conflicts of interest are not exploited even in the absence of regulation because the incentive to do so is not sufficiently high and the vast majority of bankers are decent people. Also, banks often live and die by their reputations. Any conflict that became visible would be punished as other financial organisations and clients shunned the firm. Having said that, we still need regulation because these constraints may not work on particular individuals with immediate bonuses to puff-up, or when the firm itself is excessively focused on short-term profits rather than long-term reputation.

Fraud

Financial markets present opportunities to make large profits over short periods of time; this is especially the case if a trusted professional lacks moral fibre. While the majority of people in the financial sector are honourable and of high integrity, such a honey pot is bound to attract greedy knaves who are clever enough to dream up a range of chicanery.

Incompetence

Consumers often receive poor service due to incompetence. This may be bad advice because of the inattention or ignorance of a financial adviser – see Article 26.1 for an example. There may be incompetence in managing a client's funds or their business interests. In financial services incompetence can continue

Article 26.1

Santander faces advice probe

By Tanya Powley

Santander UK is facing a regulatory investigation after a "mystery shopping" exercise by the Financial Services Authority (FSA) uncovered failings in the investment advice given by high street banks.

The FSA published the findings of 231 visits to six banks and building societies, in which assessors posed as potential customers to gauge the quality of advice given.

It found that a quarter of customers were given poor investment advice – leading Santander's UK operation to be referred to the regulator's enforcement division.

News of the FSA findings came on the same day that Santander announced it was carrying out a strategic review of its UK investment advice arm, which could result in it being closed down.

Mystery shopping exercises are set to become a more widely-used supervisory tool when the FSA is replaced by the Financial Conduct Authority (FCA) in April. In its latest review of investment advice, it found that bank advisers gave unsuitable advice to customers in 11% of cases. It also found that in 15% of cases, advisers did not gather enough information to make sure their advice was suitable.

The FSA said it found problems at all of the high street lenders it reviewed, but it was particularly concerned with the "high level of poor advice" it found in some.

undetected for years. For example, in the handling of asset fund money, the manager will render the service of investing to supply a return decades after the savers have injected funds into the scheme. It may only be after decades that it is revealed whether it has been managed well.

Contagion

The failure of a bank may result in the failure of others leading to instability in the whole system. This is called **contagion risk**. As we have seen following the collapse of Lehman Brothers in 2008 contagion can have very serious consequences for the economic health of a nation as well as for consumers of financial products. If a domino effect takes hold, where one bank's failure (or perceived likely failure) to meet its obligations to other banks or clients, leads to more bank collapses and further losses it can ruin the entire system, possibly taking us down into a 1930s-style depression. Economists would describe this as an example of an 'externality' in which the social cost of failure exceeds the private cost.

The damage caused by spreading contagion is so bad that it is well worth the effort to ensure individual banks are unlikely to collapse by regulating the amount of capital and liquid assets they hold. It is also worth insisting that they write and continuously update 'living wills' so that they can be revived or closed down in an orderly way, that none are either too big to fail or 'too big to save', where no government can raise enough money to save a bank.

Monopoly/oligopoly

Many markets will, if left to their own devices, tend toward a structure where one or a few firms exert undue market power over product pricing. Consumers need protection against monopolistic/oligopolistic exploitation.

There are many forces encouraging movement toward monopoly in financial services apart from the desire to control prices. Economies of scale are such that it makes sense for many banks and other institutions to become very large. Banks with branches in every town and with capabilities to serve multinational firms in every country have an advantage in attracting customers. There are also network effects: a single payments system linking the major banks makes more sense than a number of competing systems, because each participant needs to make as many connections within the network as possible.

The dangers to watch out for in a regulatory system

Moral hazard

The mere presence of regulation can cause **moral hazard**, which in this context is: *the presence of a safety net that encourages adverse behaviour (e.g. carelessness).*

Thus regulation can be counterproductive, in that, if consumers believe they will be bailed out by the government if things go wrong they will be tempted to take higher risk. Why not place your money in a deposit account offering an unrealistically high interest rate? The bank may go bust but your deposit is safe. In this way irresponsible, badly managed and crooked banks and other financial institutions survive, drawing society's scarce resources away from more productive investment.

Agency capture

Agency (regulatory) capture occurs when those that are supposed to be regulated take some control of the regulatory process. Then the regulation is modified to suit the interests of the producers rather than the consumers. For example, under

Basel II (see Chapter 25) the large banks managed to persuade the regulators that it would be sensible for capital requirements to be set in the mould of the banks' own internal risk models. Many people say that the banks were too influential in lowering capital limits, manipulating the rules on risk-weighting assets and in using their own models. This helped to precipitate the 2008 crisis as banks were found to have taken too much risk.

The regulated firms usually have far more financial interest in the activities of regulators than consumers, and so they apply themselves to persuading their overseers to relax constraints. In many cases the people working in the regulatory organisation are paid significantly less than the financial service high flyers, and they can sometimes be intimidated or outsmarted. Furthermore, many of the more senior regulators have come from the industry they are now regulating and therefore share many of their attitudes and values. Also, they may expect to return to work in the industry following their policing stint and may thus avoid offending potential future employers.

Excessive compliance cost

The cost to regulated firms of adhering to the rules will usually result in raised fees, lower returns or some other penalty for consumers, because the institution is likely to pass the additional burden on to clients.

Stifling innovation and growth

The requirements to be licensed and the additional costs of subsequent compliance can impose such a bureaucratic load that few or no firms dare to enter the industry. Thus inefficient monopolies are sustained and oligopolies with implicit cartel-type arrangements persist in over-charging consumers because they are not challenged by new entrants. The core elements of regulation are shown in Figure 26.1.

Regulation of UK financial services

Now that we have covered the basic principles lying behind regulation we will look at the example of the UK to illustrate the range of responsibilities typically given to regulators.

Interestingly, the UK regulatory system has gone through something of an upheaval recently. For over a decade the **Financial Services Authority (FSA)** dominated the scene. It was a 'super-regulator' with oversight of an amazing range of financial sectors. This is in contrast to some systems (e.g. in the USA) where there

Licensing/Authorisation

Is a person fit and proper to manage a provider?
Only those who have met the standards
required (integrity, honesty, capability)
are allowed to provide a service.
Training schemes and qualifications are
encouraged by regulators to raise standards.

Disclosure and monitoring

Disclosure of information about the
operations of the financial firm and on-going
monitoring may reveal whether a conflict of
interest exists, whether risk management
procedures are sound, whether the managers
are competent and the institution is run
with integrity.
This may involve off-site analysis of
information provided and on-site inspections
by the regulator

Prudential limits

For example, capital and liquidity requirements
of banks.

Exposure limits

For example, no single borrower to account
for more than 5% of a bank's loans.

Mandatory information provisions and consumer education

Customers should obtain the right information
at the right time to help them make a decision.
Financial products/services to be clearly
explained including risks, potential returns and
costs such as charges. This must be presented
in a consistent format to allow comparison.
Regulators often accept a responsibility to
educate and foster financial literacy. This is to
reduce the need for more heavy handed
regulation.

Restricting activities

Prohibiting certain firms from a line of business
or prohibiting a particular combination of
financial services within the same organisation
or a ban on anyone from engaging in the
activity (e.g. no mortgage lending without
proof of borrower's income).
Commercial companies are often not allowed
to hold large equity stakes in a bank, and
vice versa.
Regulators may insist that financial service
functions be separated. This may be by
splitting into in-house departments with
'Chinese walls' between them, or insisting on
separately capitalised group companies or
splitting up the company.
Anti-monopoly provisions restrict activity/prices.

Duty of care

Prescribing appropriate financial institution behaviour to avoid harm to customers.
No misrepresentation, fraud or mis-selling.
Knowing the financial position, investment goals, knowledge and experience of the customer
before providing advice or selling a service to ensure that it is suitable (e.g. not selling a high-risk
investment to someone needing a low-risk portfolio).
Eliminating unfair terms in contracts.
A firm must protect client assets while it holds them on behalf of the client – e.g. ringfencing them.

Penalties

In the event of non-compliance penalties may
be imposed (e.g. fines, de-licensing,
imprisonment, banning directors from the
industry). For less serious offences a private
warning or public censure may be sufficient.

Complaints handling and compensation

Put systems in place to assist consumers
pursuing a complaint against a firm and
to secure recompense.
Provide compensation if a firm is bust
(e.g. bank deposit insurance).

Figure 26.1   Core elements of regulation

are a dozen or more regulators, each looking after one or a limited range of types of financial service.

In 2013 the FSA split in two. The main body, the **Financial Conduct Authority (FCA)** remains a super-regulator covering a very wide range of financial services (see Figure 26.2). However, the important functions of the individual regulation[2] of the 1,700 biggest banks, building societies, credit unions, insurers and major investment firms on the issue of safety and soundness (micro-prudential supervision) has been transferred to the new **Prudential Regulatory Authority (PRA)**, a subsidiary of the Bank of England (BoE). It is responsible for granting permission for their activities and approving their senior management and risk-mitigation systems. It has powers to impose additional capital and liquidity requirements, change the risk weighting of assets in order to reduce the risk of failure, and to insist on a good resolution plan (living will) in the event of failure, so it is not disorderly.

The BoE previously had the responsibility, together with the FSA and the Treasury, of ensuring the systemic safety of the banking system. That is, setting rules, particularly on capital reserves, for banks across the sector as a whole and imposing other rules to reduce contagion risk. Following the financial crisis it was thought wise to concentrate this macro-prudential regulation in the hands of one regulator, the new **Financial Policy Committee (FPC)** and the micro-prudential regulation of individual banks in the hands of the PRA, rather than have the 'tripartite' approach where people in the BoE, Treasury and the FSA were not quite clear which of them should be taking charge when a systemic threat arose – as was the case up to 2008. The additional consideration is that these systemically important institutions might need access to central bank funding in an emergency and so it is best if they are regulated by the BoE.

The Bank of England's FPC, making decisions that apply to the entire sector to ensure system-wide financial stability including the avoidance of credit and asset bubbles, only meets four times a year to set rules. It might, for example, increase capital requirements above the Basel III minimum in normal times to ensure safety, and then lower them in a crisis so that the banks do not withdraw lending when the economy is already suffering (the 'countercyclical capital buffers' discussed in Chapter 25). It may impose system-wide higher risk-weights against specific classes of bank assets (e.g. residential mortgages) in markets that appear too exuberant, or vary the minimum leverage ratio across the sector ratio. It may insist that banks increase their forward-looking loss-provisioning when lending is growing fast.

The FPC has also been set the task of identifying emerging threats to the system from the 'shadow banking sector', which comprises a group of financial institutions that individually or collectively act like banks but are not as heavily regulated as banks – see later in this chapter for more on shadow banking.

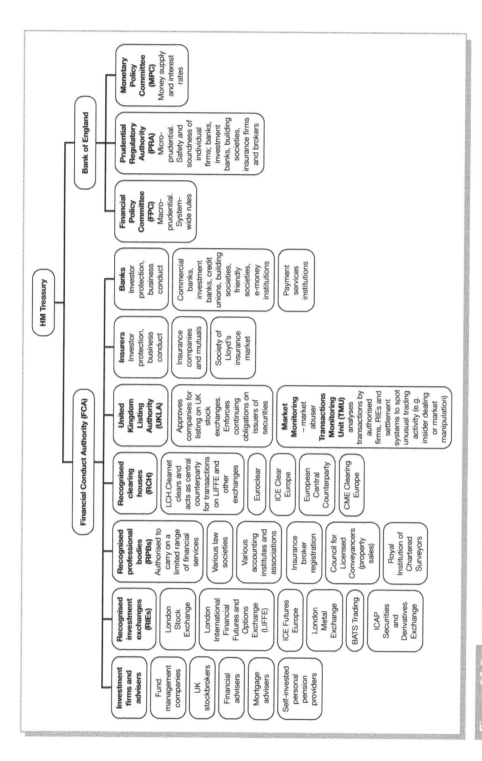

Figure 26.2 UK financial services industry regulation

So there is a division of labour: the PRA does the hard work of day-to-day handling of individual institutions to ensure firm, level stability and soundness; the FPC adjusts reserves, etc. across the system when it perceives a threat to overall stability. However there is much common ground and need for co-ordination with each other and with the organisation looking out for bad conduct such as fraud, the FCA. And, of course, the BoE also has the Monetary Policy Committee to set interest rates and adjust the money supply (see Chapter 24).

In retaining responsibility for protecting consumers and preserving market integrity the FCA covers:

- investor protection, including that for bank customers, against wrong doing such as mis-selling, incompetence and fraud;
- market supervision and regulation;
- business conduct of banks and financial services, including approval of consumer-related managers and the supervision of investment managers;
- civil and criminal enforcement of market abuse rules, e.g. putting false information into the market to benefit from a rise or fall in a share price;
- UK Listing Authority – supervision of initial public offerings and subsequent monitoring of listed companies.

While most companies will only be answerable to one regulator, the PRA-supervised firms, including all banks, will be under the supervision of two regulators. The FCA will cover the good treatment of customers and general business conduct while the PRA will cover safety and soundness of the institution.

The FCA can be described as semi-detached from government: it is financed by the industries it regulates, but its powers come from legislation; it often consults the financial services companies before deciding on principles, rules and codes of conduct, but it has basic principles approved by the government and it is answerable to the Treasury, which appoints its board, and through them to Parliament.

The FCA contributes to the following:

- maintaining and enhancing the integrity of, and confidence in, the financial system;
- an appropriate degree of protection for consumers;
- promoting effective competition in the interests of consumers;
- reducing financial crime, such as money laundering and insider dealing;
- helping people to gain the knowledge, aptitude and skills to manage their financial affairs effectively by promoting public understanding of the financial system.

While pursuing these objectives the regulators make it clear that they are not removing all risk for the investor. Risk is an inherent part of the system and those who take the benefits from an investment/bank product when everything goes right have to accept that from time to time losses will occur. Also, the complete absence of consequences for clients, should a financial firm fail, may encourage laziness in choosing a place for their money and other moral hazards, and so the FCA and the PRA do not promise to rescue failed firms, nor guarantee all money deposited/invested with them (but see Financial Services Compensation Scheme later). The regulators also try to maintain healthy competition by encouraging new players to enter the industry, and try to strike the right balance between the costs and benefits of tighter regulation.

The introduction of a single super-regulator for a country was unusual when in 2001 the FSA was given powers over several areas of financial services (it was set up in 1997 with a more limited remit). However, the advantages of a unified approach are now well-recognised, and many countries (e.g. Japan, Germany and Sweden) now have a super-regulator for their financial sectors. Increasingly, financial institutions provide a wide range of services and so a unified approach to regulation is needed. This allows greater insight into the firm's practices and avoids the problem of financial activities falling between the cracks of separate regulator's responsibilities. Also there are economies of scale in investigation and monitoring: having six different regulators visiting a firm and asking similar questions is clearly inefficient for the regulated and the regulator. Despite economies of scale the system is not cheap – see Article 26.2.

Article 26.2

'Twin peaks' regulation to cost £646m

By Brooke Masters

The UK's 'twin peaks' regulation will cost £646.3m for 2013–14, up 15% from last year's bill for the single Financial Services Authority.

The Bank of England announced that its new Prudential Regulation Authority arm will cost £214.2m on top of the £432.1m that the independent Financial Conduct Authority has already proposed.

The fees charged to the financial services industry will be slightly smaller, because £40.7m in fines will be used to offset resources spent on enforcement investigations.

The combined burden will fall most heavily on banks, insurers and large investment firms, which are all regulated by both authorities.

The PRA said the fee increase was due to a £34m rise in staff costs for both regulators that "reflects the need to embed the judgment-based, forward-looking and risk-focused supervision approach".

Authorisation

All firms or individuals offering financial advice, products or services in the UK must be authorised by the FCA.[3] Engaging in a regulated activity without authorisation can result in a two-year prison sentence. The FCA insists on high standards when assessing for authorisation. These require competence, financial soundness and fair treatment of customers. Firms are authorised to carry out specific activities, e.g. banking, giving financial advice only, managing client money in a fund or stockbroking.

Monitoring

Even after initial approval, firms cannot relax as the FCA continues to monitor adequacy of management, financial resources, internal systems and controls. It also insists that any information provided to investors is clear, fair and not misleading. If there is a failure to meet these standards the firms can be fined or even stopped from doing business. Individual managers can be held accountable – see Article 26.3. The FCA also works closely with the criminal authorities and uses civil and criminal powers.

Article 26.3

Watchdogs keep up pressure on responsibility

By Brooke Masters

Five years after the financial crisis, public anger still boils in both the US and UK that so few enforcement cases have been brought against the chief executives and directors who led their banks into catastrophe.

But London's new financial watchdogs are quietly doing their best to make sure that today's leading bankers and brokers can be held to account more easily.

Over the past five years the authorisation procedure for "significant influence functions", which include roles such as chief executives, finance directors and non-executive directors, has been sharply revamped. Would-be Sifs now have more specific responsibilities and are often called for searching panel interviews before their applications are approved.

The new Prudential Regulation Authority and the Financial Conduct Authority have also stepped up the use of a practice pioneered by their predecessor agency, and are asking individual executives to take personal responsibility for addressing specific regulatory concerns.

In some cases, the executive must "attest" that the firm either does not have or has addressed a particular industry-wide problem. In others the individual agrees to ensure that a particular redress programme has been or will be carried out properly. First used in March 2012, the technique has shown up in the FCA's work on getting banks to compensate small businesses that were mis-sold

Article 26.3 Continued

interest rate hedges and its review of conflicts of interest at fund managers. The PRA has said it is using attestations to make sure that banks are addressing particular risks to safety and soundness.

Regulators say the new techniques are a natural extension of the emphasis on personal responsibility.

"We don't see this as a reason for anybody to be nervous about taking these positions. We approve people for the Sif position pretty rigorously," said Clive Adamson, FCA director of supervision. "Ultimately, it is the firm's responsibility to satisfy themselves that the individuals they appoint are of the highest possible quality and possess the right skills for the role they perform."

The attestations also echo a technique adopted in the US during the last decade in the wake of the Enron and WorldCom accounting scandals. As part of the 2002 Sarbanes–Oxley corporate accountability law, chief executives and chief financial officers of public companies were required to sign statements personally attesting that the reported quarterly and annual results were accurate.

Higher up executives are particularly uncomfortable with having to certify that their entire organisation, which may include thousands of people around the world, is complying with particular rules.

Clifford Smout, a former UK regulator now with Deloitte, said the new demands could backfire. "If you have very tough controls and all sorts of penalties [for non-executive directors and Sifs], many of the people you put off becoming directors will be the more reflective and risk-sensitive ones".

The FCA emphasises broad principles rather than its rules. The problem with a regulator sticking strictly to rules is that they can result in inflexibility – just 'ticking boxes' – rather than concentrating the minds of the regulated on the spirit underlying the rules. Also a rule-based approach can be less flexible when it comes to permitting innovation from existing or new firms. A principles-based approach has less prescription and allows the regulator to meet new situations (e.g. new tricks by those smart people in the City) by using some degree of judgement rather than being hidebound by rules. Lawyers will forever be finding loopholes in rules; they find that more difficult if the rules are set in a framework of general principles, when the principles have greater weight.

Independent complaints scheme

Most financial services firms belong to an independent complaints scheme – the FCA insists on this in most cases.[4] These are beneficial to the system because they increase the confidence of investors and other financial clients by responding to consumers' fear that they lack knowledge or resources to be able to stand up to the financial professionals. There are two types: arbitration schemes and ombudsman schemes. Under both the complaint will be investigated and, if found to be justified, the firm will be ordered to put matters right.

Under arbitration both the complainant and the firm agree in advance to accept the arbitrator's decision. Importantly, in accepting this the complainant gives up the right to take the case to court. The advantage is that it is much quicker and cheaper than going to court.

Under the **Financial Ombudsman Scheme (FOS)** the independent and impartial ombudsman collects together the facts of the case and arrives at what seems to him or her a reasonable and fair settlement. The firm is then under an obligation to accept the decision,[5] but the complainant remains free to take the case to court. The service is free to consumers. The ombudsman's approach is less legalistic than arbitration and allows for more 'common-sense' factors of fairness. The FOS looks at complaints about most financial problems involving:

- banking;
- insurance;
- mortgages;
- credit cards and store cards;
- loans and credit;
- pensions;
- savings and investments;
- hire purchase and pawnbroking;
- money transfer;
- financial advice;
- stocks, shares, unit trusts and bonds;
- payment protection insurance.

Compensation

The complaint steps described in the last section are all well and good if the firm that has behaved badly is still in existence. But what if it is defunct? The **Financial Services Compensation Scheme (FSCS)** can compensate consumers (and small companies) if an *authorised* company is unable to pay money it owes. Note that if a consumer does business with a firm not authorised by the FCA, e.g. an offshore company,[6] he or she is not covered by the FSCS or the complaints procedure.

The FSCS service is free for the consumer and small businesses. It covers investments (e.g. bad advice, bad investment management), money deposited in accounts (at banks, building societies and credit unions), insurance products (e.g. car insurance, life insurance), mortgage advice, pensions and endowments. For investments and home finance (mortgages) the maximum payout is £50,000 per person. For deposit claims (e.g. bank accounts) the scheme pays up to £85,000 per person (per bank). For insurance the scheme pays 90% of the loss (100% for compulsory insurance).

To compensate victims of mis-selling or other malpractice the FSCS raises money from the financial service firms via a regular annual levy supplemented by additional levies in years of high compensation pay outs, and this can be very costly for them.

Money laundering

Money laundering is concealing the source of illegally obtained money. It is the process of changing money obtained from crimes, such as drug trafficking, into a form that appears to be legitimate. The process often involves multiple international transactions across currencies and financial institutions in order to obscure the source. To combat money laundering the UK regulators require that any bank, share broker or other financial firm being asked to open an account for a person or company has to verify the customer's identity. Even solicitors carrying out house conveyancing are required to see forms of identity such as passports, driving licence and utility bills of the purchasers (even if they have known the client for years and asked for the same documents only months before for an earlier transaction!). Financial firms are also required to look out for suspicious transactions and report them. The FCA penalises firms that lack adequate systems and controls to detect and report money laundering, as do the US regulators – see Article 26.4.

There are some people within the finance industry who help money launderers, using their contacts and knowledge about jurisdictions abroad where policing is lax. Criminal investigators are tasked with tracking them down. Suspected money laundering is reported to the **National Crime Agency**, which is assisted by other investigating agencies such as the police, particularly The City of London Police.

Article 26.4

HSBC to spend $700m vetting clients

By Patrick Jenkins and Tom Braithwaite

HSBC will spend $700m on a global "know your customer" programme, as part of a 26-point plan agreed with US regulators to settle money laundering and sanctions breaches. The UK bank, which signed up to the A–Z programme of management changes covering both its US and global operations, reiterated apologies for its failure to prevent Mexican money launderers and countries subject to sanctions, including Iran, from using its network.

It also agreed to pay a $1.256bn fine to the Department of Justice and a further $665m to US regulators.

HSBC confirmed it had clawed back bonuses from a number of senior US managers.

 Source: Jenkins, P. and Braithwaite, T. (2012) 'HSBC to spend $700m vetting clients', *Financial Times*, 11 December. © The Financial Times 2012. All rights reserved.

European Union regulation

As well as national financial service regulation we have another layer for the countries in the European Union. We will concentrate on the basic principles that the EU legislators are applying, and look at a few examples of the pan-European rules that have already been introduced.

The fundamental objective of the EU is to promote movement toward a single market in financial services regardless of national boundaries. It is thought that movement toward such a goal will bring about improved welfare for consumers and faster economic growth. The **Financial Services Action Plan (FSAP)** is the process devised by the European Commission to provide momentum towards a single integrated market. It includes moves to create a legal framework to allow financial institutions to offer their services throughout the EU by removing obstacles that hamper the cross-border purchasing or provision of these services (e.g. single bank account, mortgage credit). The following are examples of goals:

- reducing the charges on low-value transfers of money between EU countries by encouraging more efficient, cheaper cross-border payments system, e.g. on credit card payments;

- ensuring that consumers are provided with clear and understandable information when they are investing some or all of their savings in another country;

▨   that there are efficient and effective procedures for redress for incompetent or
     crooked practices or other malpractices in cross-border services.

There is also co-ordination on strengthening the rules on macro- and micro-prudential supervision of banks.

The two key elements for achieving the objectives are:

1 Mutual recognition. If a financial firm has been authorised to offer a service by
one EU member state it is then free to operate in other member states selling its
service there without requiring further authorisation from the host countries.

2 Minimum standards. Agreeing minimum standards for financial services. This
ensures that if a firm is authorised by its home regulator it abides by reasonably
tough rules that would protect clients throughout the EU. There is not a 'race to
the bottom' by countries deliberately offering a lax regulatory environment to
attract financial service firms to set up in their countries or to promote the growth
of their domestic firms by lowering their costs or allowing doubtful activity.

Note that there is no attempt to create either full harmonisation in which the
rules are identical in each country ('one size fits all'), or a common regulatory
structure with a large centralised bureaucracy or a single European regulator in
Brussels. The member states would not accept this level of interference in their
economies. Politically, it is far easier for them to agree to adopt minimum standards and a **'passport' system**, in which the granting of a licence in one EU country
is sufficient for a financial firm to sell its services in all EU member states.

Dozens of 'directives' have been published by the European Commission and then
implemented by member countries. Some of the most significant are:

▨   **The Capital Liberalisation Directive, 1988.** Money can be moved from one
     country to another without controls. This free movement was given a boost
     when the majority of EU states adopted the euro in 1999; it was diminished
     when Cyprus imposed controls on transferring money in 2013.

▨   **The Capital Requirements Directive, 2006.** Common minimum rules on
     bank and investment firm capital adequacy.[7] The directive links to the Basel
     rules – see Chapter 25.

▨   **The First Banking Directive, 1977.** Banks became free to open branches or
     establish subsidiaries in other member states. These were to operate under the
     supervisory rules of the host country. This limited the range of services to only
     those accepted by the host country's regulations. Thus a subsidiary of a French
     bank in Spain could only do what the Spanish regulators allowed local banks
     to do.

- **The Second Banking Directive, 1989.** A single banking licence allowed operations throughout the EU. This allowed a bank licensed in one EU country to sell its services in other EU countries regardless of whether the host country normally allows these services to be provided by its domestic banks. The activities permitted under this rule are those on an approved list, and include securities business as well as banking services. As a safeguard the home and host country supervisors exchange information as they now have to share supervision. Home country regulators have the main responsibility, but host country regulators can impose monetary policy-related rules, e.g. liquidity reserves, and supervise consumer protection.

In addition to agreeing to abide by directives, occasionally the EU states agree that they will all impose common rules on the financial sector, e.g. banker's bonuses will be limited throughout the EU.

There is now a college of national supervisors – the **European System of Financial Supervisors.** Under this, three authorities, focused on different aspects of financial services, were created in 2011:

- **The European Banking Authority (EBA).** Headquartered in London, the EBA is concerned with ensuring EU-wide co-ordination on regulatory and supervisory standards with a focus on the stability of the financial system (prudential regulation). It stress-tests European banks and will have much to say on the adoption of new capital and liquidity reserve standards over the next few years.

- **The European Insurance and Occupational Pensions Authority (EIOPA).** Based in Frankfurt, it focuses on EU co-ordination of rules for protection of insurance policyholders, pension scheme members and beneficiaries.

- **The European Securities and Markets Authority (ESMA).** Located in Paris, it tries to improve the EU regulators' co-ordination on the functioning of markets and strengthens investor protection. It is charged with harmonising the regulation of issuance and trading of shares, bonds and other securities. It covers matters of corporate governance, auditing, financial reporting, take-over bids, clearing and settlement, and derivatives issues.

The committees of these three organisations, made up of the heads of national regulators, have the responsibility of trying to achieve greater convergence of regulatory standards and practices across the EU. They produce technical standards and plan for the adoption of EU regulatory law throughout the EU – some countries have been lax in adopting the EU-wide rules in the past, and so need a little chivvying along.

Despite past attempts to gain greater co-operation at the EU level, regulation remains mostly a national affair, embedded in domestic regulation. However, these new bodies will have the power to override national authorities in 'emergency situations'. Also, the political mood seems to be to grant more powers to pan-EU regulatory bodies (outside the UK, that is), and it is thought that their powers to override national regulators will be extended into a greater range of products and markets than those listed above.

In addition to these three the **European Systemic Risk Board (ESRB)**, also set up in 2011, has powers to issue warnings and recommendations when it sees threats to economies or financial systems. The European Central Bank takes the lead role in the ESRB, but national central bankers dominate the board. We will have to wait and see if it is merely a talking shop fretting over, say house prices in Spain and excess property lending in Ireland, but with no teeth to do anything about a wayward economy.

Many people, particularly in the City of London, think that too much control over financial services and markets is being granted to pan-European regulators, who may not fully understand the needs of a financial centre like the City, and who may have political agenda, e.g. to grab business from London.

The **Financial Stability Board (FSB)** is charged with the task of developing and co-ordinating supervisory and other policies to promote financial stability on a global basis. It also co-ordinates with the **International Monetary Fund** in sounding alarm bells about vulnerabilities in financial systems. For example, it is currently working on the 'too big to fail' problem in banking.

Some gaps in the system?

One major problem is overcoming the political obstacles to effective international regulation. There is always a temptation for the country that would like to build up its financial service sector to race to the bottom, because footloose financial institutions are attracted by 'lightness of regulation', and will move. Thus regulatory arbitrage will always be with us, with some aspects of finance moving to the least-regulated jurisdiction. Hence the need for robust international agreements on minimum standards. The problem is that each country examines a proposal for a tighter rule in the light of an assessment of the impact on its competitiveness. The intention of the national policymakers too often seems to be 'to find a regulatory regime that crimps competitors more than one's own companies'.[8] Hence the slowness in achieving worldwide (or G20) agreement on issues as diverse as bankers' bonuses (the US rules are more flexible than the EU ones) or banning investment banks from proprietary trading (the US is strict, other countries less so, leaving loopholes).

On the other hand, the widespread recognition that under-regulation contributed to the 2008 financial crisis has reinforced the view that policymakers do not serve their people well if they allow too much slack. The tension between the desire for an easy-going light-touch regulated financial centre – egged on by bankers, etc. threatening to leave for more accommodating environments – and the need to protect consumers will always be with us. It will be interesting to see how the politicians resolve the tension over the next few years (it does not help that such a high proportion of political party donations in the UK, USA and other countries come from the finance sector).

Shadow banking

Another major problem is that the regulators have paid little attention to the less obvious, but powerful, sectors within the financial system. I am referring here to the **'shadow banking system'**. This is the collection of non-bank entities that move money and risk around the global financial system, by-passing the banks. The following are the usual candidates to be included in this group:

- **Hedge funds.** Raising funds directly from wealthy individuals and institutional investors, they have a large and growing role in debt, equity and derivatives markets. A failure of a large hedge fund could destabilise the markets and the banking system given that banks are often the counterparties in derivatives and other deals, and they also lend to the funds.

- **Private equity funds.** Originally set up to raise funds from long-term investors to invest in non-quoted companies, some have branched out into debt trading, and even have hedge fund arms. Failure of these ventures could pose a threat to banks and the wider system, as could a failure of a large leveraged buyout. Some funds have loan books larger than that of many banks. Much of that money was raised through bank borrowing, thus a failure to repay could imperil banks.

- **Money market funds.** These by-pass the banks by taking short-term money from investors to buy commercial paper and other securities. It was their abrupt withdrawal from lending via commercial paper, etc. following some defaults, that caused corporates and banks to be unable to roll over their debt, leading many to failure in 2008. Many money market funds supplied cash for repayment over, say, 30 days. This was used to lend out on 25-year mortgages. Thus, non-banks (money market funds and special purpose vehicles issuing long-term bonds as securitised bonds) became conduits for maturity transformation, where short-term money is lent out into long-term securities. The expectation by those who borrowed from the money market funds was that they would always be there to supply more money, every 30 days. This was a silly assumption.

▦ **Securitisation.** The securitisation of assets such as sub-prime mortgages greatly assisted the growth of the housing finance market. These securitised bonds were then repackaged which created pockets of extreme risk in the financial system and as a result many banks failed.

▦ **Commodity funds.** The banks are by-passed and money is placed at risk with large bets being taken on future movements of commodity prices using derivatives and borrowing. They might blow up resulting in huge losses, which might pose knock-on risks throughout the financial system, as banks might face bad debts.

▦ **Clearing houses.** As well as confirming deals on many financial markets these organisations usually take on a central counterparty role, that is, acting as a buyer to every seller and a seller to every buyer. This reduces risk for each side because a highly respectable organisation is now the trader's counterparty rather than another trader on the other side of the world. To protect themselves the clearing houses demand that a sum of money be left with them which is forfeit if the trader does not go through with the deal they agreed. These processors of trading activity handle billions every day, asking for only a small margin in their role as central counterparties. They tend to have little capital in reserve, so in the event of a few defaults by traders the system might be in trouble. Contagious fear could spread if investors worry about the clearing house's promise to guarantee every deal. This could halt lending and other deals for a while.

▦ **Peer-to-peer finance.** The internet has brought new ways of raising finance directly from savers, e.g. Zopa is a platform for debt for individuals and the self-employed, MarketInvoice allows investors to advance loans to firms in return for the right to collect income from customers and Crowdcube permits investment in shares.

▦ **Inter-dealer broker.** If one of these organisations standing between traders and connecting them fails then billions could be lost.

Article 26.5 describes the concerns over shadow banking in China.

China pushes lending into the shadows

By David Pilling

These days Chinese regulators spend much of their time chasing shadows. The shadows in question belong to the banking industry, the more dimly lit reaches of which have grown voluminously, some might say alarmingly. So steep has been the trajectory that almost half of all new credit is now supplied by non-banks or through off-balance-sheet vehicles of regular banks, up from just 10% a decade ago.

There is every reason to believe that much of the credit sluicing through these informal channels goes to less-than-worthy investments. Rather, shadow banking is the deformed stepchild of contradictory state policies. On the one hand, Beijing wants a financially sound banking system with tightly controlled deposit and lending rates. On the other, it seeks high economic growth, which must be fed by a stream of few-questions-asked credit. The upshot is an ill-defined and under-regulated part of the financial system that now controls assets worth about 40% of gross domestic product.

Shadow banking can take many forms, including loan sharks, investment companies known as trusts and off-balance-sheet lending by regular banks. The most important of the latter are "wealth management products", considered so potentially dangerous by some analysts that they are known affectionately as "weapons of mass Ponzi".

In return for locking up one's money for three or six months, such products offer annual rates of 4–5%, better than the 3.25% on normal deposits. Since they are "guaranteed", few depositors take much interest in the underlying asset. Typically, the money goes to other banks (which lend it on) and to property companies, small and medium-sized businesses and local governments.

Such products are potentially dangerous for several reasons. First, there is a mismatch between their short-term maturity and the longer-term projects they fund. To the depositor, the vehicle looks like quasi-cash; to the bank, it could be funding an illiquid multiyear investment. Second, the underlying asset may not be creditworthy. Reuters investigated one wealth management product which offered a more than tempting annual return of 7.2%. The asset being funded turned out to be a deserted housing estate in the middle of a rice paddy field in Jiangxi province. Third, banks often pool assets from different schemes, paying the interest and principal of maturing schemes from new deposits. It would be hard to find a better definition of a Ponzi scheme.

Paradoxically, the biggest concern may not be default, but the fact that such investments appear to be risk-free. In one recent case, investors who bought a product through Huaxia Bank were compensated in full when the investment failed. "Because they get bailed out nobody needs to worry," says May Yan of Barclays. "It's moral hazard rather than a healthy development of the market."

Thus we face the problem that the regulators are busy constructing a strong Maginot Line,[9] such as raised Basel III capital and liquidity reserves, to protect banks, while the real danger may lie to the side. Risk can and has moved from the regulated and transparent elements in the system to the less-regulated opaque sector. The shadow banks have become enormous sources of credit and may well fuel the next bubble, as they assisted with the noughties one.

Notes to chapters

Chapter 1

1. From W. N. Goetzmann and K. G. Rouwenhorst (editors) (2005) *The Origins of Value: The Financial Innovations that Created Modern Capital Markets* (OUP: Oxford), p.20.
2. The Chinese had got there first using bamboo tally sticks around 500 BC.

Chapter 2

1. Strictly, Nationwide is a building society rather than a bank. The term bank has been stretched so we need to be flexible in what we regard as a banking service. In addition to those institutions that have 'bank' in their name such as Banco Santander, this book discusses many other institutions that conduct banking activities, such as building societies and savings and loan associations, collectively known as **depository institutions** or **deposit-taking institutions (DTIs)**.

Chapter 3

1. Money market instruments are described in Chapter 20.
2. At the time of writing many European banks held unusually large balances at the European Central Bank. They were less concerned with gaining a decent return than on pure safety – they did not trust other banks, nor could they take the risk of investing in tradable financial instruments.
3. According to the Council for Mortgage Lenders.
4. According to the Federal Reserve.
5. Working capital is the difference between current assets (e.g. inventory, trade receivables) and current liabilities (e.g. trade payables, short-term debt).
6. Indeed, when the author contacted a number of banks to negotiate a loan for a company he controls, the corporate loan officers were all amazed at his cheek in not accepting a personal guarantee clause: 'but we normally get a personal guarantee, it is just standard practice', they declared. With some banks this is a firm rule sent from head office and you cannot negotiate it away if your turnover is under, say, £5m. With others there may be some leeway.

Chapter 4

1. For a report on this see http://news.bbc.co.uk/1/hi/8194241.stm.
2. Some banks may reserve 'wealth management' for the especially affluent.

Chapter 5

1. The same or similar terms, such as revolving credit or revolving loan, are often used for simple consumer borrowing where the customer is able to withdraw funds as needed. As the borrower repays the debt, the amount of available credit will increase back to the maximum. The most common type of 'revolving credit' is the credit card. Here we concentrate on large-scale corporate revolving credit.
2. The term **mandated lead arranger (MLA)** is often used for the managing bank(s). Also **'bookrunner'** or **'bookrunner group'** indicates those who solicit interest in the loan from lenders and gather offers of support. They gradually **'build a book'** – a list of confirmed buyers who do the syndication.
3. More complex larger loans can take three months.
4. An important sub-set of project finance is **infrastructure finance**, where large-scale, capital-intensive investment usually, but not always, has a government influence.
5. This means outside the jurisdiction of the currency of issue rather than the currency of the eurozone. So a US dollar issue of Euro MTNs could be issued outside the control of the US authorities in Japan.

Chapter 6

1. We live in extraordinary times, where banks offered negative interest rates to lend money out for up to one month – they paid the borrowers.
2. An alternative way of making money illegally is for traders to receive advanced word on which direction rates would move. It wasn't just banks. Some interdealer brokers, who facilitate derivative trades between banks, also came under investigation for co-ordinating manipulation.
3. 'Briefing: The LIBOR Scandal', *The Economist*, 7 July 2012, pp. 25–7.

Chapter 7

1. CDs can be issued with a maturity date of two years or longer. The instruments dated for more than one year may pay a variable rate of interest, with the rate altered, say, each year, based on the rates on a benchmark rate, e.g. LIBOR.
2. While many CDs can be sold in a highly liquid secondary market to another investor before the maturity date, other CDs are not so liquid, with few potential buyers interested in trading.
3. Many central banks now do pay interest, but it can be quite low. In July 2013 the US Federal Reserve paid 0.25% (annual rate), for example.
4. Made up of 8% of £9,100m = £728m, and 4% of £9,100m = £364m.

5. This case illustrates a domino effect. The Cypriot banks ended up in trouble and unable to pay their debts because a few years earlier they had bought a lot of bonds issued by Greek banks. Then the eurozone 'bailout' of Greece was agreed, which resulted in default on the Greek bank bonds – they lost 70% of their value. This wiped out a tremendous proportion of assets from the Cypriot banks' balance sheets.

6. This is at the top end of the usual range of ROAs for commercial banks.

Chapter 8

1. Cost of capital calculations and concepts are explained in *Corporate Financial Management*, fifth edition (2012) by Glen Arnold.

2. J.P. Morgan led on this.

3. Many books and articles get this wrong and say the VaR is a measure of the maximum amount of money at risk rather than a level that will be exceeded. In reality the loss can go much higher than the VaR figure. The VaR figure is better seen as a minimum loss on a bad day. Obviously, this misunderstanding and misrepresentation would have been read by many bankers prior to the 2008 crisis, and therefore contributed to their failure to understand the extent of their bank's risk exposure.

4. Taleb, N.N. (2001) *Fooled by Randomness: The hidden role of chance in life and in the markets* (Texere: New York); and Taleb, N.N. (2008) *The Black Swan: The impact of the highly improbable* (Penguin: London).

5. Source: Triana, P. (2009) *Lecturing Birds on Flying: Can mathematical theories destroy the financial markets?* (John Wiley and Sons: Chichester).

6. Ibid.

7. Ibid.

8. http://www.sec.gov/Archives/edgar/data/777001/000091412108000345/be12550652-10q.txt

Chapter 9

1. Lloyds 2012 Annual Report.

2. Ibid.

3. Ibid.

Chapter 10

1. An issue of new shares to current shareholders, who receive a quantity of new shares in proportion to their current holding (if you own 1% you are offered 1% of the new shares) if they are willing to pay for them. This allows the company to raise new capital.

2. Even after deducting employee cost, investment banks would routinely report returns on equity of 20–25% before the crisis. Now the figure is more like 9–13%. But employees take a large chunk of revenue before the ROSF (return on shareholders' funds) is calculated, so the pre-wage profits are still high.

3. Similar restrictions were placed on Italian and Japanese banks.

Chapter 11

1. For more on equity markets see *The Financial Times Guide to Investing* or *The Financial Times Guide to Financial Markets*, both by Glen Arnold.
2. See *The Financial Times Guide to Investing* (by Glen Arnold) Chapter 5 for more on collective investment vehicles.
3. For more on hedge funds see *The Financial Times Guide to Financial Markets*, by Glen Arnold.
4. Also known as the first-loss tranche, residual tranche or toxic waste.
5. They also invested in other long-term assets such as corporate bonds, Treasury bonds, ABS and CDOs based on credit card receivables and student debt. Also they raised money from medium-term notes as well as commercial paper.
6. With the exception of Gillian Tett at the *Financial Times* and a handful of others. Professor Nouriel Roubini of New York Stern School of Business was warning of the impending crisis in the mid-2000s. Practitioners ignored or dismissed his comments, and derogatorily called him 'Dr. Doom'.

Chapter 12

1. Only 10% of members of a credit union can be corporate members and there are limits on how much of the savings and loans in a credit union can be taken up by organisations: at least 75% of shares in a credit union must be held by individuals, as must 90% of loans.
2. Also known as building and loan associations and homestead associations.
3. Crédit Agricole S.A. owns a 25% stake in each regional bank.

Chapter 13

1. Factoring and invoice discounting are included under the umbrella term 'invoice financing'. Another term is 'sales finance'.
2. However, with many finance leases, after the asset has been leased for the great majority of its useful life (value), the lessee may have the option to purchase it.

Chapter 17

1. Assets: JPMorgan Chase $2,265,792m; Bank of America $2,136,577m; Citigroup $1,873,878m; Wells Fargo $1,313,867m.

Chapter 19

1. A strict interpretation of the word riba is usary or excessive interest.
2. For example, stamp duty on a house sale is not paid twice (when the bank buys and when the customer buys from the bank).

Chapter 20

1. Already covered: certificates of deposit, interbank transactions, commercial paper, medium-term notes, repos, banker's acceptances, bills of exchange and securitised bonds.
2. This is shown in *The Financial Times Guide to Bond and Money Markets* (forthcoming), *Corporate Financial Management* (Pearson, 2013) and *Modern Financial Markets and Institutions* (Pearson, 2012) all by Glen Arnold.
3. Some so-called 'corporate bonds' are in fact issued by business enterprises owned by the government and the biggest issuers are banks.
4. The rating agencies say that they do not in the strictest sense give an opinion on the likelihood of default, but merely evaluate relative creditworthiness or relative likelihood of default, and because rating scales are relative, default rates fluctuate over time. Thus, a group of middle-rated bonds are expected to be consistent in having a lower rate of default than a group of lower-rated bonds, but they will not, year after year, have a default rate of say 2.5% per year.
5. Alternatively they may be convertible into preference shares.
6. Although new EU rules mean that a prospectus is required if the bond is marketed at retail (non-professional) investors.
7. In some cases the issuer pays the investment bank(s) a fee to underwrite the bonds on a 'firm commitment' basis, which means that if any of the bonds are not bought by funds, etc., then the underwriter will end up holding them. In other cases the bonds are underwritten on a 'best efforts' basis: the issuer accepts that it may receive less than anticipated as the investment bank does not guarantee sales.

Chapter 21

1. Note that some futures contracts have cash delivery rather than physical delivery.
2. Initial margin is the same as maintenance margin in this case.
3. Technically 194.1023 contracts are needed but we cannot deal in a fraction of a contract so we need to round up or down.
4. Assuming that the futures price is equal to the spot price of the FTSE 100. This would occur close to the expiry date of the future.
5. All figures are slightly simplified because we are ignoring the fact that the compensation is received in six months whereas interest to Bank X is payable in 18 months.

Chapter 22

1. This is the amount payable in December for the September FRA. If the agreement is for payment to be made in September the amount will be reduced (discounted) at the annualised rate of 6.2%.
2. The Saturday paper version presents a traded option table. For the other days of the week you need to go to www.ft.com, or the original source, https://globalderivatives.nyx.com/en/nyse-liffe.

3. The expiry date is the third Wednesday of the expiry month.

4. For this exercise we will assume that the option is held to expiry and not traded before then. However in many cases this option will be sold on to another trader long before the expiry date approaches (at a profit or loss).

5. The word 'premium' gives a clue as to the underlying nature of these instruments: they are a series of options for the buyer to decide at, say three-monthly, intervals whether to exercise the option to insist that the difference between the agreed fixed rate of interest and the current LIBOR will be paid over. Thus on each three-month roll-over day throughout the five years the cap holder will compare the strike on his cap (4.5% for Oakham) with the three-month LIBOR fixing that morning and exercise the cover if it makes sense to do so.

Chapter 23

1. Non-working days do not count, so a Friday deal is settled on the following Tuesday. There are also some exceptions, e.g. the US dollar/Canadian dollar deals are settled the next day.

2. This is on the regulated exchange of the CME. Options are also available in the OTC market via banks, allowing more precise hedges, but this may be more expensive.

Chapter 24

1. Occasionally called a reserve bank, national bank or monetary authority.

2. Some central banks, e.g. the Bank of England, have moved from a fixed daily level of reserves to target balances of reserves held at the central bank on average over 'maintenance periods'. In the case of the BoE the maintenance period runs from one meeting of the committee that sets interest rates (the Monetary Policy Committee) to the next, usually one month. Smaller banks may be exempt from the system.

3. At the time of writing the usual system has been suspended in the UK and elsewhere because the supply of reserves fluctuated in response to the central bank's decisions on quantitative easing, pumping in vast amounts of fresh cash. However, by the time you read this I expect normal service to be resumed and quantitative easing will be an historical novelty. Therefore I describe the standard monetary policy responses, those applying when the central banks are not desperate to save the economy by creating bucket-loads of money.

4. A long time ago you might have been able to take along your currency notes to the central bank and receive gold or silver in exchange. Today if you took along, say, a £20 note you will only receive other notes in return, say four £5 notes. Because these notes (and coins) are generally accepted as a medium of exchange and store of value they can function as money.

5. Also called the cash reserve ratio.

6. The Bank of England asks banks to hold **target balances (reserves)** at the Bank on average over the maintenance periods (about one month).

7. Also called a **money multiplier**.
8. In the UK they earn the 'Official Bank Rate', which is the target interest rate kept at 0.5% pa for over five years through to 2014.This has a direct bearing on interest rates in the short-term money markets, particularly the overnight interest rates in the repo market.
9. Between 2008–13 the relationship between the monetary base and broad money changed considerably. Banks were supplied with cash, but they reduced lending. This was due to a combination of the banks' fear of borrower default, poor bank solvency ratios and customer reluctance to borrow in a recession. Thus we must view the credit multiplier as a model of how it works most of the time; it is reliable in an approximate way and in most economic conditions. However, when conditions are extreme it can break down.
10. In many financial systems there is a select group of security dealers (often a wing of the major commercial and investment banks) with whom the central bank buys and sells government securities. It is these security dealers' deposit accounts that are credited and debited.
11. The BoE generally uses repos with an average maturity of two weeks, but will also target long-term repos.
12. In the USA, for example, the Fed funds rate is targeted (an overnight borrowing rate).
13. On the last day on the maintenance period month it can borrow at 0.25% above the BoE Bank Rate.
14. The European Central Bank offers loans at the **marginal lending rate** rather than the discount rate, in its **marginal lending facility**.
15. Unless, of course, it too happens to be one of the buyers or sellers in the normal market.

Chapter 25

1. A **resolution regime** would need to be established and authority to control a bank's demise be given to a **resolution agency**. This might involve forcing holders of bank bonds to accept losses alongside shareholders.
2. Incentive-caused bias?
3. 'Additional Tier 1' and 'Tier 2' can contribute to the 'capital' but only in a minor way and the definition of what can be included has been considerably tightened so that the debt instruments here have to be very subordinated (toward the back of the queue to get redemption if the bank runs into trouble) to other liabilities, particularly depositors.
4. Switzerland, as a small country has to be very careful, because the assets of its banks are many times annual GDP. A slip by them could bankrupt the entire nation, as happened to Iceland.

5. For example, in 2013 the Basel committee handed the same hypothetical trading portfolio to 15 large banks in nine countries and asked them to calculate the total capital required to support it. The results ranged from €13m to €35m. Also, the chief executives of JPMorgan and Santander have complained that their competitors may be cheating under the guise of 'optimising' their models (as reported in the *Financial Times*, 1 February 2013).

6. Bank regulators regularly conduct **stress tests** to examine how a bank would look in terms of liquidity and capital reserves should a number of bad events occur. However they are flexible on what can be regarded as a liquid asset. Some equities, corporate bonds rated as low as BBB– and mortgage-backed securities can contribute up to 15% of their 'near-cash' buffers.

7. In the UK for example coins are produced by another organisation, The Royal Mint.

8. The 12 presidents of the regional Feds rotate as voting members. All 12 presidents attend the meetings; it is just that seven of them participate in discussions but do not have a vote.

Chapter 26

1. Some make the distinction between regulation (the framework of rules with penalties for non-compliance) and supervision, meaning the authorising and monitoring of activities to ensure compliance with both the formal rules and with the judgements of the supervisor, based on principles, with regard to safety, soundness, customer exploitation, etc. Here we will use the words interchangeably with each meaning both.

2. Assessing the risks that firms pose to the PRA's objectives and, where necessary, take action to reduce them.

3. Or have special exemption. A list of those registered as authorised by the FCA is at www.fca.org.uk

4. The firm's literature should set out its regulatory body and scheme.

5. Although they can appeal through the courts.

6. One based and regulated outside of UK, such as in Bermuda or Jersey.

7. The securities activities of banks require a capital reserve, separate to that for banking activities.

8. Stiglitz, J. (2010)'Watchdogs need not bark together', *Financial Times*, 10 February, p.13.

9. Defensive fortifications along the French-German border which Hitler avoided by going through Belgium in 1940.

Index